WOODROFFE & LOWE'S CONSUMER LAW AND PRACTICE

WOODROFFE & LOWE'S CONSUMER LAW AND PRACTICE

Eighth Edition

By

GEOFFREY WOODROFFE, M.A. (Cantab.)
*Solicitor, Formerly Professor and Director of the
Centre for Consumer and Commercial Law Research,
Brunel University*

and

ROBERT LOWE, LL.B.
Solicitor and training consultant

*with Precedents by
District Judge Stephen Gerlis*

LONDON
SWEET & MAXWELL
2010

First Edition 1980
Second Edition 1985
Third Edition 1991
Reprinted 1993
Fourth Edition 1995
Reprinted 1996
Fifth Edition 1999
Reprinted 2000
Sixth Edition 2004
Seventh Edition 2007
Eighth Edition 2010

Published in 2010 by
Sweet & Maxwell Limited of
100 Avenue Road, Swiss Cottage,
London NW3 3PF
http://www.sweetandmaxwell.co.uk
Typeset by Servis Filmsetting Ltd, Manchester
Printed in the UK by CPI William Clowes, Beccles, NR34 7TL

No natural forests were destroyed to make this product; only
farmed timber was used and replanted

A CIP catalogue record for this book is available from the
British Library

ISBN 9780414042407

PREFACE TO THE EIGHTH EDITION

Thirty years have elapsed since the First Edition in 1980, when consumer law as a discrete area was still developing. Much legislation was of Victorian vintage such as the Sale of Goods Act 1893 just being replaced then by the 1979 Act. The Consumer Credit Act 1974 and the Unfair Contract Terms Act 1977 were in their infancy and the European Commission was yet to make an impact on UK consumer law.

Increasingly the strengthening of consumer protection stems from Brussels and comparatively little is home grown, as will be seen from the changes which have occurred in the last three years since the 7th Edition. For example, the Consumer Protection from Unfair Trading Regulations 2008 (discussed in Chapter Seventeen and reproduced in Appendix Four) implemented the Unfair Commercial Practices Directive destroying in its wake most of the Trade Descriptions Act 1968 as well as the price provisions in Part III of the Consumer Protection Act 1987 (see Chapters Thirteen and Fourteen).

Credit has not been left untouched by the EU. Legal advisers, law students, money advice centres and finance companies are still getting to grips with the changes to the 1974 Act made by the Consumer Credit Act 2006. Soon they must grapple with the complexities added by the Consumer Credit Directive 2008 on which we comment in Chapter Eighteen and set out in Appendix Three. The UK Government should have implemented this by May 2010. However, BIS announced in its CCD Bulletin in February 2010 that it had submitted a draft set of statutory instruments to Parliamentary Counsel for scrutiny and expected "to proceed to Parliament with the new regulations . . . in March this year". It has decided to delay the final date for compliance to February 1, 2011 "in recognition of the difficulties lenders would have in being fully compliant by June this year"—a pragmatic view welcomed by the finance industry.

In these difficult economic times "ambulance chasers" such as claims management companies have been searching for technical defects to enable debtors to avoid their financial burdens on the grounds that their credit agreements are unenforceable. Two very recent cases show that this defence may give only temporary relief: *McGuffick* v *Royal Bank of Scotland* and *Carey v HSBC Bank Plc* (both discussed in Chapter Twenty-One).

The other most important cases since 2007 are also concerned with financial charges. They turn on the interpretation of reg.6(2) of the Unfair Terms in Consumer Contracts Regulations 1999 (discussed in Chapter Nine). Here the OFT has been busy. Its attack on bank charges was repelled by the banks with the support of the Supreme Court in *OFT* v *Abbey National Plc,* in which the "core or essential bargain" was examined. However, the OFT was successful in its action against overcharging estate agents in *OFT v Foxtons Ltd*, another 2009 case on core bargains.

Other changes, again by secondary legislation, include the replacement of the 1987 "Doorstep" Regulations with the neatly entitled Cancellation of Contracts made in a Consumer's Home or Place of Work etc. Regulations 2008! These consolidate the 1987 Regulations and later amendments and appear in Chapter Six.

The OFT's new regime of Approved codes is slowly expanding—all nine codes which have reached Stage Two are analysed in Chapter Ten. The relevant core criteria are set out in Appendix Two.

Again Appendix One contains a set of County Court Precedents and once more we express our gratitude to District Judge Stephen Gerlis for reviewing them and updating Chapter 11. As always the OFT and BIS receive our well-deserved thanks for their friendly cooperation and help. Sweet & Maxwell in the person of Nicola Thurlow and her colleagues still provide amiable encouragement and support. Robert Lowe, though more in the background now, remains a source of wisdom and insight. Last, but not least, my loving thanks to my wife Rosemary (a Writer to the Signet) for her invaluable assistance on research, proof checking and the many detailed tasks of an author.

I have tried to state the law as at February 28, 2010.

Geoffrey Woodroffe

PREFACE TO THE FIRST EDITION

There are many ways of writing a book on consumer protection. One can trace the historical development; one can analyse the economic and social effects; one can deal with the subject from a comparative point of view. In this book we have decided to concentrate on practical problems and remedies. The book is written primarily for law students and for those who are called upon to advise on consumer problems, whether legal or para-legal practitioners. We hope that it will also be useful to persons in industry and their legal advisers as an indication of the growing battery of controls—civil, criminal and administrative—which the law now imposes on business activity. With this aim in mind we have tried to adopt a very practical approach.

A further problem for writers on this subject is that of selection. The term "consumer protection" has no precise definition and it could quite properly be given an immensely wide meaning. Thus every citizen of this country is a consumer, or potential consumer, of welfare benefits, public utilities, health services, educational services and so on. Then again it can be argued that the term "consumer protection" should include the law relating to the supply of housing. Another relevant area is the law of competition which has an underlying consumer protection philosophy. Finally, we have had Government regulation of business activity and in particular we have had price control. In view of our basic approach outlined above we have decided not to deal in any detail with these wide areas. Indeed, we shall concentrate on the types of problem most likely to arise where an individual consumer orders goods or services from a supplier who then proceeds to render defective performance or no performance at all.

Our remedies-based approach has influenced the structure of this book. Part I is entitled "The Consumer and the Civil Law" and deals with such matters as defective performance of contracts to supply goods or services, product liability, the remedies available to the consumer, attempts to exclude them and finally the all-important question of how the remedies can be enforced. Special attention is given to the methods of extra-legal enforcement provided by the growing number of voluntary Codes of Practice. Part II of the book is entitled "The Consumer and the Criminal Law"; special consideration is given to the Trade Descriptions Act 1968 and there is also a chapter dealing with compensation orders. Part III of the book describes the most significant development of consumer protection—administrative control under the Fair Trading Act 1973. Part IV contains nine chapters dealing with "Consumer Protection in Credit Transactions". The book ends with a chapter entitled "The EEC Dimension".

This is a new venture and we would welcome suggestions for improvement. In the meantime we would like to thank the many people who took the trouble to read parts of the typescript and to answer our questions. Special thanks are due to a number of individuals at the Office of Fair Trading, Department of Trade, National Consumer Council, Society of Motor Manufacturers and Traders, Motor Agents Association and the Manchester Arbitration Scheme. The views which they expressed are necessarily personal ones but nevertheless we have found them of great value. We would also like to thank Bill Thomas (solicitor), Valerie Chiswell (consumer adviser), Malcolm Leder (Senior Lecturer at Middlesex Polytechnic), and Peter Chiswell, Peter Hawkins, Tony King, and Chris Whitehouse (all at the College of Law). All of them made very helpful suggestions and assisted in the tiresome task of proof reading.

At the time of going to press there is a Bill before Parliament entitled the Sale of Goods Bill. This is a pure consolidation measure which does not make any changes in the law. The future of the London Small Claims Court, which is discussed in Chapter 9, is still in the balance; we understand that a grant of £5,000 will enable it to survive.

We have tried to state the law as at October 1, 1979.

Robert Lowe
Geoffrey Woodroffe

CONTENTS

PART I: THE CONSUMER AND THE CIVIL LAW

PART IV: CREDIT TRANSACTIONS

TABLE OF CASES

TABLE OF STATUTES

TABLE OF STATUTORY INSTRUMENTS

INTRODUCTION

"The coffee at McDonalds was too hot" said the scalded customer
"The central heating isn't working"
"The holiday was ruined"
"The car has been off the road for a month"
"The salesman wouldn't go away until I signed"
"There was a snail in the ginger beer"

This book is concerned with complaints which consumers may have against **1.01** a supplier of goods or services and with the remedies available to them. It is a vast subject and, as indicated in the preface to the First Edition,[1] it is necessary to curtail it.

In the words of the Molony Committee on Consumer Protection (1961) "the consumer, unlike some classes with claims on public bounty, is everybody all the time". In the present book, however, the word "consumer" will be used to describe a customer who buys for personal use and not for business purposes.

A number of learned writers, e.g. Borrie and Diamond in their excellent book *The Consumer, Society and the Law*, have traced the history of the subject and have shown that, although the subject is comparatively new, its roots are old. Thus the law has imposed duties on persons exercising certain callings for many centuries, e.g. inn-keepers and carriers. Nevertheless, the explosion of interest in consumer matters was very much a creature of the second half of the 20th century. We can see this simply by looking at the dates of some of the principal reforming legislation:

Hire-Purchase Acts 1954 and 1964 **1.02**

Trade Descriptions Act 1968

Fair Trading Act 1973

Supply of Goods (Implied Terms) Act 1973

Consumer Credit Act 1974

Unfair Contract Terms Act 1977

Consumer Safety Act 1978

Supply of Goods and Services Act 1982

[1] Above, p.vii.

Consumer Protection Act 1987

Sale and Supply of Goods Act 1994

Unfair Terms in Consumer Contracts Regulations 1999

Sale and Supply of Goods to Consumers Regulations 2002

Enterprise Act 2002

Consumer Protection from Unfair Trading Regulations 2008

What is the reason for this tremendous upsurge of activity? The answer is two-fold—a combination of new business methods and changing social attitudes. The key factors on business methods are to be found in the complexity of the goods themselves and in the changing forms of advertising, marketing and distribution. To quote again from the Molony Report (p.31):

> [The last half century] has seen a growing tendency for manufacturers . . . to appeal directly to the public by forceful national advertising and other promotional methods . . . a further influence during the same period has been the development of a mass market for extremely complex mechanical and electrical goods. . . . Their performance cannot in some cases be accurately established by a short trial; shortcomings of design are not apparent to the inexpert eye; inherent faults may only come to light when the article breaks down after a period of use.

In other words, the need for what is called consumer protection has become far greater because the consumer is no longer in a position to rely on his own judgment when buying a complex article.

The second motivating force is the general move from individualism to collectivism. The 20th century saw not only consumer protection but also the Rent Acts, Financial Services and Markets Act, the massive volume of legislation protecting employees and, of course, the welfare state. The extent to which some of these measures hamper business activity is, of course, a matter of keen and continual political debate.

The scale of the problem

1.03 A government White Paper "modern markets; confident consumers" was published as our Fifth Edition went to press in July 1999. Welcoming the decision to place consumers at the heart of government policy the Director General of Fair Trading pointed out that:

> consumer complaints are now running at 900,000 a year and these are the tip of the iceberg—I believe that tens of millions of transactions for goods or services cause problems for the consumers. Rightly UK consumers expect better service and better quality and that demand is going to get stronger. (OFT Press Notice July 22, 1999)

In the following year research carried out by the OFT estimated that "defective goods, substandard service and poor information cost consumers £83 billion—with those on lower incomes particularly badly hit" (OFT Press Notices 11/00 and 12/00).

The international dimension

It is clear that the judiciary of the United States has been a long way ahead **1.04** of this country in recognising and dealing with consumer problems. In particular, the American courts have increased the manufacturer's liability in two respects (1) by moving from negligence liability to strict liability, and (2) by breaking the shackles of the privity of contract rule. In this country these changes have been left to Parliament.[2]

The subject of consumer protection is also very much alive in the European Union and most UK legislation in the last 25 years derives from EU Directives.

The original Rome Treaty did not refer specifically to consumer protection but now, under the Maastricht amendments, art.3(r) specifies "a contribution to the strengthening of consumer protection" as one of the key activities of the Community. The previous Editions of this book highlighted a number of major EU initiatives which have become part of English law—product liability, misleading advertisements, doorstep selling, package holidays, unfair contract terms, distance selling and consumer remedies. This Edition is no exception and deals with the Unfair Commercial Practices Directive in Chapter Seventeen and the Consumer Credit Directive in Chapter Eighteen. A list of consumer protection Directives and their implementation into domestic law can be found in the Enterprise Act 2002 (Pt 8 Community Infringements Specified UK Laws) Order 2003 (SI 2003/1374).

Consumer protection agencies

There is a very large number of bodies concerned with consumer protection **1.05** matters and they can be divided into Government Departments, Government-sponsored bodies, local authorities and voluntary bodies.

Government departments: BIS and OFT

The Department for Business Innovation and Skills (BIS, formerly DTI **1.06** and, briefly, BERR) has a Minister for consumers and seeks to improve consumer protection both directly (through consumer protection legislation and advice) and indirectly (through competition law). A speech given by a previous Minister (Dr Howells) to the Yorkshire Fiscal Group contains the following passage:

> "To prosper, companies need satisfied customers, but the expectations of cus-
> tomers are growing. Well-informed consumers, able to make discerning choices,
> put pressure on businesses to provide better goods and services, tailored to the
> needs of their customers and sold at competitive prices . . . The revolution in
> shopping via the Internet and digital highways will enable consumers to compare

---

[2] See paras 5.10 and 4.06 below.

prices and product quality not only against those available in the other Member States of the European Union but elsewhere in the world including the US. I have no doubt that this will change forever the ways we judge whether and if we are getting a good deal . . . We are also working on proposals to ensure that consumer law is consistently enforced and that traders who cheat consumers are quickly stopped."

He also referred to the Competition Act 1998 which brought about a long-awaited reform of competition law and gave the Office of Fair Trading much-needed, sweeping new powers to take action against "firms and cartels which try to restrict competition or rig prices ripping off the consumer". These powers were further increased by the Enterprise Act 2002 which, for the first time, imposed criminal liability on cartels.

1.07   Among its principal duties BIS makes Regulations under the Consumer Credit Act 1974 and the Consumer Protection Act 1987, Pt II. It also issues a large number of Press Releases and offers a great deal of business information and advice on issues ranging from pyramid selling ("if an offer seems too good to be true it probably is") to e-shopping and how to complain. These can be viewed on its website *www.dti.gov.uk*.

The Home Office has responsibility in certain areas including firearms and explosives and the Department of Environment, Food and Rural Affairs (DEFRA) has a number of duties under the Food Safety Act 1990. Some of these duties have been transferred to the Food Standards Agency under the Food Standards Act 1999.

1.08   Closely linked to BIS is the Office of Fair Trading (OFT) which is now a statutory body set up under the Enterprise Act 2002; it has taken over many of the powers formerly vested in the Director-General. Its duties include promoting good practice in the carrying out of activities which may affect the economic interests of consumers (s.8(1)) and approving (or withdrawing approval from) Codes of Practice. It issues a large number of press releases setting out warnings and details of enforcement action and also publications containing advice in everyday language (a guide aimed at students was entitled "wake up, wise up, speak up, don't get stuffed"). The Act also requires the OFT to respond within a specified time to a "super complaint" from a designated body. As with BIS there is a strong link with competition law on the basis that "consumers will benefit from markets which work well—and this will be so when fair dealing businesses are in open and vigorous competition for custom".

We shall see in Pt III of this book how the OFT's enforcement powers formerly contained in Pt III of the Fair Trading Act 1973 have been greatly strengthened under the Enterprise Act 2002. We shall describe in Chapter Nine the wide scope of its activities in curtailing the continued use of unfair contract terms.

The OFT also has extensive powers under the Consumer Credit Act 1974 which is dealt with in Pt IV of this book. The linchpin of control is the licensing system; every trader who carries on a consumer credit or consumer hire business needs a licence and the OFT is responsible for the grant, renewal, suspension or revocation of a licence.

In a Press Notice back in 1999 the Director-General warmly welcomed his new powers to drive disreputable traders out of business and confirmed that "safeguarding the consumer interest has always been the OFT's top priority".

Government-sponsored bodies

A number of government "quangos" now have the power to apply for a **1.09** court injunction to restrain the continued use of unfair terms in consumer contracts. This topic is considered in Chapter Nine.

There is also the National Consumer Council which had been in operation as a company since 1974. It is an independent, publicly-funded body which acts as a watchdog and pressure group to protect consumer interests. It has been restructured and its powers and functions extended by the Consumers, Estate Agents and Redress Act 2007. It may investigate complaints of general interest and took over the functions of Energywatch and Postwatch. It is now called Consumer Focus.

BIS also makes a grant to the British Standards Institute (BSI). This voluntary body has been in existence for more than 80 years. One of its functions is to lay down uniform specifications for certain products. If a product bears a BSI "kite mark" this means that it has been tested by BSI. Regular spot checks will follow and the mark will be withdrawn if these prove unsatisfactory. It can be seen on products worldwide—from manhole covers and Christmas lights to lawnmowers and cricket balls—enabling manufacturers to achieve product differentiation.

Local authorities

The county councils and the London boroughs make three major contribu- **1.10** tions to consumer protection. First they employ trading standards inspectors (their former name was weights and measures inspectors) who have extensive responsibilities in the enforcement of legislation including the Consumer Credit Act 1974. They must give the Office of Fair Trading notice of an intended prosecution and they will also keep it informed of undesirable trade practices which come to their notice. They also have enforcement powers under the Unfair Terms in Consumer Contracts Regulations 1999 (as to which see Chapter Nine) and in practice they work closely with the OFT. If we look at the OFT Bulletin No. 4 on Unfair Contract Terms we find (on p.7) the following passage:

> We recognise that local expertise and being close at hand may make it entirely appropriate for traders' home authority TSDs to guide and influence them in the drafting of their consumer contracts; clearly, this may remove the need for the OFT to invoke the threat of proceedings in the High Courts. Such informal local action can represent a speedy, cheap and informal way of achieving improvements in consumer contracts, particularly those used by small traders.

The second major field of local authority involvement lies in the field of consumer advice. They give pre-shopping advice and also give advice on complaints. Sometimes they take up individual complaints with the object of achieving a satisfactory settlement but much of this work is now undertaken by the help-line Consumer Direct. Thirdly, Environmental Health Departments are responsible for the enforcement of legislation on a number of matters including noise, pollution, waste disposal and bad housing.

Voluntary bodies

1.11 Which? (formerly the Consumers' Association) is widely known for its comparative testing of goods and services. The results are published in *Which?* magazine and are clearly of great value to prospective consumers. Which? is very active in promoting legislation dealing with consumer affairs (including consumer awareness of legal remedies). Thus it played a large part in seeing the Unfair Contract Terms Act 1977 on to the statute book. It now has enforcement powers under the Unfair Terms in Consumer Contracts Regulations 1999.

There are also a number of consumer groups at local level; their main function is to carry out research into the quality of local services and to publish the results of these surveys to their members. There is a central co-ordinating body formerly known as the National Federation of Consumer Groups and it is believed that total membership of the groups is in the region of 2,000. It became the National Consumer Federation in 2002 when it amalgamated with Consumer Congress after the DTI withdrew the funding of both organisations. Another body working in a closely related field is the Money Advice Trust which is an umbrella organisation formed in 1991 to bring together a large number of money advice bodies. Back in 1999, the Chairman Robert Colville stated that "over a million people every year seek help from money advisers and demand for their services is exceeding supply". (See DTI press notice P/99/58.)

Finally we should mention trade and professional associations (e.g. the Association of British Travel Agents). These are in no sense consumer protection agencies but many of them operate voluntary conciliation and arbitration procedures. A consumer with a complaint may well find that an approach to the relevant association will produce a more satisfactory outcome than embarking on the hazards of litigation. The codes of practice and complaints procedures operated by a number of associations are examined in Chapter Ten of this book.

One important aspect of the voluntary procedures referred to above has been the creation of an "Ombudsman" for particular business activities. The Insurance Ombudsman's Bureau was set up, on a voluntary basis, in 1981. Similar bodies were set up in relation to other sectors such as banking, building societies, funerals, estate agents, pensions and unit trusts. Many of them were brought together recently as a "one stop shop" by the Financial Ombudsman Service. They are discussed in Chapter Ten.

Part I

THE CONSUMER AND THE CIVIL LAW

The civil law assists the consumer by imposing certain obligations on manu-   **1.12**
facturers and suppliers of goods and services and by restricting attempts to
exclude or cut down these obligations or the remedies available on breach.

It must be said at once that in many key areas the law is in a very uncertain state and the case law is very sparse. This is particularly so in relation to
(1) the meaning of "satisfactory quality",[1] and (2) the circumstances in which
the buyer loses his right to reject goods by "accepting" them.[2] There is also
the question of "reasonableness" under s.3 of the Unfair Contract Terms Act
1977 where, for example, a builder seeks to avoid liability for delay or non-
performance.[3] When one thinks of the many millions of consumer contracts
concluded each day this absence of authority may seem surprising. A charita-
ble view would be that traders, for reasons of commercial goodwill, settle all
genuine complaints without litigation. A more realistic view is that consumers
are deterred from bringing proceedings by a variety of factors including ignorance, lethargy and cost.

In Chapters Two to Four we shall consider the consumer's rights against
his *immediate supplier* of goods for failure to pass title, to deliver the goods
contracted for or to deliver goods of the right quality and fitness. Then in
Chapter Five we shall discuss his rights against the *manufacturer (and other
suppliers in the distribution chain)* both under the general law and under Pt
I of the Consumer Protection Act 1987. Chapter Six deals with a number of
common consumer problems including defective performance, late delivery,
distance selling, holidays and disputes about the price. In Chapter Seven
we shall analyse and explain the remedies available to the consumer and to
members of his family (remedies which have been greatly strengthened by an
EU Directive which was incorporated into domestic law in 2003). This will
be followed in Chapter Eight by an examination of exemption clauses and in
Chapter Nine we shall consider the Unfair Contract Terms Directive and the
regulations which incorporate the Directive into English law.

The last two Chapters in this Part deal with questions of enforcement.
In Chapter Ten we shall describe ways in which the consumer can seek

---

[1] See below, para.4.09.
[2] See below, para.7.33
[3] The Unfair Contract Terms Act 1977 is examined in Ch. Eight.

redress without going to court—including arbitration schemes under codes of practice, the use of the consumer councils for public utilities and alternative dispute resolution. Finally Chapter Eleven is entitled "What happens if I go to court?"; it describes the availability of legal aid, the "no win, no fee" schemes to finance litigation and the conduct of cases under the Civil Procedure Rules which came into force in April 1999.

CHAPTER TWO

"THEY SAY IT ISN'T MINE"

(1) A owns a diamond ring. B steals it and sells it to C who sells it to D. The **2.01**
police have now traced the ring and have seized it from D's home.
(2) E takes his car to F, a car dealer, and says "Find me a buyer but don't sell
for less than £1,000." F sells to G for £600 and disappears.
(3) H, a finance house, supplies a car to I on hire-purchase. Before completing
her payments I sells the car to J, a motor dealer, who lets the car out to K on a
fresh hire-purchase agreement. H now claim from K the unpaid balance due
on the original agreement.

In unravelling this type of problem three closely connected principles must
be distinguished:

1. Does any buyer acquire title to the goods?

2. What are the rights as between each buyer and seller? This question will usually only be relevant in advising a buyer who has not
   acquired title.

3. What are the rights of a buyer who has spent money on improving
   the goods?

In this chapter it is proposed to deal separately with these three questions.
Before doing so, it may be helpful to define the term "sale of goods" which
occurs throughout this book. By s.2(1) of the Sale of Goods Act 1979:

> "A contract of sale of goods is a contract by which the seller transfers or agrees
> to transfer the property in goods to a buyer for a money consideration called
> the price."

A contract of sale must be distinguished from other supply contracts—hire,
hire-purchase, work and materials, exchange—although the law is similar in
many key areas. Hire and hire-purchase are not sales because the contract
does not "transfer the property in goods" to the other party, who merely
has a right to the use and possession of the goods and, in the case of hire-
purchase[1], an option to purchase them too. Work and materials contracts
fall outside the 1979 Act because of the presence of services as well. Finally,
an exchange of goods is not a sale as no "price" is paid. The extent to which

[1] *Helby v Matthews* [1895] A.C. 471.

computer software can be regarded as "goods" is debatable (see para.4.32 below).

1. DOES THE BUYER GET TITLE?

2.02   Where goods are sold by a non-owner the law is faced with a clear policy choice. Lord Denning M.R. has described it as follows[2]:

> "In the development of our law two principles have striven for mastery. The first is for the protection of property; no one can give a better title than he himself possesses.[3] The second is for the protection of commercial transactions; the person who takes in good faith and for value without notice should get a good title."

Faced with this choice the law has developed in a piecemeal and haphazard way with a basic rule protecting property and a number of exceptions protecting commercial transactions. The Crowther Committee on Consumer Credit described the rules as "arbitrary and capricious" and pointed out that their application depended "not on principles of equity or justice but on fine technicalities which have little rhyme and less reason".[4]

There has been only one small step to bring this area of the law into line with modern commercial life. The rules of "market overt", dating back to the 16th century, enabled a buyer in certain types of market to acquire a good title from a non-owner (e.g. a thief). This ancient rule was enshrined in s.22(1) of the Sale of Goods Act 1979 but, following a DTI consultation paper published in January 1994,[5] it was finally abolished by the Sale of Goods (Amendment) Act 1994.

The nemo dat rule

2.03   With this warning we can examine the relevant provisions. The cornerstone is to be found in s.21(1) of the Sale of Goods Act 1979. It reads:

> Subject to this Act, where the goods are sold[6] by a person who is not their owner, and who does not sell them under the authority or with the consent of the owner, the buyer acquires no better title to the goods than the seller had, unless the owner of the goods is by his conduct precluded from denying the seller's authority to sell.

If we revert to our three examples, the effect of s.21(1) is that the goods will still belong to A, E and H unless someone along the line acquired title under one of the exceptions to the basic rule. We must now consider the scope and extent of these exceptions.

[2] *Bishopsgate Motor Finance Corp Ltd v Transport Brakes Ltd* [1949] 1 K.B. 322 at 336–337.
[3] This is commonly referred to as the *"nemo dat"* rule, i.e. *nemo dat quod non habet.*
[4] Report, p.178.
[5] *Transfer of Title: Sections 21 to 26 of the Sale of Goods Act 1979*; other reforms are proposed too, broadly to extend protection to innocent purchasers.
[6] "Sold" does not cover an agreement to sell by the intermediate seller: *Shaw v Commissioner of Police of the Metropolis* [1987] 1 W.L.R. 1332, CA.

Does an exception apply?

Let us first list the principal exceptions:

2.04

> Sale under order of court
>
> Sale under a common law or statutory power
>
> Sale with the owner's consent
>
> Sale where the owner is precluded from denying the seller's right to sell ("estoppel")
>
> Disposition by a mercantile agent
>
> Sale under a voidable title
>
> Disposition by a seller in possession
>
> Disposition by a buyer in possession
>
> Disposition of a motor vehicle under Pt III of the Hire-Purchase Act 1964 (as re-worded by the Consumer Credit Act 1974)

It is now proposed to examine six of the more important of these exceptions. Nearly all of the examples chosen relate to cars; this is clearly the area where the consumer is most likely to buy goods which do not belong to the seller. There is substantial overlap between these provisions and it is often advisable to plead more than one.

(a) Is the owner estopped?

Section 21 itself displaces the basic *nemo dat* rule where the owner, by his conduct, is precluded from denying the seller's right to sell. The courts have construed this provision in a fairly narrow way. In the words of Lord Wilberforce:

2.05

> "English law has generally taken the robust line that the man who owns property is not under a general duty to safeguard it and that he may sue for its recovery any person into whose hands it has come."[7]

In *Central Newbury Car Auctions Ltd v Unity Finance Ltd*[8]:

> A distinguished looking swindler wished to acquire a car from Central Newbury Car Auctions on hire-purchase terms and intimated that he was prepared to leave his own car in part exchange. He filled in an application form for a hire-purchase agreement. If the deal went through the dealer would sell to a finance company who would let the car to him on hire-purchase. Central Newbury allowed him to take the new car and its registration book away. Within a very short time it was discovered that (i) he had given a false name, address and

---

[7] *Moorgate Mercantile Co v Twitchings* [1977] A.C. 890 at 902.
[8] [1957] 1 Q.B. 371.

employer; (ii) the car which he had left in part exchange did not belong to him; and (iii) he had sold the new car to Unity Finance. Central Newbury sued Unity Finance for the return of the car.

It was the classic situation; which of two innocent parties should suffer for the fraud of a third? Many people would agree with Lord Denning that the loss should fall on Central Newbury in view of their carelessness in parting with the car. Nevertheless this was a minority view; the majority in the Court of Appeal applied what Lord Wilberforce has described as the "robust" view.[9] All that Central Newbury had done was to hand over physical possession; that was not conduct which precluded them from setting up their ownership; the car was still theirs. The only right of Unity Finance would be an action against the swindler under s.12 of the Sale of Goods Act[10] and this would almost certainly be worthless.

2.06   In the more recent case of *Moorgate Mercantile Co v Twitchings*[11]:

> Finance companies set up a company called HPI and 98 per cent of all finance companies belonged to it. The object was to register subsisting hire-purchase agreements—some four-and-a-half million—and to pass on information to motor dealers who were associated members. Any dealer who was considering buying a car could contact HPI to find out whether a hire-purchase agreement relating to that car was registered. Several thousand inquiries were made each day. The M. Finance Co. entered into a hire-purchase agreement, but for some unexplained reason they failed to register it with HPI. The hirer offered to sell the car to T, a dealer. T contacted HPI and was told that nothing had been registered. He then bought the car from the hirer. M. Finance Co. claimed that the car was still theirs. The House of Lords, by a majority, upheld this claim.

The case was fought on two grounds—estoppel and negligence. As to estoppel the question was twofold: (i) were HPI the agents of the finance companies? (ii) did their answers amount to a representation that no finance company had an interest in the car? By a majority of four to one (Lord Salmon dissenting) the House of Lords gave a negative answer to both of these questions. The other argument was negligence—the M. Finance Company owed a legal duty of care to dealers and were in breach of that duty. This argument was accepted by the Court of Appeal and by Lords Salmon and Wilberforce but the majority of the House of Lords rejected it. One of the main reasons which influenced the majority was the fact that (i) membership of HPI was voluntary and (ii) there was no duty to register agreements. Neither of these arguments appears totally convincing but they indicate that the owner of goods will seldom lose his ownership by reason of carelessness, even though this causes serious loss to an innocent buyer. We shall see later that HPI can also be used by a prospective private buyer.[12]

---

[9] See above.
[10] Below, para.2.19.
[11] [1977] A.C. 890.
[12] Below, para.2.17.

The only type of case where the owner may be estopped is where he makes a positive representation that the seller owns the goods[13] or where he signs a document which clearly conveys that impression.[14]

Not surprisingly a document signed at gunpoint during an armed robbery does not create an estoppel.[15]

(b) Was there a disposition by a mercantile agent?

We have seen that the mere delivery of possession does not preclude the owner from setting up his ownership. There is, however, one statutory exception. The basic effect of s.2 of the Factors Act 1889 is that if the owner transfers possession to a "mercantile agent", this may amount to a representation that the agent has authority to sell. If the agent then sells in the ordinary course of business, the owner may lose his ownership even though the agent went beyond his instructions. **2.07**

The Act of 1889 starts by defining a mercantile agent. By s.1:

> 'Mercantile agent' shall mean a mercantile agent having in the customary course of his business as such agent authority to sell goods, or to consign goods for the purpose of sale, or to buy goods, or to raise money on the security of goods.

Then comes the key provision. By s.2(1):

> Where a mercantile agent is, with the consent of the owner, in the possession of goods . . . any sale, pledge or other disposition of the goods, made by him when acting in the ordinary course of business of a mercantile agent, shall . . . be as valid as if he were expressly authorised by the owner of the goods to make the same; provided that the person taking under the disposition acts in good faith, and has not at the time of the disposition notice that the person making the disposition has not authority to make the same.

This section could apply to the second example at the beginning of this chapter.[16] If the agent receives instructions not to sell for less than £1,000 or if he is merely instructed to take offers, the buyer will usually not be aware of these restrictions and will get a good title under s.2 even though the agent exceeded his authority. **2.08**

The sale by the agent must be in the ordinary course of business and the buyer must have no notice of the restrictions on the agent's authority. In practice these points are unlikely to give rise to difficulty. There are, however, two other points which could defeat the buyer's claim. Thus:

(1) The section will apply only if the agent was in possession *in his capacity of mercantile agent*. It would not apply if, for example, a garage

---

[13] See *Henderson v Williams* [1895] 1 Q.B. 521.
[14] See *Eastern Distributors v Goldring* [1957] 2 Q.B. 600.
[15] *Debs v Sibec Developments* [1990] R.T.R. 91.
[16] Above, para.2.01.

which happened to be a mercantile agent received a car for servicing or repair and then sold it.[17]

(2) The agent must have received possession of the goods with the owner's consent. The mere fact that consent was obtained by fraud[18] or that consent has ended[19] does not affect the buyer unless he knows of this—an obviously sensible rule. On the other hand, the owner may decide to keep the registration document and/or the ignition key. What happens if he accidentally leaves them with the dealer or in the car? In *Pearson v Rose and Young*[20]:

The owner of a car instructed a dealer to obtain offers. He never intended to hand over the registration book but by mistake he left it in the dealer's show-room. The dealer sold the car with its registration book to a buyer. The Court of Appeal held that (i) in the case of a second-hand car the words 'goods' included the registration book and the consent of the owner must extend to the registra-tion book as well as to the car itself; (ii) there had been no consent to the handing over of the book; (iii) the dealer must therefore be treated as if he had sold the car without the book; (iv) such a sale would not be in the ordinary course of busi-ness; (v) consequently the buyer obtained no title under section 2.[21]

(c) Did the seller have a voidable title?

2.09 Where a contract is voidable (e.g. for misrepresentation) it is a valid contract until the innocent party takes steps to set it aside, i.e. rescinds the contract. The remedy of rescission is an equitable one and in certain cases it will not be possible to rescind. One such case is concerned with third party rights— once a third party has acquired rights under the voidable contract it will be too late to rescind it. This principle now appears in s.23 of the 1979 Act as follows:

When the seller of goods has a voidable title to them, but his title has not been avoided at the time of the sale, the buyer acquires a good title to the goods, pro-vided that he buys them in good faith and without notice of the seller's defect of title.

In virtually all the reported cases under this section the goods were obtained as a result of a fraudulent misrepresentation. The position of the ultimate buyer depends on a highly technical rule—was the title of the fraudulent buyer *voidable* for misrepresentation or *void* for mistake? In the well-known case of *Ingram v Little*[22]:

---

[17] See, e.g. *Belvoir Finance Co Ltd v Harold G. Cole & Co Ltd* [1969] 1 W.L.R. 1877.

[18] *Folkes v King* [1923] 1 K.B. 282; but perhaps the position would be different if the owner was under a fundamental mistake as to the agent's identity. See *Benjamin on Sale of Goods* (7th edn), para.7.037.

[19] Act of 1889, s.2(2).

[20] [1951] 1 K.B. 275.

[21] See also *Stadium Finance Ltd v Robbins* [1962] 2 Q.B. 664, CA (log book accidentally left in car; key not handed over at all; buyer from agent not protected).

[22] [1961] 1 Q.B. 31. For a more recent case with the same result see *Shogun Finance Ltd v Hudson* [2001] EWCA 1000 which is discussed in [2002] 23(2) B.L.R. 288–290.

Three ladies agreed to sell a car to a man who called himself 'Hutchinson'. They were reluctant to take a cheque from him but he gave them the initials and address of a real Hutchinson. After checking in the telephone directory they let him take the car away in return for a cheque. He sold the car to a buyer; the cheque was dishonoured. The Court of Appeal held that (i) the offer to sell was made to the real Hutchinson and could not be accepted by anyone else; (ii) consequently the contract with the rogue was void for unilateral mistake; (iii) consequently section 23 did not apply and the buyer acquired no title.

Some years ago, the Law Reform Committee recommended that the fraudulent person should always be treated as having a *voidable* title, so that the ultimate buyer would be protected. No such legislation has been enacted but the courts have, in effect, achieved this result. In the later case of *Lewis v Averay (No. 1)*[23] the facts were somewhat similar to those in *Ingram v Little* but the decision went the other way. In that case:

> A rogue calling himself Richard Green—a well-known television actor—induced the owner of a car to sell it to him in return for a cheque. He resold the car to a buyer. The cheque was dishonoured.

The Court of Appeal held that the rogue had a voidable title, with the result that s.23 protected the buyer. They treated *Ingram v Little* as a case turning on very special facts and laid down the broad principle that where the parties were face-to-face, the seller would normally be treated as intending to deal with the actual person in front of him. If this intention was brought about by fraud or by a trick, this would make the transaction voidable but not void.

Section 23 does not apply if the owner has avoided the contract *before* the **2.10** resale takes place. In general the innocent party must give notice of rescission and this can raise a practical problem, since not all fraudulent buyers supply their sellers with a correct address. In *Car and Universal Finance Co v Caldwell*[24] the Court of Appeal held that avoidance was possible in this type of case without notifying the fraudulent buyer. In that case the seller reported the matter to the police and the AA as soon as the cheque was dishonoured and asked them to trace the car. It was held that his conduct did amount to an avoidance of contract. The practical effect of this case has however been largely undermined by the later case of *Newtons of Wembley Ltd v Williams* which is considered later in this chapter.[25] The onus is on the ultimate buyer to prove that title passed before the contract was avoided.[26]

(d) Did the seller remain in possession after a previous sale?

We have seen that the owner of goods may lose his ownership if he transfers **2.11** possession to a mercantile agent who disposes of them in the ordinary course of business.[27] We now meet two further cases where ownership and possession are

[23] [1972] 1 Q.B. 198.
[24] [1965] 1 Q.B. 525.
[25] Below, para.2.14.
[26] *Thomas v Heelas* [1988] C.L.Y. 3175.
[27] Above, para.2.07.

split. The first concerns a sale where the buyer becomes the owner but the seller retains possession. Let us assume that X, an antique dealer, agrees to sell to Y an antique vase. Y agrees to collect it on the following day. By mistake the dealer sells the same vase to Z who pays for it and takes it away. On these facts the first sale may have initially passed the ownership to Y[28] but nevertheless the second sale, coupled with delivery, may have then passed the ownership to Z. The authority for this is s.24 of the Sale of Goods Act 1979 which reads as follows:

> Where a person having sold goods continues or is in possession of the goods . . . the delivery or transfer by that person or by a mercantile agent acting for him of the goods . . . under any sale, pledge or other disposition thereof to any person receiving the same in good faith and without notice of the previous sale, has the same effect as if the person making the delivery or transfer were expressly authorised by the owner of the goods to make the same.

Thus in advising Z one would start by claiming that X was still the owner at the time of the sale to him. If this is not so (see above) Z may acquire title under s.24, provided that the sale to him was coupled with delivery. After earlier doubts it now seems clear that the nature of X's possession is immaterial—he may be in possession as seller, as repairer, as warehouseman or in any other capacity.

2.12   As already stated[29] these rules are highly technical. Consider the following problem:

> X sells a car to Y as a result of a fraudulent misrepresentation made by Y. Y pays by cheque. Y sells to Z and retains possession. When Y's cheque is dishonoured X comes to Y's premises. Y allows X to take the car back in return for a promise by X not to enforce the cheque.

The sale from Y to Z gave Z a title under s.23.[30] After that sale Y became a "seller in possession". The return of the car to X amounts to a delivery under a "sale, pledge *or other disposition*" within s.24. Consequently title is re-transferred to X.[31]

A modern example occurs where a seller raises finance by selling goods to a finance company and then leases them back. A situation can arise where a person (a) sells goods, (b) retains possession and then, (c) enters into a sale-and-lease-back operation with a finance company buyer. Where the seller acknowledges that he holds the goods on behalf of the finance company this can amount to a "delivery" to them. Consequently the sale-and-lease-back can confer a s.24 title on the finance company.[32]

(e) Was the sale by a buyer in possession?

2.13   Section 25(1) is the exact converse of s.24. It is again concerned with a split between ownership and possession but this time it is the seller who retains

---

[28] Sale of Goods Act 1979, s.18, r.1.
[29] Above, para.2.02.
[30] Above, para.2.09.
[31] See *Worcester Works Finance Ltd v Cooden Engineering Co Ltd* [1972] 1 Q.B. 210, CA.
[32] *Michael Gerson (Leasing) Ltd v Wilkinson* [2001] Q.B. 514, CA.

ownership and the buyer who obtains possession. There is, in fact, a very substantial overlap with s.23. Let us assume that B buys a car from A and pays by cheque. The contract provides that no property shall pass to B until the cheque is cleared. B obtains possession of the car with A's consent, and sells and delivers the car to C. B's cheque is dishonoured. Although C bought from a non-owner he may acquire title under s.25(1). The section reads as follows:

> Where a person having bought or agreed to buy goods obtains, with the consent of the seller, possession of the goods . . . the delivery or transfer by that person, or by a mercantile agent acting for him, of the goods . . . under any sale, pledge or other disposition thereof, to any person receiving the same in good faith and without notice of any lien or other right of the original seller in respect of the goods, shall have the same effect as if the person making the delivery or transfer were a mercantile agent in possession of the goods . . . with the consent of the owner.

This provision has been before the courts on a number of occasions and the following points emerge:

(a) The section applies only where a person has *bought or agreed to buy* goods. It does not apply where, for example, the goods have been let out on hire-purchase[33] or stolen.[34] Similarly, a buyer under a conditional sale agreement within the Consumer Credit Act 1974 is *not* (for this purpose) a person who has "agreed to buy" so that a transfer by him will not enjoy the protection of the section.[35]

(b) The first buyer must obtain possession with the *consent* of the seller; this includes consent obtained by fraud.[36]

(c) The section can apply even where the first buyer has obtained a voidable title and even if the disposition by him takes place *after* his title has been avoided (see below).

(d) What is the meaning of the obscure words "shall have the same effect as if the person making the delivery or transfer were a mercantile agent in possession. . .with the consent of the owner"? In *Newtons of Wembley Ltd v Williams*[37] the Court of Appeal reached the astonishing conclusion that the disposition by the first buyer must be in the ordinary course of business of a mercantile agent—even though that buyer is not such an agent! In that case: **2.14**

---

[33] *Helby v Matthews* [1895] A.C. 471. It is not a sale because the hirer has an option, not an obligation, to purchase. Note however that the label used by the parties is not conclusive. If therefore a "hire-purchase" agreement contains a binding obligation to pay all future instalments (and a provision that the property *will* pass when the final instalment is paid) the section *will* apply: *Forthright Finance Ltd v Carlyle Finance Ltd* [1997] C.C.L.R. 84. For a further illustration of the distinction see *Close Asset Finance v Case Graphics Machinery Ltd* [2000] C.C.L.R. 43, Q.B.

[34] *National Employers' Mutual General Insurance Association v Jones* [1990] 1 A.C. 24, HL. Lord Goff's judgment contains a clear, historical analysis of this and related statutory exceptions.

[35] See Consumer Credit Act 1974, Sch.4.

[36] *Du Jardin v Beadman Bros* [1952] 2 Q.B. 712.

[37] [1965] 1 Q.B. 560.

A agreed to buy a Sunbeam Rapier car from Newtons of Wembley. The contract provided that no property should pass to the buyer until his cheque was cleared. When the cheque was dishonoured Newtons took steps to trace the car and recover it. A then sold it to B in an open-air market in Warren Street. B resold it to Williams. A pleaded guilty to obtaining the car by false pretences and Newtons of Wembley sued Williams for the return of the car. The claim was unsuccessful.

The Court of Appeal held that A was a buyer in possession; even though he was not a mercantile agent the sale to B was in the ordinary course of business of a mercantile agent; B took in good faith; accordingly B acquired a good title which he could pass on to Williams.

It will be appreciated that the first transferee from the original buyer must take "in good faith". This condition was satisfied in this case but not in the earlier case of *Car and Universal Finance Co. Ltd v Caldwell*.[38] The effect of the *Newton* decision is to severely restrict the practical consequences of the original seller avoiding a voidable title acquired by the fraudulent buyer. The original seller may, however, recover his goods from the sub-buyer if (a) the original sale and sub-sale both reserved ownership until payment, and (b) payment has not been made.[39]

(f) Was there a disposition of a motor vehicle held on hire-purchase or conditional sale?

2.15   The problem here is caused by the fact that a hirer under a hire-purchase agreement has no title to the goods,[40] but a right to use and possession only. Thus if a consumer buys a car from such a hirer, the *nemo dat* rule applies.

The final rule, which may protect such a consumer, was introduced by Part III of the Hire-Purchase Act 1964 and verbal amendments were made to it by the Consumer Credit Act 1974. The provision was introduced after an earlier proposal had been rejected, for administrative reasons, by the finance companies. This would have provided for the retention of the registration books by the companies and the issue of cards to the hirers. One of the real problems in this area of law is that many people ignore the warning in the registration certificate guidance notes that "The registered keeper is **NOT** necessarily the legal owner of the vehicle."

Part III applies if the following conditions are satisfied:

(a) a motor vehicle is let out on hire-purchase or agreed to be sold under a conditional sale agreement; and

(b) the hirer or buyer ("the debtor") disposes of it before the property has passed to him.[41]

---

[38] Above, para.2.10.
[39] See *Re Highway Foods International, The Times*, November 1, 1994.
[40] *Helby v Matthews*, above, n.33.
[41] Where a finance company lets out goods to two or more hirers, each of them can be treated as a "debtor"; consequently a disposition by one of them can confer title under Pt III: *Keeble v Combined Lease Finance Plc* [1996] C.C.L.R. 63, CA.

The section can apply even if the hire-purchase agreement is an oral one[42] and even though it fails to satisfy the formality requirements of the Consumer Credit Act 1974.[43] On the other hand, the section will not apply if the hire-purchase agreement is void[44] or has not yet been made prior to the "disposition".[44a]

The Act then makes a distinction between:

(a) a disposition to a *private purchaser*; and

(b) a disposition to a *trade or finance purchaser.*

In the former case the purchaser may get a good title. In the words of s.27 of the 1964 Act (in its amended form):

> Where the disposition . . . is to a private purchaser, and he is a purchaser of the motor vehicle in good faith without notice of the hire-purchase or conditional sale agreement (the 'relevant agreement') that disposition shall have effect as if the creditor's title to the vehicle had been vested in the debtor immediately before that disposition.

Two points should be noted. First, the private purchaser must have no actual notice of a subsisting hire-purchase or conditional sale agreement.[45] Secondly, the "creditor's title" means the title of the person who was described as the creditor in the hire-purchase or conditional sale agreement (i.e. the person who made the relevant agreement as owner or seller).

> Suppose that X, a thief, sells a car to Y who lets it on hire-purchase to Z and Z sells it to A. Even if A takes in good faith he will only get the title which was vested in Y. Since Y had no title, the section does not protect A.

If we now assume that the hirer or buyer disposes of the vehicle to a trade or finance purchaser, that purchaser has no Pt III protection (presumably because he will be able to use the HPI facilities[46]) but if further dispositions take place the Act protects the *first private purchaser* if he takes in good faith and without notice.[47] It, therefore, becomes crucial to find out whether the original transferee was a trade or finance purchaser. A trade purchaser is defined as a person who at the time of the disposition "carries on a business" of buying motor vehicles for sale,[48] while a finance purchaser is one who **2.16**

---

[42] *Hitchens v General Guarantee Corp.* [2001] EWCA Civ 359.
[43] ibid.
[44] *Shogun Finance Ltd v Hudson*, above, n.22 (forged signature). The law was criticised as unsatisfactory.
[44a] *Rohit Kulkarni v Manor Credit (Davenham) Ltd* [2010] EWCA (Civ) 69.
[45] *Barker v Bell* [1971] 1 W.L.R. 983, CA.
[46] Above, para.2.06.
[47] The mere fact that the transaction should have aroused suspicion is not necessarily fatal (*Hall v Rover Financial Services (GB) Ltd* [2002] EWCA Civ 1514—buyer suffered from "moral blindness").
[48] This may be a part-time business: *Stevenson v Beverley Bentinck Ltd* [1976] 1 W.L.R. 483, CA. S.29(2) also includes someone buying his first vehicles for stock for a new business venture: *GE Capital Bank Ltd v Rushton* [2006] 3 All E.R. 865, CA.

provides finance by buying motor vehicles and letting them out under hire-purchase or conditional sale agreements. Any other purchaser is a private purchaser. The following points can be important:

> (i) "Private purchaser" is much wider than "private person"; thus many large public companies will enjoy the "private purchaser" protection of the Act.

> (ii) Although the purchaser is a trade or finance purchaser, he may still have Pt III protection if he buys for his private use.[49]

> (iii) The term "disposition" can include a fresh hire-purchase agreement. Thus in the third example at the beginning of this chapter the ultimate hirer will be entitled to remain in possession under Pt III even though he finds out about the original agreement before completing his payments.[50]

Conversely (and controversially) the private purchaser can rescind the agreement and recover all his payments—on the basis of total failure of consideration—if he does so before he has acquired title. In other words, it seems that he can have his Pt III cake and eat it![51]

2.17   Two final points can be made. First, there are bound to be serious practical problems in proving that the vehicle was transferred by the hirer or buyer to a private purchaser. The purchaser's job is made somewhat easier by a series of rebuttable presumptions which are to be found in s.28 of the 1964 Act. Secondly, one must always bear in mind that prevention is better than cure. A member of the public who is considering buying a car can always check with HPI.[52] HPI make their information available to the AA, RAC and Citizens Advice Bureaux.

Hire-purchase generally

2.18   X lets out goods to Y on hire-purchase and it then transpires that X is not the owner of the goods. A number of the provisions discussed in this chapter refer to a "disposition" and this is clearly wide enough to cover a hire-purchase agreement. Thus Y could, in appropriate cases, claim the protection of s.2 of the Factors Act,[53] s.24 or 25(1) of the Sale of Goods Act[54] or Pt III of the Hire-Purchase Act. He would also be protected if X had a voidable title, since it will be too late for the original owner to rescind the agreement once third party rights have been acquired.[55]

---

[49] See Moore-Bick LJ, obiter, in *GE Capital Bank Ltd. v Rushton*, above n.48.
[50] See also *Dodds v Yorkshire Bank Finance Ltd* [1992] C.C.L.R. 92, CA (car held on hire-purchase; hirer sold it as part of a loan agreement; only to take effect if he defaulted (which he did); buyer got Pt III title).
[51] *Barber v NWS Bank Plc* [1996] C.C.L.R. 30, CA.
[52] Above, para.2.06.
[53] Above, para.2.07.
[54] Above, paras2.11–2.14.
[55] Above, para.2.09.

2. Buyer's Rights Against Seller and Others

Sales of goods

We have dealt at some length with the *nemo dat* rules because it is likely **2.19** that the real battle in practice will be fought between the original owner and the buyer. We must now consider the position as between buyer and seller. The general principle is clear enough; under a contract of sale the transfer of ownership from seller to buyer is a fundamental term around which the whole contract revolves. Section 12(1) (as amended by the Sale and Supply of Goods Act 1994) spells out the seller's basic obligation with an implied condition:

> In a contract of sale, other than one to which subsection (3) below applies, there is an implied [condition][56] on the part of the seller that in the case of a sale, he has a right to sell the goods, and in the case of an agreement to sell, he will have a right to sell the goods at the time when the property is to pass.

In addition, s.12(2) implies warranties that:

(a) the goods are free, and will remain free until the time when the property is to pass, from any charge or encumbrance not disclosed or known to the buyer before the contract is made, and

(b) the buyer will enjoy quiet possession of the goods except so far as it may be disturbed by the owner or other person entitled to the benefit of any charge or encumbrance so disclosed or known.

These provisions have been before the courts on a number of occasions and the following points emerge from the cases:

(1) If the goods are delivered in such a form that any sale can be stopped by an injunction there is no "right to sell".

(2) If the seller is in breach of this essential condition, the buyer can recover the price even though he has used the goods for a considerable time.[57] The basis of his claim is a "total failure of consideration". If he asks for the return of the price his right will crystallise and will not be affected by anything done *after* this to cure the defect. If the principle of "total failure" were applied literally it would enable a buyer of stolen wine to have the best of both worlds—consume the wine and get his money back on discovering the theft![58]

(3) If the buyer has incurred other losses or expenses, e.g. the cost of necessary repairs, these can also be claimed from the seller.[59]

---

[56] s.12(1) describes it as a "term", but s.12(5A) states that it is a "condition" in England, Wales and Northern Ireland. Similarly the other "terms" in s.12(2) to (5) are "warranties".

[57] *Rowland v Divall* [1923] 2 K.B. 500, CA.

[58] If the true owner re-appeared he could, of course, sue the buyer for conversion.

[59] *Mason v Burningham* [1949] 2 K.B. 545.

2.20   An unsettled question is the precise relationship between s.12 and the *nemo dat* exceptions considered earlier in this chapter. If the seller had no title he would technically have no *right* to sell, even though the effect of the sale would be to pass title to the buyer. Nevertheless, it is inconceivable that a court would allow a claim based on "total failure of consideration" if the buyer got exactly what he paid for, i.e. the property in the goods; in a recent case the Court of Appeal has rejected such a claim.[60] If, however, he was put to trouble and expense in proving his title he might well have a claim.

Can sections 12(1) and 12(2) be excluded?

2.21   There may be cases where the seller of goods is uncertain as to whether or not he has a right to sell and he may wish the buyer to bear this risk. Section 12(3) allows the seller to give a more limited undertaking in a case where there appears from the contract or is to be inferred from its circumstances an intention that the seller should transfer only such title as he or a third person may have. In this type of case the basic title obligations referred to above are replaced by two implied warranties, i.e.:

> (4) . . . that all charges and encumbrances known to the seller and not known to the buyer have been disclosed to the buyer before the contract is made.
> (5) . . . that none of the following will disturb the buyer's quiet possession of the goods, namely—
>> (a) the seller;
>> (b) in a case where the parties to the contract intend that the seller should transfer only such title as a third person may have, that person;
>> (c) anyone claiming through or under the seller or that third person otherwise than under a charge or encumbrance disclosed or known to the buyer before the contract is made.

Subject to this, s.12 cannot be excluded.

2.22   Where goods are delivered to an auctioneer by a person who is not the owner, the question arises as to whether the conduct of the auctioneer can trigger a claim for conversion. The point arose in a recent case[61] in which the auctioneer returned the goods to the person from whom he had received them; that person, who was not the owner, subsequently sold them on. The judge ruled that, depending on the facts, the true owner might have a claim against the auctioneer. He ruled that:

> (1) liability will normally only arise where there has been a positive act withholding property from the owner;
>
> (2) nevertheless, a person who has taken possession of the goods of another can be liable if he has not acted in good faith and without notice; and
>
> (3) the onus of proving good faith is on him.

---

[60] *Freeman v Walker* (2001) EWCA Civ 923.
[61] *Marcq v Christie Manson and Woods Ltd* [2002] EWHC 2148.

Hire-purchase

The Supply of Goods (Implied Terms) Act 1973 implies title provisions into **2.23** hire-purchase agreements.[62] These are similar to those implied in a sale of goods and only one point calls for brief mention. Under the 1973 Act the condition of "right to sell" is a condition that the owner will have a right to sell when the property is to pass (this usually occurs when the hirer has completed his payments). It seems, however, that the hirer may be in an even stronger position under a term implied at common law, i.e. that the owner has the right to sell at the time of delivery to the hirer.[63] A breach of the condition gives the hirer the right to recover all his payments with no set-off for user.[64]

Other supply contracts

There may be other cases where a contract is made involving the transfer **2.24** of ownership of goods to the buyer. Examples include contracts for work and materials (installation of central heating, double glazing, etc.) and contracts of exchange. The obligations as to the right to sell, quiet possession and freedom from encumbrances are similar to those implied in a sale of goods (see s.2 of the Supply of Goods and Services Act 1982). In contrast, the contract of hire does not involve the transfer of ownership at all and consequently the only "title" terms are (a) a condition that the owner has the right to transfer possession, and (b) a warranty for quiet possession (s.7 of the 1982 Act).

3. IMPROVEMENTS AND REPAIRS

S sells goods to B who spends £200 on repairs and improvements. It then **2.25** transpires that the goods belong to C who claims them, or their value, from B. It has been well established for many years that, in assessing damages for conversion, credit must be given for improvements made by the defendant.[65] In *Greenwood v Bennett*[66] this principle was applied in interpleader proceedings between the owner and the improver. This seems fair enough but one point is unclear; if the owner seizes the goods from the improver, does the improver have a cause of action to recover the cost of the improvements from the owner? No English authority supports such a claim, although Lord Denning M.R. suggested (obiter) that such a claim would be allowed on the basis of unjust enrichment.[67]

The principle of *Greenwood v Bennett* now appears in statutory form in s.6(1) of the Torts (Interference with Goods) Act 1977. It reads:

---

[62] s.8.
[63] *Karflex Ltd v Poole* [1933] 2 K.B. 251 and more recently (and controversially) *Barber v NWS Bank Plc*, para.2.16 above.
[64] *Warman v Southern Counties Finance Corp* [1949] 2 K.B. 576, CA.
[65] *Munro v Willmott* [1949] 1 K.B. 295.
[66] [1973] 1 Q.B. 195.
[67] For further discussion, see (1973) 36 M.L.R. 89.

If in proceedings for wrongful interference against a person (the 'improver') who has improved the goods, it is shown that the improver acted in the mistaken but honest belief that he had a good title to them, an allowance shall be made for the extent to which, at the time as at which the goods fall to be valued in assessing damages, the value of the goods is attributable to the improvement.

The section goes on to give a similar right to a subsequent buyer who acted in good faith.[68] If the buyer then sues his seller under s.12 of the Sale of Goods Act[69] the seller can claim a similar reduction provided that he acted in good faith.[70]

O owns a car which is stolen by T who sells it to A. It is worth £200 but A increases its value to £900. He then sells it to B for £900. O claims the car from B.

If we assume that O has been the owner at all material times, the court may well order O to pay B the sum of £700 (the improvement figure reflected in the price paid by B to A) as a condition of getting the car back. In the result, B is out of pocket to the tune of £200. If he then sues A for the return of the £900 it seems only right that his claim should be limited to £200 and (assuming that A acted in good faith) s.6(3) allows such a reduction.

2.26   Two final points may be made. It will be seen that the section uses the words "if in proceedings . . . against a person". In other words it does not create a new cause of action. If the owner seizes the goods from the improver, there is nothing in the Act to give the improver a claim against the owner.[71] Secondly, the right to claim compensation for improvements will only be relevant where the improver or his successor in title is liable to the owner and it will not be relevant where the improver or his successor in title has himself become the owner under one of the *nemo dat* exceptions discussed at the beginning of this chapter.

---

[68] s.6(2).
[69] Above, para.2.19.
[70] s.6(3).
[71] He may of course have a claim against the seller—see *Mason v Burningham*, n.59, above.

The College of Law
of England and Wales
14 Store Street
Bloomsbury
London
WC1E 7DE

CHAPTER THREE

"IT'S A GOOD LITTLE BUS"

(1) During negotiations for the sale of a car the dealer says to the consumer **3.01** "it's a good little bus—I'd stake my life on it." The consumer then takes the car on hire-purchase from a finance company. The steering is defective and the consumer is injured.

(2) The vendor of a site of a petrol filling station tells the prospective purchaser that it should have a throughput of 200,000 gallons per year. This is far too high and the purchaser suffers severe financial loss.

(3) A prospective hirer of barges asks the owner how much they could carry and the owner replies "1,600 tonnes". The hirer makes the contract but the statement is wrong and the hirer refuses to pay the hire charges.

The supplier of goods is likely to make extravagant claims about them during negotiations. What are the remedies of the consumer if, as in the three cases cited, the statement turns out to be wrong? The position depends on how the statement is classified. There are at least five possibilities:

(1) The statement may be nothing more than "trader's puff". In this case the consumer has no remedy.

(2) The statement may be an actionable misrepresentation. In this case the consumer may have (i) a right to rescind the contract unless it is too late to do so; (ii) a right to damages at common law if the supplier was fraudulent; (iii) a right to damages under s.2(1) of the Misrepresentation Act 1967 unless the supplier can prove that he had reasonable grounds for believing, and did believe, the statement to be true.

(3) It may be a negligent misstatement giving rise to an action for damages in tort. This branch of the law of negligence is based on the House of Lords decision in *Hedley Byrne & Co Ltd v Heller & Partners Ltd*,[1] but the law has been developing slowly and the precise scope of liability has still to be determined.

(4) It may be a contractual term. In this case the consumer can claim damages; whether he can also treat the contract as discharged depends upon the importance of the term and upon the seriousness and the consequences of the breach.

(5) It may form part of the description of the goods (this overlaps with (4) above). If this is so, a breach will be a breach of condition and the

---

[1] [1964] A.C. 465.

consumer can choose between (i) treating the contract as repudiated and claiming damages, and (ii) affirming the contract and claiming damages.[2] Until recently the term "description" has been given a very wide meaning but the pendulum may be swinging the other way.[3]

It remains to add that the supplier may be in breach of the Consumer Protection from Unfair Trading Regulations 2008[4] and a criminal conviction could lead to an award of compensation.[5] Further, if the statement is a credit advertisement within the Consumer Credit Act 1974 the provisions of ss.46 and 167(2) of that Act must be borne in mind. These matters are considered in later parts of this book.

1. MERE PUFF

3.02   The praising of goods by a prospective supplier is a universal fact of commercial life and the lifeblood of the advertising industry. The following phrases are typical:

> "the most popular bike in Britain"
> "clean, healthy and alive"
> "super value for money"
> "the bathroom bargain of the year."

This is typical sales patter; it is not intended to give rise to legal liability and it does not do so. The difficulty is to know where to draw the line between (a) mere puff and (b) a representation or a term. In the above examples the statements were vague and not specific; as soon as the supplier makes an inaccurate specific statement, for example, as to measurements or ingredients, the consumer should have little difficulty in proving an actionable misrepresentation or breach of a contractual term. In an early case a seller of port who described it as "superior old port" was held liable as the maker of a contractual promise. More recently in *Andrews v Hopkinson*,[6] the facts of which appear in Example 1,[7] the dealer who described the car as a "good little bus" was liable for breach of a collateral contract (and also in tort under the rule in *Donoghue v Stevenson*).[8]

2. MISREPRESENTATION

3.03   A misrepresentation can broadly be described as a half-way house between mere puff and a contractual term. The essence of a misrepresentation is that

---

[2] Sale of Goods Act 1979, ss.11, 13.
[3] See below, para.3.14.
[4] Below, para.17.25.
[5] Below, para.16.03.
[6] [1957] 1 Q.B. 229.
[7] Above, para.3.01.
[8] [1932] A.C. 562, below, para.5.40.

it is a statement made *before* the making of the contract which *induces* the other party to enter into the contract. There can, of course, be an overlap between a misrepresentation and a contractual term; a dealer may represent a car as being a 2006 model and this may later be incorporated into the contract. Subject to this, a mere pre-contractual inducement is less potent than a term of the contract itself because damages are always available for breach of contract.

Until the 1960s it was often vital for the injured party to prove that the statement was something more than a misrepresentation; the reason was that the only remedy for misrepresentation was the equitable remedy of rescission, with no right to damages unless there was fraud. If it was too late to rescind the innocent party might find himself with no remedy at all. This is what happened in *Oscar Chess Ltd v Williams*[9] where the following facts arose:

> A consumer who was buying a car was asked by the dealer to state the age of the car which he was giving in part-exchange. He said that it was a 1948 model, as appeared from the registration book. In fact it was a 1939 model and the dealer suffered loss in that the part-exchange allowance was too high. He sued the buyer for damages.

The Court of Appeal held that the statement made by Mr Williams was a mere representation and not a contractual warranty. Accordingly, as the law then stood, no damages could be awarded. In the words of Lord Denning M.R.:

> "If, however, the seller, when he states a fact, makes it clear that he has no knowledge of his own but has got his information elsewhere and is merely passing it on it is not so easy to infer a warranty."

On these particular facts the result of this case might be the same today even after the changes made by s.2 of the Misrepresentation Act 1967 (as the consumer could prove reasonable grounds for his belief) and even after *Hedley Byrne v Heller*.[10]

If the parties are on an equal bargaining footing the courts may again be **3.04** reluctant to find a contractual promise. Thus in *Howard Marine and Dredging Co Ltd v Ogden & Sons (Excavation) Ltd*,[11] the facts of which appear in Example 3 at the beginning of this chapter,[12] the statement about the barge capacity was held to be non-contractual; in this case, however, the hirers recovered damages under s.2(1) of the Misrepresentation Act.[13]

If, however, we turn to the normal dealer-consumer situation a statement made by the dealer will frequently be classified as a contractual promise because of the dealer's special knowledge. In *Dick Bentley Productions Ltd v Harold Smith Motors Ltd*[14]:

---

[9] [1957] 1 W.L.R. 370.
[10] Below, para 3.07.
[11] [1978] Q.B. 574.
[12] Above, para.3.01.
[13] Below, para.7.06.
[14] [1965] 1 W.L.R. 623.

> A dealer told a prospective buyer that the engine of a second-hand car had done 20,000 miles. It was later discovered that the engine had done 100,000 miles. The buyer claimed damages.

The Court of Appeal gave judgment for the buyer. Here was a statement about a matter within the special knowledge of the seller. It was a contractual warranty and the seller was liable for breach of it.

In this type of case, therefore, the plaintiff should allege in the alternative (i) a contractual term, (ii) a misrepresentation, and (iii) a negligent statement.[15] The advantage of (i) is that the consumer will be entitled to damages for *any* breach of the term, even though the maker had reasonable grounds for believing the statement to be true.

3.05   The various remedies available for misrepresentation will be considered later[16] but before leaving misrepresentation three further points can be made:

(a) It may be necessary to distinguish a representation of *fact* from a mere statement of *opinion*—a problem which can cause particular difficulty on a sale of a painting which is attributed to an old master. Note however that even a statement of opinion can be treated as an actionable misrepresentation if it carries the inference that the maker knew of facts justifying the opinion.[17] A misrepresentation of law can also give rise to liability.[18]

(b) Whether a person relies on the statement is a question of fact. The maker of a statement cannot avoid liability simply by saying "the accuracy of this statement is not guaranteed and the buyer should make his own enquiries". If, in such a case, the buyer *does* rely on the statement he will have the usual remedies for misrepresentation if the statement is incorrect.[19] A recent example of reliance is *Spencer Flack v Pattinson*[20] where the buyer was induced to buy an historic car by a fraudulent misrepresentation that it was "Innes Ireland's 2.5 litre Grand Prix car". The mere fact that the claimant has an opportunity to check the statement will not absolve the maker from liability.[21]

(c) The action for damages for misrepresentation is only available where the statement was made by the other party to the contract. Thus it would not be available if, for example, a consumer bought from a retailer in reliance on a statement made by the manufacturer. There may, however, be a claim against the manufacturer if a collateral con-

---

[15] Below, para.3.07.
[16] Below, para.7.03.
[17] *Nelson Group Services (Maintenance) Ltd v BG Plc* [2002] EWCA Civ 547.
[18] *Pankhania v Hackney LBC* reported in Lawtel October 11, 2002, Ch D.
[19] *Cremdean Properties Ltd v Nash* (1977) 244 E.G. 547, CA. As to exclusion of remedies see para.8.41.
[20] [2002] EWCA Civ 1820.
[21] *Morris v Jones* [2002] EWCA Civ 1790 (defendants liable even though the claimant had three survey reports warning him of damp).

tract can be established[22] or if he is liable in negligence under the rules discussed below.

3. LIABILITY IN TORT FOR NEGLIGENCE

The history of the law of tort is one of gradual and cautious development. **3.06** Although the industrial revolution started in the 18th century, it was not until 1932 that the modern law of negligence was born. Until then it was widely accepted that where A negligently performed a contract with B and thereby caused loss to C, A was not liable to C. It was not until *Donoghue v Stevenson*[23] that the House of Lords, by a bare majority, came down in favour of a more realistic approach. In that case the House decided that in certain circumstances the manufacturer of a product owed a duty of care to the ultimate consumer. The case is also a landmark because Lord Atkin laid down his famous "neighbour" test as the basis of liability in negligence. He said:

> "The liability for negligence . . . is no doubt placed upon a general public senti-ment of moral wrongdoing for which the offender must pay. But acts or omis-sions which any moral code would censure cannot in a practical world be treated so as to give a right to every person injured by them to demand relief. In this way rules of law arise which limit the range of complainants and the extent of their remedy. The rule that you are to love your neighbour becomes in law—you must not injure your neighbour; and the lawyer's question, Who is my neighbour? receives a restricted reply. You must take reasonable care to avoid acts or omis-sions which you can reasonably foresee would be likely to injure your neighbour. Who, then, in law, is my neighbour? The answer seems to be—persons who are so closely and directly affected by my act that I ought reasonably to have them in contemplation as being so affected when I am directing my mind to the acts or omissions which are called in question."

Despite *Donoghue v Stevenson* there were, and still are, important areas of non-liability. In particular the courts have been very reluctant to hold that negligence resulting in purely economic loss gives rise to legal liability; the claimant could not succeed merely by proving that he was a "neighbour" of the defendant within Lord Atkin's test.[24] The reason for this refusal to apply *Donoghue v Stevenson* to statements was their potentially wide-ranging effect. A distinguished American judge referred to the "three indeterminates"—a careless statement might make the maker liable "in an indeterminate amount for an indeterminate time to an indeterminate class".[25] The refusal of the law to provide a remedy was not without its critics. In *Candler v Crane Christmas*[26] Lord Denning adopted a statement from an earlier case:

---

[22] *Shanklin Pier v Detel Products* [1951] 2 K.B. 854.
[23] [1932] A.C. 562. See below, para. 5.46.
[24] *Hamble Fisheries Ltd v L. Gardner & Sons Ltd, The Times*, January 5, 1999, CA and see the building cases discussed in para.5.40 below.
[25] Cardozo C.J. in *Ultramares Corporation v Touche* (1931) 255 N.Y. Rep. 170, cited in *Candler v Crane Christmas*, below.
[26] [1951] K.B. 164 at 176 (a powerful dissenting judgment).

"A country whose administration of justice did not afford redress in a case of the present description would not be in a state of civilization."

3.07   It was not until 1964 that the House of Lords altered the law. The case of *Hedley Byrne & Co Ltd v Heller and Partners Ltd*[27] shows a cautious approach and it is difficult to extract one really clear-cut principle from the five speeches. In one sense all the pronouncements in the *Hedley Byrne* case were *obiter* because the actual decision was that the defendants were absolved from liability because of a disclaimer. The facts were as follows:

> The plaintiffs were advertising agents. They placed orders on behalf of E. Ltd with various newspapers and television. They were personally liable to the sellers of the advertising space and they were anxious to make sure that E. Ltd were financially sound. The plaintiffs' bankers got in touch with the defendants who were the bankers of E. Ltd. The defendants gave favourable references "without responsibility". The plaintiffs thereupon made the contracts. The references turned out to be unjustified and the plaintiffs lost £17,000 on the contracts. They sued the defendants on the references. The House of Lords gave judgment for the defendants.

Lord Reid pointed out that a duty of care existed if there was a "special relationship"; he considered that this could be proved:

> "where it is plain that the party seeking information or advice was trusting the other to exercise such a degree of care as the circumstances required, where it was reasonable for him to do that, and where the other gave the information or advice when he knew or ought to know that the enquirer was relying on him."

It is clear from a careful reading of the speeches that the key factor was an assumption of responsibility. In the words of Lord Morris:

> "My Lords, it seems to me that if A assumes a responsibility to B to tender him deliberate advice, there could be a liability if the advice is negligently given."

The case was decided in favour of the bank because (a) the disclaimer made it clear that no responsibility was being assumed and (b) even without such disclaimer it could well be argued that the only duty expected in this type of case was a duty to be honest.

3.08   In all the decided cases since 1964 the defendants supplied information in answer to an inquiry or in the course of professional duties and the most recent cases[28] indicate that a private consumer (especially at the lower end of the market) is more likely to succeed than a businessman or professional investor; the "reliance" factor mentioned above will often be crucial.[29]

---

[27] [1964] A.C. 465.

[28] Five of them related to auditors. The leading case on non-liability of auditors is *Caparo Industries Plc v Dickman* [1990] 2 A.C. 605, HL.

[29] For a recent (and rather special) case where the plaintiff succeeded *without* reliance, see *White v Jones* [1995] 2 W.L.R. 187 (solicitors' delay in drawing will; testator died before will was ready; solicitor liable in negligence to two daughters who were due to benefit under that will). Similarly a solicitor was liable to a disappointed beneficiary when he failed to advise a testator to sever a joint tenancy: *Carr-Glynn v Frearsons* [1998] All E.R. 225, CA.

An important pair of cases related to mortgage valuations. *Smith v Bush* and *Harris v Wyre Forest DC*[30] were heard together because similar issues arose. The facts were as follows:

> Mrs Smith and Mr and Mrs Harris applied for mortgages for house purchase. In both cases they paid to the lenders a non-returnable fee for a valuation. In one case the valuer was an independent surveyor and in the other he was an in-house surveyor employed by the lender. In both cases they negligently overvalued the property by failing to discover defects and the buyers suffered loss. Mrs Smith was shown a copy of the valuer's report; the Harrises were not.

In both cases the lenders were under a statutory duty to cause a valuation to be made but the House of Lords held that this was irrelevant. They unanimously held that the negligent surveyor was liable to Mrs Smith[31] and that the council who made the advance to the Harrises were liable for the negligence of their surveyor. What emerges from the case is that the "assumption of responsibility" test is not the true one—or rather the question should be "in what circumstances will a negligent party be *deemed* to have assumed responsibility?" The language of the three substantive speeches is cautious. Lord Templeman said (at p.800):

> "In general, I am of the opinion that in the absence of a disclaimer of liability the valuer who values a house for the purposes of a mortgage, knowing that the mortgagee will rely and the mortgagor will probably rely on the valuation, knowing that the purchaser mortgagor has in effect paid for the valuation, is under a duty to exercise reasonable skill and care and that duty is owed to both parties to the mortgage for which the valuation was made."

The speech of Lord Griffiths shows a typical judicial reluctance to extend the scope of liability. He said (at pp.815–816):

> "I therefore return to the question in what circumstances should the law deem those who give advice to have assumed responsibility to the person who acts upon the advice? I would answer—only if it is foreseeable that if the advice is negligent the recipient is likely to suffer damage, that there is a sufficiently proximate relationship between the parties *and that it is just and reasonable to impose the liability*" (italics supplied).

Finally, Lord Jauncey of Tullichettle stressed the reliance factor in the following passage (at p.822):

> "The four critical facts [in the Smith case] are that the appellants knew from the outset:
>
> (1) that the report would be shown to Mrs Smith;
> (2) that Mrs Smith would probably rely on the valuation contained therein in deciding whether to buy the house without obtaining an independent valuation;

---

[30] [1990] 1 A.C. 831. The "disclaimer" aspect of the case is considered in para.8.51 below.
[31] The lender too can be sued if he "adopts" the negligent valuation: *Beresford v Chesterfield BC and Woolwich Equitable Building Society* (1990) 10 Tr.L.R. 6, CA.

(3) that if in these circumstances the valuation was, having regard to the actual condition of the house, excessive, Mrs Smith would be likely to suffer loss; and

(4) that she had paid to the building society a sum to defray the appellants' fee."

After stating that these facts gave rise to a duty of care both to the building society and to Mrs Smith he added:

"It is critical to this conclusion that the appellants knew that Mrs Smith would be likely to rely on the valuation without obtaining independent advice."[32]

3.09 In a more recent case[33] (involving a company take-over by a person who had relied on statements made by the company's financial advisers) Hoffmann J. was asked to apply the principles set out above so as to impose negligence liability on the advisers. He declined to do so and in an illuminating passage he stressed the "consumer" aspect of the *Smith* and *Harris* cases. He distinguished *Smith* from the case before him as follows (at p.335):

"First, Mr Smith [*sic*] had paid for the survey; although he had no contract with the surveyor, the relationship was, as Lord Templeman said, 'akin to contract.' [The take-over bidder], on the other hand, had not paid for the audit.

Second, the typical plaintiff in a *Smith v Bush* type case is a person of modest means and making the most expensive purchase of his or her life. He was very unlikely to be insured against the manifestation of inherent defects. The surveyor can protect himself relatively easily by insurance. The take-over bidder, on the other hand, is an entrepreneur taking high risks for high rewards and while some accountants may be able to take out sufficient insurance, others may not.

Third, the imposition of liability on surveyors would probably not greatly increase their insurance costs and push up the cost of surveys because the typical buyer who relies on a building survey is buying a relatively modest house. Take-overs on the Stock Exchange involve huge amounts and the effects on accountants' insurance and fees are unpredictable."

This "economic" distinction is not an absolute one. Thus an auditor who prepares and certifies the accounts of a company does not thereby owe a legal duty of care to individual shareholders[34] and there is no distinction for this purpose between a private and a commercial investor.

3.10 What is the relevance of all this to supplies of goods? If the statement is made by the supplier it may be useful to plead *Hedley Byrne* as an alternative to other forms of liability. It is unlikely, however, to add a great deal to consumers' chances of success, as the facts will usually disclose a *Bentley v*

---

[32] For a further case on similar facts see *Merrett v Babb* [2001] EWCA Civ 214 where the surveyor's firm had ceased to trade and the borrower successfully sued the surveyor in his personal capacity.

[33] *Morgan Crucible Co v Hill Samuel Bank Ltd* [1990] 3 All E.R. 330. The Court of Appeal subsequently held that, on the case as pleaded, a duty of care *might* arise—see [1991] 1 All E.R. 148.

[34] *Caparo Industries Plc v Dickman* [1990] 2 A.C. 605, HL.

Smith contractual term[35] or an actionable misrepresentation under s.2(1) of the Misrepresentation Act 1967[36] as well as a *Hedley Byrne* duty situation. Apart from the inherent uncertainty of establishing such a duty, the plaintiff is on stronger ground under the Misrepresentation Act because under that Act the burden is on the defendant to prove that he had reasonable grounds for believing the statement to be true. There is, however, a possibility that a *Hedley Byrne* claim could be pursued where the consumer has relied on a statement made by the manufacturer (for example, in sales literature or in a leaflet giving instructions for use). There is no doubt, however, that this would represent a major extension of the *Hedley Byrne* rule and in the only modern case in which the matter was raised the claim was rejected.[37]

There is one further possibility. If, for example, the supplier (being a limited company) has gone out of business, a consumer might have a *Hedley Byrne* claim against a director of that company if the personal expertise of that director has given rise to an "assumption of responsibility" for statements made by him.[38]

4. CONTRACTUAL TERMS

We have already seen that a statement made during negotiations may some-times be classified as a contractual term.[39] When will this occur? The leading case is *Heilbut, Symons & Co v Buckleton*[40] where Lord Moulton said:

> "An affirmation at the time of the sale is a warranty, provided it appears on evidence to be so intended."

3.11

The key word here is the word "intended" and the courts apply an objective test; they do not look into the minds of the parties but at their conduct. In the words of Lord Denning M.R.:

> "If an intelligent bystander would reasonably infer that a warranty was intended, that will suffice."[41]

To avoid confusion it must be stressed that the word "warranty" has at least two meanings. In the above examples it is used in its normal sense to mean

---

[35] Above, para.3.04. See *Huyton SA v Distributora Internacional de Productos SA* [2003] EWCA Civ 1104—the claimant had a valid claim for breach of contract, so there was no need to consider misrepresentation.

[36] Above, para.3.03 and below, para.7.06.

[37] *Lambert v Lewis* [1980] 2 W.L.R. 299 at 328, CA (the claim was actually brought by an intermediate dealer). In the House of Lords the case was decided on a different point. See also below, para.4.16. Note also that statements made by the "producer" in relation to the goods will be relevant in deciding whether they are of "satisfactory quality" (see below, para.4.28).

[38] *Ojjeh v Waller* [1999] C.L.Y. 4405 applying the principles laid down by the House of Lords in *Williams v Natural Health Foods Ltd* [1988] 1 W.L.R. 830.

[39] Above, para.3.04.

[40] [1913 A.C. 30.

[41] *Dick Bentley v Harold Smith* [1965] 1 W.L.R. 623 at 627.

"a term" or "a contractual promise". There is, however, a second meaning which is used in the Sale of Goods Act 1979. By s.61:

> . . . warranty . . . means an agreement with reference to goods which are the subject of a contract of sale, but collateral to the main purpose of such contract, the breach of which gives rise to a claim to damages, but not to a right to reject the goods and treat the contract as repudiated.

In other words it means a minor term.

If an express statement is classified as a contractual term we have seen that the innocent party can claim damages. Can he also treat the contract as repudiated and reject the goods? The answer is that he may be able to do so, provided that he has been substantially deprived of what he bargained for. Under the Sale of Goods Act 1979 terms are classified as conditions or warranties. However, the Court of Appeal has held that this rigid classification is not exhaustive.[42] The court held that there were also intermediate stipulations (sometimes called "innominate terms") where the right to reject depended on the seriousness and consequences of the breach. This decision helps to bring the law of sale of goods more into line with the rest of the law of contract and with the reasonable expectations of the parties.

5. DESCRIPTION

3.12 The final possibility is that the statement formed part of the description of the goods. By s.13 of the Sale of Goods Act 1979:

> (1) Where there is a contract for the sale of goods by description, there is an implied term that the goods will correspond with the description.
>
> (1A) As regards England and Wales and Northern Ireland, the term implied by subsection (1) above is a condition.[43]
>
> (2) If the sale is by sample, as well as by description, it is not sufficient that the bulk of the goods corresponds with the sample if the goods do not also correspond with the description.
>
> (3) A sale of goods is not prevented from being a sale by description by reason only that, being exposed for sale or hire, they are selected by the buyer.

The section is largely self-explanatory. Thus if a handbag is described as "leather" there will be a breach of s.13 if it is plastic; if a car is described as a 2006 model there is a breach of s.13 if it is a 2004 model; if the seller agrees to sell a "woollen skirt" he will be in breach if the material is cotton, rayon or linen. In this type of case the section adds nothing to the general law. It is a central obligation of the seller to supply the goods contracted for and he is guilty of non-performance if he fails to do so.

We now have to consider two problems, namely:

(1) What is a sale by description?

(2) What stipulations form part of the contract description?

---

[42] *Cehave N.V. v Bremer Handelsgesellschaft GmbH* [1976] Q.B. 44. See below, para.7.29.

[43] Inserted by the 1994 Act, Sch.2, para.5(4)(b).

What is a sale by description?

The courts have given a wide meaning to this term—in the words of the Law **3.13**
Commission "It [is] to all intents and purposes comprehensive." The following examples show how wide it is.

(a) Sales of purely generic goods, e.g. "50 rolls of hand-blocked wallpaper".

(b) Sales of specific goods[44] which the buyer has not seen where he
is relying on the description, e.g. "my 1988 wooden skis, ideal for
Alpine downhill skiing".

(c) Sales of specific goods which the buyer has seen if they are sold as
goods answering a description, e.g. "Canadian salmon".

(d) Goods selected by the buyer at a self-service store or supermarket.
This is the effect of s.13(3).[45] Thus if a packet on a supermarket shelf
is labelled "Scotch salmon" and it contains Canadian salmon there
will be a breach of s.13—so also if a label wrongly states the ingredients or quantity.

A recent case concerning the sale of a painting has confirmed that a sale
will only be "by description" if both parties intend the description to form
part of the contract.[46]

The principle that goods can describe themselves was affirmed by the **3.14**
courts in the remarkable case of *Beale v Taylor*[47] where the following facts
occurred:

> The plaintiff saw an advertisement "Herald convertible white 1961". He went to
> see it and saw a "1200" disc on the rear of the car. He agreed to buy it for £190
> in the belief that he was buying a 1961 Triumph Herald model. Unfortunately,
> he was only half right; the front part consisted of an earlier model which had
> been welded on to the rear end of a 1961 Herald 1200. He claimed damages from
> the seller, but the county court judge dismissed the claim. The Court of Appeal
> allowed his appeal.

The court held that the combined effect of the advertisement and the disc
was that the seller was offering to sell a 1961 Herald. This was, therefore, a
sale by description and the seller was in breach of s.13. Damages were agreed
at £125 (the price less the scrap value to the buyer).

It is not clear from the judgments whether the buyer would have succeeded
on the strength of the disc alone. It is clear, however, that if a seller says to
the buyer "I am offering to sell this to you—I am making no representations

---

[44] "Specific goods": see below, para. 6.38.
[45] This "supermarket" rule was first introduced in 1973 as an amendment to the original Sale of
Goods Act 1893 to reflect the changing pattern of retail trading.
[46] *Drake v Thomas Agnew & Sons Ltd* [2002] EWHC 294 (a statement that the painting was "a
Van Dyck" was held to be a statement of opinion only and not part of the description.
[47] [1967] 1 W.L.R. 1193.

and you must exercise your own judgment," there would not be a sale by
description.

This principle was recently applied and extended in *Harlingdon and Leinster
Enterprises Ltd v Christopher Hull Fine Art Ltd*[48] where the seller started by
telling the buyer that he had come to sell two paintings by one Gabrielle
Munter and then went on to say that he was not an expert in these matters
and knew nothing about that particular artist. In holding that this was *not* a
sale by description, Nourse L.J. in the Court of Appeal said (at p.18):

> "Authority apart, those words [*i.e.* s.13(1)] would suggest that the description
> must be influential in the sale, not necessarily alone, but so as to become an essen-
> tial term, *i.e.* a condition, of the contract. Without such influence a description
> cannot be said to be one *by* which the contract for the sale of goods is made."

Accordingly, the buyer will fail if, viewed objectively, the court is satisfied
that he did not rely on the description.

What statements form part of the description?

3.15   Until recently the courts have given an extremely wide meaning to the term
"description". The term has been held to include such matters as the quantity, the colour,[49] the measurements, the manner of packing and even the date
of shipment. The practical result of this can be very serious from the seller's
point of view and unduly favourable to the buyer. We have seen that if the
goods do not comply with their description there is a breach of "condition";
this means that the buyer can reject the goods, even though he has suffered no
loss. In the leading case of *Arcos Ltd v Ronaasen*[50]:

> Sellers sold a quantity of wooden staves to the buyers. The thickness was given
> as half an inch. When the goods were delivered the arbitrator found that (i) only
> 5 per cent were half an inch thick; (ii) a large proportion were between half-an-
> inch and nine-sixteenths of an inch; (iii) some were between nine-sixteenths and
> five-eighths of an inch; (iv) a very small proportion were more than five-eighths
> of an inch; (v) the staves were fit for the buyer's purpose and commercially
> within, and merchantable under, the contract specification. Despite the finding
> in (v) the buyer claimed that he was entitled to reject them. The High Court, the
> Court of Appeal and the House of Lords upheld the buyer's claim.

The judgments in the House of Lords are brief but they emphasise the need
for strict compliance. In the words of Lord Buckmaster[51]:

> "If the article they have purchased is not in fact the article that has been deliv-
> ered, they are entitled to reject it, even though it is the commercial equivalent of
> that which they have bought."

---

[48] [1991] 1 Q.B. 564. The legal effect of attribution may depend on whether the buyer was (as
here) a dealer or a private buyer (*ibid.*). Note the strong and convincing dissenting judgment
by Stuart-Smith L.J.

[49] *Ojjeh v Waller* [1999] C.L.Y. 4405, QBD—purchase of 17 purple Lalique glass car mascots—
colour not authentic—seller liable.

[50] [1933] A.C. 470.

[51] ibid. at p.474.

Lord Atkin, in a well-known passage, commented that:

> "If the written contract specifies conditions of weight, measurement and the like, these conditions must be complied with. A ton does not mean about a ton, or a yard about a yard. Still less, when you descend to minute measurements does half an inch mean about half an inch. If the seller wants a margin he must and in my experience does stipulate for it."

He did, however, go on to add that:

> "No doubt there may be microscopic deviations which businessmen, and therefore lawyers will ignore."

Another well-known illustration of the doctrine of strict compliance is *Re Moore & Co and Landauer & Co*[52] which, like the previous case, reached the courts via an arbitrator. **3.16**

> Sellers agreed to sell tinned fruit in boxes containing 30 tins. When delivered some contained only 24 tins. The arbitrator found that there was no difference in the market value of the goods whether they were packed 24 tins or 30 tins in a case. The Court of Appeal upheld a claim by the buyer that he was entitled to reject the entire consignment even though a claim for damages would have failed.

It may be, however, that the position is changing. In a passage which can be equally relevant to consumer cases Lord Wilberforce said this:

> "Some of these cases . . . I find to be excessively technical and due for fresh examination in this House. Even if a strict and technical view must be taken as regards the description of unascertained future goods (e.g. commodities) as to which each detail of the description may be assumed to be vital, it may be, and in my opinion is, right to treat other contracts of sale of goods in a similar manner to other contracts generally so as to ask *whether a particular item in a description constituted a substantial ingredient of the 'identity' of the thing sold, and only if it does to treat it as a condition.*" (italics supplied).[53]

Critical comments such as these presaged a change in law in relation to remedies, so that a non-consumer is no longer able to *reject* for slight breaches (see below, para.7.32).

Special meaning

If words have acquired a special trade meaning there will be no breach of s. 13 if they answer that meaning. Thus in the case of *Grenfell v EB Meyrowitz Ltd*[54] it was proved that the words "safety glass" had acquired a special meaning and that this was known to the buyer. It was held that the sellers were not in breach of s.13 when they supplied "safety glass" goggles which corresponded to the special trade meaning. **3.17**

[52] [1921] 2 K.B. 519.
[53] *Reardon Smith v Hansen-Tangen* [1976] 1 W.L.R. 989 at 989, HL.
[54] [1936] 2 All E.R. 1313.

Relationship between description and fitness

3.18   A final question which can be important for the consumer relates to the distinction between description and fitness for purpose. If goods are unfit for the buyer's particular purpose, can he allege that there is a breach of s.13 or must he rely on the condition of fitness for purpose under s.14? (considered in Chapter Four). This is yet another problem where the law is uncertain; the practical importance lies in the sphere of private sales.

> Suppose that the seller of a house agrees to sell to the buyer his furniture, lawnmower and television set. Both the lawnmower and the television set break down almost immediately and a cocktail cabinet collapses shortly afterwards.

As the law stands at the moment it is very unlikely that the buyer would have any remedy against the seller. Section 14 only applies to a sale "in the course of a business". There is nothing to suggest that any of the goods have been misdescribed.

One point which is clear is that unfitness for one particular use does not amount to a breach of s.13. Thus "herring-meal" in animal feed is still "herring-meal" even if it has defects making it lethal when fed to mink.[55] If, however, the goods have only one use (e.g. "touring skis") it might be arguable that fitness for purpose forms an intrinsic part of the description. Perhaps the courts might adopt the words spoken by Birkett L.J. in another context that "a car which will not go is not a car at all".[56] On the other hand, a finding that the goods are not of satisfactory quality may make it unnecessary to consider whether the seller is also in breach of s.13.[57]

6. OTHER SUPPLY CONTRACTS

3.19   We saw in Chapter Two that the Sale of Goods Act 1979 applies to sales only and that other legislation with similar provisions applies to other types of contracts for the supply of goods.[58] Thus where goods are let out on hire-purchase the condition as to description is implied by the Supply of Goods (Implied Terms) Act 1973, s.9.

Almost identical conditions apply in other cases where the property in goods is transferred to the customer (notably contracts of exchange and contracts for work and materials)[59] and in cases of hire[60]; here the relevant statute is the Supply of Goods and Services Act 1982.

---

[55] *Ashington Piggeries v Christopher Hill* [1972] A.C. 441. Such goods might, however, fail to satisfy the new (and expanded) test of "satisfactory quality" as to which see below, para.4.14.

[56] *Karsales (Harrow) Ltd. v Wallis* [1956] 1 W.L.R. 936 at 942.

[57] *Clegg v Andersson* [2003] EWCA Civ. 320 (sale of yacht with overweight keel).

[58] See above, para 2.01.

[59] s.3, 1982 Act.

[60] ibid. s.8.

Chapter Four

"IT DOESN'T WORK"

1. The Problem

(1) A buys a dishwasher. It fails to work. The seller calls on numerous occa- **4.01**
sions to try to put it right. It invariably breaks down again after a few days.
(2) B orders central heating which is installed by X. The radiators leak and
damage the carpet.
(3) C takes his suit to the cleaners. It comes back in a ruined condition.
(4) D buys a pair of new patent leather shoes for a ball. The soles come away
from the uppers almost immediately and D is unable to wear them.
(5) E takes his car to a garage for repair. The garage puts in faulty brake
linings and E is injured when the brakes fail.

By far the most common consumer complaint is that the goods or services
were not up to the expected standard. How does the law protect consumers?
There are four sets of provisions which may give them rights against the supplier:

(a) Section 14 of the Sale of Goods Act 1979 (as amended) is vitally
    important if the contract was a contract of sale.

(b) Section 10 of the Supply of Goods (Implied Terms) Act 1973 con-
    tains virtually identical provisions relating to hire-purchase agree-
    ments.

(c) Sections 4 and 9 of the Supply of Goods and Services Act 1982
    contain virtually identical provisions in relation to other contracts
    for the transfer of goods (exchange, work and materials, etc.) and
    contracts of hire.

(d) At common law, an analogous condition of fitness for purpose
    may be implied in relation to computer software (see para.4.30,
    below).

Until the passing of the 1982 Act it used to be important to distinguish **4.02**
clearly between a contract for the sale of goods on the one hand and a contract for work and materials (central heating, double glazing, loft conversion,
car repair, etc.) on the other. The need for a clear distinction has been reduced
considerably in relation to quality and fitness but it can still be important for
other purposes—including the *nemo dat* rules discussed in Chapter Two.

2. SALE OF GOODS

The general position

4.03   If a contract is for the sale of goods, the obligations of the seller in relation to quality and fitness are governed by s.14 of the Sale of Goods Act 1979 which is one of the most important provisions of the Act.[1] The Act is a consolidating Act and many of the key provisions (e.g. "merchantable quality") were originally to be found in the Sale of Goods Act 1893; that Act was passed before the consumer explosion of the last century and much of its terminology is more appropriate to a contract between two businesses rather than between a business and a consumer.

The "business-to-business" flavour can be seen not only in the terminology (see above) but also in relation to remedies. The two remedies which the consumer most wants (namely, to have the goods repaired or replaced) have only recently been introduced—see Chapter Seven. The Law Commission have commented that:

> one reason for the longevity of the provisions of the original 1893 Act may be that in many instances the Act is in practice not relied upon. For example, there are shops which will always allow customers to return recently purchased goods whether defective or not.[2]

In relation to "merchantable quality" (now "satisfactory quality") five dates are significant, namely:

1973—The Supply of Goods (Implied Terms) Act 1973 made minor changes and introduced a statutory definition.

1979—The Acts of 1893 and 1973 were consolidated.

1987—The Law Commission Report[3] made proposals for certain changes (including changes to the rules governing the buyer's right to reject, as to which see below, para.4.10 and para.4.35).

1994—The Sale and Supply of Goods Act 1994 gave effect to most of these proposed changes by amending the 1979 Act. It introduced the term "satisfactory quality".[4]

2002—A further amendment was made by the Sale and Supply of Goods to Consumers Regulations 2002.

The relevant Act remains the Sale of Goods Act 1979.

Let the buyer beware

4.04   In the light of what has been said above, the early law developed on the basis that it was for the parties to make their own bargain—it was up to

---

[1] See Law Com. No.24, p.9.
[2] Law Com. No. 160, Scot. Law Com. No. 104, para.1.9. The popularity of manufacturers' guarantees is a further example of the by-passing of the Act.
[3] Law Com. No.24.
[4] The Law Commission recommended "acceptable quality": see Report cited in n.2 above, at paras 319–322.

the buyer to decide whether the goods were merchantable and fit for their purpose before he agreed to buy them. The principle ("caveat emptor" or "let the buyer beware") has been severely eroded but is not entirely extinct. By s.14(1):

> Except as provided by this section . . . there is no implied condition or warranty about the quality or fitness for any particular purpose of goods supplied under a contract of sale.

We shall see that the Act protects the consumer if the seller sells in the course of a business. If, however, the seller is a private seller the principle of *caveat emptor* may still apply.

> Suppose that A, a private individual, sells a hedgecutter to B. It is in poor condition and breaks down after a few days. In the absence of any express promise or representation B has no claim against A.

The distinction then is between a sale "in the course of a business" and a sale which is not in the course of a business. After earlier doubts, and after referring to Hansard debates on the 1973 Act (which amended the original Sale of Goods Act 1893), the Court of Appeal held in *Stevenson v Rogers*[5] that the seller does not have to deal in the particular class of goods. Thus the conditions would apply to, e.g. the sale of surplus computer equipment by a solicitor or (as in the present case) the sale of a fisherman's boat. The words "in the course of a business" must be construed broadly and purposively; the mere fact that they have been construed differently in other contexts is immaterial.

There is one hybrid situation; what about a dealer who sells in the course **4.05** of a business as agent for a private seller? Section 14(5) makes it clear that the seller must endeavour to bring this fact to the buyer's notice to avoid liability. It provides that:

> [The conditions of quality and fitness] apply to a sale by a person who in the course of business is acting as agent for another as they apply to a sale by a principal in the course of a business except where that other is not selling in the course of a business and either the buyer knows that fact or reasonable steps are taken to bring it to the notice of the buyer before the contract is made.

A recent Scottish case illustrates that a buyer can take advantage of s.14(5) if he buys from a dealer without knowing that the dealer is acting for a non-business seller.[6]

Section 14(5) is concerned with the case where a private seller appears to be selling in the course of a business. What about the converse case—trade sellers masquerading as private sellers? An inquiry under Pt II of the Fair Trading Act 1973 disclosed that some motor traders were guilty of this—they advertised their cars for sale and gave only their private addresses. Such practices were a criminal offence under the Business Advertisements (Disclosure)

---

[5] [1999] Q.B. 1028. The court distinguished *Davies v Sumner* (trade descriptions): and *R&B Customs Brokers v U.D.T.* (U.C.T.A. 1977): see para.8.32.

[6] *Boyter v Thomson* [1995] 2 A.C. 628, HL.

Order 1977 but are now covered by the Consumer Protection from Unfair Trading Regulations 2008.[6a]

Privity of contract—new law

4.06 The conditions of quality and fitness are implied *as between seller and buyer*. If, for example, a mother buys a defective washing machine and gives it to her daughter as a present then (subject to what is said below) the daughter has no claim against the supplier if it breaks down. The mother would have a claim but she might find it difficult to prove damage flowing from the breach (although she might have a claim if she paid for the cost of repairs).[7] The question of "who made the contract?" may also be relevant if, for example, a group of people go to a restaurant for a meal. It seems that the restaurant makes a contract with each of them, so that each of them would be entitled to claim damages if the supplier was in breach of the implied term.[8]

The mother-and-daughter example given above now has to be considered in the light of the changes made by the Contracts (Rights of Third Parties) Act 1999. The Act provides that a non-party can enforce a contractual term if (a) the contract so provides or (b) the contract purports to confer a benefit on the third party—but this will not be so if, on a proper construction of the contract, it appears that the parties did not intend the third party to have enforcement rights. Thus the Act can apply if the matter is expressly dealt with when the contract is made. The following further points should be borne in mind:

(1) The supplier will have the same defences against the third party as he would have had against the original buyer.

(2) The third party must be expressly identified by name, class or description. As the Court of Appeal decided in a recent case, "the use of the word 'express' does not allow a process of construction or implication."[9]

(3) The normal rules as to causation, remoteness and mitigation will apply.

4.07 Questions of agency must also be borne in mind in this connection. A woman who does the shopping may do so as agent for her husband or cohabitee, so that *he* would have a claim in contract if the goods turn out to be defective. There is no agency case (so far) the other way round. Thus if a man buys typhoid-infected milk which injures his wife, it was held in *Frost v Aylesbury Dairy Co.*[10] that only the husband has a claim in contract. In

---

[6a] Sch.1, para.22. See below, para.A4.05.
[7] See *Jackson v Horizon Holidays* [1975] 1 W.L.R. 1468 where the Court of Appeal allowed a contracting party to recover damages for a third party's loss (the facts are given below, para.7.62). But see the comments of Lord Wilberforce in *Woodar Investment Development v Wimpey Construction UK* [1980] 1 W.L.R. 277 HL.
[8] *Lockett v AM Charles Ltd* [1938] 4 All E.R. 170.
[9] *Avraamides v Colwill, The Times*, December 12, 2006, per Waller L.J.
[10] [1905] 1 K.B. 608.

modern social conditions the courts might well hold that the husband was buying for himself and as agent for his wife. An argument on these lines should certainly be tried in appropriate cases; if it were accepted it could help to counter any argument based on the privity rule.

Strict liability

The practical importance of the point just mentioned lies in the concept of **4.08** strict liability. Section 14(2) says that the goods "are of satisfactory quality". It is clear from the case of *Frost v Aylesbury Dairy Co*, above, that the absence of negligence is no defence; the seller will not be able to avoid liability by proving that he neither knew, nor ought to have known, of the defect. It is irrelevant that the defect is latent and undiscoverable.

If, however, the privity rules bar a claim in contract an injured claimant will have to bring proceedings in *tort*. This used to mean having to prove negligence—by no means an easy task. However, since the arrival of the Consumer Protection Act 1987 and the imposition of strict liability on producers and some distributors, the claimant's position has improved.[11]

Satisfactory quality: section 14(2)

This provision is arguably the most important statutory weapon for con- **4.09** sumers. Where consumers have a complaint about defective goods—failure to work, durability, appearance, safety etc—their first line of attack will be based on the condition of satisfactory quality implied by s.14(2).

The vast majority of case law is concerned with the law as it stood before the amendments to the 1979 Act made in 1994, when the Victorian expression "merchantable quality" was still in place. In the absence of case law on the latest version of the 1979 Act we shall cite extensively earlier decisions from 1893 onwards, as the changes during the last century or so have been comparatively small.

The amended term

Section 14(2) of the 1979 Act (as amended), which is virtually identical to the **4.10** old wording apart from "satisfactory" being substituted for "merchantable", is as follows:

> Where the seller sells goods in the course of a business, there is an implied term[12] that the goods supplied under the contract are of satisfactory quality.

This definition gave rise to four problems and three of them (numbers (1), (2) and (4) below) are unaffected by the 1994 Act changes. The problems are:

(1) Is the sale in the course of a business?

(2) What is the meaning of "goods supplied"?

---

[11] Below, paras 5.10 and 5.12.
[12] "Term" means "condition" in England, Wales and Northern Ireland: s.14(6).

(3) Are the goods of "satisfactory quality"?

(4) Do any of the exceptions apply?

(1) Is the sale "in the course of a business"?

4.11 We have already considered the purposive interpretation of these words (see para.4.04, above).

Some borderline cases can be imagined. What about goods sold at a charity or tennis club jumble sale? It could be argued that such a "one-off" activity is not a business sale. Again, if a dentist or an accountant sells his private car, the mere fact that he sometimes used it for business would not, it is believed, make it a sale "in the course of a business". The Act itself merely provides that the term "trade" includes a profession and the activities of a local authority, government department or statutory undertaker. The concept of "business" is also central to the Unfair Contract Terms Act 1977[13] and to the Consumer Credit Act 1974[14] and both of these Acts merely give a limited definition similar to the one referred to above.

(2) What is the meaning of "goods supplied"?

4.12 The courts have given a sensible answer to this question by giving the words their normal meaning. Thus the condition of satisfactory quality can apply not only to the *contents* of a bottle or tin but also to the *container*, i.e. the bottle or tin itself, even if it has to be returned—it is still "supplied" under the contract even if it has not been sold.[15] Similarly, if the goods actually supplied contain a foreign body (for example, a worm, a snail or a piece of glass) the totality of the goods supplied may be unsatisfactory.[16]

(3) Are the goods of "satisfactory" quality?

4.13 As already stated (above, para.4.03) the first statutory definition was introduced in 1973. This became s.14(6) of the 1979 Act which read as follows:

> Goods of any kind are of merchantable quality . . . if they are as fit for the purpose or purposes for which goods of that kind are commonly bought as it is reasonable to expect having regard to any description applied to them, the price (if relevant) and all the other relevant circumstances.

This definition was replaced by the 1994 Act with a new definition which is to similar effect, but emphasises that the test is an *objective* one by referring to "the standard that a reasonable person would regard as satisfactory". This contrasts with the *subjective* test adopted in s.14 (3), where the question is whether the goods are fit for the buyer's *particular* purpose, which may be unusual and uncommon.[17]

---

[13] Below, para.8.23.

[14] Below, para.20.03.

[15] *Geddling v Marsh* [1920] 1 K.B. 668.

[16] See the interesting case of *Wilson v Rickett Cockerell & Co Ltd* [1954] 1 Q.B. 598 where a detonator was mistakenly included in a bag of coalite.

[17] Below, para.4.29.

New definition. The new definition is given in s.14(2A). This is amplified **4.14**
by s.14(2B) which specifies a non-exhaustive list ("among others") of five
"aspects of the quality of goods" lettered (a) to (e). Section 14(2A) and 14(2B)
are as follows:

> (2A) For the purposes of this Act, goods are of satisfactory quality if they
> meet the standard that a reasonable person would regard as satisfactory, taking
> account of any description of the goods, the price (if relevant) and all the other
> relevant circumstances.
>
> (2B) For the purposes of this Act, the quality of the goods includes their state
> or condition and the following (among others) are in appropriate cases aspects
> of the quality of goods—
>
> > (a) fitness for all the purposes for which goods of the kind in question are
> > commonly supplied,
> > (b) appearance and finish,
> > (c) freedom from minor defects,
> > (d) safety, and
> > (e) durability.

We shall consider below these "aspects" and other matters relating to the
definition. However, before doing so some general points should be made.
First, if the goods are unfit for their only proper use they will not be "satisfactory". If a thermos flask breaks when it is filled, if a refrigerator will not keep
cold, if wallpaper cannot be stuck to the wall, the seller is liable. In the words
of Lord Ellenborough in an early case[18]:

> "The purchaser cannot be expected to buy the goods to lay them on the dung-
> hill."

Again in the well-known "sulphite in the pants" case of *Grant v Australian
Knitting Mills Ltd*[19] Lord Wright commented that:

> "it [merchantable quality] does mean that the article sold, if only meant for one
> particular use, is fit for that use."[20]

Secondly, the definition uses the word "are". This confirms the ruling in
Jackson v Rotax Motor Co Ltd[21] that if goods are unsatisfactory, the mere
fact that they can be made satisfactory by a simple process is immaterial and
it is very doubtful whether the seller can legally rectify the defect after the
buyer's rejection of the goods.

Thirdly, the reference to price supports what Lord Reid said in *Brown &
Son Ltd v Craiks*,[22] namely, that if a particular description covers different
qualities of goods, a buyer who pays a price appropriate to a *superior* quality

---

[18] *Gardiner v Gray* (1815) 4 Camp. 144.
[19] [1936] A.C. 85.
[20] ibid. at 100.
[21] [1910] 2 K.B. 937.
[22] [1970] 1 W.L.R. 752, HL. If, however, the buyer relies entirely on his own judgment, the mere
fact that he makes a bad bargain will not give rise to a claim: *Harlingdon Enterprises Ltd v
Christopher Hull Fine Art Ltd*, above, para.3.14.

can reasonably expect to receive that quality, and can regard the goods as unsatisfactory if he receives an inferior quality.

Lastly, what about goods bought at a "sale" at reduced prices? There is no reported case on this point but a buyer should have no difficulty in satisfying a court that the "sale" aspect is irrelevant; it results from a commercial decision to dispose of surplus stock at bargain prices and it cannot in any way be relied on by the seller to justify the supply of inferior goods.

4.15 Multi-purpose goods: aspects (a).   The new definition makes one change of substance relating to multi-purpose goods. Cases before the 1973 Act had decided that where the goods had several purposes, and were suitable for some of those purposes, there was no breach of the condition (in effect "unmerchantable" meant "useless").[23] Then came the 1973 definition which required the goods to be fit for "the purpose or purposes" for which goods of that type were commonly used. Had the definition inadvertently changed the law, so that the goods now had to be suitable for *all* their purposes? In *Aswan Engineering Co v Lupdine Ltd*[24] the Court of Appeal decided that the law had not been changed. However, the 1994 Act did change the law (see s.14(2B)(a), above, para.4.14) by requiring the goods to be fit for *all* their common purposes.

4.16 Appearance and finish: aspect (b).   Problems may occur which upset the consumer even though the goods are still usable. A tabletop may be scratched, a refrigerator dented, the pattern on a shirt or skirt uneven or the paintwork on a car chipped or matt.

In a report[25] published by the Consumers' Association in 1979 it was pointed out that the statutory definition was unsatisfactory in two respects. In the first place, it concentrated excessively on the fitness of the goods for their purpose and ignored aesthetic considerations and appearance (dents, scratches, etc.). Secondly, the reference to the standard which a buyer might reasonably expect could open the door to an argument that a buyer could not complain if his new car had "teething troubles" since it was widely known that all new cars had them. The Law Commission Report[26] refers to a number of cases which lend some support to these fears[27] but in two recent cases these fears have been largely laid to rest. The leading modern case on the point is *Rogers v Parish (Scarborough) Ltd.*[28]

> Mr Rogers bought a Range Rover for £16,000 under a conditional sale agreement. It was sold as new but it had defects in the engine, gearbox and bodywork and the oilseals were unsound at vital junctions. In the six months following

---

[23] *Kendall v Lillico* [1969] 2 A.C. 31, HL.

[24] [1987] 1 W.L.R.I.

[25] *Merchantable Quality—What does it mean?*

[26] See n.2 above, para.4.03.

[27] *Millars of Falkirk Ltd v Turpie* (1976) S.L.T. (Notes) 66; *Spencer v Claude Rye (Vehicles) Ltd*, *The Guardian*, December 19, 1972; *Leaves v Wadham Stringer (Cliftons) Ltd* [1980] R.T.R. 308.

[28] [1987] Q.B. 933. The other case is *Bernstein v Pamson Motors (Golders Green) Ltd* [1987] 2 All E.R. 220.

delivery Mr Rogers drove the car some 5,500 miles while unsuccessful efforts were made to rectify the defects. At the end of that period he rejected the car and claimed the return of his payments and damages on the basis that the car was unmerchantable.

Counsel for the sellers argued that since the car was roadworthy, the defects   **4.17**
did not make it unmerchantable. The judge at first instance accepted this view but the Court of Appeal rejected it and found in favour of Mr Rogers. Mustill L.J. said (at 359):

> "Starting with the purpose for which 'goods of that kind' are commonly bought, one would include in respect of any passenger vehicle not merely the buyer's purpose of driving the car from one place to another *but of doing so with the appropriate degree of comfort, ease of handling and reliability and, one might add, of pride in the vehicle's outward and interior appearance* [italics supplied]. What is the appropriate degree and what relative weight is to be attached to one characteristic of the car rather than another will depend on the market at which the car is aimed.
>
> "To identify the relevant expectation one must look at the factors listed in the subsection. First, the description applied to the goods. In the present case the vehicle was sold as new. Deficiencies which might be acceptable in a secondhand vehicle were not to be expected in one purchased as new. Next, the description 'Range Rover' would conjure up a particular set of expectations, not the same as those relating to an ordinary saloon car, as to the balance between performance, handling, comfort and resilience. The factor of price was also significant. At more than £16,000 this vehicle was, if not at the top end of the scale, well above the level of the ordinary family saloon. The buyer was entitled to value for his money."

Even if the car is in the middle or lower end of the market it will still be unsatisfactory if (1) the defects have a knock-on effect so that the car can never be restored to its previous condition, or (2) the defects (e.g. oil leak) render it dangerous to drive the car.[29]

The point has now been clarified beyond doubt by the 1994 Act amendments, which include "appearance and finish" as aspect (b) of s.14(2B).

Minor defects: aspect (c).   The list of five aspects also includes aspect (c):   **4.18**
"freedom from minor defects". In many cases this will overlap (b) since, for example, a dent in the side of a refrigerator will be a minor defect and also relate to its finish. However, there are often minor defects which affect the function of a product while at the same time not preventing its general use, for example, a faulty light in kitchen equipment such as an extractor hood or oven or a faulty radio in a car. Here aspect (c) can be called in aid and will counter the "teething troubles" argument. *Farnworth Finance Facilities v Attryde*,[30] a hire-purchase case, illustrates this type of problem where a motor cycle had successively unstable panniers, a faulty headlight switch and a broken chain drive. The consumer was entitled to reject it because of a "congeries of defects".

---

[29] See the judgment of Rougier J. in the *Bernstein* case cited in n.28.
[30] [1970] 1 W.L.R. 1053. See below, para.7.47.

4.19   Effect of guarantee.   In the *Rogers* case (above) counsel for the sellers raised a further point—namely that a car was not rendered unmerchantable by defects which the buyer was entitled to have rectified free of charge under the manufacturer's guarantee (or warranty). Mustill L.J. was unimpressed. He said (at p.360):

> "Can it really be right to say that the reasonable buyer would expect less of his new Range Rover with a warranty than without one? Surely the warranty is an addition to the buyer's rights, not a subtraction from them, and, it may be noted, only a circumscribed addition since it lasts for a limited period and does not compensate the buyer for consequential loss and inconvenience.
>
> If the defendants are right a buyer would be well advised to leave his guarantee behind in the showroom. This cannot be what the manufacturers and dealers intend or what their customers reasonably understand."

4.20   Second-hand goods.   There have been four cases dealing with "merchantability" of second-hand cars (and they would have been decided in the same way after the 1994 amendments). The first was *Bartlett v Sidney Marcus*[31] where the following facts arose:

> The plaintiff bought a second-hand Jaguar car for £950. It was pointed out that the clutch was in need of repair, but the defect was believed to be a small one and the price was reduced accordingly. After driving for 300 miles the plaintiff took the car to a garage who found that the defect was more serious than the plaintiff expected. The cost of repairs came to £84 and the plaintiff claimed this amount from the seller.

The county court judge gave judgment for the buyer but the Court of Appeal allowed the seller's appeal. On the question of merchantability Lord Denning M.R. pointed out that:

> "On the sale of a second-hand car, it is merchantable if it is in usable condition, even if not perfect. . . . A buyer should realise that when he buys a second-hand car defects may appear sooner or later and, in the absence of an express warranty, he has no redress."

4.21   In *Crowther v Shannon Motor Co,*[32] which was also concerned with a second-hand Jaguar, the buyer was more successful.

> The car was eight years old; the engine had done 82,165 miles; the buyer paid a price of £390. He drove the car for another 2,300 miles in three weeks. Then the engine expired. The evidence showed that (a) the engine was in a "clapped out" state when the car was sold to the buyer; (b) the buyer of a Jaguar car could reasonably expect the engine to do 100,000 miles. On these facts the Court of Appeal held that the seller was liable.

In the third case the buyer scored a somewhat Pyrrhic victory. The case was *Lee v York Coach and Marine*[33] and the facts were as follows:

---

[31] [1965] 1 W.L.R. 1013.
[32] [1975] 1 W.L.R. 30.
[33] [1977] R.T.R. 35.

Mrs Lee bought a second-hand Morris 1100 for £355. Almost immediately it developed defects and it was off the road for a considerable time when the sellers sought unsuccessfully to mend the defects. After seven weeks her solicitors wrote to the sellers saying "we must ask you please to remedy all these defects without delay or to refund £355 to Mrs Lee". The sellers then offered to do some further work on the car; a Department of Environment examiner found very serious defects, and two weeks later a further letter was written by the solicitors. "Mrs Lee would have been justified in rescinding the contract on that basis—that is on the basis that the car was unroadworthy—in our opinion she may still be entitled to do so." Four months later the buyer brought an action claiming the return of the price. The evidence showed (*inter alia*) that the brakes were so poor that they could not have survived an attempt to test them.

The Court of Appeal held that the car, being unsafe to be driven, was clearly unmerchantable. They also held, however, that neither of the solicitor's letters amounted to a rejection of the car. By the time that the buyer finally sought to reject (the start of the proceedings) it was too late to reject.[34] Accordingly, she was only entitled to damages and the figure of £100 was not disputed. Presumably Mrs Lee would have seen none of the £100 since the court made no order for costs in the Court of Appeal.

Finally, in the most recent case[35] the Court of Appeal applied the *Rogers* ruling (above) that roadworthiness was not the correct test. Each case would turn on the application of the statutory definition to the particular facts and on the extent to which the actual condition of the vehicle matched the buyer's reasonable expectations.

Acts to be done before use.   If both parties contemplate that some act will **4.22** be done to the goods before use, they must be satisfactory *after* this has been done but not necessarily before. Thus in *Heil v Hedges*[36] the buyer of pork chops failed to cook them properly and became ill as the result of the chops becoming infected by worms. Had she cooked them properly the infection would not have occurred. Her claim for damages failed. On the other hand in the underpants case[37] the pants were sold for immediate use. Therefore the fact that the sulphite might have been removed by washing was held to be irrelevant.

Safety: aspect (d).   It is self-evident that the average buyer of goods will be **4.23** dissatisfied, if they prove to be dangerous and cause death, injury or damage to property or make it necessary to spend money to make them safe. We have already mentioned many cases concerning unsafe goods. For example, in the leading case on strict liability *Frost v Aylesbury Dairy Co.*[38] milk was infected by typhoid. In the previous paragraph we referred to *Grant v Australian Knitting Mills* where underpants impregnated with a noxious chemical

---

[34] See below, para.7.44.
[35] *Business Application Specialists v Nationwide Credit Corporation* [1988] R.T.R. 332.
[36] [1951] 1 T.L.R. 512.
[37] *Grant v Australian Knitting Mills* [1936] A.C. 85. The facts appear in para.5.45.
[38] Above, paras 4.07 and 4.08.

caused dermatitis. In the next paragraph we consider *Lambert v Lewis* where a tow bar broke resulting in a serious accident.[39]

These cases clearly show that if goods are unsafe, they are not of satisfactory quality. Even so, in line with the policy adopted in 1994, when the definition was redrafted so as to underline some important features of quality, "safety" appears as aspect (d) in s.14(2B). No change in the law results.

Of course, many products are intrinsically dangerous. Some are so obviously so that no warnings or instructions for use are needed—knives, handsaws and other tools. However, in other cases such as cars, domestic electrical equipment, power tools, gardening machinery, pesticides and medicines it may be difficult or impossible to use them, or to use them safely, unless clear and unambiguous instructions[39a] are supplied with the goods. If these are not followed and damage occurs, consumers have no one but themselves to blame. The legal position about instructions under s.14(2) is identical to that under s.14(3).[40] Comparable problems occur in relation to manufacturers' product liability in tort, which is considered in Chapter Five.[41]

4.24   **Durability: aspect (e).**   It is clear from commercial cases involving the sale of rabbits and potatoes that if defects appear soon after purchase this may show that the goods were unsatisfactory at the time of the contract.[42] What does that mean in the consumer context? A vacuum cleaner breaks down after one month, a freezer after six months, a carpet starts to wear away after 14 months and a dishwasher ceases to operate after 18 months. The consumer *may* be able to show that the goods were unsatisfactory right at the beginning but it will not be easy. If the seller wishes to resist a claim, he will point out that all sorts of things could have caused the breakdown and that it is up to the buyer to produce evidence[43] linking the breakdown to the condition of the goods when he bought them. The buyer will argue, "I used the goods in the normal way—a freezer should not break down after only six months." A House of Lords case lends support to the consumer's argument. In *Lambert v Lewis*[44]—a case concerning a tow bar on a Land Rover—Lord Diplock said:

> "The implied warranty [*sic*] of fitness for a particular purpose . . . is a continuing warranty that the goods will continue to be fit for that purpose for a reasonable time after delivery. . . . What is a reasonable time will depend on the nature of the goods but I would accept that in the case of the coupling the warranty was still continuing up to the date, some three to six months before the accident, when it

---

[39] For two recent cases where a lack of safety was a key factor in a successful claim see *Clegg v Andersson* [2003] EWCA Civ 320 (below, para.7.43) and *SW Tubes Ltd v Owen Stuart Ltd* [2002] EWCA Civ 854.

[39a] See *Vacwell Engineering*, below, para.5.44.

[40] Below, para. 4.33.

[41] Below, paras 5.18 and 5.44.

[42] See *Beer v Walker* (1877) 46 L.J.Q.B. 677; *Mash & Murrell v Joseph I Emanuel Ltd* [1961] 1 All E.R. 485.

[43] See below, para.7.18, for the reversal of the burden of proof during the first six months: s.48A(3).

[44] [1982] A.C. 225. See also para. 5.43.

first became known to the farmer that the handle of the locking mechanism was missing."[45]

Now the considerable uncertainty in this area (especially at the level of consumer complaints) has been dispelled. The Law Commission recommended[46] an express reference to durability in the Act. This has been done by the inclusion of aspect (e) in s.14(2B).

A further change has recently been made by reg.5 of the Sale and Supply of Goods to Consumers Regulations 2002. We shall deal with this shift in the onus of proof when we come to consider the buyer's remedies—see below, para.7.18.

Spare parts. A consumer may find that his goods become useless because, **4.25** for example, the retailer does not have a supply of spare parts and the manufacturer has discontinued that particular product or has gone out of business altogether. There is no legal obligation on the seller or manufacturer to carry spare parts[47], although some trade associations have adopted Codes of Practice which require their members to do so.[48]

(4) Do any of the exceptions apply?[49]

Three exceptions, which operate in quite narrow limits, appear in s.14(2C) **4.26** and are as follows:

> (2C) The term implied by subsection (2) above does not extend to any matter making the quality of the goods unsatisfactory—
> (a) which is specifically drawn to the buyer's attention before the contract is made,
> (b) where the buyer examines the goods before the contract is made, which that examination ought to reveal, or
> (c) in the case of a contract for sale by sample, which would have been apparent on a reasonable examination of the sample.

The first exception in s.14(2C)(a) applies where defects are *specifically* drawn to the buyer's attention before the contract is made. This could apply if, for example, a defective clutch or a dent or scratch or other defect was pointed out to the buyer—perhaps with an abatement in price. This is quite common where stores sell shop-soiled showroom models at a discount with labels drawing attention to the particular damage. There could, of course, be room for argument—the buyer might say "the seller told me that the clutch was rather worn but I had no idea I would have to spend £450 on it a week after buying the car."

The second exception in s.14(2C)(b) relates to examination where the buyer has examined the goods *before* the making of the contract. The condition does not apply as regards defects which that examination ought to reveal. Two

---

[45] At p.276.
[46] Op. cit. at pp.10, 31–33.
[47] See Law Com. No.160, p.34.
[48] See below, para.10.26.
[49] The first two were s.14(2)(a) and (b) before the 1994 Act amendments.

points can be made with regard to this exception. First, it applies only to a buyer who has *actually* examined the goods—not to a buyer who has declined an opportunity to do so. Secondly, what is the meaning of "defects which that examination ought to reveal?" This wording was first introduced in 1973 and differs slightly from the wording of the original 1893 Act, i.e. "defects which such examination ought to have revealed". In either case the words appear to refer solely to the examination actually made. If, for example, the buyer of a handbag only examines the outside, he will still be able to complain if on arriving home he finds that the inside has numerous defects including a broken zip (but he could not claim for an external defect which he should have seen, e.g. a broken handle). There is a Court of Appeal case which appears to confirm this view.[50] However, in *Thornett & Fehr v Beers & Son*[51] Bray J. at first instance appeared to treat the words "such examination" as if they read "a reasonable examination". He held that (a) the buyers had examined the goods; (b) an examination would "in the ordinary way" have revealed the defect; (c) accordingly, the quality condition was not implied.

It is possible that this decision is wrong on the wording of the Act and it appears to be inconsistent with the *Bristol Tramways* case (which was not cited). It can also be argued that if the case was wrong on the original wording of the Act, it may be even more incorrect on the amended wording. Thus, the courts may well refuse to follow it. Nevertheless, the moral is clear for consumers—examine goods thoroughly before purchase or not at all.

The Law Commission Report and the 1994 Act: a footnote

4.27   The Law Commission have acknowledged that there is no magic formula to cover all cases[52] because:

> Sale transactions may take an almost infinite variety of forms. A sale may be of a new jet aircraft from the manufacturers to an international carrier, of a washing machine still in its packing from a department store to a young married couple, of a catapult to a child, of an old motor car by a back-street garage to a student, of a breeding ewe from one farmer to another, of thousands of tons of a primary product (such as wheat) from one trader to another (neither of whom will ever see the goods), of a newspaper or box of matches from a street-vendor to a passer-by.[53]

In the Third Edition of this book we forecast that the Law Commission's proposals were likely to be given statutory force before the next decade was much older. That was written in 1990 and four years later the Sale and Supply of Goods Act 1994 was passed.

Although, as we have seen, no dramatic changes in the law resulted, the use of the expression "satisfactory quality" is more appropriate to modern times and the inclusion of the five aspects in s.14(2B) alerts consumers and their advisers more directly to these important facets.

---

[50] *Bristol Tramways v Fiat Motors* [1910] 2 K.B. 831.
[51] [1919] 1 K.B. 486.
[52] Op. cit., p.24.
[53] ibid. at p.23.

A further change

The Sale and Supply of Goods to Consumers Regulations 2002 incorporated **4.28** into English law the provisions of EU Parliament and Council Directive 1999/44. Most of the key provisions relate to remedies and will be considered in Chapter Seven but there is one further amendment to s.14(2)—an amendment that can be significant in these days of high-pressure advertising on television, the internet and elsewhere. Section 14(2C) is followed by two further provisions which read as follows:

> (2D) If the buyer deals as consumer . . . the relevant circumstances mentioned in subsection (2A) above include any public statements on the specific characteristics of the goods made about them by the seller, the producer or his representative, particularly in advertising or on labelling.
> (2E) A public statement is not by virtue of subsection (2D) above a relevant circumstance for the purpose of subsection (2A) above in the case of a contract of sale, if the seller shows that—
>
> > (a) at the time the contract was made, he was not, and could not reasonably have been, aware of the statement,
> > (b) before the contract was made, the statement had been withdrawn in public or, to the extent that it contained anything that was incorrect or misleading, it had been corrected in public, or
> > (c) the decision to buy the goods could not have been influenced by the statement.

The moral is obvious; any prospective consumer buyer who is attracted by an advertisement or other public statement made by the producer should bring this to the notice of the seller before the contract is made.

However, this provision may cause problems for a retailer caught between a consumer buyer and his own supplier (e.g. a producer or wholesaler). If the consumer makes a successful claim against the retailer based on s.14(2D), the retailer as a non-consumer cannot pass the buck to his seller — a piggy in the middle! The retailer's solution is to include an express indemnity in his contractual terms.

Fitness for particular purpose: section 14(3)

Section 14 of the Sale of Goods Act implies a condition of reasonable fitness **4.29** as well as the condition of satisfactory quality which has just been considered. Section 14(3) reads as follows:

> Where the seller sells goods in the course of a business and the buyer, expressly or by implication, makes known
>
> > (a) to the seller, or
> > (b) where the purchase price or part of it is payable by instalments and the goods were previously sold by a credit-broker to the seller, to that credit-broker
>
> any particular purpose for which the goods are being bought, there is an implied term[54] that the goods supplied under the contract are reasonably fit for that

---

[54] In England and Wales and in Northern Ireland that term is a "condition": s.14(6). It was s.14(1) in the 1893 Act and amended in 1973.

purpose, whether or not that is a purpose for which such goods are commonly supplied, except where the circumstances show that the buyer does not rely, or that it is unreasonable for him to rely, on the skill or judgment of the seller or credit-broker.

A number of rules are common to both subsections. Thus (a) in both cases liability is strict; (b) in both cases the seller is only liable if he supplied the goods "in the course of a business"; (c) both conditions apply to all goods "supplied" under the contract; (d) in both cases the condition only applies as between seller and buyer; and (e) in both cases the seller may be relieved from liability if the buyer fails to do something to the goods before use.

What is the need for s.14(3)? The key is to be found in the words "any *particular* purpose . . . whether or not that is a purpose for which such goods are commonly supplied".

Suppose that a law student goes to a bookseller and says "I want to buy some books which are suitable for the Solicitors examinations." The seller supplies books which are only suitable for the Bar or University examinations. On these facts the seller would clearly be liable under s.14(3); but there might well be no breach of s.14(2). Common examples are tyres, windscreen wipers or wing mirrors for cars, bags for vacuum cleaners or mobile phone chargers, where the spares or accessories are not defective but are not suitable and do not fit the particular model.

4.30   The subsection applies where the purpose is made known "expressly or by implication". In the case of single purpose goods such as a bun or a hot water bottle,[55] the buyer does not have to go through the ritual of spelling out his purpose—this will be implied because it is self-evident. In this type of case the courts would not give much weight to a clause in a standard form contract (even if signed by the buyer) stating that "the buyer has not made known the purpose for which the goods are required." This type of clause was used in the hire-purchase case of *Lowe v Lombank*,[56] a case involving a car with numerous defects. The Court of Appeal found no difficulty in holding that the supplier (the finance company) was liable under the implied condition of fitness. The purpose was obvious and the clause was inconsistent with the facts. If, however, the purpose is a special one (for example, a textbook suitable for a particular course) then the seller will be liable only if that purpose was *expressly* made known. In *Griffiths v Peter Conway Ltd*[57]:

> A lady bought a Harris tweed coat. She had an abnormally sensitive skin and contracted dermatitis from wearing the coat. The evidence showed that the coat would not have caused problems apart from this one special fact. It was held that as this fact had not been disclosed to the seller, he was not liable.

---

[55] See *Preist v Last* [1903] 2 K.B. 148—the case of a bursting hot water bottle. The seller would also be liable under s.14(2), above.

[56] [1960] 1 W.L.R. 196.

[57] [1939] 1 All E.R. 685. See also *Aswan Engineering Establishment Co v Lupdine Ltd* [1987] 1 W.L.R. 1. and *Slater v Finning* [1997] A.C. 473.

Reliance

In the 1893 Act the wording required the buyer to show that he relied on the sell-   **4.31**
er's skill and judgment, but the 1973 Act reversed the burden of proof. Thus the
condition of fitness is not implied if the seller can prove that the buyer did not rely
on the seller's skill or judgement. Suppose that John, an amateur jeweller, goes
to a general hardware store and asks for glue suitable for jewellery-making. The
seller might say "I have no idea whether this brand is suitable—you must decide
for yourself and not rely on me." In such a case he would escape liability under
s.14(3) (and perhaps also under s.14(2)[58] since the circumstances surrounding
the purchase would be one of the "circumstances" in s.14(2A)). The buyer's reliance on the seller's skill or judgment may well be partial. If the goods turn out to
be unfit for the buyer's particular purpose, the seller will be liable unless he can
prove that the defect fell outside the area of reliance.[59]

A recent non-consumer case provides a good modern illustration. In
Jewson Ltd v Kelly[60]

> A developer claimed that boilers installed in flats had a low rate of energy reten-
> tion and that this resulted in a number of prospective buyers dropping out. He
> sued the supplier of the boilers under s.14. The action failed.

The Court of Appeal held that (1) there was nothing intrinsically wrong with
the boilers and accordingly they were of "satisfactory quality"; (2) the case
therefore turned on their fitness for a particular purpose under s.14(3); (3) it
was not reasonable for the buyer to rely on the seller's skill or judgment and
accordingly the action failed.

Computer software

In the recent case of *St. Albans DC v ICL*[61] the Council ordered software from   **4.32**
ICL in order to calculate the size of the local population so that they could
set the appropriate community charge. Owing to an error in the software, the
population figure was overstated and the Council suffered a substantial and
irrecoverable loss by setting too low a charge. The judge and the Court of
Appeal decided the case in favour of St. Albans on the basis that ICL were in
breach of an express term. In the Court of Appeal, and in a double obiter, Sir
Ian Glidewell considered that (1) where a disk containing software is supplied
by one person to another, the disk is "goods" for the purposes of s.14 and (2)
if the software on the disk is defective, the transferee will have the benefit of
the implied condition of reasonable fitness. The exemption clause aspects of
the case are considered in Chapter Eight (see para.8.57).

---

[58] But see *R & B Customs Brokers Co Ltd v United Dominions Trust* [1988] W.L.R.321, CA
below at para.8.32. Claim succeeded under s.14(3), but failed under s.14(2) because of
customer's awareness of the fault under the exception in s.14(2C) (as it now is), above,
para.4.26.
[59] *Ashington Piggeries Ltd v Christopher Hill Ltd* [1972] A.C. 441.
[60] [2003] EWCA Civ. 1030.
[61] *St. Albans City and DC v International Computers Ltd* [1996] 4 All E.R. 481. ICL had inserted
the software into the St. Albans computer without supplying a disk.

Warnings and instructions

4.33   If the instructions supplied with the goods are wrong or misleading this can
make the goods unfit for their purpose. If, however, there is a clear warning
(e.g. "Do not use after July 1") a buyer who ignores this cannot complain
merely because the damage which he suffers is different from that mentioned
in the warning.[62] The position will depend on a number of factors including
the experience of the buyer and any previous course of dealing.[63]

Credit-broker

4.34   The term "credit-broker" is taken from the Consumer Credit Act 1974
which is considered in Part IV of this book (below, para.18.01). The type
of case contemplated by s.14(3) is that of a consumer who goes to a dealer
and tells the dealer the purpose for which he wants the goods. The dealer
then sells the goods on to a finance house which in turn sells the goods to
the consumer on instalment terms. Although the consumer has bought the
goods from the finance company (which he has probably never heard of
until they write to him demanding payment) he will enjoy the protection of
s.14(3) if he makes his purpose known to the dealer (credit-broker) unless he
did not rely, or it was not reasonable for him to rely, on the credit-broker's
skill or judgment.

The Law Commission

4.35   In their Report No.160, which has been discussed earlier in this chapter in
relation to merchantable quality, the Law Commission did not make any
proposals for the amendment of the fitness condition in s.14(3). They did,
however, make a number of proposals in relation to remedies and these will
be dealt with in Chapter Seven.

3. CONDITIONAL SALES AND CREDIT SALES

4.36   These transactions where the buyer pays the price by instalments (as to which
see below, para.18.09) are treated in the same way as any other sales.

4. HIRE-PURCHASE

4.37   We saw earlier that a hire-purchase agreement is not a sale of goods because
the hirer has not agreed to buy.[64] The implied terms as to fitness and quality
are virtually the same as in a sale of goods but the relevant provision is s.10
of the Supply of Goods (Implied Terms) Act 1973. The hirer will usually

---

[62] *Wormell v RHM Agriculture (East)* [1987] 1 W.L.R. 1091 (herbicide failed to kill farmer's
wild oats because it was used too late in the season).
[63] *Medivance Investments Ltd v Gaselane Pipeworks Ltd* [2002] EWCA Civ 500.
[64] Above, paras.2.01 and 2.13.

conduct the negotiations with a "credit-broker" (see above) and once again it is sufficient if he notifies his purpose to that credit-broker.[65]

5. WORK AND MATERIALS

We saw at the beginning of this chapter that certain contracts may be clas- **4.38** sified as contracts for "work and materials" rather than "sale of goods" because, in addition to the transfer of goods, significant services are supplied too. Contracts to repair a house or car, or to insulate a loft, are obvious examples. In the words of Stable J. in a case where a hairdresser applied a hair dye to the head of a customer:

> "[It] is really half the rendering of services and, in a sense, half the supply of goods."[66]

The law applies different standards to the two halves of the contractual obligation. On the first half (i.e. the provision of work or services) there is an implied duty to take reasonable care[67]; on the second half (i.e. the provision of materials or goods) there is strict liability under s.4 of the Supply of Goods and Services Act 1982 in respect of satisfactory quality[68] and fitness for purpose.

The Act confirms the common law position; thus in *Samuels v Davis*[69] the defendant was liable when the denture which he had made did not fit the mouth of the plaintiff's wife. The Court of Appeal found it unnecessary to decide whether it was a sale of goods or work and materials contract. The important point is that the dentist was liable even though the county court judge had found that he was not negligent. The court approved the reasoning in the earlier Divisional Court case of *GH Myers & Co v Brent Cross Service Co.*[70] In that case:

> The plaintiff asked the defendant to "knock-in" the engine of his car and to renew any parts which required replacement. In the course of the work the defendant bought six connecting rods and fitted them. Owing to a latent defect one of the rods broke and damage of nearly £70 was caused. When the plaintiff claimed damages, the defendant argued that he was not liable because the defect could not have been discovered by the exercise of reasonable care and skill. The defence was rejected.

The Divisional Court made it clear that if the consumer relied on the repair- **4.39** ers' skill and judgment then liability was strict. In the words of du Parcq J.:

---

[65] s.10(3).
[66] *Watson v Buckley Osborne & Co* [1940] 1 All E.R. 174 at 180.
[67] Supply of Goods and Services Act 1982, s.13. Below, para.6.44.
[68] But see s.18(3) for the five "aspects".
[69] [1943] K.B. 526.
[70] [1934] 1 K.B. 46. The principles set out in this judgment are now statutory—see Supply of Goods and Services Act 1982, s.4. A detailed discussion can be found in Woodroffe, *Goods and Services—the New Law*, Ch.3.

"I think that the true view is that a person contracting to do work and supply materials warrants that the materials which he uses will be of good quality and reasonably fit for the purpose for which he is using them, unless the circumstances of the contract are such as to exclude any such warranty. There may be circumstances which would clearly exclude it. A man goes to a repairer and says 'repair my car; get the parts from the makers and fit them.' In such a case it is made plain that the person ordering the repairs is not relying upon any warranty, except that the parts used will be parts ordered and obtained from the makers. On the other hand if he says 'do the work—fit any necessary parts' he is in no way limiting the person doing the repair work, and the person doing the repair work is in my view liable if there is any defect in the materials supplied, even if it was one which reasonable care would not have discovered."

Thus, for example, the repairer will be liable where the defect was due to the faulty work of a sub-contractor—unless this was a person selected by the customer.[71]

One area of increasing concern is the sale by builders or developers of houses or flats with fully equipped kitchens and central heating. Here again the 1982 Act applies, so that if the equipment such as a dishwasher is faulty, the builder will be strictly liable for breach of the condition of satisfactory quality in s.4(2).

6. HIRE

4.40   The rules relating to the quality or fitness of goods let out on hire were somewhat uncertain but the matter is now governed by s.9 of the Supply of Goods and Services Act 1982. Once again the rules are virtually identical to those which apply to sale, hire-purchase and the "materials" element of work and materials contracts and the liability of the supplier is strict.[72]

7. SOFTWARE

4.41   In the *St. Albans* case (para.4.32 above) Sir Ian Glidewell considered (obiter) that the insertion of software into a customer's computer was subject to an implied common law condition of reasonable fitness analogous to that set out above. The comment was obiter because the court found that the installers (ICL) were in a breach of an express term. This is clearly a developing area of law.[73]

---

[71] *Stewart v Reavell's Garage* [1952] 2 Q.B. 545.
[72] See Woodroffe, above, n.70.
[73] See, e.g. unreported case of *Horace Holiman Ltd v Sherwood International Group Ltd* noted on (2000) Lawtel November 14, 2001 (TCC).

CHAPTER FIVE

"IT WILL COST £1,000 TO MAKE THEM SAFE"

Scheme of this chapter

In the previous chapter we examined the consumer's contractual rights **5.01**
against his immediate supplier where the goods were faulty. In this chapter
we move further afield to consider the consumer's rights against other
persons in the distribution chain—including in particular the manufacturer.
Such rights can be important for at least three reasons:

(1) A buyer may find that his rights under a manufacturer's guarantee
are easier to enforce than his Sale of Goods Act rights against his
supplier, where he may have considerable difficulty in proving that
the goods were of unsatisfactory quality.

(2) A supplier may be unable to meet the claim—perhaps because he has
gone out of business.

(3) The injured party may not have a contract at all; thus a badly constructed car may cause death or injury to passengers and pedestrians
while a child may suffer pre-natal injuries caused by a drug supplied
to the mother.

This chapter will deal first with *poor quality* goods and then with *dangerous*
goods. The distinction is crucial.

Example 1

A buys goods from B which were manufactured by C. They are of very *poor* **5.02**
quality, do not work and are useless to A unless he spends money on repairing
them. The goods are *not* dangerous.

Example 2

The goods in the previous example cause death or personal injury or damage to **5.03**
other property. The goods are *dangerous*.

A. POOR QUALITY GOODS

1. INTRODUCTION

It is clear from the cases that the law of negligence in tort will not help the **5.04**
consumer where the goods are not dangerous, but of poor quality, i.e. safe but
shoddy (as in Example 1 above). It is equally clear that Pt I of the Consumer

Protection Act 1987 (below, para.5.11) will not help either. That leaves just two rights which exist side by side—a claim under the contract of supply[1] and a contractual claim under a manufacturer's guarantee (in Example 1 against B and C respectively).

2. MANUFACTURERS' GUARANTEES[2]

The nature of a guarantee

5.05   A guarantee is familiar to millions of consumers and it has become an integral part of the purchase of durable goods. The manufacturer usually agrees to replace defective parts for a specified period (for example, 12 months). The attraction of this for the consumer may be cut down by further clauses requiring the consumer to pay the cost of carriage and sometimes even the cost of labour. Subject to this, a guarantee can have very real commercial advantages for both parties. For the manufacturer, it helps to promote his product and the card which the customer signs and returns may be valuable for the purposes of market research. For the customer, the guarantee may be a valuable way of sidestepping the hazards of litigation, especially as the remedy which he *really* wants—repair or replacement—may not always be available against the retailer.[3]

There have been very few cases on guarantees and until recently their precise legal status was uncertain; there were (at least in theory) doubts as to how a manufacturer's guarantee could satisfy the legal requirements of offer, acceptance and consideration. Attempts to clarify the position, and to strengthen the consumer's rights, were made by Office of Fair Trading,[4] the Department of Trade and Industry and the National Consumer Council and we summarised them in paras 5.06–5.07 of the Fifth Edition of this book. These domestic initiatives were overtaken by developments in Europe which are now to be found in the Sale and Supply of Goods to Consumers Regulations 2002. By reg.2: "'consumer guarantee' means any undertaking to a consumer by a person acting in the course of his business, given without extra charge, to reimburse the price paid or to replace, repair or handle consumer goods in any way if they do not meet the specifications set out in the guarantee statement or in the relevant advertising".

5.06   It will be noted that this definition is wide enough to cover a guarantee given by a supplier as well as one given by a manufacturer. Regulation 15, which in para.(1) finalises the arguments about their legal status by stating that they take effect as a "contractual obligation", reads as follows:

---

[1] See Chapter Four. Or possibly under a collateral contract: consider Example 1 in para 3.01 and *Andrews v Hopkinson* [1957] 1 Q.B. 229.

[2] In practice guarantees are sometimes also given by retailers and by suppliers of services (as, e.g. by suppliers of motor vehicles and electrical appliances). They are often called "warranties".

[3] Below, para.7.19. For the interrelationship between guarantees and the condition of satisfactory quality see, above, para.4.19.

[4] See the OFT Discussion Paper *Consumer Guarantees* published in August 1984, pp.21–23.

(1) Where goods are sold or otherwise supplied to a consumer which are offered with a consumer guarantee, the consumer guarantee takes effect at the time the goods are delivered as a contractual obligation owed by the guarantor under the conditions set out in the guarantee statement and the associated advertising.

(2) The guarantor shall ensure that the guarantee sets out in plain intelligible language the contents of the guarantee and the essential particulars necessary for making claims under the guarantee, notably the duration and the territorial scope of the guarantee as well as the name and address of the guarantor.

(2A) The guarantor shall also ensure that the guarantee contains a statement that the consumer has statutory rights in relation to the goods which are sold or supplied and that those rights are not affected by the guarantee.

(3) On request by the consumer to a person to whom paragraph (4) applies, the guarantee shall within a reasonable time be made available in writing or in another durable medium available and accessible to him.[4a]

(4) This paragraph applies to the guarantor and any other person who offers to consumers the goods which are the subject of the guarantee for sale or supply.

(5) Where goods are offered with a consumer guarantee, and where those goods are offered within the territory of the United Kingdom, then the guarantor shall ensure that the consumer guarantee is written in English.

(6) If the guarantor fails to comply with the provisions of paragraph (2) or (5) above, or if a person to whom paragraph (4) applies fails to comply with paragraph (3) above, then the [the Office of Fair Trading or any local weights and measures authority in Great Britain] may apply for an injunction . . . against that person requiring him to comply.

(7) The court on an application under this Regulation may grant an injunction . . . on such terms as it thinks fit.

The value of the guarantee to the consumer depends on its terms. The most generous ones provide that:

> If owing to a defect in workmanship or material your appliance breaks down within one [or two] years of purchase we will repair or replace it free of charge.

We have seen, however, that the consumer may sometimes be required to pay the cost of transporting the goods; occasionally he even has to pay the cost of labour which can render the guarantee virtually useless. There is also the possibility that the manufacturer may say "there is nothing wrong with this appliance—you have mishandled it". (A similar argument is sometimes advanced by a seller when a buyer complains that the goods are unsatisfactory.) In such a case the consumer might have to negotiate an independent

---

[4a] Added by CPRs, Sch.2, para.97 (below, para.17.06).

examination of the goods, with the manufacturer paying the whole or part of the cost. The provisions of the various codes of practice (e.g. for new cars) are also relevant.

Further provisions relating to guarantees

5.07   There is still widespread misunderstanding about who is legally responsible for defective products. Such widespread ignorance should have decreased, if not disappeared, as the result of an Order made in 1976[5] whereby a supplier commits a criminal offence if a document setting out his obligations (e.g. the guarantee) fails to draw the consumer's attention to his rights against the retailer. This Order was revoked by the Consumer Protection from Unfair Trading Regulations 2008 and replaced by including a new reg.15(2A) in the 2002 Regulations (above, para.5.06).[5a]

Another feature of guarantees aroused fierce criticism in the past; many guarantees were used not to extend the customer's rights (as he not unreasonably expected) but to cut them down. The Unfair Contract Terms Act 1977 makes void such exemption clauses in consumer guarantees.[6]

Further reforms?

5.08   A discussion paper published by the OFT in August 1984 highlighted some of the main problem areas. Attention was drawn in particular to the following matters:

(1) The consumer may buy an "extended guarantee"[7] or "extended warranty" which may become worthless if the "guarantor" goes out of business during the extended period.

(2) Guarantors delay in dealing with complaints and in carrying out or authorising repairs.

(3) Consumers take guarantees at their face value (with bland assurances as to "peace of mind") only to find later, when they seek to enforce them, that the small print makes them far narrower than expected; the guarantee may, for example, exclude liability for consequential loss and a warranty for a second-hand car will almost certainly not extend to the clutch or gear box.

(4) A consumer wishing to sell a house or car with the benefit of a long-term guarantee may find, to his horror, that it is not transferable.

In the case of extended warranties and long-term guarantees the OFT proposed that the consumer should have a direct contractual relationship

---

[5] Below, para.17.06.
[5a] 2008 Regulations, Sch.2, Pt 2, para.97.
[6] Below, para.8.40.
[7] See a Report prepared for the OFT on extended warranties for electrical goods (July 2002). See also the Supply of Extended Warranties on Domestic Electrical Goods Order 2005 (SI 2005/37).

with a duly authorised insurer. These proposals have been incorporated in the Code of Practice for Mechanical Breakdown Insurance Schemes, but this covers motor vehicles only. The Supply of Extended Warranties on Domestic Electrical Goods Order 2005 (SI 2005/37) should also be borne in mind.

Conclusion

It cannot be stressed too strongly that any rights which the consumer may **5.09** have under a manufacturer's guarantee do *not* cut down his rights against the supplier. In virtually all cases retailers seek to create the false impression in the minds of their customers that the legal responsibility is that of the manufacturer and that, if the guarantee has expired, the retailer is no longer liable. The consumer must be on his guard against this and must be prepared to say (in a loud voice if necessary) "it's *your* responsibility under the Sale of Goods Act". The question of remedies (and their enforcement) is considered in greater detail in Chapters Seven, Ten and Eleven.

B. DANGEROUS GOODS

1. INTRODUCTION

In the Second Edition of this book it was pointed out that proposals to **5.10** increase manufacturer's liability from negligence to strict liability had been made by no less than four different bodies—the Law Commission, the Pearson Commission, the Council of Europe and the European Commission. At the time of publication (March 1, 1985) some seven years had gone by without any progress; negotiations on the EC draft directive were stalled over the so-called "development risks" defence. It was, however, only a matter of months before a workable compromise emerged and on July 25, 1985 the EC Council of Ministers adopted the Product Liability Directive whereby Member States were required to pass the appropriate legislation by July 30, 1988 (but with the option of excluding the development risks defence). The United Kingdom responded before the deadline by passing the Consumer Protection Act 1987. Part I is designed to implement the Directive and came into force on March 1, 1988.

It is important to appreciate that Pt I exists side by side with the general law of contract and negligence. In a contract case the consumer will have his (largely non-excludable) rights under the Sale of Goods Act 1979, and in this situation the 1987 Act is virtually irrelevant. As regards non-contractual claims the basic rule is that the consumer will be in a stronger position under the Act because strict liability is the new regime and the need to prove negligence has disappeared. The provisions of Pt I will be examined in detail in the next section of this chapter. It will be seen that there are some situations where the Act does not apply and in these cases the non-contractual consumer will have to fall back on the general law of negligence, which will be briefly considered in the final part of this chapter.

2. PART I OF THE CONSUMER PROTECTION ACT 1987 ("THE ACT")

5.11 EU Directives generally start off with a large number of recitals and the second recital of this one declares its policy explicitly:

> Whereas liability without fault on the part of the producer is the sole means of adequately solving the problem, peculiar to our age of increasing technicality, of a fair apportionment of the risks inherent in modern technological production.

We have seen that Pt I is designed to give effect to the EC Product Liability Directive and s. 1(1) expressly so provides.

> This Part shall have effect for the purpose of making such provision as is necessary in order to comply with the product liability Directive and shall be construed accordingly.

In the light of section 1(1) above the adviser must refer to the Directive if the drafting of the Act is in any way ambiguous.

The basic rule

5.12 By section 2(1):

> Subject to the following provisions of this Part, where any damage is caused wholly or partly by a defect in a product, every person to whom subsection (2) applies shall be liable for the damage.

The words "shall be liable" impose strict liability — a vital change.
In advising the consumer a number of questions must be asked:

(1) Has a *product* been *supplied*?

(2) If yes, did it contain a *defect*?

(3) If yes, did the defect cause *damage*?

(4) If yes, is it the *type* of damage to which the Act applies?

(5) If yes, *who* is liable to the consumer?

(6) Are there any *defences* which may cut down the consumer's rights?

(7) Are there any special *time-limits* for bringing a claim?

Burden of proof

5.13 The Act is silent on this but on general principle the burden will fall on the claimant and a recent case confirms that this is so.[8] This is reinforced by art.4 of the Directive which states that:

---

[8] *Foster v Biovil* [2001] B.M.L.R. 178—a breast implant case decided at the Central London CC by Recorder Cherie Booth Q.C.

The injured person shall be required to prove the damage, the defect and the causal relationship between defect and damage.

In practical terms the abolition of the need to prove negligence may often be of limited value because the task of proving causation (which still exists) can be difficult—especially in medical and pharmaceutical cases.[9]

It will be appreciated from the wording of s.2(1) that partial causation is sufficient.

Example 3

Goods manufactured by M injure C; this is due partly to the goods being defec-   **5.14**
tive and partly to C not following M's instructions. C can recover damages from
M under the Act—but subject to a reduction for contributory negligence under
section 6(4).

What is a product?

We must first consider whether it was a "product" which was defective.   **5.15**
Section 1(2) provides that the term "product" means any goods or electricity
and it is clear that components are included.

Example 4

CM supplies a defective component to M who incorporates it into a product
which he then supplies to D. Both CM and M have supplied a "product" and, if
the component makes M's product defective, both CM and M are liable under
the Act.

The term "goods" is defined in s.45 to include "substances,[10] growing crops
and things comprised in land by virtue of being attached to it and any ship,
aircraft or vehicle". What about houses and land? The effect of s.46 is that
the seller of a house built with defective bricks does not supply "goods", but
if the house collapses and causes "damage",[11] the brick manufacturer can be
liable to the injured party under the Act.

Agricultural products

Although the definition of "goods" includes crops (see above), s.2(4) created   **5.16**
an important (and politically sensitive) exception from liability. It excluded
liability under the Act "in respect of any defect in any game or agricultural
produce if the only supply . . . by that person to another was at a time when
it had not undergone an industrial process." However, as a result of the 10
year review of the Directive this exception was removed, so that agricultural
crops are covered.[12]

---

[9] See, e.g. *Kay v Ayrshire and Arran Health Board* [1987] 2 All E.R. 417, HL (penicillin given to
child; child became deaf; causal link not proved).
[10] This is not itself defined in the Act.
[11] Below, para.5.21.
[12] Consumer Protection Act 1987 (Product Liability) (Modification) Order 2000. For a discussion of the previous position, see Fifth Edition, para.5.16.

Is the product defective?

5.17   Section 3 rephrases art.6 of the Directive in the following words:

> (1) Subject to the following provisions of this section, there is a defect in a
> product for the purposes of this Part if the safety of the product is not
> such as persons generally are entitled to expect; and for these purposes
> "safety," in relation to a product, shall include safety in respect to [com-
> ponents] and safety in the context of risks of damage to property, as well
> as in the context of risks of death or personal injury.
>
> (2) In determining . . . what persons generally are entitled to expect . . . all the
> circumstances shall be taken into account, including—
>
>> (a) the manner in which, and purposes for which, the product has been
>> marketed, its get-up, the use of any mark in relation to the product,
>> any instructions for, or warnings with respect to, doing or refrain-
>> ing from doing anything with or in relation to the product;
>>
>> (b) what might reasonably be expected to be done with or in relation to
>> the product; and
>>
>> (c) the time when the product was supplied by its producer to
>> another;
>
> and nothing in this section shall require a defect to be inferred from the
> fact alone that the safety of a product which is supplied after that time is
> greater than the safety of the product in question.

5.18   The above definition of "defective goods" is broadly similar to the definition of "satisfactory quality" in s.14(2A) of the Sale of Goods Act 1979.[13]
However, one major distinction must be reiterated. Whereas satisfactory
quality covers both unsafe and shoddy, poor quality products, "defective"
goods in the 1987 Act mean only unsafe or dangerous products; so "defective" is used in an unusually narrow sense. The following points can be
made:

> (1) "Persons generally" can be contrasted with "a person" in art.6 of
> the Directive; the expectation standard will be an objective one in
> the light of the matters mentioned in the section—notably any safety
> representations in advertising material. Thus the mere fact that the
> producer was unaware of the defect is immaterial.[14]
>
> (2) The standard of safety that the public are entitled to expect is an
> objective one and it will be decided by the judge as an informed rep-
> resentative of the public at large.[15]
>
> (3) Instructions for use and warnings, referred to in s.3(2)(a), now
> proliferate, e.g. in a car handbook and the engine compartment. A
> warning can make a product safe—provided that it is sufficiently
> clear; conversely the absence of a warning can make it unsafe. The
> massive cigarette litigation in the United States has largely turned
> on the warning factor—and in a class action on behalf of 500,000

---

[13] Above, para.4.14.
[14] Burton J. (as he then was) in *A v National Blood Authority* [2001] 3 All E.R. 289.
[15] *Abouzaid v Mothercare (UK) Ltd, The Times*, February 20, 2001—defective attachment to
push-chair—producer liable.

Florida smokers a US jury found a large number of leading tobacco companies liable for deception (see *The Times*, July 8, 1999).

(4) Sometimes products, which are safe when properly used, are misused and for that reason prove to be dangerous. Producers have the unenviable task of trying to anticipate how users may mishandle their products by placing warnings against such misuse on the products or in the instructions. It is significant that s.3(2)(b) asks "what might reasonably be expected" to be done. The position of the adverb is crucial: the question is not whether what is done with the goods is reasonable. People have been known to cut their hedges with rotary mowers or use a metal ladder while undertaking electrical wiring: if the producer reasonably expects this to happen, a warning should be given – and the best place for a warning is on the product itself, as it is the user who may be in danger and the user may be someone to whom the original buyer sold, gave or lent the product without passing on the instruction leaflet. The interrelation between s.3(2)(a) and (b) is a close one.

(5) The question of what safety persons are entitled to expect brings in what is known as the "cost-benefit" analysis. In relation to medicines a DTI explanatory note contains the following passage: **5.19**

> Establishing the existence of a defect in a medicine administered to a patient is complicated by the fact that not only is the human body a highly complex organism, but at the time of treatment it is already subject to an adverse pathological condition. . . .
>
> The more active the medicine, and the greater its beneficial potential, the more extensive its effects are likely to be, and therefore the greater the chances of an adverse effect. A medicine used to treat a life-threatening condition is likely to be much more powerful than a medicine used in the treatment of a less serious condition, and the safety that one is reasonably entitled to expect of such a medicine may therefore become correspondingly lower.

If, however, a product is found to be defective, the mere fact that it is of public benefit is irrelevant.[16]

(6) The relevant time for assessing the safety factor specified in s.3(2)(c) (and this is important for two reasons) is the time when the product was supplied by its *producer*—not by the retailer. This is often called "the state of the art" factor.

Example 5

In April 2004 M sells to D a car manufactured by him. In August 2004 D sells it to R who sells it to C in 2006. While C is driving the car in 2009 it veers out of control and P is injured. In considering the safety aspects two questions arise, namely (1) what degree of safety could reasonably be expected of a five-year-old car? and (2) what were the relevant safety standards in April 2004? The fact that safer models have been introduced since that time is irrelevant.

---

[16] *A v National Blood Authority* [2001] 3 All E.R. 289.

(7) In deciding whether a product is "defective" expert evidence is crucial. This can be seen from two cases concerning contraceptives. In one of them[17] a class action was brought alleging that a particular type of oral contraceptive had created an increased risk of thrombosis and other serious injuries. The other case[18] concerned a single contraceptive which had burst during intercourse resulting in a pregnancy. In both cases the court, after considering the expert evidence, rejected the claim. In the former case (which lasted for 42 days) the judge described his own role in the following words:

> "The judge cannot transform himself into some form of super-scientist with access to a level of expertise superior to those who have given the evidence. His role. . .and my role here is to evaluate the witnesses and decide. . .which parts of the evidence are sound and reliable and which are not."

The case of the contaminated blood

5.20 One of the very few cases so far decided under Pt I of the 1987 Act involved a class action brought by persons who had received blood which was found to be infected with Hepatitis C. The case was heard by Burton J. (as he then was) and his judgment in favour of the claimants was based not on the Act but on the underlying Directive. He described the threefold objective of the Directive, namely:

(1) to increase consumer protection;

(2) to introduce an obligation on the producer which was irrespective of fault by way of strict liability (but not absolute liability); and

(3) to render the compensation of an injured party easier by removing the concept of negligence as an element of liability

A number of points arising from this judgment have already been mentioned and every point raised by the defendant was rejected. Thus, for example, he held that the producer could not rely on the fact that the medical profession who administered the blood were aware of the risk. He doubted whether a warning would be sufficient to exonerate the defendant from liability. He also rejected a claim that the risk of infection was inherent in all blood. Finally, he gave the development risks defence (as to which see below) a very narrow interpretation. Writing in (2001) 151 N.L.J. 647 Alison McAdams (a member of the legal team representing the defendant) expressed the view that the judge sought to achieve the object of the Directive "by an alarmingly strained reading of the language of Article 6. The finding is extremely close to one of absolute liability". We do not share that alarm.

---

[17] *X v Schering Health Care Ltd* [2002] EWCH 1420, QBD.
[18] *Richardson v LRC Products Ltd* [2000] P.I.Q.R. P.114, QBD. For criticism see Charles Lewis, "Wrongful Birth; Rubber-dub-dub" (2000) Med. Lit. 2 (Feb) 8.

What damage is covered?

Section 5, which is based on art.9, makes it clear that only three types of **5.21** damage are covered, namely death, personal injury and damage to "private" (as opposed to business) property, i.e. property is excluded if at the time of the loss or damage it is not—

    (a) of a description of property ordinarily intended for private use, occupation or consumption; and

    (b) intended by the person suffering the loss or damage mainly for his own private use, occupation or consumption.

Example 6

    A defective heater explodes and damages X's office premises. He cannot recover under the Act.

Two other restrictions must be noted. First (and this is an echo of the **5.22** distinction between shoddy and dangerous goods)[19] the Act does not cover loss of or damage "to the product itself" or to "the whole or any part of any product which has been supplied with the [defective product] comprised in it."[20]

Example 7

    C buys a defective car. It crashes and injures C. The car is a write-off. C can recover for his injuries but not for the cost of replacing the car.

Example 8

    Suppose in the above example the accident is caused by a defective tyre. If the tyre formed part of the car as originally supplied, the answer is the same as in Example 7. If, on the other hand, the tyre was fitted at a later date, the car replacement cost will be "damage to any property" and recoverable under the Act against the tyre manufacturer.

The second restriction (designed to exclude small claims) is set out in s.5(4); **5.23** the Act will not apply where the total damages awarded, exclusive of interest, in respect of *property* do not exceed £275. What if the damages are, say, £1,000? The wording of the Act is unambiguous—no deduction is made and £1,000 would be awarded. However, art.9(b) talks of "a lower threshold of 500 ECU". It could be argued—and the French version of the Directive and the EU Commission support this view—that a deduction should be made from *every* award in respect of property. It will be interesting to see how the courts interpret this provision.

It is clear from the wording that any reduction for contributory negligence must be made first.

---

[19] Above, para.5.01 and below, para.5.46.
[20] s.5(2).

Example 9

> C's damages in respect of private property are assessed at £500 but this figure falls to be reduced by 50 per cent for contributory negligence so that the final figure is £250. The Act does not apply.

Whom can the consumer sue?

5.24   Section 2(2) imposes liability on:

(1) The "producer" (see below).

(2) Any person who, by putting his name on the product or using a trade mark or other distinguishing mark in relation to the product, has held himself out as the producer of the product.

Example 10

> S, a supermarket, puts its own brand mark on a bottle of wine which it sells to B. Unknown to the seller the wine has been mixed with antifreeze. C becomes violently ill when drinking the "wine" at B's house. C can sue S under the Act. But if S makes it clear that a third party is the producer, e.g. with a label stating "produced for S by M", S is not caught—there is no "holding out".

5.25   (3) Any person who imported the goods into a Member State of the EC from a place outside the Member States in order, in the course of a business, to supply it to another.

Example 11

> F, a French company, imports lethal toys from Taiwan which it then exports to England where one is sold by R to C. C's child is injured.
> The English importer is *not* liable under the Act because he imported the toys from another Member State (i.e. France). F, however, *is* liable under the Act and can be sued in England.[21]

(4) A person to whom s.2(3) applies—see below.

5.26   Returning to para.(1) above, s.1(2) defines a "producer" in relation to a product as—

(a) the person who manufactured it;

(b) in the case of a substance which has not been manufactured but has been won or abstracted, the person who won or abstracted it; (this covers mining and quarrying.)

---

[21] Under a revised version of the EC Jurisdiction and Judgments Convention (operative as from March 1, 2002) a defendant domiciled in a Contracting State can be sued in tort in another Contracting State where the damage is suffered (see art.5). A claim under Pt I of the Act is a claim in tort—see s.6(7). The Act gives the injured consumer a wide choice of where to sue (this is known as "forum shopping"); this can be important because the development risks defence (below, para.5.34) applies in some EU countries but not all.

(c) in any other case, a person who has applied an industrial or other process affecting the essential characteristics of the product.[22]

The section 2(3) defendant: anonymous goods

There may well be cases where the injured party will have great difficulty in identifying the "producer" or the person importing the product into a Member State. To deal with this situation s.2(3) allows him to seek information from another supplier in the chain and makes that other supplier liable if the information is not supplied. Such liability will arise if the following conditions are satisfied: **5.27**

(1) the injured party asks the supplier to identify one or more of the persons listed in s.2(2) (above, para.5.24)—whether still in existence or not; and

(2) the request is made within a reasonable time after the damage and at a time when it is not reasonably practicable for the person making the request to identify all those persons; and

(3) the supplier fails within a reasonable time after receiving the request either to comply with the request or to identify the person who supplied the product to him.

Example 12

The facts are as in Example 11 except that the only person known to the injured party is the retail supplier R. The injured party can ask R to identify the manufacturer and/or the EC importer. R can supply this information or alternatively he can say "I bought from X Ltd" (whereupon the injured party can approach X Ltd with a similar request). If R does neither of these things within a reasonable time he will be liable under the Act.   **5.28**

Conclusion

It will be apparent that the injured consumer has a large number of persons to sue—especially bearing in mind the co-extensive liability of a component supplier and an end-product supplier. He can sue them alone or together and their liability is joint and several; each of them is liable to him for the full amount of his "damage" (see s.2(5)).   **5.29**

What defences are available?[23]

Section 4(1) lists six possible defences lettered (a) to (f), namely: **5.30**

(a) That the defect is attributable to compliance with any statutory or EC *requirement.*

---

[22] The term "industrial or other process" is not defined.
[23] The defences must be narrowly confined: *Veedfald v Arhus Amtjkommune, The Times,* June 4, 2001—a case on art.7 of the Directive.

5.31   (b) That the person proceeded against did not at any time supply the product to another.

Example 13

> M manufactures a crane. While it is being tested on M's premises it collapses and P is killed. P's estate has no claim under the Act.

The term "supply" is widely defined in s.46. In a hire-purchase case involving dealer—hire-purchaser—finance company the section provides that the *dealer* (and not the finance company) is to be treated as supplying the product to the hire-purchaser—which is what happens in practice (although not in the law of contract).

5.32   (c) That the only supply was not in the course of the supplier's business *and* that either s.2(2) does not apply to that person or does so only as the result of things done otherwise than with view to profit.

Example 14

> Mrs Jones makes jam for a private function. The jam is defective and a guest is taken ill. There is no liability under the Act.

5.33   (d) That the defect did not exist in the product at the relevant time.[24]

Example 15

> M manufactures a car and sells it to D. D sells it to C. C has it serviced by S. C crashes because S left the wheel nuts loose. M is not liable.

5.34   (e) That the state of scientific and technical knowledge at the relevant time was not such that a producer of products of the same description as the product in question might be expected to have discovered the defect if it had existed in his products while they were under his control.

It will be recalled[25] that the dispute over this "*development risks*" defence was the prime reason why the EC draft Directive took nearly 10 years to become a Directive. There was strong lobbying from United Kingdom industries (especially pharmaceuticals) on the basis that without such a defence research and development would be severely hampered. The argument on the other side is equally compelling—such a defence would leave victims of a future Thalidomide-type tragedy without a remedy. In the event the Directive adopted a compromise—the defence was introduced by art.7(e) but individual Member States were left free to exclude it (art.15(1)(b)) and a few of them have exercised their right to do so, e.g. Luxembourg.

The drafting of this provision was hotly debated in Parliament and the Government forced through the present wording in the dying days of the

---

[24] "Relevant time" means the time when the "producer" supplied it to another: s.4(2).
[25] See above, para.5.10.

1986–1987 session just before the 1987 General Election. It is widely felt that the wording is less strict than art.7(e) of the Directive which reads:

> "that the state of scientific and technical knowledge at the time when he put the product into circulation was not such as to enable the existence of the defect to be discovered."

There is an immense gap between what a producer might be *"expected"*   **5.35** to discover in a particular sector of industry and what he *could* ("enable") discover with all the technical resources available. Nevertheless the ECJ has ruled that the two provisions are not inconsistent.[26]

In one case[27] (involving an attachment to a push-chair) the producer argued that he was unaware of the defect because "scientific and technical knowledge" in the form of accident reports had not existed at the time of the accident. The argument was rejected; the reports did not amount to "scientific and technical knowledge" and this had not changed since the date of the accident. It has also been held (in the infected blood case, para.5.20) that the defence ceases to apply once the risk is known—even if the risk from a particular product is unavoidable.

(f) That the defect: **5.36**

     (i) constituted a defect in a subsequent product in which the product in question (i.e. a component) was comprised; and

     (ii) was wholly attributable to the design of the subsequent product or to compliance with instructions given by the producer of the subsequent product.

This defence protects a component producer where the reason for the end product being defective is the design or instructions of the end producer.

Example 16

    CM supplies a component to M. The component makes the end product faulty but only because M's design is faulty. CM is not liable.

When must the claim be brought?

There are two rules—a consumer rule and an overriding supplier rule. For   **5.37** the *injured party* the basic limitation period is three years from (1) the date on which the cause of action accrued, or (2) (if later) the date on which he first discovered (or should have discovered) the relevant facts.[28] There is no distinction between injury and property damage—the period is the same in both cases.

As regards the *supplier* there is a 10-year cut-off period for each supplier.[29]

---

[26] *EC v UK* [1997] All E.R. (EC) 481.

[27] *Abouzaid v Mothercare (UK) Ltd*, *The Times*, February 20, 2001.

[28] Sch.1, para.1, amending Limitation Act 1980, s.11.

[29] ibid. This is a "period of limitation" and accordingly the court can exercise its power to substitute a new party under s.35(5) of the Limitation Act 1980 even though the 10-year period has expired: *Horne-Roberts v Smith Kline Beecham* [2001] EWCA Civ 2006. See also *O'Byrne v Aventis Pasteur MSD Ltd* [2008] UKHL 34.

This "period of repose", as it is called in the United States, relates to the particular product, not to the product line; so producers must keep precise records (showing the exact date when each item was sold) to enable them to rely on this provision. Traceability is crucial.

Example 17

5.38   CM supplies a component to M in April 2000. M sells the end product to R in April 2001.

       The 10-year period expires in April 2010 as regards CM and in April 2011 as regards M. The fact that no injury has occurred by the cut-off date is immaterial.

3. NEGLIGENCE

5.39   It will be appreciated that there will be a limited number of cases where the regime introduced by the Act will not apply and in these cases the injured party must fall back on the general law of negligence. This will be so where, for example:

    (1) the damage sustained by the claimant (e.g. to business property) is not covered by the Act;

    (2) the damage to property is £275 or less;

    (3) the claim is out of time.

In considering negligence we must stress once again what we said at the beginning of this chapter—namely the crucial distinction between shoddy goods of poor quality and dangerous goods. The courts have always been very cautious to extend the boundaries of liability and one weapon which they have used has been the weapon of "economic loss". They have held that where the only damage is to the product itself, this loss is "economic" and not recoverable in the tort of negligence.[30] This is so even though the financial loss may be the cost of repairing goods to make them safe (see below, para.5.46).

5.40   In relation to dangerous goods the starting point must be the so-called "narrow rule" in *Donoghue v Stevenson*.[31] The facts were as follows:

A lady took a friend for refreshment to a café in Paisley, near Glasgow. She bought a bottle of ginger beer and two ice creams. The bottle was made of dark, opaque glass, so the contents were invisible. They put the ice creams into tumblers, poured some of the ginger beer on top and drank the concoction. They then poured the rest of the ginger beer into a tumbler and out slid the body of a decomposed snail. They both suffered shock and gastroenteritis. The friend could not sue the café under the Sale of Goods Act 1893 because of the privity of

---

[30] The first of three House of Lords cases on this point (all concerned with defective construction of buildings) is *D. & F. Estates Ltd v Church Commissioners* [1989] A.C. 177. Note the similar exclusion under the Act: s.5, above, para.5.22. A similar result was reached in the other two cases that are cited in n.53 to para.5.46 below.

[31] [1932] A.C. 562.

contract rule, so she sued the manufacturers in tort ("delict" in Scotland). They argued that their only duty was a contractual duty to their buyers, e.g. the café and other distributors. The House of Lords disagreed.

The principle of law was stated by Lord Atkin in the following well-known passage:

> "A manufacturer of products, which he sells in such a form as to show that he intends them to reach the ultimate consumer in the form in which they left him with no reasonable possibility of intermediate examination, and with the knowledge that the absence of reasonable care in the preparation or putting up of the products will result in an injury to the consumer's life or property, owes a duty to the consumer to take that reasonable care."

Lord Atkin added that this was a self-evident proposition which no one who was not a lawyer would for one moment doubt. **5.41**

The duty outlined above is merely one particular type of "duty situation" in the context of the general law of negligence. The cases decided since 1932 show a gradual extension of liability. Thus:

(1) There is no limit to the type of goods covered by the rule. Examples include hair dye, underpants, cars, lifts and even a tombstone.

(2) Liability has been extended beyond manufacturers to cover, for example, repairers and assemblers. In one case even a car dealer was held liable.[32]

(3) The word "consumer" is not confined to the ultimate buyer; it means anyone likely to be injured by the lack of reasonable care. Perhaps the best illustration is provided by *Stennett v Hancock and Peters*[33] where part of the wheel of a lorry came off and struck a pedestrian on the pavement. She recovered damages from the second defendant who had negligently repaired the wheel shortly before the accident.

(4) The "possibility of intermediate examination" will only defeat the claim if there was a real likelihood of a type of examination which would (or should) reveal the defect. Thus in *Evans v Triplex Safety Glass Co*[34] the buyer of a Vauxhall car was injured when the windscreen shattered. His action against the manufacturers of the windscreen failed for various reasons; one reason was the likelihood of an intermediate examination by Vauxhall before it was fitted into the car; another reason was a failure to prove that the windscreen was defective when it left the manufacturer.

This case can be contrasted with the sale of goods case of *Wren v Holt*[35] where beer containing arsenic was sold by a publican to a customer. The case was fought on s.14(2) of the Sale of Goods

---

[32] *Andrews v Hopkinson* [1957] 1 Q.B. 229.
[33] [1939] 2 All E.R. 578.
[34] [1936] 1 All E.R. 283.
[35] [1903] 1 K.B. 610.

Act[36] and the publican was liable (and strictly so) even though the customer had examined the beer before drinking it; the defect was not discoverable by any normal examination. Presumably the same reasoning would have applied if the buyer had sued the brewer, i.e. the manufacturer would not have been liable unless negligence could have been proved.

Proof of negligence and causation

5.42   As the law stands at present the task facing the injured consumer is not an easy one. He must prove (a) that the product was defective when it left the manufacturer; (b) that this was due to negligence and (c) that this was the cause of his injury. If the article is completely destroyed in the accident, the claimant's task may well be insuperable unless the court is prepared to make a dangerous use of circumstantial evidence.

Was the product defective?

5.43   In many cases this should present no problem; a bun containing a stone, a loaf of bread containing a piece of glass or a car with faulty brakes—these are obvious examples. There may, however, be other cases which are less obvious. Thus in *Evans v Triplex Safety Glass Co*, the facts of which have already been given,[37] the plaintiff failed to prove that the windscreen was dangerous when it left the manufacturer.

In the examples previously given (for example, arsenic in the beer)[38] the product was out of line with the general run of goods produced by the manufacturers. Alternatively, it may be possible to argue that there is a fault in manufacture or design affecting all goods of a particular type. The cost of such a finding could be potentially astronomic for the manufacturer and for intermediate suppliers; they could be faced with a very large number of claims when the decision became known, and they might have to recall all the defective goods for repair.[38a] In view of this the courts (both here and in the United States) have been cautious to base a negligence finding on this ground. There have, however, been cases in which the injured party has been successful. Thus in *Lambert v Lewis*[39] the manufacturer of a defective towing hitch which broke and caused a serious accident was held liable to the victims because its design was negligent.

Has the manufacturer been negligent?

5.44   This question and the previous one are closely linked. Thus in *Vacwell Engineering Co Ltd v B.D.H. Chemicals Ltd*[40] the defendants, who manufac-

---

[36] Above, para.4.09.
[37] Above, para.5.41.
[38] ibid.
[38a] e.g. the Toyota accelerator problems in 2009.
[39] [1982] A.C. 225. See above, paras 3.10 and 4.24.
[40] [1971] 1 Q.B. 88. On warnings, see also *Coal Pension Properties Ltd v Nu-Way Ltd* [2009] EWHC 824 (Tcc).

tured a chemical, were liable in negligence for failing to undertake adequate research to discover, and to warn prospective users, that contact with water could lead to an explosion. Similarly, in *Wright v Dunlop Rubber Co Ltd and ICI*[41] the Court of Appeal held that ICI were liable in negligence for continuing to market a product with knowledge that it constituted a serious health hazard. Finally in *Fisher v Harrods Ltd*[42] Mrs Fisher recovered damages from Harrods when they sold an untested bottle of cleaning fluid to her husband. She suffered personal injury when it came into contact with her eyes.

The duty owed by the manufacturer does not involve it in strict liability—it is merely a duty to take reasonable care. This is particularly relevant where a manufacturer of (say) a car buys components such as brake linings or wheel bearings[43] which prove to be defective and cause injury to the ultimate consumer. If the manufacturer sources its components from a reliable supplier, has an adequate inspection system and an adequate system for checking faults this may well be sufficient.

A case from another branch of the law of negligence (employer's liability) is highly relevant here. In *Davie v New Merton Board Mills*[44] an employer supplied his employee with a tool which the employer had bought from a reputable supplier. The tool had a latent defect which the employer had no means of discovering. The employee was injured when the tool broke and he sued the employer for damages for negligence. The House of Lords dismissed the claim on the ground that the employer had not been negligent. In the employment field the principle underlying this case has been reversed by statute[45] but in the product liability field the principle still stands.

As already stated, the onus of proving negligence is on the injured party and it can be immensely difficult, especially in the case of a highly complex piece of equipment or a chemical or drug. Evidence of previous accidents caused by the same product is highly relevant and should be sought. Sometimes the facts themselves point to negligence; if a consumer loses a tooth through eating a cake containing a stone this suggests that the manufacturer had been negligent and, under the doctrine of *res ipsa loquitur*, the manufacturer will have to adduce evidence from which the inference of negligence can be rebutted.[46] He may say "the defect was in a component and I myself took all reasonable care" or even "I have no idea how the acid got into the lemonade bottle but I had a foolproof system of inspection" (this latter argument was successfully raised in *Daniels v White Ltd and Tarbard*[47] but the decision has been criticised and is unlikely to be followed).[48]

When studying all the vast number of reported cases on negligence

[41] (1972) 13 K.I.R. 255.
[42] [1966] Lloyds L.R. 500.
[43] But in *Walton v British Leyland* (unreported) the defendants were liable in negligence for failure to recall cars when they discovered unexpected defects in wheel bearings.
[44] [1959] A.C. 604.
[45] Employers' Liability (Defective Equipment) Act 1969.
[46] *Moore v R. Fox & Son* [1956] 1 Q.B. 596.
[47] [1938] 4 All E.R. 258.
[48] For a case where the court refused to follow the *Daniels* decision see *Hill v James Crowe (Cases) Ltd* [1978] 1 All E.R. 812.

(perhaps far too many are reported) one point must never be forgotten; whether a defendant has performed his duty of care is a pure question of fact and a decision on this point is not a binding precedent for any future case.[49]

Did the defendant's negligence cause the claimant's injury?

5.45   The injured claimant must be able to prove a causal link between the defect, the negligence and his injury. This again can be a difficult matter in practice and the result of the case may turn on the inferences which the court is willing to draw from the facts. In the leading case of *Grant v Australian Knitting Mills*[50] where the claimant, a doctor, contracted dermatitis, the Privy Council accepted his argument that it was caused by an excess of sulphite in underpants manufactured by the defendants. The court reached this decision even though the evidence showed that more than four million of these pants had been sold without complaint. On the other hand, the claimant will fail if the injury would have occurred in any event. Thus, to borrow again from employment law, an employer is generally not liable for failing to provide safety equipment if he can show that the employee would not have worn it.[51] Similarly, a manufacturer of a car will not be liable for faulty brakes if the claimant was driving so fast that the accident would have occurred even if the brakes had been in perfect working order. A "class action" brought by smokers against Gallaghers was dismissed as causation could not be proved.[52]

For what damage can the plaintiff recover?

5.46   Reverting once again to the poor quality/dangerous dichotomy, the final question relates to *potentially* dangerous goods. On which side of the line do they fall? Can the buyer of a car claim in negligence for the cost of repairing brakes in order to avert a serious accident? In the Second Edition of this book we expressed the view that such a claim should be allowed but in two later cases, concerning potentially dangerous buildings, the House of Lords have classified such repair costs as irrecoverable economic loss.[53]

[49] *Qualcast (Wolverhampton) Ltd v Haynes* [1959] A.C. 743.
[50] Above, para.4.22.
[51] *Qualcast (Wolverhampton) Ltd v Haynes* [1959] A.C. 743; *McWilliams v Arrol* [1962] 1 W.L.R. 295, HL.
[52] *Hodgson v Imperial Tobacco Ltd* (1999) N.L.D. March 8, Q.B.D. For another non-liability case see *Hamble Fisheries Ltd v L Gardner & Sons Ltd, The Times*, January 5, 1999, CA.
[53] *Murphy v Brentwood DC* [1990] 3 W.L.R. 414; *Department of the Environment v Thomas Bates & Son Ltd* [1990] 3 W.L.R. 457.

CHAPTER SIX

"DO I HAVE TO PAY?"

If the supplier of goods or services is guilty of a misrepresentation or a serious **6.01** breach of contract the consumer may be able to rescind the contract or treat it as repudiated. In either case this will relieve him of his obligation to pay the price. Some examples of this were examined in Chapters Two to Four and the matter will be considered again in Chapter Seven. This chapter is concerned with a group of eight unrelated but important topics on which the consumer may seek legal advice. The topics are:

(1) Delivery of unordered goods.

(2) Contracts concluded "at a distance" including internet shopping.

(3) Cancellation of doorstep and distance contracts.

(4) Loss of or damage to goods after contract but before delivery.

(5) Unsatisfactory performance of services.

(6) Late performance.

(7) A dispute about the price.

(8) A holiday dispute.

1. I NEVER ORDERED THESE GOODS

An aggressive salesman may try to boost his sales by delivering goods which **6.02** the customer has never ordered, followed by an invoice demanding pay-ment.[1] He clearly hopes that the consumer will be induced, by a combination of ignorance, lethargy and fear, to pay the price. Some years ago there was a considerable outcry at these and similar practices, and there was a growing demand for legislation to curtail them. Eventually this demand was met by the Unsolicited Goods and Services Act 1971. The rights of the consumer are now to be found in reg.24 of the Consumer Protection (Distance Selling) Regulations 2000 (SI 2000/2334).

Before considering these provisions it may be useful to dispose of one problem which has arisen under the general law: is the consumer legally liable if the goods are lost or damaged while they are in his possession? Under the tort of negligence the plaintiff must prove that the defendant owed him a legal

---

[1] For a recent example where a company allegedly guilty of this was wound up in the public interest see *Re Forcesun Ltd* [2002] EWHC 443, Ch.

duty of care.[2] A person receiving unordered goods is known as an "involuntary bailee" and does not owe a duty of care. Therefore he will generally not be liable for accidental loss or damage.[3] On the other hand he may be liable for the tort of conversion if he deliberately destroys the goods or converts them to his own use. Where is the line to be drawn? If a tradesman delivers an unordered 10-volume encyclopedia the consumer might well be liable if he puts them outside his house and allows them to disintegrate. The editors of a leading textbook[4] have suggested that the consumer might be entitled to destroy the goods in an emergency.

The Act of 1971 and the Regulations

6.03   The 1971 Act imposed both civil and criminal sanctions but s.1 (which dealt with the civil sanctions) was repealed and replaced in 2000 by the regulation referred to above. Under the heading "Inertia Selling" reg.24 applies where (a) unsolicited goods are sent to a person (the recipient) with a view to his acquiring them and (b) the recipient has no reasonable cause to believe that they were sent with a view to their being acquired for the purpose of a business and (c) he has neither agreed to acquire nor agreed to return them. The effect is that the consumer gets a free gift! The regulation provides that:

> (2) the recipient may, as between himself and the sender, use, deal with or dispose of the goods as if they were an absolute gift and
> (3) the rights of the sender to the goods are extinguished.

Note that (unlike the Act) the regulation has immediate effect; thus if the goods are sent by mistake it will be too late for the sender to recover them. The recipient is not completely safe, however, because the regulation only applies as between himself and the sender; if therefore the goods belong to a third party (for example, a finance company) the rights of that party are unaffected.

6.04   As regards the criminal sanctions[5] these are to be found in reg.24(4) and (5) and in s.2 of the 1971 Act; the former is slightly wider in that it also applies to services. An offence is committed where a trader (a) makes a demand for payment for what he knows are unsolicited goods/services which are sent/supplied to another person with a view to his acquiring them otherwise than for the purposes of a business, and (b) he has no reasonable cause to believe that there is a right to payment. An offence is also committed where a person in such a case (1) asserts a right to payment, (2) threatens to bring legal proceedings, (3) places, or threatens to place, the name of any person on a defaulters' list, or (4) invokes, or threatens to invoke, any other collection procedure.

---

[2] *Bourhill v Young* [1943] A.C. 92.
[3] See *Howard v Harris* (1884) Cab. & E. 253.
[4] *Winfield and Jolowicz on Tort* (17th edn, 2006) para.17.10.
[5] See also the criminal sanctions for sending unsolicited credit tokens in para.24.03 below.

2. I Ordered Them From the Internet

Introduction to Distance Selling Regulations

In the previous section we were concerned with the obsolescent (or obsolete?)   **6.05**
marketing practice of sending the goods themselves unasked to consumers
with the result that the consumers receive an unexpected present. That is the
effect of the Consumer Protection (Distance Selling) Regulations 2000 (SI
2000/2334).

Much more frequent nowadays—indeed, so frequent that it is a constant
source of irritation to many—is the importunate marketing of goods or
services by various physical and electronic means. Mail order catalogues
and leaflets constantly drop through letter-boxes; magazines and newspapers are littered with advertisements for everything from cosmetic surgery
to a holiday in Thailand (or both); continual interruptions are caused by telephone calls from call centres pushing telecommunications, utilities, double
glazing or fitted kitchens; commercial breaks on television stridently market
their wares; and last, but not least, the internet with emails and the web is a
fertile source of advertising.

In none of these examples are the trader and customer face to face. This
is where the Distance Selling Regulations really begin to bite, i.e. where a
"distance contract" is concluded by "means of distance communication"
defined by reg.3(1) as "any means without the simultaneous physical presence of the supplier and the consumer". The Regulations give effect to the
EU Directive 97/7/EC on the protection of consumers in respect of distance
contracts. We discuss below the provisions about information for consumers, both pre-contractually and at the contract stage, and some other related
matters. The cancellation provisions will be covered separately in section 3B
of this chapter.

What practices are caught?

All the practices given as examples in the previous paragraph are caught by   **6.06**
the Regulations, as they fall within the definition of "distance contract" in
reg.3(1):

> "distance contract" means any contract concerning goods or services concluded
> between a supplier and a consumer under an organised distance sales or service
> provision scheme run by the supplier who, for the purpose of the contract, makes
> exclusive use of one or more means of distance communication up to and includ-
> ing the moment at which the contract is concluded;

Three points need to be made. (1) They apply only to an "organised. . .
scheme", not to a casual service provided by a supplier, e.g. a telephone
order to the local butcher or plumber. (2) If pre-contractually there is a face-
to-face meeting, the Regulations will not bite, even though the contract was
concluded remotely. (3) The general words of regs 3(1) and 4 are important
in that, although Sch.1 contains an "Indicative list of Means of Distance
Communication" caught by the Regulations, it is not an exhaustive list. For

example, internet contracts are not mentioned, presumably because on-line purchasing was rare when the Directive was drafted, and yet they clearly fall within the meaning of "distance contract".

The list in Schedule 1 is as follows:

1. Unaddressed printed matter.
2. Addressed printed matter.
3. Letter.
4. Press advertising with order form.
5. Catalogue.
6. Telephone with human intervention.
7. Telephone without human intervention (automatic calling machine, audiotext).
8. Radio.
9. Videophone (telephone with screen).
10. Videotext (microcomputer and television screen) with keyboard or touch screen.
11. Electronic mail.
12. Facsimile machine (fax).
13. Television (teleshopping).

Regulations' requirements

6.07 The Regulations contain detailed requirements about providing information to consumers and various other matters.

Pre-contract information

6.08 Regulation 7 entitles the consumer to specified information "in good time prior to the conclusion of the contract", e.g. identity of the supplier, main characteristics of the goods or services, price, delivery costs, arrangements for delivery, performance or payment and cancellation rights. It must be provided "in a clear and comprehensible manner" but not necessarily in writing—it can, for example, be a telephone call. The supplier must have regard to the principles of good faith in commercial transactions and the principles governing the protection of those who are unable to give their consent such as minors.

Written confirmation

6.09 Regulation 8 states that the supplier must provide in writing "or in another durable medium which is available and accessible to the consumer" most of the information set out above. Unless the information has already been supplied in that form, it must be given in good time—and in any event not later than the time of delivery.

Performance

6.10 Unless otherwise agreed, the supplier must perform within thirty days beginning with the day after the day on which the consumer sent his order to the supplier (see reg.19). Where the goods are not available to the supplier he can provide substitute goods of equivalent value and price if his right to do so formed part of the pre-contractual information referred to in reg.7.

Enforcement

Regulation 26 requires the Office of Fair Trading, or any other enforcement authority, to consider complaints (unless frivolous or vexatious). If they find that there has been a breach they are likely to seek an undertaking from the supplier. If a satisfactory undertaking cannot be obtained, or if it is broken, reg.27 enables them to apply to the court for an injunction and the court may grant it on such terms as it thinks fit to secure compliance with the Regulations. **6.11**

No contracting out

A term contained in any contract to which the Regulations apply is void if, and to the extent that, it is inconsistent with any provision for the protection of the consumer contained in these regulations (see reg.25). **6.12**

Exceptions

A few contracts are excepted from the Regulations by reg.5, e.g. the sale of an interest in land, financial services and contracts via vending machines. Some others are partially exempt by reg.6, e.g. the supply of food by regular round-smen (milk etc), accommodation, transport,[6] catering and leisure for specific dates (hotel bookings etc). **6.13**

Making distance contracts

The Regulations frequently refer to a contract being "concluded" and some-times the word "made" is used instead (e.g. reg.6): they appear to mean the same—the moment when the contract is formed. Not surprisingly they do not set out the contractual principles governing the formation of contracts and it may be helpful briefly to analyse the common law rules. This involves a discussion of offer and acceptance. Two questions have to be answered: (a) who makes the offer? and (b) when does acceptance occur? **6.14**

(a) Who makes the offer?

It is important to decide whether the supplier or consumer is the offeror. If the supplier were the offeror, then as soon as the consumer accepted the offer (e.g. by posting an order form) a contract would be made. This could pose difficult, if not insuperable, problems for the supplier. A seller of goods would usually have limited stocks and be unable to meet an unexpected demand. Conversely, if it is the consumer who makes the offer when placing an order, the supplier will be in a position to choose whether to accept or reject it. **6.15**

---

[6] See reg.6(2). "Transport" includes car hire: *easyCar(UK) Ltd v OFT*, *The Times*, March 15, 2005, ECJ.

We take the view that the latter solution is correct and the presumption should be that the consumer is the offeror and the supplier the offeree. Case law on the distinction between an invitation to treat and an offer supports this view.[7] Thus a supplier is merely giving an invitation to treat when including goods or services in a mail order catalogue, newspaper advertisement, door to door flyer or letter. The same is true of advertisements on radio or television or the use of fax.

How do email and the internet fit into the rules? The virtue of the common law is its flexibility—there is no need for legislation when a new medium of communication is brought into use. Where suppliers contact consumers electronically, the medium is a modern version of the mail order catalogue and so merely an invitation to treat, so that the consumer's offer to buy may be rejected if the supplier so decides. Thus if, as happened with a well-known retailer, a colour television is advertised at the price of £29.90 with a misplaced decimal point, the supplier is entitled to refuse to accept orders (in that case the other defence was unilateral mistake, as the error was self-evident).

(b) When does acceptance occur?

6.16 There are a number of reasons why it is vital to identify the precise moment when the contract is made. At that time, both parties become bound (subject to the consumer's cancellation rights: see para.6.35), so that neither the supplier nor the consumer can change their minds with impunity. Further, any later attempt by the supplier to introduce protective terms of business will be ineffectual (see paras. 8.08 to 8.11). (Thus supplies of goods such as software delivered shrink-wrapped, so that the buyer cannot read the conditions of sale until after the contract is made, are not subject to such hidden terms.)

The general common law principle of acceptance is that it must be communicated to the offeror, i.e. no agreement is made until the offeror is, or could be, aware of the acceptance. The posting rule is exceptional whereby the acceptance is effective as soon as the letter is put in the pillar box.[8] This principle applies whenever the method of communication is fast so that there is no significant interval between the sending and receipt of the acceptance.

6.17 **(i) Mail order.**   The postal rule applies where the supplier accepts the order by posting an acknowledgment of order; otherwise the delivery of the goods or commencement of the services will be an act of acceptance.

6.18 **(ii) Telephone.**   There can be no hard and fast rule, as during the negotiation either party may make an offer or counter-offer. However, if the line goes dead or the signal fails, so that the offeror does not hear the acceptance, no contract results. Of course, evidential problems are enormous.

---

[7] Goods in shop window—*Fisher* v *Bell* [1961] 1Q.B.394; on supermarket shelf—*Pharmaceutical Society of GB* v *Boots Cash Chemists (Southern)* [1952] 2 Q.B. 795.
[8] *Adams v Lindsell* (1818) 1 B. & Ald. 681.

(iii) Fax. The general principle applies: the contract is made where and **6.19** when the communications are received. If the premises are empty during ordinary office hours, but the offeror could have read the messages, had he been there, presumably the contract will still be made on receipt by the equipment. However, consumer contracts by this mode are rare.

Internet: email and the world wide web

Although there is no authority on this point, we consider that the offer is **6.20** made by the consumer, e.g. by clicking on "submit" or "order", and the acceptance occurs if—and only if—the supplier accepts by a further communication to the consumer, e.g. by sending an email acknowledgment or confirmation with a reference for the order or booking. We take this view because, as we stated earlier, this type of transaction is just an up-to-date version of paper mail order. As with fax, whether the offeror/consumer has accessed the computer server and actually read the email acceptance is irrelevant, provided it is accessible.[9]

Terms and conditions

The principles explained above are, of course, subject to any terms and con- **6.21** ditions incorporated into the contract by the supplier. It is almost inevitable that internet purchasing via the web will involve such express terms. For example, one well-known retailer states that they "will confirm receipt of your order by sending an email, . . . however this will not bring into existence a legal binding agreement between us . . . No contract will exist . . . until your credit/debit card has been charged". Amazon, perhaps the best known internet retailer, has the following clause lurking amongst its many pages of terms of business:

> Your order represents an offer to us to purchase a product which is accepted by us when we send an e-mail confirmation to you that we've dispatched that product to you. That acceptance will be complete at the time we send the Dispatch Confirmation E-mail to you.

These and other web suppliers seem to agree with our view that the consumer makes the offer, which is accepted when the supplier does something further, e.g. charging the price to a credit card, emailing confirmation that the goods have been sent or, in one reputable High Street chain's terms, the actual sending of the goods.

The legal effect is that neither party is bound during the interval between sending the order and its acceptance, so that meanwhile the consumer may change his mind and revoke his offer—there will be no need to resort to the statutory cancellation rights at that stage.

It is by no means clear that such terms of business will always be successfully incorporated by the supplier. It often takes a time consuming search

---

[9] See above, para.6.19.

to find the terms and conditions among the list of other information on the website and then a more detailed search through many pages of terms to discover the relevant provision. The courts may well take the view that the supplier has not taken sufficient or reasonable steps to bring the clause to the consumer's attention;[10] if so, the principle stated in para.6.20 will apply.

OFT study and code

6.22   The scale of the internet shopping revolution can be seen from the OFT website (www.oft.gov.uk; see also www.dti.gov.uk). In the five years to 2006 online sales rose by 350 per cent and were shared between 130,000 businesses. In April 2006 the OFT launched a fact-finding study into this area. The report *Internet Shopping* (OFT 921, 169 pp.) was published in June 2007. The questions included whether consumers are aware of their rights and receive the right level of regulatory protection. The study concentrated on four sectors:

- Airline tickets.
- Domestic electrical equipment.
- Music sales and downloading.
- Online auctions.

Finally one point is noteworthy on consumer redress: a code of practice. The Safebuy Code has reached stage 1 of the OFT code approval regime and will be of eventual help to consumers in this area if it reaches stage 2 (see para.10.14).

3. I HAVE CHANGED MY MIND

6.23   In the Second Edition of this book we referred to an EC draft Directive which conferred cancellation rights for contracts "which have been negotiated away from business premises". We commented then on this somewhat surprisingly wide approach and in the event a number of changes were made before it was adopted as Council Directive 85/577. It was incorporated into English law by the Consumer Protection (Cancellation of Contracts Concluded away from Business Premises) Regulations 1987.[11]

The 1987 Regulations have now been revoked and replaced by the Cancellation of Contracts made in a Consumer's Home or Place of Work etc. Regulations 2008,[12] which came into force on October 1, 2008.

The 2008 Regulations (which we shall refer to as the Doorstep Regulations) are quite distinct from the Distance Selling Regulations which also confer cancellation rights. The former regulations catch face-to-face selling to consumers in their homes, whereas the latter involve no such physical confrontation. We shall now summarise them in turn.

---

[10]   See paras 8.08 to 8.11 and in particular *Interfoto*.
[11]   SI 1987/2117 (as amended).
[12]   SI 2008/1816.

A. THE DOORSTEP REGULATIONS

We pointed out in para.6.23 that the 2008 Regulations have replaced the **6.24**
1987 Regulations. The main change effected by the 2008 Regulations was the
extension of cancellation rights from unsolicited to solicited visits requested
by the consumer (reg.6(3), pursuant to the Consumers, Estate Agents and
Redress Act 2007, s.59). Rather than amend the 1987 Regulations yet again,
the opportunity was taken to consolidate the earlier amendments with a new
set of Regulations.

At the outset it is to be noted that reg.2(1) contains 14 definitions, e.g.
"cancellable agreement," "solicited visit".

Relationship with Consumer Credit Act

Since 1985 a consumer has had the right to cancel a regulated consumer credit **6.25**
or consumer hire agreement (subject to minor exceptions) where oral representations are made in his presence and the prospective agreement is signed
by the debtor or hirer away from business premises (as defined). This right
is conferred by s.67 of the Consumer Credit Act 1974.[13] It is clear from the
Regulations that s.67 and the cancellation right conferred by the Regulations
are intended to be mutually exclusive (see reg.6(1)).

What agreements are caught?

Subject to what has been said above, and subject also to the exceptions set **6.26**
out below, the Regulations (which are aimed primarily at cold callers and
high-pressure doorstep salesmen) apply to a contract for the supply by a
trader of goods or services to a consumer where the *contract*, written or oral,
is made in any of the cases set out in reg.5:

(a) During a visit by a trader to the consumer's home or the home of
another person or to the consumer's place of work.

(b) During an excursion organised by the trader away from his business **6.27**
premises.

Example 1

A timeshare company organises a visit to one of its sites. While relaxing in a
restaurant after the visit a customer is induced to sign a timeshare contract. The
Regulations apply.

(c) After an *offer* by the consumer was made at such premises or during **6.28**
an excursion.

Example 2

During a visit by Charles to David's place of work, David offers to acquire a personal computer. The contract itself is concluded a week later at Charles' shop.
The Regulations apply.

---

[13] Below, para.22.04.

Business "consumers"

6.29 Even if the consumer carries on a business, the Regulations will still apply if in making the contract he is acting for purposes which can be regarded as outside his business (reg.2(1)).

Excepted contracts

6.30 Regulation 6(1) and Sch.3 contain a long list of contracts to which the Regulations do not apply. They include:

- contracts for the construction, sale or rental of immovable property; but contracts for (i) extensions, patios, conservatories or driveways or (ii) repair, refurbishment or improvement are specifically included in the Regulations;
- catalogue selling with continual contact between the parties;
- food, drink and other goods intended for current consumption in the household and supplied by regular roundsmen;
- contracts of insurance;
- investment agreements under the Financial Services and Markets Act 2000; and
- price or credit of £35 or less.

The cancellation notice

6.31 Any agreement to which the Regulations apply is unenforceable against the consumer unless the trader has delivered to him a notice in writing, informing him of his right to cancel and containing the information (including a cancellation form) set out in the Regulations.[14] This notice must be given at the time of the contract or, in offer cases, at the time of the offer.

Under the Regulations, a trader who enters into a contract without delivering this notice commits an offence. The trader has the usual "due diligence" defence in appropriate cases and the Regulations "lift the corporate veil" by providing that, where an offence is committed by a body corporate, the directors and other officers will also be guilty if the offence took place with their connivance, consent or neglect. The trading standards departments of local authorities are given the task of enforcement.

Time for cancellation

6.32 The consumer can cancel by serving a notice in writing (not necessarily in the form set out in the Schedule) within seven days following the making of the contract.[15] It is important to note that a notice sent by post or e-mail takes

---

[14] Reg. 7 and Sch.4, Pt I.
[15] Reg.7(1), The "cancellation period" is defined in reg.2(1). cf. the five-day period in relation to consumer credit: below, para.22.08.

effect at the time of posting or sending—even though it never reaches the trader (see reg.8(5),(6)).

Specified contracts   **6.33**

Regulation 9 contains special provisions to enable a supplier, if the consumer wishes, to commence performance of "specified contracts" during the cancellation period. The list of these in reg.9(4) includes:

- newspapers and magazines;
- advertising;
- emergency supplies;
- perishable goods;
- funerals; and
- services of any other kind.

In such cases the consumer must so request in writing and, if he then cancels, must pay for goods and services already supplied.

Effect of cancellation

The rules are very similar to those under the Consumer Credit Act.[16] Thus: **6.34**

(a) the cancelled contract is treated as if it had never been made (reg.8(2)) and any security is extinguished;

(b) sums paid by the consumer are repayable to him and he can refuse to hand over the goods (in legal terminology he has a "lien" over them) until those sums have been repaid (reg.10);

(c) subject to exceptions, he must have the goods available for collection by the dealer (reg.13);

(d) reg.14 deals with the return of part-exchange goods to the consumer;

(e) where the consumer has already had the benefit of a loan or overdraft, then cancellation will not extinguish his repayment obligation (reg.12).

B. THE DISTANCE SELLING REGULATIONS

We considered above in paras 6.05 to 6.22 various other provisions of the   **6.35**
Consumer Protection (Distance Selling) Regulations 2000. We now consider cancellation. The reg.8 information must give details of the consumer's

---

[16] Below, para.22.10.

cancellation rights including (if appropriate) any duty to return the goods and who is to bear the cost of this. The cancellation rights under these Regulations are to be found in regs10–18 and they can be summarised as follows:

1. Subject to exceptions (as to which see reg.13) the consumer can cancel a contract for the supply of goods by giving a notice in writing or other durable form available and accessible to the supplier (or other person nominated by him) indicating a desire to cancel the contract.

6.36
2. Regulations 10 and 11[17] contain detailed rules as to the ways in which, and the time within which, the notice must be given. Thus:

   (a) the notice period begins when the contract is concluded;
   (b) where the supplier has complied with his reg.8 obligation, the period ends on the expiry of the period of seven working days beginning with the day after the day on which the consumer receives the goods;
   (c) where (b) above does not apply, but where the supplier complies within three months from the consumer receiving the goods, the seven day cancellation period referred to above starts to run on the day after the day on which the consumer receives the information;
   (d) in any other case the consumer will have a cancellation period of three months and seven working days from the day after the day on which the contract was concluded;
   (e) the notice can be given by leaving it at the last known address of the supplier (in which case it takes effect when it is left) or by posting it to that address (in which case it takes effect at the date of posting) or by fax or email (in which case it takes effect when it is sent).

3. By reg.14 the supplier must, within 30 days, reimburse any sum paid by the consumer and he must do this without making any charge—except that he may sometimes recover the direct cost of recovering the goods if the contract requires the consumer to return them and he fails to do so.

4. Cancellation will also operate to cancel any related credit agreement.

5. Regulations 17 and 18 (relating to the consumer's duties to take reasonable care of goods and to restore them to the supplier, and to his rights relating to goods taken in part exchange) are similar to the rules which apply to the cancellation of credit agreements (as to which see paras 22.12 and 22.13 below).

---

[17] Reg.12 contains similar provisions for supplies of services. Amended from April 6, 2005 by the Consumer Protection (Distance Selling) (Amendment) Regulations 2005 (SI 2005/689).

4. THE SELLER'S ENTIRE STOCK HAS BEEN DESTROYED IN A FIRE

We have already seen that where goods are supplied in the course of a busi-   **6.37**
ness, they must be of satisfactory quality. What happens if they were clearly
satisfactory at the time of the contract but are accidentally damaged or
destroyed at a later date? We must distinguish between total destruction and
damage, and the precise form of the contract is also highly relevant.

What has the consumer agreed to buy?

The law draws a distinction between three types of goods: **6.38**

1. **Specific goods.** These are defined as "goods identified and agreed on
   at the time a contract of sale is made" (Sale of Goods Act 1979, s.61).
   If therefore a consumer goes into a store and selects a specific DVD
   player from the shelf, this would be a contract for specific goods.
2. **Purely generic goods.** An example would be where a buyer places an
   order for a DVD model without identifying any particular unit.
3. **Generic goods from an identified source.** An example would be "ten
   cases of wine from the stock in your warehouse".

In 2 and 3 alone the goods are "unascertained".

Total destruction

In case 1 above the goods are said to "perish" and s.7 of the Sale of Goods   **6.39**
Act provides that:

> Where there is an agreement to sell specific goods and subsequently the goods,
> without any fault on the part of the seller or buyer, perish before the risk passes
> to the buyer, the contract is avoided.

So in advising the consumer we must consider (a) fault, (b) risk, and (c) the
legal position if s.7 applies.

(a) Fault—if, for example, the seller has been negligent in failing to
    provide adequate fire precautions, s.7 would not apply and the
    buyer could sue the seller for damages for negligence and/or non-
    delivery.
(b) Risk—until recently there were some highly technical rules in
    ss.16–20 of the Act under which the risk of accidental loss or damage
    was geared to the passing of property, so that the risk would some-
    times pass to the buyer even before delivery. This is still the position
    for sales to a non-consumer, but in consumer sales a new s.20(4)
    (inserted by reg.4(2) of the Sale and Supply of Goods to Consumers
    Regulations 2002) provides that

> in a case where the buyer deals as consumer . . . the goods remain at the
> seller's risk until they are delivered to the consumer.

(c) Effect of s.7—The contract is frustrated but the Law Reform (Frustrated Contracts) Act 1943 does not apply in a case where specific goods perish and the legal rights of the parties will be governed by the common law rules. Under these rules (a) the buyer does not have to pay the price, (b) if he has paid it, or any part of it, he can recover it on the basis that there has been a "total failure of consideration", (c) he cannot claim damages for non-delivery, and (d) the unfortunate seller cannot claim anything for work done to the goods nor for storage charges.

6.40 The position is different in cases 2 and 3 above. Where the goods are purely generic (case 2 above) the fact that the seller's premises have been destroyed by fire will not cut down his liability to the buyer. Unless he has protected himself by an effective exemption clause he must find goods from elsewhere or pay damages for non-delivery. If, however, the source of the goods is specified in the contract (case 3 above) the destruction of that source before the risk has passed to the buyer will operate to frustrate the contract and in this situation the 1943 Act will apply. The rules are similar to those discussed above except that adjustments can be made for expenses incurred by the seller and benefits received by the buyer before the frustrating event.

Damage

6.41 What happens if goods are accidentally damaged while they are still at the seller's risk? This problem could arise if, for example, the DVD player ordered by the buyer is damaged when the delivery van is involved in a road accident for which the seller is not responsible. Presumably the buyer can refuse to accept the damaged goods and then bring an action for non-delivery. The precise nature and the precise legal basis of the buyer's rights do not appear to have been analysed in any reported case; perhaps it is based on an implied undertaking by the seller that the quality of the goods delivered will correspond precisely with the quality of the goods when the buyer agreed to take them.[18]

Risk and delivery

6.42 One final point relates to cases in which the buyer authorises or requires the seller to send the goods to him. Where the buyer is a consumer, the law now makes it clear that delivery of the goods to a carrier for transmission to the buyer is not to be treated as delivery to the buyer (Sale of Goods Act, s.32(4) inserted by reg.4(3) of the Sale and Supply of Goods to Consumer Regulations 2002). Accordingly the goods will remain at the seller's risk until actual delivery to the consumer.

---

[18] For a somewhat similar principle in a slightly different context see *Financings Ltd v Stimson* [1962] 1 W.L.R. 1184, CA (damage to car between hirer's initial offer and its acceptance by the finance company).

5. THE PLUMBER WAS A COWBOY

Contracts for services

The contract of "work and materials" (installation of central heating, double-   **6.43**
glazing, etc.) was briefly examined in Chapter Four.[19] It will be recalled that
such a contract can be divided into two parts—the "goods" part and the
"work" part and the legal rules for the two parts are different. The "work"
part of such a contract can be classified as a contract for services. The list of
such contracts includes repair, decoration, servicing, maintenance, cleaning,
building, storage, carriage of goods and passengers, insurance, the provision of accommodation, entertainment and the whole range of professional
services—legal, banking, accountancy, medical, dental, surveying, valuing
and so on. A report published by the National Consumer Council (*Service
Please*)[20] in 1981 highlighted three main areas of dissatisfaction—the quality
of the work, the time it took to do it and the cost. This section of this chapter is
only concerned with the first of these—unsatisfactory performance (Time and
charges are dealt with in sections six and seven.) The report referred to above
shows that, for example:

(1) Out of 50 garages only two came anywhere near to carrying out a full
     service in line with the maker's specifications.

(2) Out of 10 repair men called in to mend defective washing machines
     only two did so effectively.

(3) A "plumber" connected a drinks vending machine to a lavatory pipe.

1982 Act, s.13

There used to be no statutory[21] obligation on the supplier of a service to carry   **6.44**
out his work with reasonable care and skill but this was rectified by s.13 of the
Supply of Goods and Services Act 1982.[22] It reads:

> In a contract for the supply of a service where the supplier is acting in the course
> of a business there is an implied term that the supplier will carry out the service
> with reasonable care and skill.

Section 13 imposes merely a duty of care and skill on a business supplier of
services and the "term" is an intermediate stipulation (see para.7.31). This
contrasts with the implied statutory obligations imposed on suppliers of
goods by such Acts as the Sale of Goods Act 1979 and Pt I of the 1982 Act
which result in strict liability and are "conditions" and "warranties" (see
paras 4.08 and 7.29).

---

[19] Above, para.4.38.
[20] Above, para.1.09.
[21] This section codified the existing common law duty.
[22] For the background to, and commentary on, the 1982 Act see Woodroffe, *Goods and
      Services—The New Law* (1982). It was a Private Member's Bill and Geoffrey Woodroffe was
      the draftsman of Pt II (the work or services sections).

The implied term then requires the supplier of services to be careful only. However, the express terms of the contract may go further and impose liability even though the supplier has not been negligent. In *Platform Funding Ltd v Bank of Scotland plc (formerly Halifax plc)*[22a]

> The defendants carried on business as valuers and surveyors (trading as "Colleys"). The claimants instructed them to inspect and report on the condition and value of a new house, 1 Bakers Yard. The borrower misled them into inspecting another house nearby. The claimants made an advance and, when the borrower defaulted, repossessed the house and sold it. They sought to recover a shortfall of over £30,000 from the defendants.

The defendants argued that, as their mistake was caused by the borrower's fraud, they were not liable in the absence of negligence. The claimants contended that the obligation to inspect the specified property was unqualified. The Court of Appeal (Sir Anthony Clarke M.R. dissenting) held that the obligation was unqualified. "By accepting instructions to inspect and value 1 Bakers Yard they undertook an unqualified obligation to inspect the property and were in breach of contract in failing to do so", said Moore-Blick L.J.

Of course, usually such an error will result from negligence, but strict liability applies to the identification of the correct property. It is likely that the courts will limit this higher standard to very special facts. The case does not erode substantially the general principle in s.13.

The section was intended to confirm and codify the existing common law. It was not intended to enlarge existing areas of liability. Accordingly, s.12(4) gives the Secretary of State power to make orders excluding particular groups of persons from the "services" provisions of the Act (i.e. ss.13–15). An Order has been made (SI 1982/1771) which provides that s.13 shall not apply to the following services:

  (i) the services of an advocate in court or before any tribunal, inquiry or arbitration or in carrying out any preliminary work directly affecting the conduct of the hearing[23]; or

  (ii) the services rendered to a company by a director of the company in his capacity as such.

Another Order (SI 1985/1) has been made taking arbitrators outside the scope of s.13.[24]

6.45   We revert now to the basic question—does the consumer have to pay the full price if the work of the plumber, electrician, etc., is unsatisfactory? In the vast majority of cases the answer will be "no"; the plumber, etc., will be in breach of the implied duty of care and skill under s.13 and the consumer

---

[22a] [2008] EWCA Civ 930.
[23] See now *Hall v Simons* [2002] 1 A.C. 615 where the House of Lords abolished the immunity previously enjoyed by litigation advocates as illustrated by *Rondel v Worsley* [1969] 1 A.C. 191.
[24] An arbitrator is immune from liability unless he acts in bad faith: Arbitration Act 1996, s.29.

may well be able to treat himself as discharged from the contract altogether or alternatively he can set off his claim for damages against the claim for the charge or fee. The matter is examined more fully in Chapter Seven (below, paras 7.31, 7.65, et al.).

Section 16 of the Act enables the parties to exclude s.13 by express agreement or by course of dealing, or by usage if it is such as to bind both parties. Such exemption clauses may, however, be controlled by statute: see Chapters Eight and Nine below.

6. THEY TURNED UP LATE

Late performance, whether by sellers, electricians, builders, plumbers, carriers or tour operators, is a frequent source of complaint by consumers. The legal principles governing this topic can be summarised as follows: **6.46**

(1) If the contract specifies a date for performance, a supplier of goods or services who fails to perform by that date will be liable in damages for breach of contract (unless this liability has been effectively excluded or unless the contract is frustrated). This claim for damages can be pleaded by way of set-off or counter-claim in an action by the supplier for the price.[25]

(2) If the contract does not specify a date for performance the supplier must perform within a "reasonable" time. This statutory obligation is imposed on business suppliers of services by s.14 of the Supply of Goods and Services Act 1982.[26] The question of reasonableness is a question of fact[27]; even a long delay will not necessarily amount to a breach of contract if it was due to circumstances beyond the supplier's control.

In one case a car owner took his car to a garage for repair following an accident. A competent repairer would have taken five weeks; the garage gave priority to other work and took eight weeks. It was held by the Court of Appeal that they had failed to carry out the work within a reasonable time and were therefore liable in damages.[28]

(3) Can the consumer go further and claim to be discharged from the contract altogether? This depends on whether time is "of the essence", i.e. a vital term or, in sale of goods language, a condition. The following statement in *Halsbury's Laws of England* has received judicial approval: **6.47**

> Time will not be considered to be of the essence unless (1) the parties expressly stipulate that conditions as to time must be strictly complied with, or (2) the nature of the subject-matter of the contract or the surrounding circumstances show that time should be considered to be of the essence.[29]

---

[25] For the assessment of damages, see below, paras 7.51–7.64.

[26] This section codified the existing common law rule.

[27] ibid.

[28] *Charnock v Liverpool Corp.* [1968] 1 W.L.R. 1498; s.14 would now apply to such a case. The exclusion provisions of s.16 also apply to s.14 cases (see para.6.44 above).

[29] *Halsbury's Laws of England* (4th edn), Vol.9, para.481, approved by Lord Simon in *United Scientific Holdings Ltd v Burnley Council* [1978] A.C. 904, HL. See also *Bunge Corp. v Tradax S.A.* [1981] 1 W.L.R. 711, HL.

It is probably true to say that under a contract to supply goods or services to a consumer a failure to observe the agreed performance date is not of itself a repudiation of the contract. There can, of course, be difficult cases; what about an operator who agrees to provide his client with a 15-day holiday in Majorca starting on August 1, but is prevented from carrying out that obligation by reason of industrial action for which he is not responsible? It could be argued that if he is unable to transport his clients on August 1, he will have broken an essential term of the contract which enables the clients to treat the contract as discharged; alternatively, it might be argued that the contract has been frustrated.[30]

(4) If a reasonable time has elapsed, or if the breach of an essential time clause has been waived, the consumer can serve a notice fixing a time for performance. The time limit in this notice must itself be a reasonable one, but subject to this the consumer can treat the contract as discharged if the supplier fails to perform by the date specified in the notice.[31]

(5) Thus the consumer should always make it clear, in appropriate cases, that the date for performance is vital, e.g. by stating expressly that "time is of the essence".

7. THE PRICE SEEMS RATHER HIGH

6.48   In the case of sale of goods it is fairly rare to find an agreement without a price; indeed the absence of a price may indicate that the parties are still negotiating and that consequently there is no contract at all.[32] Section 8 of the 1979 Act, which is more appropriate to a commercial contract, provides that the price can be fixed by the contract itself, in manner thereby agreed or by usage. It then goes on to provide that if the price is not fixed in this way, the buyer must pay a reasonable price for the goods.

In the case of services, it is rather more common to call in a repairer, or to take a suit to the cleaners or a car for a service without agreeing a charge in advance. In such a case the supplier is entitled to claim a reasonable charge by virtue of s.15 of the Supply of Goods and Services Act 1982.[33] This, of course, is much easier said than done. If a consumer feels that the charge is too high the onus will be on him to find expert evidence to substantiate his claim. He will also be put to great practical inconvenience if the supplier has the goods in his possession and refuses to release them until he has been paid. The consumer should also be very careful to limit his potential liability. Instead of saying "the car is starting badly—put it right" he should say "tell me if the work is going to cost more than £50".

6.49   Incidentally, what about an "estimate"? If an estimate amounts to an

---

[30] In practice the contract will usually deal with the matter in accordance with the ABTA Code of Practice.

[31] *Charles Rickards Ltd v Oppenheim* [1950] 1 K.B. 616, CA.

[32] *May and Butcher v R.* [1934] 2 K.B. 17.

[33] Provided that there is a "contract" for the service it does not have to be in the course of a business—although it usually is. Once again exclusion is possible: see s.16 noted in para.6.44 above.

offer which is accepted, the estimate will become the contract price.[34] This, however, is rather unusual and the general rule is that the estimate is not legally binding but merely an indication of the likely charge; if however the estimate is a long way short of the final bill, the court might take the estimate into account in fixing a "reasonable price". In contrast, a quotation is more likely to be an offer to do the job for the quoted price.[35]

Can a supplier of services claim an additional amount if additional work is required? This again depends on what the parties have agreed. If, for example, a builder is employed to convert a loft at a fixed price, the onus will be on him to ensure that the work will comply with the local bye-laws and building regulations. If it turns out that the local authority require extra work to be done (for example, fireproofing) he will generally be unable to recover any additional payment for this extra work from the owner—he should have checked on the point before fixing his price.

There may also be special rules to protect the consumer in particular professions. Thus, for example, a client who is dissatisfied with a solicitor's bill for non-contentious business can insist that the solicitor has the bill assessed by the Law Society (a "remuneration certificate") or by an official of the court (a "detailed assessment" of the bill).

8. THE HOLIDAY WAS A NIGHTMARE

Legal relationship between the parties

The Law Commission Second Report on Exemption Clauses[36] touches on an interesting and difficult question—the precise legal relationship between the customer and the other organisations involved in providing his package holiday (the travel agent, the tour operator, the hotel and the airline).   **6.50**

It is suggested that generally the position is as follows. The customer makes only one contract with one legal entity—the tour operator.[37] This is effected via the travel agent who acts on behalf of the tour operator, not the customer.[38] As the agent is normally known to be acting for a named principal, he will incur no personal responsibility to the customer on the contract.

The contracts for accommodation and transportation are made by the tour operator on his own account: only he is responsible to the hotelier and airline for these costs, even though the services will be supplied by them to the tour operator's customer. Clearly the tour operator is under an implied obligation to his customer to pay the necessary sums to the carrier and hotelier to enable the customer to travel and to stay at his chosen resort without additional payment; if he fails to do so, so that the carrier or hotelier refuse to provide their services to the customer unless the customer himself pays

---

[34] *Croshaw v Pritchard* (1899) 16 T.L.R. 45.
[35] See, e.g. VBRA Code, below, para.10.29.
[36] Law Com. No. 69 (1975), para.126.
[37] See Lord Scarman in *Wings Ltd v Ellis* [1984] 3 All E.R. 577 at 586.
[38] For a discussion of this tripartite relationship, particularly in relation to payment by credit card, see *Connected Lender Liability* (OFT, March 1994), pp.28–30.

for them direct, the tour operator will have broken his contract with the customer and be liable in damages for such additional charges. Of course, if he does not provide the promised accommodation and facilities, he will be liable for breach of contract too.[39]

6.51   Although the travel agent is not a party to the main holiday contract, he may incur liability to the customer in other ways. If he makes untrue statements to the customer about the subject-matter of the contract, for example, hotel amenities, he may be liable (1) in tort for deceit or negligence, or (2) for breach of an implied warranty of authority if the statement is outside his actual or ostensible authority. Further, he may be in breach of a collateral contract between himself and the customer—a contract collateral to the main contract between the tour operator and the customer. Such rights against the travel agent are unlikely to be needed unless the tour operator is unable to meet his responsibilities under the main contract, e.g. because he is bankrupt or in liquidation.

Package Travel Regulations

6.52   The consumer's position has been considerably strengthened by legislation passed to comply with the EC Directive on Package Travel, Package Holidays and Package Tours (90/314). This was adopted by the EC Council in June 1990 and had to be brought into force by the end of 1992.

The Directive was implemented in the United Kingdom by the Package Travel, Package Holidays and Package Tours Regulations 1992.[40] They keep closely to the wording of the Directive. Clearly the Government was anxious not to be taken to the European Court of Justice, as happened in the field of employment law and sex discrimination, for failure properly to translate European law into national law; the safest route then is to use the same phrases as the Directive (so-called "copy out").

We shall comment on the main provisions, particularly where they improve the consumer's position.

Package

6.53   The Regulations do not apply to travel or accommodation booked separately, for example, a flight or hotel. Regulation 2(1) defines "package" as follows:

> 'package' means the pre-arranged combination of at least two of the following components when sold or offered for sale at an inclusive price and when the service covers a period of more than twenty-four hours or includes overnight accommodation:
>
> (a) transport;
> (b) accommodation;
> (c) other tourist services not ancillary to transport or accommodation and accounting for a significant proportion of the package.

---

[39] See the cases cited below, para.7.63.
[40] SI 1992/3288.

It can be seen that there must be at least two of the three elements. Generally, of course, the package will comprise travel by aircraft, coach, ship or train coupled with accommodation[41] in a hotel, apartment or even on the ship itself in the case of a cruise. However, it is not vital for transport to be included as the package may consist of items (b) and (c). An example given in the Consultation Document *Implementation of EC Directive on Package Travel, Package Holidays and Package Tours (arts. 1–6)* (February 1992) by the Department of Trade and Industry suggests that a weekend at a hotel where the price included access to fishing rights or to a golf course, where residents do not generally have these benefits, would be "other tourist services" thus making the arrangement a "package".

Organiser and retailer

These terms are used in reg.2(1) to describe the tour operator and travel agent. **6.54**

Information

There are a number of regulations about information to be given to the **6.55** consumer. Regulation 5 coupled with Sch.1 prescribes the information to be included in brochures, e.g. type of accommodation, inclusion of meals, itinerary, price and deposit.

Regulation 7 deals with information to be provided "before a contract is concluded". This covers such matters as passport and visa requirements, health formalities, and importantly "the arrangements for security for the money paid over and (where applicable) for the repatriation of the consumer in the event of insolvency". This is supplemented by reg.8 which deals with information to be provided "in good time before the start of the journey", for example, the times and places of intermediate stops and transport connections, and the name, address and telephone number of any local representative or agent.

We now come to the contents and form of the contract itself which is governed by reg.9. A written copy of the terms of the contract must be supplied to the consumer. Depending on the nature of the package, the contract must contain at least the elements specified in Sch.2. This is set out verbatim below in view of the importance of these details to the consumer or adviser.

Elements to be included in the contract if relevant to the particular package

(1) The travel destination(s) and, where periods of stay are involved, the rel- **6.56** evant periods, with dates.
(2) The means, characteristics and categories of transport to be used and the dates, times and points of departure and return.
(3) Where the package includes accommodation, its location, its tourist category or degree of comfort, its main features and, where the accommodation is to be provided in a member State, its compliance with the rules of that member State.

---

[41] In *Administrative Proceedings Concerning AFS Intercultural Programs Finland RY, The Times,* March 4, 1999, the ECJ decided that the Directive did not apply to a student exchange, where the student was treated as a member of the host family free of charge.

(4) The meals which are included in the package.

(5) Whether a minimum number of persons is required for the package to take place and, if so, the deadline for informing the consumer in the event of cancellation.

(6) The itinerary.

(7) Visits, excursions or other services which are included in the total price agreed for the package.

(8) The name and address of the organiser, the retailer and, where appropriate, the insurer.

(9) The price of the package, if the price may be revised in accordance with the term which may be included in the contract under regulation 11, an indication of the possibility of such price revisions, and an indication of any dues, taxes or fees chargeable for certain services (landing, embarkation or disembarkation fees at ports and airports and tourist taxes) where such costs are not included in the package.

(10) The payment schedule and method of payment.

(11) Special requirements which the consumer has communicated to the organiser or retailer when making the booking and which both have accepted.

(12) The periods within which the consumer must make any complaint about the failure to perform or the inadequate performance of the contract.

Regulation 9(3) states that it is "an implied condition" that the other party complies with the provisions of the regulation, so the consumer will be able to rescind the contract in the event of non-compliance—a serious sanction which should encourage organisers to keep to the rules.

Prices

6.57 Regulation 11 deals with price revisions. Prices are fixed unless the contract "states precisely how the revised price is to be calculated". Even then price revisions are permitted only for variations in transport costs, taxes or exchange rates. No increase can be made during the 30 days before departure or if less than two per cent.

Cancellation and alteration

6.58 There are provisions in regs 12 and 13 entitling the consumer to cancel or to accept an alternative package, with compensation if appropriate, e.g. if the organiser "is constrained to alter significantly an essential term"; force majeure excuses the organiser.

Implied warranties

6.59 Regulation 6 also provides that "the particulars in the brochure . . . shall constitute implied warranties . . . for the purposes of any contract to which the particulars relate." The effect is that a consumer will be able to recover damages for breach of warranty, where the services provided by the organiser do not precisely match their description. There will be no need for the consumer to resort to the Supply of Goods and Services Act 1982, s.13, by proving that the organiser had not exercised reasonable care and skill in the provision of the services, for the warranty implied by reg.6 imposes strict liability. There is one catch, however, for the consumer: there is no implied warranty where the brochure contains an express statement that changes may be made in the particulars contained in it and such changes are "clearly communicated to the consumer before a contract is concluded".

Liability

Regulation 15 provides that the organiser "is liable to the consumer for the proper performance of the obligations under the contract, irrespective of whether such obligations are to be performed by that other party or by other suppliers of services". This covers liability for sub-contractors too which, as explained above, is already the legal position in the United Kingdom, but it does no harm for the regulation to spell this out.   **6.60**

"Proper performance" does not impose strict liability on the organiser or retailer: it is fault-based.[42]

Unfortunately it goes on to permit limitation clauses which are "not unreasonable". This is the same as the UK position under s.3 of the Unfair Contract Terms Act 1977.

One point for the consumer to watch is that complaints must be speedy—"at the earliest opportunity" to the organiser and to the supplier of the services.

Assignment

One valuable new right is that the consumer may transfer his booking to a third party. However, reg.10 confines this possibility to a case where "the consumer is prevented from proceeding with the package". Will this cover only force majeure circumstances, e.g. illness? It would appear so. A change of mind would not be enough.   **6.61**

Insolvency

Article 7 of the Directive requires the organiser to prove that there is "security" for refunds and repatriation in the event of insolvency. Regulation 16 obliges the other party to the contract to "be able to provide sufficient evidence of security" for these matters. The organiser is given the option of pursuing a number of different routes: regs 17 to 20 permit bonds, insurance[43] or trust funds to be used. Further, none of these requirements apply where the package is covered by the Civil Aviation (Air Travel Organisers' Licensing) Regulations.[44]   **6.62**

Consumers can protect themselves by paying the tour operator (or hotel, airline etc, if it is not a "package") by credit card to gain the benefit of s.75 of the Consumer Credit Act 1974.[45] This is vital in these difficult economic times with unexpected insolvencies such as Globespan.

---

[42] *Hone v Going Places Leisure Travel Ltd* [2001] 1 All E.R. (D) 102, CA. See also *Codd v Thomson Tour Operators Ltd, The Times*, October 20, 2000 (local, not British, safety standards applied where boy injured in Spanish hotel lift).
[43] See Package Tours (Amendment) Regulations 1995 (SI 1995/1648).
[44] SI 1972/223.
[45] Below, para.23.07. See also, Rutherford, "*Travel agents and the use of credit cards in the travel trade*" (1994) 144 N.L.J.668.

Enforcement and penalties

6.63   Apart from giving the consumer certain contractual rights for breach of the implied terms the Regulations may result in criminal sanctions against the organiser or retailer. Various criminal offences are scattered throughout the Regulations. As usual with consumer protection legislation they are enforced by trading standards officers. The penalty for contravention is a fine; a prison sentence cannot be imposed even where the defendant is convicted on indictment.

Distress

6.64   If the tour operator, hotel, airline or other supplier breaks the contract with the customer, then the customer may recover damages for breach of contract. We discuss remedies in Chapter Seven including the important head of damages in this context—mental distress, upset, disappointment and injured feelings (the cases in paras 7.59 and 7.63 are particularly relevant).

Airline overbooking and delays

6.65   Passengers are frequently delayed at airports in two situations. (1) Sometimes the delay is caused by overbooking. The airlines assume that some passengers will prove to be "no shows" and, if more passengers turn up than anticipated, the surplus passengers are "bumped" onto later flights. (2) More often delays in take-off or cancellations are caused by incoming aircraft arriving late or having technical faults.

EC Regulation 261/2004 has provisions that help passengers in both cases, provided they fly (a) from outside the EU to an EU airport on an EU airline, or (b) from an EU airport on any airline.

In case (1) (overbooking) "denied boarding" compensation is payable on a scale set down in the Regulation: it depends on the length of the flight and of the delay in reaching the destination; for example, EUR 250 for up to 1,500km and more than two hours.[46] In case (2) (other delay) the compensation is in kind and again depends on the distance and delay; using the same example, refreshments and two free telephone calls, emails, etc.[47] If cancellation results, compensation must be paid on the above scale.[48]

Details of the Regulation can be found on the Air Transport Users Council section of the Civil Aviation Authority website (*www.caa.co.uk*).

6.66   The airline need not pay compensation where the cancellation was caused by "extraordinary circumstances which could not have been avoided even if all reasonable measures had been taken". A recent example is aircraft grounded by volcanic ash from Iceland. There are particular problems where a technical fault is the cause. Are these "extraordinary circumstances"? Happily for passengers the answer to the last question is "no". In *Wallentin-Hermann v Alitalia-Linee Aeree Italiane SpA* Case C – 549/07[49] the European Court of Justice decided that "technical problems which came to light during maintenance of aircraft, or on account of failure to carry out such maintenance, could not constitute, in themselves, "extraordinary circumstances"".

---

[46] arts 5, 7, 8 and 9.
[47] arts 6, 8 and 9.
[48] arts 5, 7, 8 and 9.
[49] *The Times*, February 16, 2009.

Chapter Seven

"WHAT ARE MY REMEDIES?"

In the previous five chapters we have considered some of the supplier's basic **7.01** obligations. We now come to the subject of remedies which, as stated in the Preface to the First Edition, is what this book is all about; it is also the area in which the consumer is most likely to seek legal advice. In practice three questions most frequently arise, namely (a) what are the consumer's remedies, (b) can they be excluded, and (c) how can they be enforced? These topics are considered in this chapter and the four following ones.

One preliminary point can be made. This chapter and the next two are concerned with questions of strict law. In Chapter Ten we shall see that in many cases consumers may be able to sidestep the worry, uncertainty and expense of litigation as a result of voluntary codes of practice drawn up by a number of trade and professional associations with the encouragement of the Office of Fair Trading. We shall also see that a complaint to a trading standards inspector can lead to a prosecution in certain cases and that this, in turn, can lead to a compensation order.[1]

This chapter is divided into three main parts, namely: **7.02**

1. Remedies for misrepresentation.
2. Remedies for breach of contract.
3. Remedies in tort.

In relation to the supply of goods there have been significant developments in the past ten years. The Sale and Supply of Goods Act 1994, which we have already considered when dealing with "satisfactory quality" in Chapter Four, also made changes to the rules governing acceptance and rejection. Then on March 31, 2003 the EU-inspired Sale and Supply of Goods to Consumers Regulations 2002 came into force introducing new remedies for consumers. All of these topics will be analysed and explained in this chapter.

1. REMEDIES FOR MISREPRESENTATION

The remedies for misrepresentation can be summarised as follows: **7.03**

(1) Fraudulent misrepresentation:
   (a) damages in tort for deceit;
   (b) rescission.

---

[1] Below, para.16.02.

(2) Negligent misrepresentation:

    (a) damages under s.2(1) of the Misrepresentation Act 1967;

    (b) rescission (or damages in lieu under s.2(2) of the 1967 Act).

(3) "Innocent" misrepresentation (i.e. neither fraudulent nor negligent):

    rescission (or damages in lieu under s.2(2) of the 1967 Act).

These matters will now be considered.

Fraudulent misrepresentation

7.04 A person commits the tort of deceit (or fraud) if he makes a false statement of fact knowingly, without belief in its truth, or recklessly (i.e. careless whether true or false) with the intention that it should be acted upon by the claimant who does act on it and thereby suffers damage.[2] In practice, fraud is notoriously hard to prove. If, however, the consumer can prove that, for example, the dealer deliberately misrepresented the age or mileage of a car then, as we have seen, he may have the remedies of damages and/or rescission.[3] If he rescinds the contract he can claim to be put back into his pre-contractual position so that, for example, he can recover any part of the price which he has paid. The action for damages can be considered (a) if the innocent party does not wish to rescind, (b) if it is too late to rescind,[4] or (c) if he has suffered damage over and above the price.

What is the measure of damages for fraudulent misrepresentation? The rules are designed to prove compensation for all loss flowing directly from the fraud, whether reasonably foreseeable or not. Thus, in a sale of goods or land the starting point is the difference (if any) between the price paid by the consumer and the true value of the goods or land.[5] Money spent on repair and improvement before discovering the fraud can also be recovered[6] but not damages for loss of bargain.[7] Damages for personal injury or damage to property can also be recovered.[8] The onus is on the consumer to prove loss and his action will fail if he cannot do so.[9]

Negligent misrepresentation

7.05 Until the passing of the Misrepresentation Act 1967 the court had no general power to award damages for a non-fraudulent misrepresentation—hence the importance of proving that there had been a breach of a contractual term.[10]

---

[2] See the leading case of *Derry v Peek* (1889) 14 App.Cas. 337, HL.
[3] Above, para.3.03.
[4] See below, paras 7.07–7.08.
[5] *Doyle v Olby (Ironmongers) Ltd* [1969] 2 Q.B. 158—a case of the sale of a business.
[6] *ibid.*
[7] *East v Maurer* [1991] 1 W.L.R. 461 (another business sale; damages awarded for the profits which the plaintiff would have earned if the false statement had not been made).
[8] *Langridge v Levy* (1838) 4 M. & W. 337—exploding gun.
[9] *Latkter v General Guarantee Finance Ltd* [2001] EWCA Civ 875—a case involving the purchase of a Triumph Thunderbird motorbike and a (disputed) representation that it was a 1997 model.
[10] See above, para.3.04.

A Law Reform Committee recommended a change in the law and accordingly s.2(1) of the 1967 Act was passed to give a statutory right to damages in certain cases. It reads:

> Where a person has entered into a contract after a misrepresentation has been made to him by another party thereto and as a result thereof he has suffered loss then if the person making the representation would be liable in damages in respect thereof had the representation been made fraudulently, that person shall be so liable notwithstanding that the misrepresentation was not made fraudulently, unless he proves that he had reasonable grounds to believe and did believe up to the time that the contract was made that the facts represented were true.

It is clear from the case of *Howard Marine & Dredging Co Ltd v A Ogden &* **7.06** *Son (Excavation) Ltd*[11] that a s.2(1) claim is a claim in tort, and the approach in relation to a claim for damages is the same as for fraud.[12] Accordingly a misrepresentation will not be easily found and the courts will take a broad view.[13] We have seen that the object of damages in tort is to put the innocent party in the same position *as if the contract had never been made*. This can be contrasted with a different rule in contract where the damages are designed to put the innocent party in the same position *as if the contract had been performed*. Thus damages for loss of bargain are appropriate to contract but not to tort; the case of *Watts v Spence*,[14] where damages for loss of bargain were awarded under s.2(1) of the 1967 Act, must be regarded as wrongly decided and the judge in a later case has refused to follow it.[15]

Rescission

We can now turn to the equitable remedy of rescission. This has already **7.07** been mentioned[16] and it only remains to consider the cases where it is not available. There are four well-established bars to rescission and these can be summarised as follows:

(a) where the parties can no longer be restored to their previous position. Thus the right to rescission would disappear if goods were destroyed before the buyer had elected to rescind;

(b) where third party rights have been acquired. Perhaps the clearest example is where B, by misrepresentation, persuades S to sell the goods to B and then resells the goods to C[17];

(c) where the innocent party has affirmed the contract with knowledge of the misrepresentation[18];

---

[11] [1978] Q.B. 574. See also *Naughton v O'Callaghan* [1990] 3 All E.R. 191 (misdescription of racehorse).
[12] ibid. at p.197. See also *Royscot Trust Ltd v Rogerson* [1991] 2 Q.B. 297, CA.
[13] *Avon plc v Swire Fraser (a firm)* unreported, applying the *Royston* case mentioned above.
[14] [1976] Ch. 165
[15] *Cemp Properties (UK) v Dentsply Research and Development Corp (No. 2)* [1989] 37 E.G. 126.
[16] Above, para.7.04.
[17] See Sale of Goods Act 1979, s.23, above, para.2.09.
[18] *Long v Lloyd* [1958] 2 All E.R. 402. Cf. Acceptance and loss of the right to reject for breach of condition, where knowledge is irrelevant: below, para.7.37.

(d) where the innocent party has been guilty of unreasonable delay. In the well-known case of *Leaf v International Galleries*,[19] the buyer of a painting which was described as by J. Constable sought to rescind for misrepresentation five years after making the contract on discovering that it was the work of another artist. The Court of Appeal held that it was far too late to rescind. In the words of Jenkins L.J.:

> "If he is allowed to wait five, ten or twenty years and then re-open the bargain, there can be no finality at all."

If the buyer had claimed damages under s.13 of the Sale of Goods Act[20] the claim would presumably have been unanswerable.

Statutory restriction on rescission

7.08 If none of these four bars applies, the general rule is that the innocent party can rescind the contract. The exercise of this remedy can have far-reaching results.

> Suppose that P buys a house from V for £200,000. V makes a non-fraudulent misrepresentation relating to the drains; the defect will cost £800 to put right. V has spent the whole of the £200,000 in buying another house.

If P were to rescind, V would have to find £200,000 (and might well be rendered homeless) because of a statement which caused damage of only £800. It was clearly with this kind of case in mind that s.2(2) of the Misrepresentation Act was enacted. It provides that:

> where a person has entered into a contract after a misrepresentation has been made to him otherwise than fraudulently, and he would be entitled, by reason of the misrepresentation, to rescind the contract, then, if it is claimed in any proceedings arising out of the contract, that the contract ought to be or has been rescinded, the court or arbitrator may declare the contract subsisting and award damages in lieu of rescission, if of opinion that it would be equitable to do so, having regard to the nature of the misrepresentation and the loss that would be caused by it if the contract was upheld, as well as to the loss that rescission would cause to the other party.

Thus, in the above example, the court would probably refuse rescission and award P damages of £800.

This power to award discretionary damages only applies where a person "would be entitled . . . to rescind the contract". In earlier editions of this book we suggested that damages could only be awarded under s.2(2) if the innocent party had a subsisting right to rescind at the date of the hearing and there are conflicting decisions as to whether this is so.[21]

---

[19] [1950] 2 K.B. 86.
[20] Above, para.3.13. But see *Harlingdon and Leinster Enterprises v Christopher Hull Fine Art*, above, para.3.14.
[21] *Thomas Witter Ltd v TPB Industries Ltd* [1996] 2 All E.R. 573 and contrast *Zanzibar v British Aerospace (Lancaster House) Ltd* [2002] 1 W.L.R. 2333.

"Innocent" misrepresentation

If the misrepresentation is neither fraudulent nor negligent, the only pos- **7.09** sible remedy is rescission. This is subject to the usual equitable bars[22] and the court's discretionary power under s.2(2) to award damages in lieu of rescission.

Exclusion clauses

A clause excluding liability for misrepresentation or cutting down the con- **7.10** sumer's remedies for misrepresentation is only valid if it satisfies the test of "reasonableness".[23]

Misrepresentation and breach of contract

It is clear from s.1 of the Misrepresentation Act 1967 that the innocent party **7.11** will have remedies for misrepresentation even though the representation has become a term of contract. The precise relationship between the two sets of remedies has yet to be worked out but presumably they are complementary.[24] It has been held that a clause stating "this agreement contains the whole contract between the parties" does not oust a claim for misrepresentation.[25] The court expressly decided that such a clause was not an exemption clause.

2. REMEDIES FOR BREACH OF CONTRACT

These remedies have recently been radically altered in the consumer's favour **7.12** by the Sale and Supply of Goods to Consumers Regulations 2002 which give effect to Directive 1999/44 by amending the Sale of Goods Act 1979 and comparable legislation. Since the new law is EU-based, the consumer will have similar remedies elsewhere in the European Union for goods bought there. In the remainder of this section a reference to a regulation is a reference to the 2002 Regulations. It is proposed to consider first the new remedies and then the other possible remedies available under the general law.

A. AN OVERVIEW

The remedies conferred by the amending Regulations exist alongside those **7.13** available under the general law. The position can be summarised as follows:

(1) Under the Regulations the remedies are:

    (a) repair or replacement of the goods;
    (b) reduction of the price;
    (c) rescission.

---

[22] Above, para.7.07.
[23] Below, para.8.41.
[24] See *Naughton v O'Callaghan*, above, para.7.06, n.11. See also n.35 in para.3.10 above.
[25] *McGrath v Shah* (1989) 57 P. & C.R. 452. This is called an "entire agreement" clause.

(2) Under the general law the remedies are:

    (a) (occasionally) specific performance;
    (b) rejection for breach of a major term;
    (c) damages.

These remedies will only be available if certain conditions are satisfied and we shall see that the Regulations give the court wide discretionary powers if the case comes to court.

Guarantees

7.14 For completeness we should also mention remedies which the consumer may have under a contract of guarantee. This is distinct from the other remedies because the consumer will not have to prove a breach of contract. The precise scope of the remedies will depend on the terms of the guarantee. We have considered some aspects of guarantees in Chapter Five.

Practical considerations

7.15 (1) The supplier will invariably require proof of purchase and the consumer should always insist on getting a sales receipt. He should then keep it in a safe place; his legal remedies will be very difficult to enforce without one, although other evidence such as a witness at the time of purchase or a credit card slip will do instead.

(2) Faced with a consumer complaint the supplier may offer a credit note. This can be useful to the consumer in some cases but he or she must realise that a credit note cannot be used by the supplier to cut down the remedies dealt with in this Chapter. Thus where consumers are entitled to their money back, they can refuse to accept a credit note instead.

B. THE NEW STATUTORY REMEDIES

(1) Introduction

7.16 One point must be stressed: the Regulations amend existing legislation so that, for example, the Sale of Goods Act 1979 must be cited, not the Regulations themselves.

(2) Sale of goods

When are the new remedies available?

7.17 Regulation 5 amends the Sale of Goods Act 1979 by adding six new sections (48A to 48F). Section 48A tells us that the new remedies are available if (a) the buyer deals as consumer and (b) "the goods do not conform to the contract of sale at the time of delivery." This must be read with s.48F which provides that:

For the purposes of this Part goods do not conform to a contract of sale if there is, in relation to the goods, a breach of an express term of the contract or a term implied by sections 13, 14 or 15 above.

The Regulations are silent on the nature of the "express term"—so perhaps even a minor term will trigger the statutory remedies (including rescission in some cases). This is very different from the existing law. Readers will recall from Chapter Four that promotional material published by a third party (e.g. a manufacturer) will be taken into account in deciding whether goods are of "satisfactory quality".

The burden of proof: six months rule—s.48A(3) and (4)

If the goods break down or develop faults at some point after delivery, the **7.18** most difficult legal task for the consumer and his or her advisers is to prove that the goods were defective when they were first supplied. This ties in with the rules as to durability which we have considered in Chapter Four (see para.4.24 above). The DTI guidance gives the following example:

If a central heating system stopped working—because of its pump failing— four years after the sale, having had average usage, then it might not be due to an inherent fault (latently there on the day of the sale) but due to it expiring at the end of its normally accepted working life. This is especially so if the relevant trade association had advice that such pumps only worked for an average of two years. If, however, the pump had lasted only half the expected life, having been subject to average use, then the consumer would, no doubt, wish to seek an opinion as to whether the item had contained a latent fault or been constructed with sub-standard raw materials that made it not durable enough to pass the satisfactory quality test of our Sale of Goods Act legislation.

Section 48A(3) now assists the consumer by reversing the burden of proof during a six month period. It reads;

. . . goods which do not conform to the contract of sale at any time within the period of six months starting with the date on which the goods were delivered to the buyer must be taken to have not so conformed at that date.

However s.48A(4) provides that this will not be so if:

(a) it is established that the goods did so conform at that date;
(b) its application is incompatible with the nature of the goods or the nature of the lack of conformity.

An obvious example of (b) above would be goods which have a very short life and which break down or deteriorate after that time. Thus a buyer who consumes food after the recommended "use by" date may well be without a remedy.

Repair or replacement—s.48B

7.19 This section brings the law into line with reality by giving the consumer, in many cases, the remedy that he really wants—namely to have the goods repaired or replaced (the term "repair" in this context means bringing the goods into conformity with the contract—see s.61(1)). Previously the question of repair or replacement was a matter of business practice rather than law—and it was very rare for some items (especially cars) to be replaced. The seller's duty is amplified by s.48B(2) and (5) which provide that:

> (2) If the buyer requests the seller to repair or replace the goods, the seller must—
>
> > (a) repair or, as the case may be, replace the goods within a reasonable time but without causing significant inconvenience to the buyer;
> > (b) bear any necessary costs incurred in doing so (including in particular the cost of labour, materials or postage).
>
> (5) Any question as to what is a reasonable time or significant inconvenience is to be determined by reference to—
>
> > (a) the nature of the goods, and
> > (b) the purpose for which they were acquired.

7.20 The "reasonable time" requirement will depend on the facts of the particular case. In some cases (a wedding dress being an obvious example) the number of days involved in repair/replacement will be critical and, perhaps, decisive (see DTI guidance, p.10).

The right to insist on repair or replacement is subject to three restrictions. By s.48B(3) the buyer must not require the seller to repair or, as the case may be, replace the goods if that remedy is—

> (3) (a) impossible, or
> > (b) disproportionate in comparison to the other of those remedies, or
> > (c) disproportionate in comparison to an appropriate reduction in the purchase price under paragraph (a), or rescission under paragraph (b), of section 48C(1) below.

Thus if a replacement would cost £50 but repair would cost £100, the buyer would not be entitled to insist on repair (unless perhaps repair, but not replacement, is possible within a critical time-frame). This is confirmed by s.48B(4) which reads as follows:

> (4) One remedy is disproportionate in comparison to the other if the one imposes costs on the seller which, in comparison to those imposed on him by the other, are unreasonable, taking into account—
>
> > (a) the value which the goods would have if they conformed to the contract of sale,
> > (b) the significance of the lack of conformity, and
> > (c) whether the other remedy could be effected without significant inconvenience to the buyer.

If the buyer asks the seller to repair the goods, he cannot change his mind and ask for replacement until he has given the seller a reasonable time for the repair; the converse (repair rather than replacement) is equally true: see s.48D.

What happens if the seller fails to comply with his statutory repair or replacement obligation? This can have two consequences. First, the court can make an order requiring the seller to perform (see s.48E(2)).[26] Secondly, the failure can trigger the abatement/rescission rights conferred by s.48C which we must now consider.

Price reduction and rescission—s.48C

Section 48C gives the buyer a right to (a) require the seller to reduce the **7.21** purchase price by an appropriate amount or (b) rescind the contract. This right is very much secondary. By s.48C(2) it is only available in two sets of circumstances:

(a) where repair/replacement is not available—see s.48B(3) above, or

(b) where a request for repair/replacement has been made and the seller is in breach of his obligation to do so within a reasonable time and without significant inconvenience to the buyer.

The secondary nature of this new "money back" right can be contrasted with the primary right under the general law to terminate the contract for breach of condition and obtain a full refund, which we shall consider later in this Chapter.

If the buyer has the right to rescind the contract, his right to claim a full reimbursement may be cut down by reference to any use which he has had of the goods since they were delivered to him (see s.48C(3)).

Remedies and the powers of the court—s.48E

There may be cases where the buyer chooses one of his new statutory rights **7.22** but the seller can satisfy the court that another remedy is appropriate. In this situation s.48E(4) allows the court to treat the buyer as if he had opted for that other remedy. Thus the court can, in an appropriate case, substitute replacement for repair or price abatement for rescission. Any such order can be made unconditionally, or on such terms and conditions as to damages, payment of the price and otherwise as the court thinks just. If, for example, a freezer is not of satisfactory quality and breaks down, the court could award compensation for any ruined food. The consumer should report any fault as soon as possible. If he fails to do so then (1) it will be more difficult to prove that the fault was present at the time of the contract and (2) the retailer will not be liable for any additional damage resulting from the delay.

---

[26] This can be contrasted with the general reluctance of the courts to grant specific performance—see para.7.25 below.

(3) Other supply contracts

7.23   Where goods are transferred to a customer under a contract which is not a contract of sale (notably contracts for exchange or for work and materials) we have seen that the supplier's obligations are governed by the Supply of Goods and Services Act 1982. Regulation 9 contains provisions which insert six new sections, 11M to 11R into the 1982 Act and which (with one addition) mirror exactly the provisions which we have just considered. The addition in s.11S (which can, for example, apply to contracts for the installation of double glazing or central heating) provides that goods will not comply with the contract if (1) installation forms part of the contract and (2) the transferor, or a person under his responsibility, fails to install the goods with reasonable care under s.13 of the 1982 Act (see para.6.44 above) or under any other rule of law.

Surprisingly, the new remedies which we have discussed above do not apply to contracts of hire or hire-purchase—although the new "promotional material" provisions must be taken into account when considering satisfactory quality.

C. REMEDIES AVAILABLE UNDER THE GENERAL LAW

7.24   The remedies which we have just described exist alongside the remedies available to the consumer under the general law pre-dating the Regulations; they do not replace them. They can be considered by attempting to answer three questions on which a consumer may seek advice, namely:

(1) Can I make them perform the contract?

(2) Can I get my money back?

(3) Can I get compensation?

(1) Can I make them perform the contract?

7.25   Let us suppose that a consumer has ordered goods from a supplier, or work from a builder, and the supplier or builder has failed to carry it out. We have already seen that the consumer may be able to serve a notice making time of the essence; if the supplier or builder then fails to perform by the stipulated date the consumer may be able to treat the contract as discharged.

Let us suppose, however, that the consumer does not want to do this—what he wants is to compel the supplier or builder to perform the contract. In practical terms this may be more trouble than it is worth—the consumer may be better advised to obtain the goods or work elsewhere and claim compensation from the defaulting party.[27] If, however, the consumer insists on performance, can the law help him? Historically the courts of common law granted only the remedy of damages, but the courts of equity supplemented this by granting decrees of specific performance in cases where damages

---

[27] Below, paras 7.51–7.65.

would not be an adequate remedy. In the case of sale of goods the power to award specific performance is enacted in s.52 of the Sale of Goods Act 1979 as follows:

> In any action for breach of contract to deliver specific or ascertained goods the court may, if it thinks fit, on the plaintiff's application . . . direct that the contract shall be performed specifically, without giving the defendant the option of retaining the goods on payment of damages. . . .

Two points must be stressed. In the first place the goods must be specific or **7.26** ascertained. We have already seen that goods are specific if they are identified and agreed upon at the time of the contract.[28] Although the term "ascertained" is not defined in the Act it probably refers to goods which are identified *after* the making of the contract.[29] Thus if a consumer merely orders "a Bosch dishwasher" or "a heated trolley" and the seller, who is out of stock, fails to obtain one, the remedy of specific performance would not be available.[30] Secondly, the remedy of specific performance is, and has always been, a discretionary remedy and a court will not grant it if damages would be an adequate remedy. In the vast majority of consumer contracts the buyer can get similar goods elsewhere and any loss can be compensated by an award of damages, e.g. for the extra cost. Accordingly, specific performance would not be granted. It follows that the scope of the remedy, in practical terms, is extremely limited.

There are only two situations in which specific performance is likely to be granted. The first is where the article is unique (perhaps a painting, sculpture or manuscript). The second is where the property in specific or ascertained goods has passed to the buyer and the seller becomes bankrupt or goes into liquidation. Under general principles of insolvency law a creditor can enforce his rights against the estate of an insolvent debtor if those rights are proprietary rather than personal. The consumer should immediately get in touch with the liquidator or trustee in bankruptcy to demand delivery of the goods.

In the case of a contract for services (e.g. building, cleaning or repairing) the remedy is even less appropriate[31] and it is difficult to think of any case in which it will be granted.

(2) Can I get my money back?

When a consumer makes a contract for the purchase of goods or services he **7.27** is under a basic obligation to pay the contract price. Thus, if he has booked a holiday at a seaside hotel, he cannot simply cancel his booking. If he does so then, as a matter of strict law, the hotel can keep any deposit, and can

---

[28] para.6.38 above.
[29] See Atkin L.J. in *Re Wait* [1927] 1 Ch. 606.
[30] ibid.
[31] There used to be a rule that specific performance (or a mandatory injunction) would not be granted if this required constant supervision of the defendant's work (*Ryan v Mutual Tontine Westminster Chambers Ass.* [1893] 1 Ch 116). The rationale of this rule has always been questionable and it is clear that it no longer exists: *Shiloh Spinners Ltd v Harding (No. 1)* [1973] A.C. 721 at 691, HL.

even sue him for damages if they have suffered additional loss by reason of his cancellation and have been unable to mitigate the loss by reletting the room.

There may, however, be cases where the consumer is relieved of his basic duty to pay the price; in these cases he can recover the price (or a deposit) if he has already paid it. This will be so in at least four cases:

(a) where the contract is rescinded for misrepresentation[32];

(b) where specific goods perish before the risk has passed to the buyer[33];

(c) where a contract for the sale of goods is discharged as a result of the supplier's breach;

(d) where the consumer exercises a contractual or statutory right of cancellation.[34]

Discharge by breach

7.28 If one party breaks a contractual term (express or implied) the innocent party can claim damages. In some cases he can go further and claim that the entire contract has been discharged by the breach. Once that happens the innocent party can regard himself as excused from further performance and can also claim damages in respect of the past breach.

In deciding whether a contract has been discharged by breach we must start by looking at the general law and then at the special rules which apply to the sale of goods and (probably) to analogous contracts. Under the general law, a contract is discharged by a breach if the innocent party has been deprived of substantially the whole benefit which it was intended that he should obtain from the contract.[35] In other words the question is not "how was this term classified when the contract was made?" but—much more sensibly—"what effect did the breach have on the innocent party?" Even if the breach was a repudiatory breach, the innocent party may well have received *some* benefit under the contract and therefore has no right to recover money paid by him—although he will have a claim for damages which could well be equal to, or greater than, the amount of payments made.

Sales of goods

7.29 If we now turn to sales of goods we find the matter complicated by the condition/warranty classification. By s.61(1) of the 1979 Act a warranty is defined as:

> . . . an agreement with reference to goods which are the subject-matter of a contract of sale, but collateral to the main purpose of such contract, the breach of

---

[32] Above, para.7.04.
[33] Above, para.6.39.
[34] For examples see Ch.6, para.6.23.
[35] per Diplock L.J. in *Hong Kong Fir Shipping Co Ltd v Kawasaki* [1962] 2 Q.B. 26 at 66.

which gives rise to a claim for damages but not to a right to reject the goods and treat the contract as repudiated.

In contrast, s.11(3) states that:

> Whether a stipulation in a contract of sale is a condition, the breach of which may give rise to a right to treat the contract as repudiated, or a warranty . . . depends in each case on the construction of such contract.

This wording, with its emphasis on "the construction of the contract" appears to leave no scope for the flexibility shown by the *Hong Kong* case (above), where the remedies available to the innocent party depend on the severity and consequences of the breach. (We use the words "appears to leave" because neither the courts nor the Law Commission seem to have considered the word "may" in the above definition—this might enable the *Hong Kong* principle to apply after all.)

Nevertheless in the case of *express* terms the courts have succeeded[36] in breaking out of the statutory straitjacket by holding that a clause could be neither a condition nor a warranty but an "intermediate stipulation" or "innominate term" to which the *Hong Kong* principles apply.

There is no scope for such flexibility in the case of the statutory *implied* terms and, as we have seen in Chapters Two to Four, the most important of the implied terms are classified as conditions. It remains to add that a buyer who rejects the goods for breach of condition can recover the price paid in full[37] because there has been a total failure of consideration (see s.54).

Other supply of goods contracts

In the case of hire-purchase, hire, work and materials, and other contracts **7.30** for the supply of goods the relevant statutes[38] use the condition/warranty terminology but do not define it. It is possible therefore (but unlikely) that a court would feel free to construe the words in a more flexible way. The case law makes it clear that a breach relating to fitness for purpose, etc., does not necessarily amount to a total failure of consideration. Accordingly the innocent party has no direct cause of action to recover payments made but instead must seek to recover them indirectly by means of an action for damages.[39] If, however, the hirer under a hire-purchase agreement discovers the owner has no right to sell, we have seen that he *can* recover all his payments on the basis of total failure of consideration (see para.2.16 above).

Supplies of services

Finally in contracts for services the statutory obligations as to care and skill, **7.31** time for performance and price are referred to by the neutral word "term".[40]

---

[36] *Cehave v Bremer* [1976] Q.B. 44, CA.
[37] Compare new s.48C(3) where reduction for use is possible (above, para.7.21).
[38] Supply of Goods (Implied Terms) Act 1973 for hire-purchase and the Supply of Goods and Services Act 1982 for the other types of contract.
[39] See Law Commission Working Paper No.85, paras 2.41–2.43 and cases there cited.
[40] Supply of Goods and Services Act 1982, ss.13–15.

It is clear therefore that the flexible *Hong Kong* test will apply to them: they are intermediate stipulations.

Slight breaches—s.15A

7.32   Minor defects can create a problem. On the one hand, a consumer should not be required to take goods which have minor defects (such as scratches on the bodywork of a car). On the other hand, the remedy of rejection may be so out of proportion that a court might be tempted to hold that the condition of "satisfactory quality" was not broken at all[41]—with the result that the buyer could neither reject nor claim damages. We pointed out this problem in relation to the implied condition as to description in Chapter Three (above, para.3.10).

The Law Commission in their report recommended that the law be changed for non-consumers[42] but not for consumers[43], since the remedy of rejection for *any* breach of the implied conditions is a vital weapon in the battle between consumers and business suppliers. Their proposals have now been enacted in the Sale and Supply of Goods Act 1994. Section 4(1) inserts into the Sale of Goods Act 1979 a new s.15A(1) which provides that:

> Where in the case of a contract of sale—
>
>   (a) the buyer would, apart from this subsection, have the right to reject goods by reason of a breach on the part of the seller of a term implied by section 13, 14 or 15[44] above, but
>   (b) the breach is so slight that it would be unreasonable for him to reject them,
>
> then, if the buyer does not deal as consumer, the breach is not to be treated as a breach of condition but may be treated as a breach of warranty.

This section broke new ground by drawing a distinction for the first time between consumers and non-consumers; a similar distinction can be found in the six new sections introduced by the 2002 Regulations[45] which apply only to consumer sales. The rest of the Act applies indiscriminately to consumers and non-consumers alike.

Loss of right to reject—sale of goods

7.33   Section 11(4) of the 1979 Act cuts down the buyer's rights if the goods (or part) have been accepted. As originally drafted s.11(4) read as follows:

> Where a contract of sale is not severable and the buyer has accepted the goods or part of them . . . the breach of any condition to be fulfilled by the seller can only be treated as a breach of warranty, and not as a ground for rejecting the goods

---

[41] *Cehave v Bremer* (above, n.36, para.7.29) is a commercial example, where the buyer was awarded damages for breach of an *express* term.
[42] op. cit. para.4.21.
[43] op. cit. para.4.41.
[44] s.15 relates to sale by sample which is irrelevant for consumers.
[45] See paras 7.17 to 7.23 above.

and treating the contract as repudiated, unless there is an express or implied term of the contract to that effect.

The changes made by the Sale and Supply of Goods Act 1994 now allow the buyer a right of partial rejection in certain cases (see below, para.7.45).

When is a contract severable?

The opening words of the subsection refer to a contract which is "sever- **7.34** able". Thus, if a consumer made a contract with a supplier for the delivery of a 12-part encyclopedia, one part to be delivered each month and to be *separately paid for*, this would be a severable contract. The result would be that the acceptance of one instalment would not prevent the buyer from rejecting a later one on the grounds that, for example, a number of pages were blank.

A further question then arises; does a breach with regard to one or more instalments amount to a repudiation of the entire contract or is it merely a severable breach? In other words, can a buyer who rejects instalment number two be compelled to accept the remaining 10 instalments? There is no clear cut answer to this question; by s.31(2):

> ". . . it is a question in each case depending on the terms of the contract and the circumstances of the case."

In this example the buyer might well be able to refuse further instalments if, for example, the set as a whole is useless without the missing part. This raises a further unsettled point; if a seller tenders a defective instalment which is lawfully rejected, can he put the matter right by delivering a non-defective instalment? On principle, the answer ought to be "yes", provided that he is not in breach of an essential time clause, but it is uncertain whether the innocent buyer must allow the seller, who has broken a condition, a second bite of the cherry.

What is acceptance?

In the overwhelming majority of consumer sales the contract will be non- **7.35** severable so that the buyer will lose the right to reject when he accepts the goods.[46] The 1994 Act makes a number of changes in favour of the buyer as proposed by the Law Commission. The statutory provisions are contained in ss.34 and 35(1) of the 1979 Act (as amended). Section 34 gives buyers the right to examine the goods. It now reads as follows:

> Unless otherwise agreed, when the seller tenders delivery of the goods to the buyer, he is bound on request to afford the buyer a reasonable opportunity of examining the goods for the purpose of ascertaining whether they are in conformity with the contract and, in the case of a contract for sale by sample, of comparing the bulk with the sample.

---

[46] But the right to damages remains untouched. See below, para.7.51.

This section is clearly of considerable importance to consumers. It would apply, for example, to a purchase by mail order; it would also apply to a purchase of a cooker or washing machine where the consumer had merely examined a demonstration model. In practice, the goods themselves are usually delivered in a large closed box and the consumer is asked to sign a form stating that the contents are satisfactory.

7.36   In the Third Edition of this book we felt that the court would look at the reality of the situation. The problem has now been resolved in the consumer's favour by s.2(1) of the 1994 Act which inserts two new subsections in s.35 as follows:

> (2) Where goods are delivered to the buyer, and he has not previously examined them, he is not deemed to have accepted them . . . until he has had a reasonable opportunity of examining them for the purpose—
>> (a) of ascertaining whether they are in conformity with the contract, and
>> (b) in the case of a contract for sale by sample, of comparing the bulk with the sample.
>
> (3) Where the buyer deals as consumer . . . the buyer cannot lose his right to rely on subsection (2) above by agreement, waiver or otherwise.

The three types of acceptance

7.37   The remainder of the revised s.35 (inserted by s.2(1) of the 1994 Act) reads as follows:

> (1) The buyer is deemed to have accepted the goods subject to subsection (2) below—
>> (a) when he intimates to the seller that he has accepted them, or
>> (b) when the goods have been delivered to him and he does any act in relation to them which is inconsistent with the ownership of the seller.
>
> (4) The buyer is also deemed to have accepted the goods when after the lapse of a reasonable time he retains the goods without intimating to the seller that he has rejected them.
>
> (5) The questions that are material in determining for the purposes of subsection (4) above whether a reasonable time has elapsed include whether the buyer has had a reasonable opportunity of examining the goods for the purpose mentioned in subsection (2) above.
>
> (6) The buyer is not by virtue of this section deemed to have accepted the goods merely because—
>> (a) he asks for, or agrees to, their repair by or under an arrangement with the seller, or
>> (b) the goods are delivered to another under a sub-sale or other disposition.
>
> (7) Where the contract is for the sale of goods making one or more commercial units, a buyer accepting any goods included in a unit is deemed to have accepted all the goods making the unit; and in this subsection "commercial unit" means a unit division of which would materially impair the value of the goods or the character of the unit.

Let us now examine the three forms of "acceptance".

(i) Intimation of acceptance. There has been no reported case on this topic; **7.38** it is felt that there must be conduct on the part of the buyer which makes it clear to the seller that the goods have been accepted. One example might be a letter asking the seller to carry out modifications. On the other hand, a form signed by the consumer stating "I accept these goods" would only amount to "acceptance" if the conditions of s.35(2) (see above) were satisfied.

(ii) Act after delivery inconsistent with the seller's ownership. The leading **7.39** cases are concerned with commercial contracts under which a delivery to a sub-buyer has destroyed the right to reject.[47] The underlying principle appears to be an inability to restore the goods to the seller. Thus, if a consumer receives a large consignment of wood and starts sawing it up in order to build a shed, the act of cutting it up would destroy his right to reject, if he then discovers that, for example, the wood does not answer the contract description. Another grey area concerns negligent damage. What happens if the buyer of a defective suit stains it with ink when he wears it for the first time? If the stain is indelible it could affect his right of rejection, since it would prevent him from returning the goods in their original form. Merely using the goods, though, is not an inconsistent act.

It must, however, be remembered that all forms of acceptance are now subject to the "opportunity to examine" rule in subs.(2). Under the statutory wording an act done by the buyer before he has had a reasonable opportunity of examination will not destroy the right to reject; it is possible that some of the earlier cases[48] might now be decided differently.

(iii) Retention beyond a reasonable time—the _Bernstein_ case. This is the most **7.40** contentious type of acceptance in the consumer context. The main bone of contention is whether "a reasonable time" begins to run only after the buyer has _discovered_ the defect (or other breach of contract) or at some earlier stage. This is of crucial importance if the goods contain a latent defect which will not show up until some months or even years of use have elapsed.

Suppose that a carpet wears through or a bed collapses after only a year or two of normal use. What if the bearings of a washing machine or the motor of a lawn mower break down after 18 months? Even though it can be shown that the goods must have been unsatisfactory at the date of delivery—this is evidenced by their subsequent failure to be durable enough—can the buyer still reject the goods? The consumer's answer would be "Of course! How can the right to reject for breach of condition be lost before the consumer can realise that there has been a breach?" The legal answer, however, may well be otherwise. The misunderstanding arises from confusing "acceptance" in s.35 with affirmation, waiver, laches, etc., which operate at common law or

---

[47] See, e.g. _Ruben v Faire Bros_ [1949] 1 K.B. 254 but note that s.35(6)(b) above has altered the law on this point.

[48] ibid. The earlier cases were decided under the 1893 Act. As originally drafted, an "inconsistent act" destroyed the right to reject even though the buyer had not had a reasonable opportunity of examination.

in equity to bar rescission[49] only if the claimant treats the contract as continuing *after discovery* of the breach or misrepresentation.

7.41   It must be remembered that we are dealing with a commercial statute which has to do service in consumer transactions too. "The general legal proposition that there should, wherever possible, be finality in commercial transactions" was stressed by Rougier J. in *Bernstein v Pamson Motors (Golders Green) Ltd.*[50]

> B bought a new Nissan Laurel from P for £8,000. It was delivered on December 7, 1984. B was ill over Christmas and unable to use it. On January 3 with 140 miles on the odometer the car broke down with a seized camshaft. Next day B wrote to P rejecting the car on the grounds that it was not merchantable. P resisted B's claim on the grounds that (1) the car was merchantable and (2) anyway it was too late to reject the car as B had accepted it. P repaired the car under the manufacturer's warranty. B sued for rescission and damages.[51]

Giving judgment for B on the first point (the car was unmerchantable) and for P on the second (it was too late to reject) Rougier J. upheld P's submission that "once a buyer has had the goods for a reasonable time, *not*, be it noted, related to the opportunity to discover any particular defect, he is deemed to have accepted them."

He went on to say:

> "In my judgment, the nature of the particular defect, discovered *ex post facto*, and the speed with which it might have been discovered, are irrelevant to the concept of reasonable time in s.35 as drafted. That section seems to me to be directed solely to what is a reasonable practical interval in commercial terms between a buyer receiving the goods and his ability to send them back, taking into consideration from his point of view the nature of the goods and their function, and from the point of view of the seller the commercial desirability of being able to close his ledger reasonably soon after the transaction is complete. The complexity of the intended function of the goods is clearly of prime consideration here. What is a reasonable time in relation to a bicycle would hardly suffice for a nuclear submarine."[52]

Applying those principles to the facts, Rougier J. held that three weeks (discounting the period of illness) was a reasonable time for a new car:

> "Reasonable time means reasonable time to examine and try out the goods in general terms."[53]

7.42   The decision seems a harsh one and some commentators regard it as suspect on the basis that an appeal was settled out of court on terms which acknowledged that the right to reject had not been lost (see (1987) 137 N.L.J. 962). Nevertheless, it must be admitted that the alternative view (i.e. that the buyer has a continuing right to reject until he discovers the defect) has one

---

[49] *Long v Lloyd*, see n.18 in para.7.07 above.
[50] [1987] 2 All E.R. 220.
[51] The action was really fought between the AA, backing B, and Nissan, backing P.
[52] At 230.
[53] ibid.

fundamental weakness—it would enable a buyer to reject and *recover the full price* even though he had used the goods for months, or even years. The Law Commission considered the problem extensively in their Report[54] and reached the conclusion that the present rule should continue; for no one had suggested, and no other common law system provided, a better answer.

Considerable room for judicial maneouvre exists because "what is a reasonable time is a question of fact".[55] This gives flexibility although, as three weeks was reasonable for a complex piece of machinery (a new car), an even shorter period might be reasonable for simple products like a pen, pie or pair of pants.

It is easy to concentrate so fiercely on the loss of the right to reject that damages are forgotten. In the *Bernstein* case the car was repaired free of charge. In addition damages were awarded: £33 for the taxi fare home and a wasted tank of petrol, £50 for five days' loss of use until a hire car was made available and £150 "for a totally spoilt day, comprising nothing but vexation".

Is Bernstein still good law? The question arises as to whether the *Bernstein* decision is still good law after the changes to s.35 which we have just considered. The Court of Appeal has recently given a negative answer to this question in a case where, however, the facts were very special. In *Clegg v Andersson*[56] the following facts arose:

7.43

> Mr Clegg agreed to buy a yacht for £260,000. The contract provided that the shoal draught keel would comply with the manufacturer's specification. On delivery in August Mr Clegg realised that the keel was too heavy. He asked the seller for information so that he could decide on whether or not repair should be carried out. He also insured and registered the yacht. The information was not supplied until February 15 and within three weeks of that date Mr Clegg purported to reject the yacht. The Court of Appeal (reversing the trial judge) held that he was entitled to do so.

The court first had to decide whether the correspondence between the parties amounted to an intimation of acceptance. They also considered whether the acts of insurance and registration amounted to acts inconsistent with the seller's ownership. All these points were decided in favour of Mr Clegg. The final point was whether he had retained the goods beyond a reasonable time without intimating rejection. The Court of Appeal held that (a) in the light of the changes made by the 1994 Act (and in particular subsections (5) and (6)[57] of the redrafted section) the five months of waiting for the information had *not* amounted to acceptance under the "reasonable time" rules and (b) even if (without deciding) *Bernstein* was correct when it was decided, it was no longer good law now.

---

[54] op. cit. paras.5.14 to 5.19.
[55] s.59.
[56] [2003] EWCA Civ320.
[57] See *J&H Ritchie Ltd v Lloyd Ltd* [2007] 2 All E.R.353, H.L. Buyer entitled to reject even after repair, as seller refused to explain cause of defect; so buyer unable to make informed choice between acceptance and rejection.

7.44   As stated above, the facts of this case were very special, because the buyer discovered the defect as soon as the yacht was delivered. Accordingly the wider question of whether the buyer has a continuing right to reject where the goods break down during their expected working life is still unsettled. It is strongly arguable that a buyer who waits too long before examining the goods will have lost the right to reject them. In practice the problem is unlikely to arise, because the consumer will usually have a right of repair or replacement under the amendments made by the 2002 Regulations or, if this is not possible, an appropriate reduction in the price that he has paid.

A related point concerns the effect of complaints. Let us suppose that an expensive camera fails to work. The consumer will usually ask the supplier (or manufacturer) to repair it. What happens if the defect persists after (say) four attempts to repair it? Alternatively, what happens if a large number of different defects manifest themselves after purchase? The buyer is certainly entitled to wait for a time to see if the defects can be put right. Thus in *Lee v York Coach and Marine Ltd* the critical factor which destroyed the right to reject was the delay of six months after the final repair. It will be recalled that a mere request for repair is not of itself acceptance, but if the defect does persist for a substantial time, the buyer will have to decide "do I keep the goods or not?" Accordingly, the buyer should make it clear at the outset that he will reject the goods if the defects are not rectified.[58]

Rejection of part

7.45   Subject to the "commercial unit" point in s.35(7) (above, para.7.37), the buyer can now reject part of goods supplied under a non-severable contract. Section 3 of the 1994 Act introduced a new s.35A and the four subsections of that section provide as follows:

> (1) If the buyer—
>> (a) has the right to reject the goods by reason of a breach on the part of the seller that affects some or all of them, but
>> (b) accepts some of the goods, including, where there are any goods unaffected by the breach, all such goods,
>> he does not by accepting them lose his right to reject the rest.
>
> (2) In the case of a buyer having the right to reject an instalment of goods, subsection (1) above applies as if references to the goods were references to the goods comprised in the instalment.
>
> (3) For the purposes of subsection (1) above, goods are affected by a breach if by reason of the breach they are not in conformity with the contract.
>
> (4) This section applies unless a contrary intention appears in, or is to be implied from, the contract.

Absence of title

7.46   If the seller of goods has no right to sell, the consumer can recover the price on the basis of total failure of consideration. His right to do this is not lost

---

[58] As happened in the hire-purchase case *Farnworth Finance Facilities v Attryde*, below, para.7.47.

by "acceptance"—as Atkin L.J. pointed out in *Rowland v Divall.*[59] He will, however, lose his right to get his money back if the defect in title is put right before he purports to reject.[60] This is reasonable enough—it would obviously be wrong to allow a claim based on "total failure of consideration" if the buyer has received substantially what he paid for, i.e. the property in the goods.

Loss of right to reject—other supply contracts

There is nothing in the Consumer Credit Act 1974 nor in the Supply of **7.47** Goods (Implied Terms) Act 1973 nor in the Supply of Goods and Services Act 1982 regulating the remedies of the consumer. The position is governed by the common law principles of waiver or affirmation which, unlike acceptance, operate only when the consumer becomes *aware* of the defect in the goods. The cases at common law show a fairly broad approach. In *Farnworth Finance Facilities v Attryde*[61]:

> Mr Attryde took a new motorcycle on hire-purchase terms on July 11, 1964. There was a large number of defects and finally on November 23 he rejected it and claimed the return of all payments.

Counsel for the defendants argued that by driving the motorcycle for 4,000 miles, Mr Attryde had affirmed the contract so as to lose his right to reject. The Court of Appeal rejected this argument. In the words of Lord Denning M.R.[62]:

> "Affirmation is a matter of election. A man only affirms a contract when he knows of the defects and by his conduct elects to go on with the contract despite them. In this case Mr Attryde complained from the beginning of the defects and sent the machine back for them to be remedied. He did not elect to accept it unless they were remedied. But the defects were never satisfactorily remedied. When the rear chain broke it was the last straw."

As already stated, there is nothing in hire-purchase law comparable to **7.48** s.11(4) of the Sale of Goods Act. The Law Commission acknowledge that the right to reject is more readily available than in a sale and recommend that this regime, which is more favourable to customers than the sale of goods regime, should not be disturbed.[63]

Where a "conditional sale agreement" (below, para.18.09) is a "consumer sale" (below, para.8.30) the rules governing rejection are similar to those for hire-purchase: see the Supply of Goods (Implied Terms) Act 1973, s.14. In *Rogers v Parish (Scarborough) Ltd* (above, para.4.16) the buyer was allowed to reject after using the car for six months and driving 5,500 miles. It must

---

[59] [1923] 2 K.B. 500 and see, above, para.2.19.
[60] *Butterworth v Kingsway Motors* [1954] 1 W.L.R. 1286.
[61] [1970] 1 W.L.R. 1053.
[62] p.1059.
[63] Report No.160, paras.5.43 to 5.46.

be noted, however, that the seller's counsel did not raise the matter[64] and one wonders what would have happened if he had done so.

Section 30: additional remedies

7.49   What happens if some of the goods are satisfactory while others are not? We have seen that under a non-severable contract the buyer can now accept part and reject part.[65]

It is also necessary to refer to s.30 which can be summarised as follows:

(a) If the seller supplies *too many* goods, the buyer can (i) reject all the goods, (ii) reject the surplus, or (iii) keep all the goods and pay for them at the contract rate.

(b) If the seller tenders *too little*, the buyer can (i) reject the goods, or (ii) keep them and pay at the contract rate.

(c) If the seller tenders the contract goods *mixed* with goods of a different description, the buyer can (i) reject all the goods or (ii) reject the goods not answering the description. There is no statutory right to keep the latter goods, but the courts might treat the delivery as an offer to sell them. If the buyer accepted this offer, he would be liable to pay a reasonable price.[66] Alternatively if the buyer did not initially accept the offer, he might be able to take advantage of reg.24 of the Distance Selling Regulations 2000 which was considered in Chapter Six.

Section 4(2) of the 1994 Act added a new s.30(2A) which prevents a non-consumer from exercising his right to reject where the shortfall or excess is so slight that rejection would be unreasonable. This adds little to s.15A above[67] because the quantity of the goods will normally form part of their description (above, para.3.12).

Practical considerations

7.50   There will, in many cases, be practical barriers to repudiation in cases where the price has already been paid. Section 36 of the 1979 Act provides that where the goods are delivered to the buyer, he need not return them but may send the seller a notice of rejection; if the property and risk have passed to the buyer the effect of the notice is to re-transfer them to the seller. In practice, however, the seller is likely to dispute the buyer's right to reject. This can mean that the buyer will have neither his money nor the use of the goods until his right to reject has been upheld by a court and until the judgment for the return of the price has been satisfied.

---

[64] The Court of Appeal refused to allow him to do so because he had not done so in his defence or in the court below.

[65] Above, para.7.45.

[66] s.8.

[67] Above, para.7.32.

(3) Can I get compensation?

The consumer is entitled to damages if the other party has broken a term **7.51**
of the contract, express or implied, and the consumer has suffered loss. It is
irrelevant whether the term is a condition, warranty or intermediate stipulation. When we turn to the difficult question of quantifying the claim we must
consider two closely related problems, namely (a) for what items of loss is
the defendant liable? and (b) on what principles should the compensation be
assessed?

For what loss is the defendant liable? Remoteness

The general rules governing remoteness of damage were laid down more than **7.52**
150 years ago in *Hadley v Baxendale*[68] and more recently by the House of Lords
in *Koufos v Czarnikow Ltd (The Heron II)*.[69] The defendant is clearly liable for
damage arising naturally from the breach (normal loss—first rule). He is also
liable for other damage which can fairly and reasonably have been within the
contemplation of both parties, at the time they made the contract, as the prob-
able result of the breach of it (unusual loss—second rule). It has been held that
where the general *type* or kind of damage was within the contemplation of the
parties, the defendant is liable even though the precise *extent* of the damage,
or the precise form of the damage, was outside his contemplation.[70]

Mitigation

Another basic rule is that of mitigation—the injured party must take reason- **7.53**
able steps to mitigate his loss. Thus, to take an obvious example, a buyer of
a defective product could not sue the seller for the cost of having it repaired
by a third party if the seller had previously offered to repair it free of charge
or presumably if a free repair (parts *and* labour) was available under a manufacturer's guarantee.

General principles of compensation

If the damage is not too remote under the rules set out above, the general **7.54**
principle is that damages should, so far as possible, place the injured party
in the same position as if the contract had been performed properly. Thus,
where a negligent survey causes a buyer to pay too much for a house the
damages will be the difference between the price paid and the lower (defective) value; in *Watts v Morrow*[71] a claim based on the cost of repair when the
defects were discovered was rejected.

---

[68] (1854) 9 Ex. 341 at 354.
[69] [1969] 1 A.C. 350.
[70] *Parsons (Livestock) Ltd v Uttley Ingham & Co* [1978] 1 Q.B. 791 (sale and construction of
hopper for feeding nuts to pigs; ventilator left unopened; nuts became mouldy; pigs died; supplier of hopper liable). See also *Vacwell v B.D.H. Chemicals* [1971] 1 Q.B. 88.
[71] [1991] 1 W.L.R. 1421, CA. See also *Ruxley Electronics v Forsyth* [1996] A.C. 344, below,
para.7.65.

Non-delivery

7.55   In the case of sale of goods the buyer may have an action for damages against the seller (a) if the seller fails to deliver, or (b) if the seller breaks a condition or warranty. In all these cases the general principles laid down in *Hadley v Baxendale*[72] appear in statutory form. Thus s.51(2) which deals with non-delivery provides that:

> The measure of damages is the estimated loss directly and naturally resulting, in the ordinary course of events, from the seller's breach of contract.

As an example of this, s.51(3) provides that:

> Where there is an available market for the goods in question the measure of damages is prima facie . . . the difference between the contract price and the market or current price of the goods at the time or times when they ought to have been delivered, or (if no time was fixed) at the time of refusal to deliver.

7.56   Let us suppose that John agrees to buy a new Ford Focus car from a dealer for £12,000. The contract provides that the car must be delivered by May 1 but the dealer fails to deliver. By that date the price has increased by £500. If John has to pay an extra £500 to buy one from another dealer, this sum will prima facie be his damages under s.51(3). If, however, he can obtain an identical model elsewhere for the same or a lower price, his loss is nil.

The second rule of *Hadley v Baxendale*, damage within the reasonable contemplation of the parties, is preserved by s.54 which reads:

> Nothing in this Act affects the right of the buyer or the seller to recover interest or special damages in any case where by law interest or special damages may be recoverable. . . .

Thus if, as a result of the non-delivery of the car, John loses a valuable business contract, that would be "special damages" and the defaulting dealer will only be liable for it, if it was brought to his attention before the agreement was made.

Non-acceptance

7.57   Consumers should be aware of their duty to take delivery and their liability in damages for non-acceptance. Sometimes they believe incorrectly that, having placed an order for goods — a car, carpet, furniture — they can change their minds and "cancel" the order with impunity. Such cancellation rights are available only where the doorstep selling or distance selling regulations apply (see Chapter Six).

If in the example in para.7.56 John refuses to take delivery, he will be in breach of contract and liable in damages to the dealer. Section 50 provides:

---

[72] Above, para.7.52.

(1) Where the buyer wrongfully neglects or refuses to accept and pay for the goods, the seller may maintain an action against him for damages for non-acceptance.

(2) The measure of damages is the estimated loss directly and naturally resulting, in the ordinary course of events, from the buyer's breach of contract.

(3) Where there is an available market for the goods in question the measure of damages is prima facie to be ascertained by the difference between the contract price and the market or current price at the time or times when the goods ought to have been accepted or (if no time was fixed for acceptance) at the time of the refusal to accept.

Section 50 (2), like s.51(2) above, puts into statutory form rule one of *Hadley v Baxendale*. Section 50(3), like s.51(3) above, gives an example. "Available market" means that demand exceeds supply. Thus if the dealer mitigates his loss and resells the car to another buyer at the same price, his loss is nil and so are his damages—he had only one car to sell and has done so. However, if supply exceeds demand, as is usually the case, s.50(3) is inapplicable and under s.50(2) the dealer will recover his loss of profit on the sale to John, for he could supply all comers and has lost a sale. [72a]

Section 50 applies where the seller is left with the goods on his hands by the buyer's refusal to take delivery. If, however, the buyer takes delivery and the property passes to him, the seller will recover the full price under s.49.

Damages for breach of warranty

In this situation damages arising naturally are covered by s.53(2) while abnormal damages are covered by s.54.[73] Where the warranty relates to quality the damages are prima facie the difference between the actual value of the defective goods and their value if they had answered the warranty. This will usually be the cost of repairing the defect.[74] It is clear, however, that damages are not necessarily confined to that amount. Thus, for example, damages for personal injury or death can be recovered on a sale of a defective toy.[75] Then, if a defective car is "off the road" for repair, the buyer will be able to recover from the seller not only the cost of repair but also the cost of hiring a substitute car[76] during this period. The magazine *Which?* has cited a case where a buyer of a leaking caravan spent large sums of money on petrol on numerous journeys to have it repaired. He also planned to have a caravan

7.58

[72a] *Charter v Sullivan* [1957] 2 Q.B.117; cf. *Thompson v Robinson (Gunmakers)* [1955] 2 W.L.R.185.

[73] Above, para.7.56.

[74] s.53(3) and see *Lee v York (Coach and Marine) Ltd*, above, para.4.21.

[75] *Godley v Perry* [1960] 1 W.L.R. 9.

[76] *Bernstein v Pamson Motors*, above, para.7.41. Some car hire companies provide cars free of charge on condition that the consumers co-operate with them in bringing proceedings and pay the hire-charges out of damages awarded. The deferment of the hirer's payment obligation amounts to "credit" and the hire agreement will usually be regulated under the Consumer Credit Act 1974 (para.19.08 below). If the agreement is "improperly executed" (para.21.02 below) the hirer cannot recover the hire charges from the other driver: *Dimond v Lovell* [2002] 1 A.C. 384. Some 40,000 cases were stayed until the House of Lords had given its ruling in this case.

holiday but was compelled to move into a guest house when the defects reappeared. He successfully recovered both the cost of petrol and the guest house expenses in county court proceedings.

If the seller is in breach of the condition of "right to sell",[77] the damages recoverable by the buyer can include not merely the price paid but also the cost of necessary repairs.[78]

The principles set out above apply equally where the seller is in breach of a condition which the buyer elects to treat, or is compelled to treat, as a breach of warranty under s.11(2) and (4).

Mental distress

7.59   A novel head of damages which no legal adviser should forget in a consumer dispute is mental distress, upset, disappointment and injured feelings. The seminal case on this topic was *Jarvis v Swans Tours*, a heart-rending case.[79]

> A solicitor on a fortnight's holiday in the Swiss Alps spent an entire week surrounded by people who could not speak English! As a further insult instead of Swiss cakes he was served crisps and desiccated nut rolls. (As their Lordships pointed out during the hearing, "You don't have to go to Switzerland to get those": Stephenson L.J. "You can get them at Crewe": Edmund Davies L.J.—*The Times*, October 19, 1972.) Damages of £125 were awarded, double the cost of the holiday, by the Court of Appeal. The description of facilities (including the promise of a fun house party) in the tour operator's brochure was an express term of the contract.

Holiday contracts continue to be a fruitful area for this type of loss.[80]

Damages have also been awarded in proceedings for negligence against a solicitor who failed to obtain a non-molestation injunction for a client.[81]

The first sale of goods case was *Jackson v Chrysler Acceptances*.[82] This has been followed by two other car cases where the damages were by no means nominal.[83]

7.60   Even so, the courts approach this area cautiously, as can be gleaned from the remarks of Staughton L.J. in *Hayes v Dodd*[84] where the Court of Appeal disallowed this head of damage in a business dispute:

> "Damages for mental distress in contract are, as a matter of policy, limited to certain classes of case. I would broadly follow the classification provided by Dillon

---

[77]   Above, para.2.19.
[78]   *Mason v Burningham* [1949] 2 K.B. 545.
[79]   [1973] 1 Q.B. 233.
[80]   For further examples, see below, para.7.63.
[81]   *Heywood v Wellers* [1976] Q.B. 446. See also *Channon v Lindley Johnstone* [2002] EWCA Civ 353, CA.
[82]   [1978] R.T.R. 474. A consumer told a dealer that he wanted a car for a holiday. The car was defective. The county court judge awarded (inter alia) £75 for a spoilt holiday. Although the award was varied on appeal there was no suggestion that such damages could not be recovered.
[83]   *Bernstein v Pamson Motors*, above, para.7.41: £150 for spoilt day. *UCB Leasing v Holtom* [1987] R.T.R. 362, CA: £500 for distress where the hire car had three complete electrical failures in four months.
[84]   [1990] 2 All E.R. 815 at 824. *Channon v Lindley Johnstone*, above.

L.J. in *Bliss v South East Thames Regional Health Authority* [1987] I.C.R. 700 at 718:

'. . . where the contract which has been broken was itself a contract to provide peace of mind or freedom from distress . . ..'

It may be that the class is somewhat wider than that. But it should not, in my judgment, include any case where the object of the contract was not comfort or pleasure, or the relief of discomfort, but simply carrying on a commercial activity with a view to profit."

In *Watts v Morrow*[85] the Court of Appeal rejected the argument that a contract for the survey of a house was a contract to buy peace of mind. In this type of case damages for distress should be limited to a modest sum for physical discomfort and disruption; the Court reduced the award from £4,000 to £750.

It is clear from the cases that damages for distress will be kept within narrow limits. Thus it has been held[86] that customers suing a bank could not claim damages for distress resulting from alleged unauthorised withdrawals from service-till machines. Similarly, the undoubted pleasure of a car owner in driving a Rolls Royce did not give rise to a distress claim when the car was badly repaired.[87]

However, in *Farley v Skinner*[87a] the House of Lords extended the param-   **7.61**
eters for distress.

> The claimant wanted to buy a gracious country residence for retirement—"a property offering peace and tranquillity was the raison d'être of the proposed purchase" (Lord Steyn). He became interested in Riverside House, in the country near the Sussex village of Blackboys. It had a tennis court, croquet lawn, swimming pool and extensive grounds. As it was only 15 miles from Gatwick Airport, when instructing the defendant surveyor he asked whether it would be affected by aircraft noise. The surveyor reported "We think it unlikely that the property will suffer greatly from such noise". He then bought it in 1991 for £420,000 and spent £125,000 on modernisation. After moving in he quickly discovered that the property was affected by aircraft noise as it was not far away from the Mayfield Stack, a navigation beacon where aircraft circled waiting to land. The trial judge found that the surveyor had been negligent and awarded £10,000 for discomfort. The Court of Appeal, by a majority, allowed the defendant's appeal.

The claimant's appeal to the House of Lords was allowed unanimously. They rejected the argument that the object of the *entire contract* must be to give pleasure, relaxation and peace of mind as being a narrow reading of the dicta of Bingham L.J. in *Watts v Morrow*. Lord Steyn stated (at p.750) that, it is sufficient if it is "a major or important object of the contract". The award of the £10,000 was "at the very top end of what could possibly be regarded as appropriate damages . . . I consider awards in this area should be

---

[85] [1991] 1 W.L.R. 1421.
[86] *McConville v Barclays Bank, The Times,* June 30, 1993. The court formerly known as the Official Referee Court has now been renamed the Technology and Construction Court.
[87] *Alexander v Rolls Royce Motor Co Ltd* [1996] R.T.R. 95.
[87a] [2002] 2 A.C. 732. See also *Yearworth v North Bristol NHS Trust, The Times,* February 10, 2009, CA: bailment of sperm–lost by hospital.

restrained and modest". However, the court would not interfere with the judge's evaluation.

It is unlikely that earlier cases would be decided differently now, as it is still essential for pleasure or peace of mind to be an important ingredient of the contract. However, in future consumers may succeed if they emphasise at the outset that such a factor is important to them, even though the contract may not be, on the whole, a pleasurable one.

Hire-purchase

7.62 The principles set out above are equally relevant to hire-purchase transactions. Thus in *Yeoman Credit Ltd v Apps*[88] the hirer of a car which took one-and-a-half hours to do three or four miles successfully sued for damages. The damages were assessed at the difference between what the car should have been worth and what it was actually worth; on that basis the hirer recovered all his payments, less a very small allowance for use.

Holiday contracts

7.63 If the customer finds, on arrival at his resort, that his room has been double-booked, or that the hotel does not exist, he can claim the extra cost of having to stay at an equivalent hotel plus (as already stated) damages for mental distress. If the hotel exists but does not have the promised facilities, the remedy will again be damages. In appropriate cases damages can include losses suffered by members of the claimant's family.[89]

An interesting recent case is *Spencer v Cosmos Air Holidays*.[90]

> The plaintiff booked two weeks' holiday in Spain with the defendants for £266. After about a week the hotelier wrongfully ejected her and her two female companions. They spent two nights sleeping on the beach before the defendants found them alternative, inferior accommodation at a less pleasing resort.

The Court of Appeal awarded her £1,000 for her distress, misery and humiliation, reducing by half the award made by the trial judge.

Cleaners

7.64 If a cleaner negligently ruins or loses a carpet or a suit, the damages will be based on the cost of acquiring a replacement, but this will be subject to a discount for age and use.

---

[88] [1962] 2 Q.B. 508.
[89] *Jackson v Horizon Holidays* [1975] 1 W.L.R. 1468, CA. A four-week family holiday in Sri Lanka proved to be a disaster, with very distasteful food apparently cooked in coconut oil, and a shower and no bath. The holiday price was £1,200. Damages of £1,100 were awarded for breach of contract to cover the distress of the husband, wife and child.
[90] *The Times*, December 6, 1989.

Builders

If a builder, decorator or plumber does a job badly, the damages will nor-   **7.65**
mally include not only the money paid to another firm to have it put right but
also damages for the resulting inconvenience.[91] If the work is done extremely
badly, the consumer may be entitled to refuse to pay anything at all.[92] If,
however, the cost of repair or reconstruction is out of all proportion to the
resulting benefit, the court will award damages based on "diminution of
value" of the property (if any) plus a modest sum for loss of amenity.[93]

3. REMEDIES IN TORT

Perhaps the most likely case of a tort claim would be where the consumer   **7.66**
has a claim against the manufacturer for negligence or under the Consumer
Protection Act 1987. In personal injury cases the damages would include loss
of actual and future earnings, medical expenses, pain and suffering and loss
of amenities. For further details readers are referred to the standard text-
books on tort and to *McGregor on Damages*.

In a case where the same facts give rise to liability in both contract and tort
the rules as to damages are being brought very close together.[94]

---

[91] See, e.g. *Batty v Metropolitan Realisations* [1978] Q.B. 554.
[92] See, e.g. *Bolton v Mahadeva* [1972] 1 W.L.R. 1009.
[93] See the swimming pool case of *Ruxley Electronics v Forsyth* [1995] 3 All E.R. 268, HL.
[94] *Parsons (Livestock) Ltd v Uttley Ingham & Co*, above, para.7.52.

CHAPTER EIGHT

"THEY SAY THAT I HAVE SIGNED AWAY MY RIGHTS"

Exemption clauses have been widely used in standard form contracts in the **8.01** past 50 years or so and have come in for severe criticism from the courts and other bodies. The courts have developed certain techniques to control the legal effect of these clauses. Unfortunately the control exercised by the courts has been unsatisfactory because, with the exception of Lord Denning M.R., they have felt themselves unable to break out of the straitjacket of freedom of contract.

Accordingly, the use of exemption clauses has been increasingly controlled by statute and the overwhelming majority of these clauses are now controlled by the Unfair Contract Terms Act 1977. These controls are supplemented by the Unfair Terms in Consumer Contracts Regulations 1999, which are dealt with in Chapter Nine. The problem for legal advisers and consumers is the complexity resulting from two concurrent statutory regimes which partly overlap. We elaborate on this problem in Chapter Nine.

Examples

The first three examples are taken from Law Commission Working Paper **8.02** No.39, pp.74–88.

(1) The shipowner shall be exempt from all liability in respect of any detention, delay, overcarriage, loss, expenses, damage, sickness or injury of whatever kind, whenever and wherever occurring, and however and by whomsoever caused of or to any passenger, or of or to any person or child travelling with him or her or in his or her care, or of or to any baggage, property, goods, effects, articles, matters or things belonging or carried by, with or for any passenger or any such person or child.

(2) [The ferry company] shall not be liable for the death or any injury, damage, loss, delay or accident . . . wheresoever, whensoever and howsoever caused and whether by negligence of their servants or agents or by unseaworthiness of the vessel.

(3) The contractors shall not under any circumstances be liable for any loss or damage caused by or resulting from or in connection with fire, howsoever caused.

(4) All cars parked at owner's risk.

(5) In the case of loss or damage the liability of the company is limited to the value of the garment.

(6) All claims within seven days.

Justification

8.03 In deciding on the price of his product a supplier is bound to consider the question of loss apportionment. He can also cut down very substantially on administration overheads by having standard form contracts (thus avoiding the need to negotiate each contract separately) and by avoiding litigation. A survey carried out by Yates in *Exclusion Clauses in Contracts* contains the following passage (2nd edn, p.25).

> The desire to avoid court proceedings in the event of a dispute was also a reason advanced for using exemption clauses which, it was often felt, gave each party a clearer indication of where they stood. . . . Distrust of lawyers' and more especially judges' ability to understand the businessman's problems was very marked.

Criticism

8.04 When due allowance has been made for the points set out above there is no doubt that exemption clauses are open to abuse. The following passage is taken from the Law Commission's Second Report on Exemption Clauses No. 69, para.11, on which the Unfair Contract Terms Act 1977 was based:

> We are in no doubt that in many cases they operate against the public interest and that the prevailing judicial attitude of suspicion, or indeed of hostility, to such clauses is well founded. All too often they are introduced in ways which result in the party affected by them remaining ignorant of their presence or import until it is too late. That party, even if he knows of the exemption clause, will often be unable to appreciate what he may lose by accepting it. In any case he may not have sufficient bargaining strength to refuse to accept it. The result is that the risk of carelessness or of failure to achieve satisfactory standards of performance is thrown on to the party who is not responsible for it or who is unable to guard against it. Moreover, by excluding liability for such carelessness or failure the economic pressures to maintain high standards of performance are reduced.

Scheme of this chapter

8.05 It is proposed to start by examining the attitude of the courts to exemption clauses and then to consider the statutory controls imposed by the Unfair Contract Terms Act. The broad scope of the Act has made the former topic far less important and accordingly it will be examined fairly briefly. A short reference to other legislation will be made at the end of this chapter.

1. JUDICIAL CONTROL OF EXEMPTION CLAUSES

8.06 The reasons for judicial hostility to exemption clauses have already been mentioned: ignorance, non-negotiation and inequality of bargaining power. Perhaps the first of these points is the strongest. After all, the law of contract is, or should be, about agreement. If the consumer were asked "do you know that you have signed away your right to complain if the cleaners lose the carpet?" or "do you know that you will receive no compensation at all if the carriers damage your furniture?" it is unlikely that his reply could be printed in this book; at all events it is likely to include the word "no". When he made the contract he would reasonably have expected that the work would be done with reasonable care, and that he would receive compensation if this was not so. His expectations may have been increased by a glowing advertisement in a newspaper or magazine or on television or the internet. Accordingly exemption clauses, which are often inconsistent with his reasonable expectations, are closely scrutinised by the courts.

The courts have to decide two basic problems, namely:

(1) was the clause duly incorporated into the contract? and

(2) does it, on its true construction, cover the event which has occurred?

(1) Incorporation[1]

The general contractual principles relating to incorporation have been well established for a considerable time. **8.07**

(a) Signed document

If the contractual document is signed, this operates as an incorporation of all the terms which appear in that document or which are referred to in it.[2] The signatory will not be bound, however, if by mistake he signed the document without negligence and it turns out to be a document of a fundamentally different kind from the document which he thought that he was signing.[3] **8.08**

(b) Unsigned document or notice

If the consumer has not signed a contractual document, a clause will only be incorporated if reasonable steps were taken before contract to bring it to his notice. The following cases illustrate how this principle has been applied. **8.09**

(i) In the case of *Thompson v L.M.S. Railway*[4] a lady bought a railway excursion ticket containing the words "For conditions see back". The back of the ticket referred to conditions in the railway timetables which were available for purchase. Had Mrs Thompson obtained and read them (by which time she would certainly have missed her train) she would have seen an exclusion clause excluding liability for negligence. The Court of Appeal held that the exemption clause had been incorporated into the contract.

(ii) The case of *Chapelton v Barry U.D.C.*[5] concerned an exclusion clause on a deckchair receipt. It was held that there was no incorporation; this was

---

[1] For a summary of the rules see the judgment of Boreham J. in *John Snow & Son Ltd v Woodcroft Ltd* [1985] B.C.L.C. 48.

[2] The leading case is *L'Estrange v Graucob* [1934] 2 K.B. 394.

[3] *Saunders v Anglia Building Society* [1971] A.C. 1039, in which the House of Lords emphasised that this so-called "*non est factum*" defence must be confined within narrow limits.

[4] [1930] 1 K.B. 41. Such a clause might now be "unfair" under Sch.2 of the 1999 Regulations: see below, para.9.31.

[5] [1940] 1 K.B. 532. In any case it was post-contractual and so ineffective.

not the type of document on which the consumer could reasonably expect to find conditions and therefore the local authority had not taken sufficient steps to bring the clause to the consumer's attention. The court reached a similar "no incorporation" result in two more recent cases where words appeared on the inside of a cheque book[6] and on time sheets.[7]

(iii) In *Olley v Marlborough Court Hotel*[8] a consumer booked a hotel room. After he had done so he saw an exemption notice in the bedroom. It was held that there was no incorporation since the clause had been introduced too late. The position might have been different if the notice was prominently displayed at the reception desk or if the customer had stayed at the hotel on previous occasions. In the latter case the notice might have been incorporated on the basis of a previous course of dealing. Nevertheless, this principle, which can readily be implied in commercial contracts,[9] is very rarely applied in consumer contracts.[10]

8.10   (iv) *Thornton v Shoe Lane Parking Co Ltd*[11] is perhaps the best modern example of how the basic rules of "contract" are being adapted, in a realistic way, to standard form consumer transactions.

> Mr Thornton went to park his car at a new multistorey car park—he had not been there before. When he arrived opposite the ticket machine a ticket popped out, the light turned from red to green and he went through and parked his car. The ticket referred to conditions displayed on the premises. These conditions (inter alia) excluded liability for personal injuries caused by negligence. There was an accident caused partly by the defendants' negligence and Mr Thornton was injured.

The Court of Appeal held that the defendants had not taken reasonable steps to bring this particular clause to the notice of Mr Thornton. In the words of Lord Denning M.R. at p.170:

> "It is so wide and destructive of rights that the court should not hold any man bound by it unless it is drawn to his attention in the most explicit way. . . . In order to give sufficient notice, it would need to be printed in red ink with a red hand pointing to it—or something equally startling."

Megaw L.J. gave an equally vivid example when he said at p.173:

> "It does not take much imagination to picture the indignation of the defendants if their potential customers . . . were one after the other to get out of their cars leaving the cars blocking the entrance to the garages in order to search for, find and peruse the notices! Yet unless the defendants genuinely intended that potential customers should do just that it would be fiction, if not farce, to treat those

---

[6] *Burnett v Westminster Bank* [1965] 3 All E.R. 81.

[7] *Grogan v Robin Meredith Plant Hire* [1996] C.L.C. 1127, CA.

[8] [1949] 1 K.B. 532.

[9] *Spurling v Bradshaw* [1956] 1 W.L.R. 461.

[10] See, e.g. *McCutcheon v David MacBrayne Ltd* [1964] 1 W.L.R. 125, HL, a notable case, if only because of the appearance in it of a Mr McSporran!

[11] [1971] 2 Q.B. 163. The case was considered in the context of wheel-clamping. The car owner cannot recover damages where there was a clear and prominent sign indicating the risk and the penalty: *Vine v Waltham Forest LBC* [2000] 1 W.L.R. 2383.

customers as persons who have been given a fair opportunity, before the contracts are made, of discovering the conditions by which they are to be bound."

Lord Denning M.R. went so far as to hold that the contract was made when the customer dropped his money into the machine, thereby accepting their offer to park with the result that the conditions on the ticket were introduced too late.[12] The trouble with this approach is that in many cases the customer does *not* put money into the slot—he merely collects a ticket and pays later. Nevertheless both Lord Denning M.R. and Sir Gordon Willmer were influenced by the finality of a contract made with a machine. To quote again from Lord Denning:

"The customer pays his money and gets a ticket. He cannot refuse it. He cannot get his money back. He may protest to the machine, even swear at it. But it will remain unmoved. He is committed beyond recall."

These interesting problems may never be decided because it may be unnecessary to do so. If the facts of *Thornton* were to recur, a clause excluding liability for death or personal injury resulting from negligence would in any event be void[13] and accordingly the question of incorporation would have no practical importance. The point might, however, remain relevant if the customer suffered damage to his property. In that case the exemption clause would be valid if reasonable[14] and accordingly the customer might well raise the argument of "no incorporation" as his first line of attack.

(v) In *Interfoto Picture Library Ltd v Stiletto Visual Programmes Ltd*[15] (a **8.11** non-consumer case) the Court of Appeal had to consider the situation where one clause in a set of conditions was particularly onerous.

SVP, an advertising agency, telephoned IPL, a photographic library, requesting photographs of the 1950s for a presentation for a client. IPL sent by hand 47 transparencies in a bag with a delivery note stating that they must be returned within 14 days.
Across the bottom of the note were printed nine conditions in four columns, under the fairly prominent heading "CONDITIONS". Condition 2 stated that all transparencies must be returned within 14 days and that "A holding fee of £5.00 plus VAT per day will be charged for each transparency which is retained by you longer than the said period of 14 days. . . ."
SVP accepted delivery, but did not use them and by an oversight kept them for 28 days. When IPL sent an invoice for £3,783.50, SVP refused to pay, for most libraries charged less than 50p per day.

Hitherto the general approach in the "ticket cases" had been to ask whether the supplier has taken reasonable steps to bring the conditions *as a whole* to the notice of the consumer. However, Lord Denning M.R. had signposted

[12] cf. *Olley v Marlborough Court Hotel*, above, para.8.09.
[13] Unfair Contract Terms Act 1977, s.2(1): below, para.8.28.
[14] ibid. s.2(2).
[15] [1988] 1 All E.R. 348. For a recent (unsuccessful) attempt to apply this case to the terms of a scratch-card competition see *O'Brien v M.G.N. Ltd* [2001] EWCA Civ 1279. The court held that there was nothing unusual about the term.

a different route with his "red ink—red hand" approach in *Thornton v Shoe Lane Parking Ltd*.[16] Following that route the Court of Appeal held in the *Interfoto* case that condition 2, imposing an exorbitant holding fee, was not part of the contract. Dillon L.J. stated the principle thus[17]:

> "It is in my judgment a logical development of the common law into modern conditions that it should be held, as it was in *Thornton v Shoe Lane Parking Ltd*, that, if one condition in a set of printed conditions is particularly onerous or unusual, the party seeking to enforce it must show that that particular condition was fairly brought to the attention of the other party."

Bingham L.J., agreeing that "the plaintiffs did not do what was necessary to draw this unreasonable and extortionate clause fairly to their attention", seemed to be of the view that a more general principle of fairness was being applied[18]:

> "The tendency of the English authorities has, I think, been to look at the nature of the transaction in question and the character of the parties to it; to consider what notice the party alleged to be bound was given of the particular condition said to bind him; and to resolve whether in all the circumstances it is fair to hold him bound by the condition in question. This may yield a result not very different from the civil law principle of good faith, at any rate so far as the formation of the contract is concerned."

8.12   The actual decision (treating the clause as unduly onerous merely because other libraries charged less) is certainly debatable but, subject to this, three final points can be made. First, the clause was not an exemption clause[19] and it will be interesting to see how far the courts will use this "non-incorporation" tool to protect consumers in areas where Parliament has chosen not to do so. Secondly, we have already seen how non-incorporation can outflank an argument based on the "reasonableness" test under the 1977 Act. Finally, it remains to be seen how far the principle discussed in *Interfoto* (and particularly the fairness point raised by Bingham L.J.) can be called in aid by someone who has *signed* a contract—even though up to now the principle of bringing the conditions to the notice of the consumer has not been relevant in this situation. In other words, *L'Estrange v Graucob*[20] may not be an impassable barrier.

(2) Does the clause cover the event which has occurred?

8.13   Even if the clause has been incorporated into the contract it is not automatically effective. The courts have evolved a number of techniques to counter their effect. These techniques may still be relevant in some cases but it must

---

[16] Above, para.8.10. See also his dictum to similar effect in *J. Spurling Ltd v Bradshaw* [1956] 1 W.L.R. 461 at 466, and the comments of Bramwell and Mellish L.JJ. in *Parker v South Eastern Rly. Co* (1877) 2 C.P.D. 416.

[17] At p.620.

[18] ibid. The concept of "good faith" in the context of the Unfair Terms in Consumer Contracts Regulations is considered below, see para.9.18.

[19] The Unfair Contract Terms Act 1977 could not be used to control the clause for that very reason—see below, para.8.22.

[20] Above, para.8.08.

be strongly emphasised that times have changed and, with the arrival of the Unfair Contract Terms Act 1977, the courts will be less concerned with these matters (see below, para.8.21).

(a) Privity

After earlier doubts, the House of Lords decided that an exemption clause **8.14** between A and B could not protect C—even though C was an employee or contractor engaged by B to perform the contract.[21] This was outflanked by a drafting technique whereby B contracted as agent for his employees/contractors, so that they could enjoy the benefit of the exemption clause.[22] As a matter of strict legal analysis this creates a separate contract between the employees/contractors and the other party, and the performance of the contract would provide the consideration. Presumably such convoluted drafting will now be a thing of the past; the parties will now be able to use the Contracts (Rights of Third Parties) Act 1999 (see para.4.06 above) under which an exemption clause may benefit a third party (s.1(6)).

(b) Strict construction and the contra proferentem rule

A party seeking the protection of an exemption clause must show that the **8.15** wording is clear enough to cover the alleged breach. This is well illustrated by three cases involving sale of goods.

In *Wallis, Son and Wells v Pratt and Haynes*[23] a commercial contract for the sale of seed excluded "all warranties". The seller supplied seed of a different description and the buyer claimed damages. The House of Lords held that the seller had broken a *condition* and that a clause referring only to *warranties* did not protect him. The mere fact that the buyer, in ignorance of the breach, had "accepted" the goods, and was therefore compelled to treat the breach as a breach of warranty,[24] was immaterial.

In *Andrews Bros (Bournemouth) Ltd v Singer & Co. Ltd*[25] the seller sold a "new Singer car" with a clause excluding "implied conditions and warranties". The seller supplied a car which was not new. The Court of Appeal held that he had broken an *express* condition and accordingly a clause which merely referred to *implied* conditions did not protect him.

In *Nichol v Godts*[26] the sellers agreed to supply rape oil "warranted only equal to sample". They supplied a mixture of rape oil and hemp oil which matched the sample. It was held that the exclusion clause did not protect them from their overriding duty to supply rape oil in accordance with the description.

---

[21] *Scruttons v Midland Silicones Ltd* [1962] A.C. 446.
[22] *New Zealand Shipping Co Ltd v Satterthwaite & Co Ltd* [1975] A.C. 154, P.C. See also *Southern Water Authority v Carey* [1985] 2 All E.R. 1077 where the same result was reached by a different route.
[23] [1911] A.C. 394.
[24] Above, para.7.33.
[25] [1934] 1 K.B. 17.
[26] (1854) 10 Exch. 191.

8.16   The rule of strict construction leads on naturally to the so-called *"contra proferentem"* rule which provides that an ambiguity must be construed against the party who introduced the clause. Thus if a claimant has two distinct claims against the defendant (one in contract and one in tort for negligence) an exemption clause may well be construed so as to cover only the former and not the latter.[27] Even words like "the company will not be liable for damage caused by fire" may merely operate as a warning that the company will only be liable if negligent.[28] It follows that clear words are required to cover liability for negligence, for example, "howsoever caused" or "whether or not due to negligence".

(c) Inconsistent oral promise

8.17   An exemption clause will be overridden by an oral promise which is inconsistent with it. Thus in *Mendelssohn v Normand*[29] a suitcase was stolen from a car which the plaintiff had parked at the defendants' car park. An employee of the defendants promised the plaintiff that he would lock the car, but he failed to do so. The Court of Appeal held that a clause excluding "loss or damage howsoever caused" was ineffective.

(d) Misrepresentation

8.18   The courts will not allow a party to rely on an exemption clause if he has misrepresented its effect to the consumer.[30] On the other hand, the consumer may find himself faced with a clause which says that "no employee of the company has any authority to add to or vary these terms." Such a clause is legally binding.[31]

(e) Fundamental breach

8.19   In a number of cases decided before the Unfair Contract Terms Act 1977 the courts sought to relieve the consumer from the harsh effects of an exemption clause by holding that it did not cover the breach of a fundamental term[32] or a fundamental breach.[33] The legal reasoning for this doctrine was highly dubious. The House of Lords has twice rejected it[34] and

---

[27] See, e.g. *White v John Warwick* [1953] 1 W.L.R. 1285. See also *Casson v Ostley P.J. Ltd* [2001] EWCA Civ1013 (a building case) where a similar result was reached.

[28] *Hollier v Rambler Motors (AMC) Ltd* [1972] 2 Q.B. 71. For a more recent example of the *"contra proferentem"* rule see *Stent Foundation Ltd v MJ Gleeson Group plc* [2001] B.L.R. 134.

[29] [1970] 1 Q.B. 177. See also *J Evans & Son (Portsmouth) Ltd v Andrea Merzario Ltd* [1976] 1 W.L.R. 1078, CA.

[30] *Curtis v Chemical Cleaning and Dyeing Co* [1951] 1 K.B. 805, CA.

[31] *Overbrooke Estates Ltd v Glencombe Properties Ltd* [1974] 1 W.L.R. 1335 (a case on auction particulars). In practice, however, the exemption clause can sometimes be overridden by the employee's apparent authority.

[32] "Something narrower than a condition—something which underlies the whole contract:" *per* Devlin J. (as he then was) in *Smeaton Hanscomb & Co Ltd v Setty (Sassoon) Sons & Co (No. 1)* [1953] 1 W.L.R. 1468 at 1470.

[33] See, e.g. *Karsales (Harrow) Ltd v Wallis* [1956] 1 W.L.R. 936.

[34] *Suisse Atlantique v N.V. Rotterdamsche Kolen Centrale* [1967] 1 A.C. 361; *Photo Production v Securicor Transport* [1980] A.C. 827.

reaffirmed the basic rule that the scope of an exemption clause is always a question of construction and that there is no rule of law preventing the exclusion of a fundamental breach. In a more recent case the House of Lords has warned against the danger of reintroducing the doctrine under another name.[35]

(f) The new approach

The most recent cases herald a new approach to the construction of exemp- **8.20** tion clauses; in future the courts will be less willing to adopt a policy of judicial control of exemption clauses because the need for it has gone. Thus in a case decided on the previous law (but with knowledge that the 1977 Act had been passed) Lord Diplock said as follows:

> "My Lords the reports are full of cases in which what would appear to be very strained constructions have been placed upon exclusion clauses, mainly in what today would be called consumer contracts or contracts of adhesion. As Lord Wilberforce has pointed out, any need for this kind of distortion of the English language has been banished by Parliament, having made these kinds of contract subject to the Unfair Contract Terms Act."[36]

Quite apart from this, it seems that a clause limiting damages to a fixed amount (a "limitation clause") will not be construed as strictly as a full exclusion clause.[37] It must be said, however, that the reasoning is not convincing although to accept some liability rather than none may be more reasonable.[38]

2. UNFAIR CONTRACT TERMS ACT 1977

Scope of the Act

The Act operates in five overlapping areas, namely: **8.21**

    (a) negligence;

    (b) contractual obligations;

    (c) terms implied in contracts for the sale of goods, hire-purchase and certain analogous contracts for the supply of goods;

    (d) guarantees and indemnities;

    (e) misrepresentation.

Before considering these areas it is necessary to mention some preliminary points.

---

[35] *George Mitchell (Chesterhall) Ltd v Finney Lock Seeds Ltd* [1983] 3 W.L.R. 163.
[36] *Photo Production Ltd v Securicor Transport* [1980] A.C. 827 at 851.
[37] *Ailsa Craig Fishing Co Ltd v Malvern Fishing Co and Securicor (Scotland)* [1983] 1 W.L.R. 964—a House of Lords decision on appeal from Scotland.
[38] ibid. at 966 (Lord Wilberforce) and at 970 (Lord Fraser).

Preliminary matters

8.22   (1) The Act does not create new duties—it merely controls clauses which cut down a duty which would otherwise exist or which exclude or modify the remedies available on breach of that duty.

> Let us suppose that Richard parks his car in a car park and keeps the key. There is a large notice at the entrance "The company is not liable for any loss or damage to vehicle or contents, whether or not due to negligence of the company or its servants or agents." When Richard comes back to collect his car it cannot be found.

The notice set out above would be controlled by s.2 of the Act[39] and would be subject to the reasonableness test. This, however, is likely to be completely irrelevant; the company can avoid liability on the more basic ground that the transaction was a mere licence and not a bailment and therefore they owed Richard no duty of care. That was the position before the Act[40] and, as already stated, the Act does not create new duties.

(2) The name of the Act is misleading—it is both too narrow and too wide. It is too narrow because it only refers to "contract"; the Act also applies to tortious negligence both at common law and under the Occupiers' Liability Act 1957. It is too wide because it does not control all "unfair terms"; it merely controls exemption clauses and notices. These are two major distinctions between the Act and the Unfair Terms in Consumer Contracts Regulations 1999, whose title is accurate (see Chapter Nine).

8.23   (3) With very minor exceptions the key provisions of the Act (ss.2–7) only apply to "business liability". By s.1(3) this means:

> liability for breach of obligations or duties arising—
>
> (a) from things done or to be done by a person in the course of a business (whether his own business or another's); or
> (b) from the occupation of premises used for business purposes of the occupier.

When we turn to s.14 we find that the term "business" includes a profession and the activities of any government department or local or public authority.

The term "business" crops up at various points in this book. Thus we have already come across it in connection with (a) supply of goods—implied conditions of quality and fitness,[41] and (b) unsolicited goods and services.[42] We shall meet it again later in this chapter when considering the phrase "deals as consumer".[43] It is also critical for certain provisions of the Consumer Credit Act, for example, non-commercial agreements[44] and the licensing provisions.[45]

There are bound to be borderline cases. Is a landlord carrying on a "busi-

---

[39] See below, para.8.28.
[40] *Ashby v Tolhurst* [1937] 2 K.B. 242.
[41] Above, para.4.11.
[42] Above, para.6.03.
[43] Below, para.8.30.
[44] Below, para.19.10.
[45] Below, para.20.03.

ness" when he lets a block of flats? Is a charity fête a business? The tax cases show that the key factors include the frequency of the transaction, the manner of operation and the profit motive. It is felt that, on these criteria, a charity fête would not be a business, whereas a landlord might well be carrying on a business—especially if he provided services for the tenants.

Reverting now to s.1(3) the question arises as to whether the Act would apply to the premises of a professional man who worked from his home. The answer is "yes", because the Act does not require the premises to be used *exclusively* for business purposes. The point is rather academic since the home is unlikely to be plastered with exclusion notices.

(4) Sections 2 to 4 do not apply to certain contracts listed in Sch.1. For the **8.24** consumer the two most important are (a) contracts of insurance, and (b) any contract so far as it relates to the creation, transfer or termination of an interest in land.[46] The words "so far as" are important. If, for example, a landlord of a block of flats remains the occupier of the common staircase, a notice stating that "visitors enter these premises at their own risk" would be controlled: thus if the landlord negligently allows the staircase to fall into disrepair, he would be liable in damages to an injured visitor under the Occupier's Liability Act 1957, s.2(2), and the exemption notice would be void by the Act of 1977, s.2(1) (below, para.8.28).

In relation to insurance the industry successfully lobbied the Government to exclude insurance policies from the Act and in return they issued their Statements of Practice covering life and non-life insurance respectively. There is no corresponding exemption from the Unfair Terms in Consumer Contracts Regulations 1999.

(5) The Act repeatedly refers to a clause which "excludes or restricts liabil- **8.25** ity". This clearly covers a clause that "no liability is accepted for any loss or damage howsoever caused" or "liability shall be limited to the cost of replacing the appliance and all liability for consequential loss is excluded". Then when we turn to s.13(1) we find that:

> To the extent that this Part of this Act prevents the exclusion or restriction of any liability it also prevents
>
> (a) making the liability or its enforcement subject to restrictive or onerous conditions;
> (b) excluding or restricting any right or remedy in respect of the liability, or subjecting a person to any prejudice in consequence of his pursuing any such right or remedy;
> (c) excluding or restricting rules of evidence or procedure.

Thus the following would be caught:

(a) "all claims within seven days";

"before starting proceedings the customer must pay £1,000 into a joint bank account";

---

[46] See *Electricity Supply Nominees v IAF Group* [1993] 3 All E.R. 372—clause in lease excluding tenant's right of set-off not controlled by the Act.

(b) "no rejection";

"no money back on sale goods: credit note only";

(c) "the report by our engineer shall be conclusive".

8.26   Section 13(1) then concludes with these words:

> ... and (to that extent) sections 2 and 5 to 7 also prevent excluding or restricting liability by reference to terms and notices which exclude or restrict the relevant obligation or duty.

What does this mean? How can the Act control a clause which prevents a duty from arising? What is "the relevant obligation or duty"? In the earlier editions of this book we suggested that the answer is to adopt the approach of Lord Denning M.R. in *Karsales (Harrow) Ltd v Wallis*[47] and look at the contract or activity apart from the clause. If, for example, it is a contract giving rise to a condition of reasonable fitness or a duty of reasonable care, the Act would control a clause or notice providing that "no condition of fitness is implied herein"[48] or "the occupier shall be under no duty of care". The House of Lords has recently confirmed in *Smith v Eric S Bush*[49] that this is the correct interpretation. Affirming the decision of the Court of Appeal[50] that the disclaimers did not prevent the surveyors having a duty of care Lord Jauncey commented on the concluding words in s.13(1) as follows[51]:

> "These words are unambiguous and are entirely appropriate to cover a disclaimer which prevents a duty coming into existence."

Lord Griffiths adopted a "but for" test[52]:

> "They indicate that the existence of the common law duty to take reasonable care . . . is to be judged by considering whether it would exist 'but for' the notice excluding liability."

Three final points can be made on this topic. First, an agreement in writing to submit present or future disputes to arbitration is *not* a clause "excluding or restricting liability".[53] Secondly, it is thought that the Act does not apply to a genuine "liquidated damages" clause where there is an intention to forecast loss rather than to exclude or restrict liability. Thirdly, the courts have held[54] that the Act does not control a genuine settlement out of court ("I accept this sum [or credit note] in full and final settlement of all claims").

---

[47] [1956] 1 W.L.R. 936.
[48] See, for example, the first two cases discussed in para.8.15. Those exclusion clauses would now fall within s.13(1).
[49] [1989] 2 All E.R. 514. The facts are given above, para.3.08. A similar construction was adopted by Slade L.J. in *Phillips Products Ltd v Hyland* [1987] 1 W.L.R. 659, CA.
[50] [1987] 3 All E.R. 179.
[51] At 543.
[52] At 530.
[53] s.13(2).
[54] *Tudor Grange v Citibank* [1991] 4 All E.R. 1.

(6) The common law rules as to incorporation, privity and construction **8.27** mentioned earlier in this chapter remain unaffected, although, as already stated,[55] they will become of far less practical importance. There may, of course, be cases where the common law rules will still be relevant. Thus if the exemption clause is controlled by the reasonableness test[56] this gives the court a wide discretion; so if the consumer can prove non-incorporation, this will of itself defeat the exemption clause and the question of discretion will not arise.

The five areas affected by the Act

(a) Negligence: s.2

Section 1(1) defines negligence as the breach: **8.28**

    (a) of any obligation, arising from the express or implied terms of a contract, to take reasonable care or exercise reasonable skill in the performance of the contract;

    (b) of any common law duty to take reasonable care or exercise reasonable skill (but not any stricter duty);

    (c) of the common duty of care imposed by the Occupiers' Liability Act 1957. . . .

This provision encompasses both a contractual and tortious duty of care. In practice the most important example of (a) is to be found in s.13 of the Supply of Goods and Services Act 1982 (above, para.6.44).

We can now consider s.2—one of the most important sections of the Act. It reads as follows:

    (1) A person cannot by reference to any contract term or to a notice given to persons generally or to particular persons exclude or restrict his liability for death or personal injury resulting from negligence.

    (2) In the case of other loss or damage, a person cannot so exclude or restrict his liability except in so far as the term or notice satisfies the requirement of reasonableness.

    (3) Where a contract term or notice purports to exclude or restrict liability for negligence a person's agreement to or awareness of it is not of itself to be taken as indicating his voluntary acceptance of any risk.

The scope of s.2 is wide. Examples include architects, surveyors, builders, carriers, dry cleaners, cinemas, garages, decorators and holiday tour operators. In all these cases—and there are many more—an exemption clause or notice will be totally void in cases of *death or personal injury*.

If the negligence results in damage to *property* or economic loss, the clause or notice will only be effective if it satisfies the reasonableness test.[57] No distinction is made between contracts with consumers and contracts with businesses—in either case the test is the same.[58]

---

[55] Above, para.8.20.

[56] Below, para.8.43.

[57] s.11, below, para.8.43.

[58] cf. ss.3, 4, 5, 6 and 7, where the distinction is crucial.

The words "contract term" and "term" cover contractual cases and "notice" covers tortious cases.

(b) Contractual obligations: s.3

8.29   The other really far-reaching provision in the Act—and one bristling with problems—is s.3. It reads as follows:

> (1) This section applies as between contracting parties where one of them deals as consumer or on the other's written standard terms[59] of business.
>
> (2) As against that party, the other cannot by reference to any contract term—
>
>   (a) when himself in breach of contract, exclude or restrict any liability of his in respect of the breach; or
>   (b) claim to be entitled—
>   (i) to render a contractual performance substantially different from that which was reasonably expected of him, or
>   (ii) in respect of the whole or any part of his contractual obligations, to render no performance at all,
>
> except in so far as (in the cases mentioned above in this subsection) the contract term satisfies the requirement of reasonableness.

This section is based on the recommendation of the Law Commission in their Second Report on Exemption Clauses[60] and is discussed on pp.52 to 62 of that Report. It applies to a contract (1) between a business and a person dealing as consumer, or (2) between two businesses where it is made on the written standard terms of business of one of them. Thus in the consumer situation there is no distinction between a standard form contract and a negotiated contract (although a negotiated contract is more likely to be upheld as being "reasonable").

8.30   **Deals as consumer.**   The term "deals as consumer" is defined in s.12. As originally drafted it read:

> (1) A party to a contract "deals as consumer" in relation to another party if—
>   (a) he neither makes the contract in the course of a business nor holds himself out as doing so; and
>   (b) the other party does make the contract in the course of a business; and
>   (c) in the case of a contract governed by the law of sale of goods or hire-purchase, or by section 7 of this Act, the goods passing under or in pursuance of the contract are of a type ordinarily supplied for private use or consumption.
>
> (2) But on a sale by auction or competitive tender the buyer is not in any circumstances to be regarded as dealing as consumer.
>
> (3) Subject to this, it is for those claiming that a party does not deal as consumer to prove that he does not.

---

[59] See article in Professional Negligence (1993), Vol. 9, No. 1 at p.28 citing *The Chester Grosvenor Hotel Co Ltd v Alfred Macalpine Management Ltd* (1992) Building Law Reports 115. See also *South West Water Services v ICL* (1999) B.L.R. 420 where a contract was held to have been made on the defendant's written standard terms of business despite extensive negotiation which left the conditions effectively untouched.

[60] Law Com. No.69.

Two changes have recently been made by reg.14 of the Sale and Supply of Goods to Consumers Regulations 2002. Thus:

(1) Section 12(1)(c) will not apply where the person claiming to "deal as consumer" is an individual (which will usually be the case), so where there is a contract for the supply of goods, the *type* of goods being supplied is now irrelevant (new s.12(1A)).

Before the amendment to s.12(1)(c) there were potential problems in the case of DIY materials such as wiring, cisterns, cement, cement mixers and other builders' tools of that type. Where the buyer is an individual these problems have now been laid to rest.

(2) Section 12(2) is replaced by the following section:

> (2) But the buyer is not in any circumstances to be regarded as dealing as consumer—
>
>> (a) if he is an individual and the goods are second hand goods sold at public auction at which individuals have the opportunity of attending the sale in person;
>> (b) if he is not an individual and the goods are sold by auction or by competitive tender.

Before this change, a purchase at *auction* could never be classified as a consumer contract—but this will no longer be so. The auction exception is still significant even where the buyer is an individual e.g. at a car auction.

If a private individual buys a camera from a shop, acquires a car on hire-purchase from a finance company, has central heating installed in his house by British Gas or books a holiday with a tour operator, in each case he "deals as consumer". **8.31**

Equally obviously a manufacturing company does not deal as consumer where it buys machinery for its factory, leases cars for its sales force or uses a security company to provide guards for its premises. Thus a customer will *not* be dealing as consumer where:

(a) the customer is a business customer; or

(b) the supplier is a private person (although exemption clauses are rare here, except perhaps "sold as seen" on a used car).

There are two main areas of difficulty, both concerned with the precise meaning of "in the course of a business" in s.12(1)(a) and (b). First, suppose a solicitor, accountant or other professional person buys a car through his business, but to be used for mixed business and private use. Secondly, assume that a retailer or estate agent buys a carpet or chair for his office—an infrequent event. In none of these cases are the goods part of their stock-in-trade, but the goods are ordered through the business and doubtless tax allowances are claimed. Are the goods bought "in the course of a business"? On a straightforward reading of the words, particularly in view of use of the indefinite article, the answer is "yes". The Act does not require the business to deal in goods of the relevant type. Surprisingly the Court of Appeal has decided that cases of this type will be classed as consumer transactions.

8.32   In *R & B Customs Brokers Co Ltd v United Dominions Trust*[61]:

> R & B, shipping brokers, was a private company whose only directors and shareholders were a married couple. R & B bought a Colt Shogun for personal and company use from UDT under a conditional sale agreement. (R & B had previously acquired one or two other vehicles on credit terms.) They both signed the agreement on behalf of the company. It contained an exemption clause excluding (*inter alia*) the implied condition as to fitness for particular purpose. The vehicle leaked badly in breach of the Sale of Goods Act 1979, s.14(3). When UDT sought to rely on the exclusion clause, R & B argued that it was void under the UCTA, s.6(2), as R & B was "dealing as consumer".

The Court of Appeal gave judgment for R & B. On first impression the court was convinced by the argument put forward above that the company bought in the course of a business.[62] In the end, however, the court was persuaded that there should be consistency of meaning for the same words in different statutes dealing with consumer protection (a line of reasoning which has since been disapproved—see para.4.04 above) and that they should follow the guidance given by the House of Lords in *Davies v Sumner*,[63] a case on the Trade Descriptions Act 1968. The court did not overlook the point that the techniques of construction of criminal and civil Acts are different; the judgment of Dillon L.J. underlines the court's approach most clearly[64]:

> "Under the Trade Descriptions Act 1968 any person who in the course of a trade or business applies a false trade description to goods is, subject to the provisions of that Act, guilty of an offence. It is a penal Act, whereas the 1977 Act is not, and it is accordingly submitted that decisions on the construction of the 1968 Act cannot assist on the construction of s.12 of the 1977 Act. Also the legislative purposes of the two Acts are not the same. The primary purpose of the 1968 Act is consumer protection, and the course of business referred to is the course of business of the alleged wrongdoer. But the provisions as to dealing as a consumer in the 1977 Act are concerned with differentiating between two classes of innocent contracting parties (those who deal as consumers and those who do not) for whom differing degrees of protection against unfair contract terms are afforded by the 1977 Act. Despite these distinctions, however, it would, in my judgment, be unreal and unsatisfactory to conclude that the fairly ordinary words 'in the course of business' bear a significantly different meaning in, on the one hand, the 1968 Act and, on the other hand, s.12 of the 1977 Act. In particular, I would be very reluctant to conclude that these words bear a significantly wider meaning in s.12 than in the 1968 Act."

8.33   So when is a purchase by a business customer outside s.12? The answer is that it must be an *integral part of the business carried on* (see below). This will be so if (a) it is a one-off adventure in the nature of a trade, or (b) a regular pattern of purchases has emerged. So presumably a dentist buying chairs for the waiting room or a firm of accountants buying carpets for its offices would be "dealing as consumer" unless a regular pattern of such purchases could be

---

[61] [1988] 1 All E.R. 847.
[62] ibid. at 857, per Neill L.J.
[63] [1984] 1 W.L.R.1301.
[64] ibid. at 853. See also Neill L.J. at 859.

shown. Referring to the words of Lord Keith in *Davies v Sumner*[65] and of Lord Parker C.J. in *Havering LBC v Stevenson*,[66] Dillon L.J. said[67]:

"In the 1977 Act also, the words 'in the course of business' are not used in what Lord Keith called 'the broader sense.' I also find helpful the phrase used by Lord Parker C.J. and quoted by Lord Keith, 'an integral part of the business carried on.' The reconciliation between that phrase and the need for some degree of regularity is, as I see it, as follows: there are some transactions which are clearly integral parts of the businesses concerned, and these should be held to have been carried out in the course of those businesses; this would cover, apart from much else, the instance of a one-off adventure in the nature of trade where the transaction itself would constitute a trade or business. There are other transactions, however, such as the purchase of the car in the present case, which are at the highest only incidental to the carrying on of the relevant business; here a degree of regularity is required before it can be said that they are an integral part of the business carried on and so entered into in the course of that business."

One final comment of Dillon L.J. is worthy of note—that if the husband had personally bought the car for domestic and business use, it would have been difficult to argue that he was not dealing as consumer; so it would be anomalous to reach a different result just because it was bought by a company for such use by its two directors: "It could well be appropriate to pierce the corporate veil and look at the realities of the situation."[68]

While we should applaud this interpretation by the Court of Appeal on the grounds that it assists the consumer, the quirky and unexpected effect on the supplier seems to have been overlooked. The use of such a written exemption clause is a *criminal* offence.[69] Yet how can a supplier know whether the customer has regularly bought such goods in the past or whether they are an essential part of the business? Such a careful examination of the extrinsic circumstances of the sale would be impracticable.

The trader's solution to this danger is perhaps to be found in the wording of the defendants' exemption clause in the *R & B Customs Brokers* case: "If the buyer deals as consumer within section 12 of the Unfair Contract Terms Act 1977 . . . the buyer's statutory rights are not affected" by the exemption clause. Thus the trader gets it both ways, but leaves the buyer in doubt as to whether or not he is protected by the 1977 Act.

Returning to s.3 itself, let us assume that the client does deal as consumer. **8.34** In that case s.3 applies the reasonableness test in three cases. The first case is where the trader is in breach of contract and the clause excludes or restricts his liability (for example, liability limited to £100). Section 3 is particularly useful where suppliers of goods or services attempt to excuse themselves from liability for late delivery or performance. The second case is where the trader relies on a clause giving him the right to render a contractual performance

---

[65] See above, para.8.32.
[66] Another Trade Descriptions Act case: [1970] 1 W.L.R.1375.
[67] ibid. at 854.
[68] ibid. at 855.
[69] Consumer Transactions (Restrictions on Statements) Order 1976 (now revoked), below, para.17.06. Remember that neither *R & B* nor *Davies v Sumner* affect the words "in the course of a business" in s.14 of the Sale of Goods Act—*Stevenson v Rogers*, para.4.04, above.

substantially different from that which was reasonably expected of him. This would apply to a condition on a theatre ticket whereby "the management reserve the right to alter the performance of any member of the cast". In the case of holidays the section would apply to a clause like the one in *Anglo-Continental Holidays Ltd v Typaldos Lines (London) Ltd*[70] "Steamers, Sailing Dates, Rates and Itineraries are subject to change without notice."

The final case covered by s.3 is where a contractual term gives the trader the right to offer no performance at all. It would seem that this provision may be wide enough to cover the so-called "force majeure" clause which is very common in practice. It may provide that "the seller shall not be liable for non-delivery if delay is caused by strikes, lockouts or other acts beyond the seller's reasonable control". Even a clause giving the right of cancellation or termination might be caught by this provision.[71]

One final comment may be made: if a trader tenders a performance substantially different from that "reasonably expected of him", can the clause which allows him to do so ever be reasonable? The question of reasonableness is considered later[72] but it might be reasonable if it formed part of an arm's-length business contract between two traders where the trader attacking the clause had exactly the same provision in his own standard terms.

(c) Implied terms: ss.6,7

8.35 Sale of goods. In Chapters Two, Three and Four we examined the terms implied by ss.12 to 14 of the Sale of Goods Act 1979. Until 1973 the parties had complete freedom to exclude these obligations, because s.55, as it appeared in the original Sale of Goods Act 1893, provided that "where any right, duty or liability would arise under a contract of sale by operation of law it can be modified or varied by express agreement or by the course of dealing between the parties or by usage if the usage be such as to bind both parties to the contract". This provision was radically altered by the Supply of Goods (Implied Terms) Act 1973 and the controls introduced by that Act are substantially re-enacted by s.6 of the Unfair Contract Terms Act. There are three basic rules:

(i) The conditions and warranties in s.12 (right to sell) can *never* be excluded.

(ii) Where the buyer deals as consumer (above, para.8.30) the conditions under ss.13 (description), 14 (quality and fitness) and 15[73] can never be excluded. Hence they are often called the consumer's "inalienable rights".[74]

(iii) Where the buyer does not deal as consumer, a clause excluding or restricting the obligations referred to in (ii) above will only be valid if it satisfies the test of reasonableness.

---

[70] [1967] 2 Lloyd's Rep. 61.
[71] See Law Com. No.69, para.146.
[72] Below, para.8.43.
[73] This relates to sales by sample.
[74] Such an exemption clause is a criminal offence: below, para.17.06.

Despite s.6 a limited amount of "contracting out" is permitted by the sec-   **8.36**
tions themselves. Thus it will be recalled that under s.12 the seller can agree
to transfer only such title as he himself has, while s.14(2) allows the seller
to avoid liability for satisfactory quality in relation to particular defects by
drawing the buyer's attention to those defects before the contract is made.

As an exception to the general rule s.6 also applies where the seller is *not*
acting in the course of a business.[75] This is unlikely to be of great practical
importance because private sales are unlikely to contain exemption clauses
and because, in relation to quality and fitness, there will be nothing to
exclude.[76] Thus the significance of this provision is limited to attempts to
exclude liability under ss.13 and 15.

Hire-purchase.   The terms implied into a hire-purchase agreement are virtu-   **8.37**
ally identical to those set out above[77] and s.6 of the 1977 Act controls them in
exactly the same way as it does in sales of goods.

Other supply of goods contracts.   We saw in para 8.35 that the attack   **8.38**
launched by the 1973 Act on exemption clauses in sale and hire-purchase
contracts was re-enacted by s.6. This attack was extended to other supplies of
goods by s.7: hire, work and materials and exchange.

(1) Title.   It will be recalled that under a contract of hire the owner does not
give an undertaking that he has a "right to sell".[78] An exemption clause controlling the more limited form of title undertaking in hire cases is controlled
by the reasonableness test and is not subject to an outright ban.[79] Subject to
this, the controls are virtually identical to those for sale and hire-purchase.[80]

(2) Description, quality, fitness.   It will also be recalled that the implied
terms are virtually identical to those implied in sale and hire-purchase cases.[81]
Similarly, the controls on exemption clauses contained in s.7 of the 1977 Act
are virtually identical to those in s.6—the exemption clause is void where the
buyer "deals as consumer" and it is controlled by the reasonableness test in
other cases.

If a consumer has a complaint relating to a "work and materials" contract
(e.g. repairs to a car) it will be necessary to find out what was wrong. If the
materials themselves were defective, there is strict liability and an exemption
clause would be void under s.7. If, however, the complaint relates to the *work*
itself, the supplier will only be liable if negligent and a clause excluding this
liability will be subject to the "reasonableness" test under s.2(2) (or totally
void if the negligence causes personal injury or death).

---

[75] See s.6(4).
[76] Above, para.4.04.
[77] Above, paras 2.23, 3.19 and 4.37.
[78] Above, para.2.24.
[79] Act of 1977, s.7(4).
[80] ibid. s.7(3A).
[81] See Supply of Goods and Services Act 1982, above, paras 3.19 and 4.38–4.40.

(d) Guarantees and indemnities: s.4

8.39   **(i) Indemnities.**   Perhaps one of the most unreasonable clauses imaginable
was formerly used by a ferry company. It said in effect "if we (the company)
incur liability to a third party in carrying your car, you (the consumer) must
indemnify us—even if the liability was entirely due to our negligence". Not
surprisingly such clauses are now controlled—perhaps the only surprising
thing is that they are not subject to an outright ban. Section 4(1) provides
that:

> A person dealing as consumer cannot by reference to any contract term be made
> to indemnify another person (whether a party to the contract or not) in respect
> of liability that may be incurred by the other for negligence or breach of contract,
> except in so far as the contract term satisfies the requirement of reasonableness.

The section is widely expressed so as to apply not only where the liability
is to a third party but also where the liability is to the consumer himself. This
could give rise to a conflict between s.4 and other provisions of the Act. To
take an extreme case let us suppose that goods are supplied subject to the following condition: "the buyer agrees that if the goods are unsatisfactory the
buyer will indemnify the seller against any damages and costs payable under
any judgment obtained by the buyer against the seller". This would be an
attempt to exclude the non-excludable condition of satisfactory quality[82] and
would be totally void under s.6 (read with the definition of exemption clause
in s.13). It would be perverse if the clause were saved by s.4.

8.40   **(ii) Guarantees.**   As already stated,[83] it was common practice for a manufacturer's guarantee to exclude negligence liability. The result was that the consumer, who thought that he was gaining valuable rights, was in effect giving up
valuable rights in return for something which might well be far less valuable.
Lord Denning M.R. severely criticised such clauses in *Adams v Richardson*.[84]
In ringing tones he declared that "If he wished to excuse himself from liability
he should say so plainly. Instead of heading it boldly 'GUARANTEE' he
should head it 'NON-GUARANTEE'; for that is what it is."

Fortunately, this type of problem should now be a thing of the past in
respect of the supply of goods because s.5 of the 1977 Act nullified a large
number of such clauses. By s.5(1):

> In the case of goods of a type ordinarily supplied for private use or consumption,
> where loss or damage—
>
> (a) arises from the goods proving defective while in consumer use; and
> (b) results from the negligence of a person concerned in the manufacture or
>   distribution of the goods,
>
> liability for the loss or damage cannot be excluded or restricted by reference to
> any contract term or notice contained in or operating by reference to a guarantee
> of the goods.

---

[82]   Above, para.8.35.
[83]   Above, para.5.07.
[84]   [1969] 1 W.L.R. 1645 at 1649.

These provisions should be read together with the changes to consumer guarantees which we considered in Chapter Five (see para.5.06).

Two further points should be noted. First, goods are "in consumer use" when a person is using them, or has them in his possession for use, otherwise than exclusively for the purpose of a business.[85] Thus if the buyer of a car and his wife are injured while the car is being used on a combined business-and-pleasure journey, s.5 would control a clause in the guarantee excluding liability for the manufacturer's negligence. Presumably, if the negligence resulted in damage to property, the outright ban in s.5 would override the s.2 "reasonableness" test. Secondly, the section does not apply as between the parties to a contract under or in pursuance of which possession or ownership of the goods passed.[86] In such cases the consumer would have the benefit of s.2 in relation to negligence and ss.6 and 7 in relation to the implied terms.

(e) Misrepresentation

Exemption clauses relating to misrepresentation have been controlled since the passing of s.3 of the Misrepresentation Act 1967. Section 3 is redrafted by s.8 of the Unfair Contract Terms Act so that it now reads as follows: **8.41**

> If a contract contains a term which would exclude or restrict—
>
> (a) any liability to which a party to a contract may be subject by reason of any misrepresentation made by him before the contract was made; or
> (b) any remedy available to another party to the contract by reason of such a misrepresentation,
>
> the term shall be of no effect except in so far as it satisfies the requirement of reasonableness as stated in section 11(1) of the Unfair Contract Terms Act 1977; and it is for those claiming that the term satisfies that requirement to show that it does.

The first point to notice here is that the law is to be found in s.3 of the Misrepresentation Act 1967 (as amended) and not in the Unfair Contract Terms Act. It follows that the section applies to all contracts (including those excluded from the Unfair Contract Terms Act[86a]) and it is not confined to "business liability".   **8.42**

What type of clauses are caught by s.3? Some cases are obvious: "The purchaser shall have no right to rescind this agreement" or "All liability for misrepresentation is excluded". On the other hand a clause stating that "no employee of the company has any authority to make representations on the company's behalf" might be effective.[87] Finally, the contract might state that "although every care has been taken the vendors do not warrant the accuracy of these particulars and the purchaser shall not rely on them." If such a clause

---

[85] s.5(2)(a). See the example given by Neill L.J. in *R & B Customs Brokers Co Ltd v U.D.T.* (above, para.8.32) at 858.

[86] s.5(3).

[86a] Unless it is an international supply contract within s.26: *Trident Turboprop (Dublin) Ltd v First Flight Couriers Ltd* [2009] EWCA Civ 290, CA.

[87] See *Overbrooke Estates Ltd v Glencombe Properties Ltd* [1974] 1 W.L.R. 1335, above, para.8.18.

were outside s.3 it would severely limit the scope of the section. It seems that if the other party does rely on the incorrect particulars there will be a misrepresentation and the clause will be treated as an exemption clause to which s.3 applies.[88] A clause which is wide enough to exclude liability for fraudulent misrepresentation will not pass the "reasonableness" test.[89]

The reasonableness test

8.43   Sections 2, 3, 4, 6, 7 and 8 all refer to the reasonableness test. The concept is not a new one; it has applied to misrepresentation since 1967 and it has applied to the implied terms of sale of goods and hire-purchase contracts since 1973. Section 11 draws a distinction between contractual clauses and non-contractual notices. In the case of a contract the person claiming that the term is reasonable must prove that:

> the term shall have been a fair and reasonable one to be included having regard to the circumstances which were, or ought reasonably to have been, known to or in the contemplation of the parties when the contract was made.[90]

Thus the critical date is the date of the contract. For example, a limitation of damages clause which was reasonable at the date of the contract will be upheld even though by the time of the hearing it has become hopelessly inadequate by reason of inflation or by reason of the claimant's loss being far greater than expected.

8.44   Three more preliminary points are significant. First, the question is whether the clause is reasonable in relation to *this particular contract*[91]; so what may be reasonable between a supplier and one customer may be unreasonable as against another, e.g. because there may be equality of bargaining power in the one case and not in the other. This poses considerable problems for the draftsman of standard form contracts in that there is no such thing as a clause which is fair and reasonable in itself.

Secondly, the burden of proving reasonableness lies on the supplier; if the factors are evenly balanced, the customer wins the day.[92]

This point equally applies to non-contractual notices and disclaimers where the party relying on the notice (e.g. a building society surveyor with a potential liability to a house buyer in the tort of negligence) must show that:

> it should be fair and reasonable to allow reliance on it, having regard to all the circumstances obtaining when the liability arose or (but for the notice) would have arisen.[93]

Finally, the term must be looked at *as a whole*. Thus in *Stewart Gill v Myer*[94] the plaintiff sought to rely on a clause excluding various remedies

---

[88] *Cremdean Properties Ltd v Nash* (1977) 244 E.G. 547, CA.
[89] *Thomas Witter Ltd v T.B.P. Industries Ltd* [1996] 2 All E.R. 573.
[90] s.11(1).
[91] See Slade L.J. in *Phillips Products Ltd v Hyland* [1987] 2 All E.R. 620 at 628.
[92] ibid. See s.11(5).
[93] s.11(3).
[94] [1992] 2 All E.R. 257.

including a right of set-off. The Court of Appeal held that the clause read as a whole was unreasonable. However, the court may sever one clause leaving a separate (reasonable) one intact.[94a]

The role of the courts

The concept of reasonableness appears in many areas of the law, includ- **8.45** ing unfair dismissal, matrimonial finance, negligence claims and housing. In relation to the Unfair Contract Terms Act Lord Bridge has emphasised that more than one view is possible. His Lordship dealt with the matter as follows:

> "The court must entertain a whole range of considerations, put them in the scales on one side or the other and decide at the end of the day on which side the balance comes down. There will sometimes be room for a legitimate difference of judicial opinion as to what the answer should be and where it will be impossible to say that one view is demonstrably wrong and the other demonstrably right. It must follow in my view that when asked to review such a decision the appeal court should treat the decision with the utmost respect and refuse to interfere unless it is satisfied that it proceeded upon some erroneous principle or was plainly and obviously wrong."[95]

Guidelines

In any case involving the reasonableness test the court has a wide discretion **8.46** and must consider all the relevant circumstances; presumably if the matter comes to court the defendant should be advised to plead the facts on which he relies to support his claim of reasonableness. Schedule 2 contains a non-exhaustive list of guidelines. They apply only to contracts controlled by ss.6 and 7, i.e. to supplies of *goods* where the claimant's claim relies on the *statutory implied* terms.[96] They are as follows:

"GUIDELINES" FOR APPLICATION OF REASONABLENESS TEST

The matters to which regard is to be had in particular for the purposes of ss. 6(3), **8.47** 7(3) and (4), 20 and 21 are any of the following which appear to be relevant—

  (a) the strength of the bargaining positions of the parties relative to each other, taking into account (among other things) alternative means by which the customer's requirements could have been met;
  (b) whether the customer received an inducement to agree to the term, or in accepting it had an opportunity of entering into a similar contract with other persons, but without having to accept a similar term;
  (c) whether the customer knew or ought reasonably to have known of the existence and extent of the term (having regard, among other things, to

---

[94a] *Regus (UK) Ltd*, n.98 below.
[95] *George Mitchell (Chesterhall) Ltd v Finney Lock Seeds Ltd* [1983] 3 A.C. 803 at 816. The case was actually decided on an earlier Act but this does not reduce its importance in the present context.
[96] Section 11(2). Where the customer is "dealing as consumer", any exemption clause is void in respect of such terms: above, paras 8.35–8.38.

any custom of the trade and any previous course of dealing between the
parties);
   (d) where the term excludes or restricts any relevant liability if some condition is not complied with, whether it was reasonable at the time of the
contract to expect that compliance with that condition would be practicable;
   (e) whether the goods were manufactured, processed or adapted to the special
order of the customer.

The first three are of greatest importance. Their broad effect is that if a business buyer, large enough to have bargaining power and with a choice of
potential suppliers with whom to negotiate terms, enters into a disadvantageous contract with his eyes open, the court is unlikely to rush to his assistance. The buyer has made a bad bargain and is stuck with it. In contrast if the
buyer is a small business, perhaps dealing with a monopoly or with a supplier
who belongs to a trade association whose members all adopt standard terms,
and does not notice or cannot understand the exemption clause, then the
court will probably strike down the clause. He had no real choice—it was a
"take it or leave it situation".[97]

8.48   No specific guidelines are laid down by the Act in other cases, e.g. contracts
for *services,* breach of *express* terms. However, by analogy the courts are
applying similar guidelines with particular emphasis on the first three criteria—bargaining power, choice and knowledge. Lord Wilberforce stressed the
significance of the first factor in the pre-Act case of *Photo Production Ltd v
Securicor Transport*[98]:

> "After this Act, in commercial matters generally, when the parties are not of
> unequal bargaining power, and when risks are normally borne by insurance, not
> only is the case for judicial intervention undemonstrated, but there is everything
> to be said, and this seems to have been Parliament's intention, for leaving the
> parties free to apportion the risks as they think fit and for respecting their deci-
> sions."

The size of print would also be relevant,[99] and a clause is unlikely to be
upheld if it is out of line with a Code of Practice adopted by the trader's trade
association.[100] It may be that a clause that "the seller can cancel this agreement in the event of strikes, etc." should now be redrafted so as to give a
mutual right to rescind. It is also helpful for the contract to specify the factors
on which the trader relies in support of his claim of reasonableness. Perhaps
we shall see the emergence of a dual price contract, £X with full responsibility or £Y without it. We already see "split clauses"—different clauses dealing

---

[97] See Slade L.J. in *Phillips Products Ltd v Hyland* at 629 (clause was one of 43 clauses of plant
hire company's terms; used by all members of trade association; not fair and reasonable).
[98] [1980] A.C. 827. The respondents' employee purposely set fire to a factory which he was supposed to be guarding! See also *Regus (UK) Ltd v Epcot Solutions Ltd* [2008] EWCA Civ 361,
CA.
[99] In *The Zinnia* [1984] 2 LL.L.R. 211, Staughton J. was minded to strike down the clause on
the grounds of (a) size of print, and (b) complexity of language. Unfortunately counsel for the
party attacking the clause did not raise this point!
[100] Below, para.10.05.

with property damage, financial loss, limitation of liability and time-limits for claims.

Limitation of damages clauses

A number of small traders (including travel agents) felt very uneasy about **8.49** the possibility of having to meet very large, unlimited claims and accordingly during the passage of the Bill Lord Hailsham introduced a new clause which is now s.11(4). Unlike the Sch.2 guidelines, these factors apply to all limitation clauses. It reads:

> Where by reference to a contract term or notice a person seeks to restrict liability to a specified sum of money, and the question arises (under this or any other Act) whether the term or notice satisfies the requirement of reasonableness, regard shall be had in particular . . . to—
>
> (a) the resources which he could expect to be available to him for the purpose of meeting the liability should it arise; and
> (b) how far it was open to him to cover himself by insurance.

This provision is bound to cause problems. Do the "resources" of a sole trader or partner include his private assets? How far afield does he have to search to find insurance? What happens if the premium would destroy or seriously reduce the commercial viability of the transaction? In spite of such difficulties it seems likely that the courts will view more sympathetically a limitation clause, whereby the supplier accepts some liability, than an exclusion clause where the supplier in cavalier fashion refuses to contribute at all to the consumer's loss.[101]

Illustrative cases

The Act was passed to give added protection to consumers who are nearly **8.50** always in a weak bargaining position. The problem of widely drawn exemption clauses has not gone away[102] but we are not aware of a single post-Act consumer case in which an exemption clause has been upheld as reasonable. The following cases show the attitude of the courts.

The first one is the most important in that the House of Lords has given valuable guidance on the operation of the reasonableness test in a consumer context.

Smith v Bush.[103] We have already discussed the first point in this case, **8.51** namely, whether the surveyors owed a duty of care in tort to the house buyers. To this question the House of Lords unanimously answered "yes".

We now turn to the second point—were the surveyors able to prove

---

[101] See *Ailsa Craig Fishing Co v Malvern Fishing Co*, above, para.8.20, n.37. See also *St. Albans DC v ICL* (below, para.8.57) where a limitation clause was held to be unreasonable: the resources of the company and its insurance were relevant factors.
[102] See Ch. Nine below.
[103] [1990] 1 A.C. 831, above, para.3.08.

that their exemption clauses satisfied the reasonableness test? Again the
House of Lords answered the question in favour of the consumers: "no".
The judgments of Lords Griffiths and Templeman deserve careful examination. Although Lord Griffiths admitted that it is impossible to draw up
an exhaustive list of relevant factors for the court to take into account
when applying the reasonableness test, the following extract is crucial
for the legal adviser, since he states that these matters should "always be
considered"[104]:

> "(1) Were the parties of equal bargaining power? If the court is dealing with a
>   one-off situation between parties of equal bargaining power the require-
>   ment of reasonableness would be more easily discharged than in a case
>   such as the present where the disclaimer is imposed on the purchaser who
>   has no effective power to object.
> (2) In the case of advice, would it have been reasonably practicable to obtain
>   the advice from an alternative source taking into account considerations
>   of costs and time? . . .
> (3) How difficult is the task being undertaken for which liability is being
>   excluded? When a very difficult or dangerous undertaking is involved
>   there may be a high risk of failure which would certainly be a pointer
>   towards the reasonableness of excluding liability as a condition of doing
>   the work. A valuation, on the other hand, should present no difficulty if
>   the work is undertaken with reasonable skill and care. . . .
> (4) What are the practical consequences of the decision on the question
>   of reasonableness? This must involve the sums of money potentially at
>   stake and the ability of the parties to bear the loss involved, which, in its
>   turn, raises the question of insurance. There was once a time when it was
>   considered improper even to mention the possible existence of insurance
>   cover in a lawsuit. But those days are long past. Everyone knows that all
>   prudent professional men carry insurance, and the availability and cost of
>   insurance must be a relevant factor when considering which of two parties
>   should be required to bear the risk of a loss."

The effect of this decision is that an exemption clause will not protect a
surveyor "in respect of a dwelling house of modest value". The position may
well be different where other types of property are valued "such as industrial
property, large blocks of flats or very expensive houses",[105] where it may be
reasonable for the mortgagee's surveyor to exclude or limit his liability to the
buyer/mortgagor.

8.52   *Spencer v Cosmos Air Holidays.*[106]   We discussed this case earlier in relation to damages for distress. The agreement contained a clause whereby the
defendants excluded responsibility "for any injury, death, loss or damage
which is caused by any negligence of the management or employees of an
independent contractor". Without amplifying their reasons the Court of
Appeal brushed the clause aside. In the words of Farquharson L.J.:

---

[104] At 858. See also the Scottish case of *Bank of Scotland v Fuller Peiser* (2002) S.L.T. 574 where
    the court upheld a clause providing that a surveyor was not to be liable to anyone except the
    borrower.
[105] per Lord Griffiths, at 859.
[106] *The Times*, December 6, 1989, CA, above, para.7.63.

"It does not bear upon the case at all and does not affect the plaintiff's contractual rights against the defendants—namely, to enjoy 14 days' holiday in the hotel she had chosen."

Walker v Boyle.[107] During negotiations for the sale of V's house V told P **8.53** that there was no boundary dispute. This was an innocent misrepresentation which induced P to buy. On discovering the facts P refused to proceed whereupon V claimed specific performance in reliance on Condition 17 of the National Conditions of Sale, which provided that "no misdescription can annul the sale". P claimed that the clause was unreasonable. His claim was upheld. Even though the clause was in the National Conditions of Sale it was not the product of negotiation between the parties or their representatives.

South Western General Property Co v Marton.[108] Property was described in **8.54** auction particulars as "long leasehold building land". The particulars failed to disclose major restrictions on development and the buyer would never have bought the property if he had known of this. The particulars provided that the statements were made without responsibility and were statements of opinion only and that it was up to intending purchasers to satisfy themselves as to their accuracy. Croom-Johnson J. held that the clause failed to pass the reasonableness test. His Lordship laid great stress on the vital importance of the matter for the buyer. He also pointed out that many prospective buyers attended auctions at short notice and would obviously have no opportunity to check out the particulars.

Waldron-Kelly v British Railways Board.[109] The defendants agreed to carry **8.55** the plaintiff's suitcase on "owner's risk" terms. It disappeared. The Board sought to limit their liability by a clause which referred only to the weight of the suitcase (equal to £27) and not to its value (£320). The learned county court judge held that the clause failed to pass the reasonableness test.

Woodman v Photo Trade Processing Ltd.[110] Mr Woodman took photographs **8.56** of a friend's wedding. The shop to which he brought the film for development displayed a notice limiting liability to the cost of the film. The film came back ruined and Mr Woodman (with the support of the Consumers' Association) claimed that the clause was unreasonable. The learned county court judge upheld his claim and awarded £75 for disappointment.

St Albans DC v ICL.[111] Although not a consumer case (and nearly all the **8.57** recent cases on the "reasonableness" test have involved "business to business" contracts), it provides helpful guidance on the "reasonableness" test.

---

[107] [1982] 1 W.L.R. 495.
[108] (1982) 263 E.G. 1090.
[109] [1981] C.L.Y. 303.
[110] *Times Business News*, June 20, 1981; *Which?*, July 1981.
[111] [1996] 4 All E.R. 481. The case is also relevant on the meaning of "written standard terms of business" (see paras 4.32 and 8.49 above), see [1997] F.S.R. 251.

ICL were a very substantial company with turnover of £1109 million, profit of £100 million and world-wide liability insurance of £50 million. The contract contained a clause limiting liability to £100,000 (less than their normal standard clause). Scott-Baker J. after considering the bargaining strength of the parties, the likely losses of the plaintiffs and other factors, held that the clause failed the reasonableness test: "I do not think it is unreasonable that he who stands to make the profit should carry the risk."[112] The Court of Appeal agreed.

The message from these cases comes through loud and clear—the standard form, non-negotiated consumer exemption clause has had its day. In none of the above cases was there any negotiation; in none of them was the clause expressly brought to the consumer's notice. In only one of them (*Waldron-Kelly*) did the consumer have anything in the nature of a choice. Indeed the most significant feature of the *Woodman* case was the fact that, in the opinion of the learned judge, it should have been possible for the processing industry to offer their customers a choice—£X with limited liability or £Y with greater liability.[113]

The Act may therefore mark a return to basic principles of contract law by destroying the fiction that a party has "agreed" to a term (1) if he did not know it was there, (2) even if he had known, he would not have understood it, and (3) even if he would have understood it, he would never have agreed to it without modification.

3. Other Controls

8.58   Although the Unfair Contract Terms Act 1977 is by far the most important example of statutory control of exemption clauses there are many other statutory controls. One of these, s.3 of the Misrepresentation Act 1967, has already been mentioned. There are also a number of other Acts relating to the carriage of passengers by public service vehicle, rail and air (see particularly the Carriage by Air Act 1961). Other examples include the Occupiers' Liability Act 1957, the Defective Premises Act 1972, the Road Traffic Act 1988 and the Consumer Credit Act 1974. For a summary of the statutory controls readers are referred to *Chitty on Contracts*.

4. The EU Dimension

8.59   The EU has been active in promoting consumer protection by banning unfair terms. We shall deal fully with this important topic in the next chapter.

---

[112] ibid. at 711.
[113] The so-called "two-tier system".

Chapter Nine

"THESE SMALL PRINT TERMS SEEM VERY UNFAIR"

On July 1, 1995 the Unfair Contract Terms Directive became part of English **9.01** law. This was done by Statutory Instrument, namely the Unfair Terms in Consumer Contracts Regulations 1994. They were reproduced with minor drafting amendments, and one change of substance, by the Unfair Terms in Consumer Contracts Regulations 1999. In the remainder of this Chapter, unless otherwise stated, a reference to a Regulation is to that Regulation in the 1999 Regulations.

The Regulations break new ground by enabling a consumer to challenge certain clauses in a contract on the ground that they are "unfair". They also enable the OFT, and certain other bodies, to seek an injunction banning the continued use of such clauses. The Regulations, and many examples of their use, will be covered in the following pages. This topic should be read together with the new powers to seek "enforcement orders" under the Enterprise Act 2002. They are considered in Part III of this book.

For the English lawyer/adviser it is vital to appreciate that the new legisla- **9.02** tion exists alongside the other controls, notably the Unfair Contract Terms Act 1977 which has been fully discussed in the previous chapter. Four points can be made:

(1) In some respects the Regulations go beyond the 1977 Act (UCTA) because (a) UCTA is largely concerned with *exemption clauses* whereas the Regulations are not so limited in that they cover unfair terms and (b) the Regulations control a number of contracts (such as insurance) to which UCTA does not apply at all.

(2) In three respects UCTA is wider than the Regulations. Thus (a) UCTA is not limited to contracts—it also covers non-contractual disclaimers; (b) UCTA is not limited to non-negotiated terms; and (c) UCTA applies not only to consumer sales but also to business sales.

(3) There is a substantial area of overlap and Art.8 of the Directive pro- vides that: "Member States may adopt or retain the most stringent provisions compatible with the Treaty in the area covered by this Directive, to ensure a maximum degree of protection for the con- sumer." It follows that if a clause is struck down as *void* by UCTA, the consumer is not concerned with the Regulations. If, however, the clause is controlled by the "reasonableness" test (e.g. UCTA, s.3), the court will have to decide whether the test of "fairness" goes beyond

the test of reasonableness. The language of art.3, which refers to a clause causing a "significant imbalance in the parties' rights and obligations arising under the contract to the detriment of the consumer", is strikingly similar to paras 1 and 4 of Lord Griffiths' UCTA guidelines in *Smith v Bush* (above, para.8.51).

(4) The Law Commission in their Final Report Unfair Terms in Contracts (LC No.298, February 2005) criticised these "inconsistent and overlapping provisions". It contains a draft bill rewriting UCTA and the Regulations and also extending protection to small businesses with nine or fewer employees.

In the decade or so since the 1994 Regulations came into force there had been hardly any cases which came to court but, as we shall see, there has been a great deal of activity out of court—and on that basis consumers have been in a much stronger position than before. Recently the OFT has flexed its muscles in court, notably; against the banks with varying success.[1]

1. THE EUROPEAN BACKGROUND

9.03 The Directive had an (interrupted) gestation period of some 19 years. Work on it started as long ago as 1975, but it was then halted when a large number of Member States (including the UK) introduced domestic legislation in this area. When the dust of this legislation had been given a chance to settle work on the Directive started again; not surprisingly the comments (especially from industry) were not entirely uncritical.

An EU Directive is normally preceded by Preambles setting out the thinking behind the Directive. This one has a very large number and in this book we have numbered them 1 to 40 for ease of reference. There seems little doubt that these Preambles will be referred to by a court faced with a problem of interpretation. Preambles 5 to 9 provide some of the flavour:

(5) Whereas, generally speaking, consumers do not know the rules of law which, in other Member States than their own, govern contracts for the sale of goods or services;

(6) Whereas this lack of awareness may deter them from direct transactions for the purchase of goods or services in another Member State;

(7) Whereas, in order to facilitate the establishment of the internal market and to safeguard the citizen in his role as consumer when acquiring goods and services under contracts which are governed by the laws of Member States other than his own, it is essential to remove unfair terms from those contracts;

(8) Whereas sellers of goods and suppliers of services will thereby be helped in their task of selling goods and supplying services, both at home and through the internal market;

(9) Whereas competition will thus be stimulated, so contributing to increased choice for Community citizens as consumers.

[1] See paras 9.10 and 9.26.

One general observation can be made; the attempt by the Directive to boost cross-border trade is unlikely to succeed, because the Directive has nothing to say on the vital question of enforcement. In most cases[2] a consumer who is dissatisfied with his purchase must sue in the supplier's home state: see the amended Convention on Jurisdiction and the Enforcement of Judgments (which now forms part of English law under the Civil Jurisdiction and Judgments Act 1982 as amended by SI 2001/3929).

Interpretation

This Directive (like all Directives) is addressed to Member States and requires **9.04** them to enact the relevant legislation by a specified date (in this case December 31, 1994). A question may then arise as to what remedies are available to a consumer if a Member State fails to implement the Directive correctly, or in time, or at all. This is a very live issue; in two cases involving the rights of employees on a business transfer and in the case of collective redundancies the EU Commission took the UK Government before the European Court which held that the UK Government had failed to implement Directives correctly in no less than six respects.[3] Where does this leave the consumer under the Directive which we are discussing? The emerging case law has established a number of points:

(1) The English courts must construe domestic law (the Regulations) in such a way as to give effect to the *purpose* of the Directive. This principle was laid down by the House of Lords in *Litster v Forth Dry Dock*[4] and by the European Court in *Marleasing*[5] and more recently in *Faccini Dori*.[6] Since one of the objects of the Directive is to approximate the laws of Member States the courts may well give particular words such as "good faith" a European meaning; anyone putting forward an argument in this area should not do so in purely Anglo-Saxon terms (see also (3) below).

(2) If the Regulations cannot be construed as set out in (1) above, the question arises as to what remedy (if any) is available to a consumer if the Directive has not been correctly implemented. As previously stated, the European Court has been extremely creative and as a result the consumer may have two possible remedies:

(a) If the claim is brought against a public body (an "emanation of the State") the claimant can enforce the Directive directly in the English courts; the public body cannot shelter behind the Government's failure to implement it. The leading case[7] concerned a Health Authority and the concept of "public

---

[2] The position is different in relation to credit transactions—see the statutory instrument referred to in this paragraph.
[3] *Commission v UK* [1994] I.R.L.R. 392 and 412.
[4] [1990] 1 A.C. 546.
[5] *Marleasing SA v La Commercial* [1992] 1 C.M.L.R. 305.
[6] [1995] All E.R. (EC) 1, ECJ.
[7] *Marshall v Southhampton Area Health Authority (No. 1)* [1986] Q.B. 401.

body" has been widely interpreted to cover public utilities both before[8] and after[9] privatisation.

(b) Quite apart from this, an aggrieved party may sue the Government for failure to implement the Directive correctly, if the relevant provision was enacted for his benefit and if the failure has caused him loss. The full ramifications of the historic *Francovitch* decision on this point[10] have recently been clarified.[11]

9.05   (3) These Regulations are just one example of domestic Regulations passed to implement EU Directives. We have already met three others—two in Chapter Six and one in Chapter Seven. In this connection the comments by Newman J. in the recent case of *Khatun v London Borough of Newham and the Office of Fair Trading*[12] are highly instructive. One of the issues in the case was whether the Regulations could be construed as giving effect to the Directive; accordingly what mattered was the effect of the Directive. He then said this:

> "In my judgment it is important not to lose sight of the character of the instrument under interpretative scrutiny. It is not to be construed by the Court as it would construe domestic legislation which is the product of a close, legislative process of debate and amendment and approval by a legislative chamber. It is an autonomous instrument drawn up for implementation by domestic legislation in each Member State. In this context the expressed purpose of the Directive is of paramount significance and is not to be narrowed by legislative or semantic interpretation. Where the Directive will be available in the language of each Member State, too close attention to semantics will place too great a weight upon the problems which can arise from translation. The initial text of the Directive is French but it has no status as the authoritative text."

The last part of this quotation highlights an important point for advisers. In construing any EU Directive the English language version is by no means the end of the story; each of the other languages is equally authentic. In arriving at his decision that the Directive did apply to land contracts the judge took into account the following matters:

(a) the text of the Directive in French, Italian, Spanish and Portuguese;

(b) the use of the French word "biens" (which includes immovable property) in the Directive and also in the European Convention on Human Rights;

---

[8] *Foster v British Gas* [1988] C.M.L.R. 697.
[9] *Griffin v South West Water Services* [1995] I.R.L.R. 15.
[10] *Francovitch v Italian Republic* [1992] I.R.L.R. 84, ECJ.
[11] In the *Factortame* case [1991] A.C. 603, the UK Government was held to be in breach of EC law because the Merchant Shipping Act 1988 discriminated against non-UK nationals. Spanish fishermen have sued the UK Government under *Francovitch* (n.10, above) and the courts have held that they were entitled to compensation for their economic loss in an action for breach of statutory duty. Subsequently they accepted a very large offer from the Government to settle their claims.
[12] [2003] EWHC Admin 2326.

(c) a conversation between an EU official responsible for the Directive and an OFT official in the period shortly before the 1994 Regulations were amended;

(d) the text of the "doorstep" Directive under which land contracts were expressly excluded;

(e) legislation and case law in other Member States; and

(f) an OFT argument that the exclusion of land contracts would leave a large gap in the consumer protection aims of the Directive, since 30 per cent of households live in rented accommodation.

2. WHAT CONTRACTS ARE CAUGHT?

The Regulations apply to "unfair terms in contracts concluded between a seller or a supplier and a consumer." When we turn to the definitions in reg.2(1) we find that: **9.06**

> "consumer" means any natural person who, in contracts covered by these Regulations, is acting for purposes which are outside his trade, business or profession;
>
> "seller or supplier" means any natural or legal person who, in contracts covered by these Regulations, is acting for purposes relating to his trade, business or profession, whether publicly owned or privately owned.

Several points call for comment. The first two both relate to the *R & B* case (above, para.8.32). This case would be decided differently under the Regulations because (a) a company can never be a "consumer" for the purpose of the Regulations as it is not a "natural" person,[13] and (b) in any event the buyer would be unable to prove that he was acting for purposes outside his business. It follows that a sole trader buying a car for his manager would not have the protection of the Regulations. To avoid confusion, we must repeat that the non-application of the Regulations will not affect the rights of a consumer under UCTA where that Act applies. In other words, the actual decision in *R & B*, based on UCTA, would be unaffected.

This leaves three unsettled questions. First, what about mixed use? What happens if a solicitor or doctor buys a car for private use but uses it occasionally for business purposes? Secondly, what happens if the private nature of the purchase is unknown to the supplier (as where the order is given on business stationery)? In the light of what has been said above (para.9.05) the court can be directed to other European texts where similar terms appear.[14] On that basis, the first question may well be answered by applying a proportionality test, so that if the car was employed overwhelmingly for private use the Directive would apply. On the second point the obvious inference must be that a buyer who leads the seller to believe that it is a business sale must take the conse-

---

[13] See *Barclays Bank v Kufner* [2008] EWHC 2319 (Comm).
[14] See, e.g. the Official Report (Guilano-Lagarde) on the Rome Choice of Law Convention, where the point is discussed in relation to art.5 of that Convention.

quences. Finally, the wording is wide enough to cover a case where the business "seller" is acting as a buyer in the particular transaction, e.g. a part exchange deal. This is the DTI view (Guidance Notes para.4.8) and we agree.

3. WHAT CONTRACTS ARE EXCLUDED?

9.07 The somewhat curious provisions of Preambles 14 and 15 read as follows:

> (14) Whereas [uniform rules of law in the matter of unfair terms] should apply to all contracts concluded between sellers or suppliers and consumers;
> (15) Whereas as a result *inter alia* contracts relating to employment, contracts relating to succession rights, contracts relating to rights under family law and contracts relating to the incorporation and organization of companies or partnership agreements must be excluded from this Directive.

These contracts were expressly excluded in Sch.1 of the 1994 Regulations, but this Schedule is not reproduced in the 1999 Regulations. The latter were designed to bring the drafting more closely into line with the *substantive* provisions of the Directive. The exclusions in the original Sch.1 did not form part of those substantive provisions—they merely appeared in recitals and consequently there was no need to include them in the Regulations. It is a pure drafting amendment; after all, none of the listed contracts can be regarded as contracts between a "seller or supplier" and a "consumer".

Until very recently there was some doubt as to whether land contracts were included. The DTI were somewhat cautious but considered it prudent to assume that the Regulations did apply (Guidance Notes para.3.20). The OFT also took the view that they were covered and dealt with more than 350 cases on that basis. As previously stated (para.9.05 above) Newman J. has now upheld the OFT view.

4. WHAT TERMS ARE NOT CAUGHT?

9.08 Three points must be noted.

(1) The Regulations apply only to terms which have not been "individually negotiated". This is considered below.

(2) The Regulations do not apply to a term incorporated in order to comply with or which reflects (a) mandatory, statutory or regulatory provisions of the United Kingdom or (b) the provisions or principles of International Conventions to which the Member States or the Community are party. An obvious example of (a) would be a contractual term inserted to comply with the Consumer Credit Act (as to which see below, para.18.01). A further example would be a contract incorporating terms laid down by a regulatory authority under the Financial Services and Markets Act. An example of (b) above would be a clause giving effect to the Warsaw Convention on carriage by air.

(3) The Regulations are only designed to cover ancillary clauses rather than "core" terms falling within reg.6(2) to which we now turn.

5. THE CORE TERMS

Regulation 6(2) provides:

> In so far as it is in plain, intelligible language, the assessment of fairness shall **9.09**
> not relate:—
>
> (a) to the definition of the main subject-matter of the contract, or
> (b) to the adequacy of the price or renumeration, as against the goods or services sold or supplied in exchange.

The basic principle is clear enough; a consumer cannot allege unfairness merely because he has made a bad bargain. That said, there is bound to be scope for argument as to which terms are core terms. If one takes the case of a clause in a motor policy stating that "the car can only be used by a driver over 25 for social, domestic or pleasure purposes and the insured must pay the first £100 of any claim", it would be a "core" provision, whereas a clause stating that "all claims must be notified within 48 hours" would be non-core. Even in the former case the exception would not apply unless the core provision was expressed in plain, intelligible language as required by the first line of reg. 6(2).

OFT and the Banks

The recent running battle between the OFT and the banks culminated in one **9.10** of the earliest decisions of the new Supreme Court, *Office of Fair Trading v Abbey National plc* [2009] UKSC6. The battleground was reg.6(2). The issue, in the words of Lord Phillips, was whether certain bank charges (detailed below) constituted "the price or remuneration, as against the services supplied in exchange".

Credit card and bank charges

First it is necessary to explain the background to the dispute. Almost every con- **9.11** sumer has at some time made a complaint about the amount of charges (often £30 or more) levied by banks, building societies and credit card issuers when a customer draws a cheque which bounces or misses a credit card payment.

The credit card problem was solved in April 2006 when the OFT, after discussions with the eight card issuers, produced a statement of principles for them to follow in setting fair default charges. These should not exceed the administrative costs in the reasonable contemplation of the consumer. The OFT will not take legal action where charges do not exceed £12, which has generally proved to be the norm.

This left open the level of bank charges on current accounts. In March 2007 the OFT began a formal investigation. Four charges were relevant (the "relevant charges"):

- an unpaid item, where a cheque is dishonoured;

- a paid item, where the bank honours a cheque though the account is not in funds;

- a guaranteed paid item, where the bank pays because of a cheque guarantee card though no funds are available; and

- an overdraft excess, where the account is overdrawn without prior authority.

About 20 per cent of the 54 million current account customers incur such charges.

The High Court[15]

9.12   In July 2007 the OFT issued proceedings in the Commercial Court seeking a declaration that reg.6(2) did not apply to such charges. They claimed that the "relevant charges" were (1) penalties at common law; and (2) fell within the Regulations. The eight defendant banks took the opposite view and in particular argued that the charges fell within the exception in reg. 6(2).

Andrew Smith J. held that (1) the relevant charges were not penalties, as the customers were not in breach of contract in relation to the events giving rise to the charges; and (2) such payments were not made in exchange for the whole package of services supplied by the banks when operating current accounts, so reg.6(2) did not apply to them. The OFT could assess their fairness.

Andrew Smith J.'s judgment runs to 69 pages. It includes a long, detailed analysis of the eight banks' terms and charges to decide whether they were "in plain, intelligible language" (reg.7), which they were except in "relatively minor aspects". The court declined to make any declaration as to the meaning and effect of the requirement of good faith in reg.5(1).

The Court of Appeal[16]

9.13   The banks appealed against the finding on reg.6.(2). The Court of Appeal dismissed the appeal unanimously. The "relevant charges" were not part of the core or essential bargain between bank and customer.

The contingent nature of the charges and the fact that the relevant terms were not specifically negotiated were strong pointers to the conclusion that the charges were not "the price or remuneration" within the meaning of art.4(2) of Directive 93/13 and reg.6 (2) (b). Accordingly an assessment of the fairness of the relevant charges was not excluded by reg.6(2)(b).

The purpose of reg.6(2)(b) was to limit the exclusion to the essence of the price. It was to be construed narrowly or restrictively because it was an exception to what would otherwise be the position. It was not intended to cover incidental or auxiliary terms.

The Supreme Court

9.14   The banks appealed again. The Supreme Court unanimously upheld the appeal. The OFT having won the first two rounds was knocked out in round three!

---

[15] [2008] EWHC 875 (Comm).
[16] [2009] EWCA Civ 116.

The court agreed that all the relevant charges fell within the exception in reg. 6(2)(b) as being part of "price or remuneration". Lord Walker considered (at para.47):

> "Charges for unauthorised overdrafts are monetary consideration for the package of banking services supplied to personal current account customers. They are an important part of the banks' charging structure, amounting to over 30 per cent of their revenue stream from all personal current account customers. The facts that the charges are contingent, and that the majority of customers do not incur them, are irrelevant. . . Even if the Court of Appeal's interpretation had been correct, I do not see how it could have come to the conclusion that charges amounting to over 30 per cent of the revenue stream were (para.111) "not part of the core or essential bargain." "

The court was not persuaded by the view of the Court of Appeal that the package should be divided into the "core or essential bargain" comprising those matters to which the typical consumer would have regard when deciding whether to enter into the agreement with the bank and those provisions which were "incidental or ancillary" such as overdrawing on his current account and so fell outside reg.6(2). [17]

While this decision prevents the OFT from intervening in relation to the adequacy or appropriateness of the price (provided plain, intelligible language has been used) the charges "will still be open to attack by the OFT on the ground that they are "unfair" as defined by reg.5(1), but that attack cannot be founded on an allegation that the Relevant Charges are excessive by comparison with the services which they purchase, for that is forbidden by Regulation 6(2)(b)" (per Lord Phillips at para.57).

The Supreme Court agreed that the charges were not penalties. As Lord Phillips explained at para.83, "It is not a breach of any of the standard form contracts under consideration to overdraw, or attempt to overdraw, on a current account."

Future solutions

On December 27, 2009, shortly after the Supreme Court judgment, the OFT **9.15** announced in a press release that it had "concluded that any investigation it were to continue into the fairness of current unarranged overdraft charging terms under the UTCCRs would have a very limited scope and low prospects of success." Other options ranged from voluntary action to legislation. It would "discuss these issues intensively with banks, consumer groups and other organisations" and report on progress by the end of March 2010.

The Supreme Court itself suggested legislation. Lord Walker, reflecting on the fact that the Government had decided to transpose the EU Directive as it stood rather than to confer the higher degree of consumer protection afforded by the national laws of some other Member States—for example, Netherlands and Spain—wondered whether "Parliament may wish to consider whether to revisit that decision." Lady Hale, though, considered

---

[17] See Lord Phillips at paras 69 and 80 and Lord Mance at para.98.

"it may not be easy to find a satisfactory solution."[18] We await the OFT's next steps with interest.

OFT v Foxtons

9.16   The OFT was more successful in its claim against Foxtons, the well-known estate agents. In *Office of Fair Trading* v *Foxtons Ltd*[19] F's terms provided for the payment by landlords of commission on the introduction of a tenant and on a renewal by or a subsequent sale to the tenant. The OFT claimed that (1) the renewal and sales commissions were not part of "the main subject matter of the contract" within reg.6(2)(a) so as to escape an assessment of fairness; (2) the terms were not "in plain, intelligible language" as required by reg.7; and (3) the provisions relating to such commissions were unfair.

Mann J. decided all these issues in the OFT's favour. (1) The renewal and sales commissions were not part of the core bargain. A typical consumer would approach F to find a tenant for an initial term; a renewal or sale would be a subsidiary matter. (2) The terms had not been drafted in plain and intelligible language. Parts of the renewal terms were too vague and hidden away in the document. (3) All the relevant provisions were unfair.

6. NOT INDIVIDUALLY NEGOTIATED

9.17   We have seen that the Regulations only control a term which has not been individually negotiated. Regulation 5 tells us that:

> (2) A term shall always be regarded as not having been individually negotiated where it has been drafted in advance and the consumer has therefore not been able to influence the substance of the term.
>
> (3) Notwithstanding that a term or certain aspects of it in a contract has been individually negotiated these Regulations shall apply to the rest of a contract if an overall assessment of it indicates that it is a pre-formulated standard contract.
>
> (4) It shall be for any seller or supplier who claims that a term was individually negotiated to show that it was.

If a consumer contract contains any express terms at all (other than subject matter, price and time for performance) all such terms will in practice be controlled except in those very rare cases where the consumer persuades the supplier to alter the terms. The words "in advance" presumably mean "before the document was presented to the consumer" and the word "therefore" was added by the 1999 Regulations in order to bring the wording more closely in line with the wording of the Directive.

If the consumer's request for a variation is met with the reply "sorry, we can't change these terms" the clause would clearly be controlled. The same would apply if the supplier said "we can't alter the term but we will give you £20 off the price"; this will be relevant in deciding whether the term was fair.

---

[18] Lord Walker at para.52. Lady Hale at para. 93.
[19] [2009] EWHC 1681 (Ch).

7. When is a Term Unfair?

Regulations 5 and 6 give effect to art.3.1 of the Directive. They provide as **9.18**
follows:

> 5 (1) A contractual term which has not been individually negotiated shall be
> regarded as unfair if, contrary to the duty of good faith, it causes a significant
> imbalance[20] in the parties' rights and obligations arising under the contract, to
> the detriment of the consumer.
> (5) Schedule 2 to these Regulations contains an indicative and non-exhaustive
> list of the terms which may be regarded as unfair.
> 6(1) Without prejudice to Regulation 12, the unfairness of a contractual term
> shall be assessed taking into account the nature of the goods or services for
> which the contract was concluded and by referring, at the time of conclusion of
> the contract, to all the circumstances attending the conclusion of the contract
> and to all the other terms of the contract or of another contract on which it is
> dependent.

It is clear from the Directive and the Regulations that the fairness of a
term must not be looked at in isolation but in the context of the contract as a
whole—including the price and the consumer's reasonable expectations. The
reference to "another contract on which it is dependent" would enable the
court to examine the terms of a contract between a lender and a debtor when
assessing the fairness of a term in a contract of guarantee or indemnity. The
Regulations mirror s.11 of UCTA (see above, para.8.43) by making the time of
the contract the critical time for assessing fairness. This time is also crucial in
deciding what damage is reasonably foreseeable (see Chapter Seven, para.7.52,
above).

The concept of "good faith" is familiar to continental lawyers: it involves
fair dealing and the absence of "sharp practice".[21] The 1994 Regulations contained a number of "good faith" guidelines—most of which were similar to
those in Sch.2 of UCTA (see para.8.47 above). They were taken from recitals
to the Directive but they did not form part of the substantive provisions and
do not appear in the 1999 Regulations.

It is to be noted that reg.5(5) above refers to "an indicative and non-
exhaustive list" of unfair terms contained in Sch.2. These are discussed
below in paras 9.31 to 9.55.

8. Plain Language and Construction

We have already come across a reference to plain language in relation to the **9.19**
core terms. Regulation 7 contains two provisions of general application. It
provides that:

> (1) A seller or supplier shall ensure that any written term of a contract is
> expressed in plain, intelligible language.

---

[20] *UK Housing Alliance (North West) Ltd v Francis* [2010] EWCA Civ 117: sale and lease back
of house fair–good faith and imbalance discussed.
[21] See the judgment of Bingham L.J. in the *Interfoto* case [1988] 2 W.L.R. 615 at 620.

(2) If there is doubt as to the meaning of any written term, the interpretation which is most favourable to the consumer shall prevail, but this rule shall not apply in proceedings brought under Regulation 12.

As the Regulations are essentially concerned with standard form contracts, the words "plain, intelligible language" will presumably be given an objective meaning so that a clause which meets the standards of the "Plain English campaign" should pass the reg.7 test. Knowledge that the particular consumer does not speak English, or that English is not his first language, will be taken into account in assessing good faith and fairness.

9.20   The requirement of plain language is greatly to be welcomed. Although the Regulations do not provide any sanction for the use of obscure language (apart from subjecting the "core terms" to statutory scrutiny) it seems clear that lack of plain language will be highly relevant to good faith and fairness.

Many clauses are being challenged on this ground. Thus the OFT Bulletins 21 and 22 list a total of 765 clauses which have been amended or deleted and of these no less than 110 related to plain, intelligible language (the second highest category, exceeded only by exemption clauses which totalled 153). It is heartening to note that from the very beginning the OFT has taken a purposive and positive approach to the issue of plain, intelligible language. For example, they have filled out the Regulations by taking the view that the "plain language" exclusion of core terms in reg.6(2) will only apply if the terms are brought to the attention of the consumer (Bulletin 1, p.8). Indeed there is a strong emphasis throughout on the principle that "before they enter into any contract consumers must be able to read and understand all its written terms" (Bulletin, 2 para.2.7 reproduced in Bulletin 4, p.13).

The following points are also worthy of note:

(1) Some firms are tending to use forms which were drafted with business customers in mind and which use language which is inappropriate to consumers.

(2) The terms must be within the understanding of ordinary consumers without legal advice.

(3) Legal jargon must be avoided. There is all the difference in the world between "all conditions and warranties are excluded" and "we are not legally responsible if the machine breaks down". Other terms to avoid include "consequential loss", "vicarious liability", "mitigation" and "this is without prejudice to your statutory rights".

(4) The need for "plain, intelligible language" goes beyond mere vocabulary and covers such matters as using short sentences, avoiding double negatives, minimizing cross-references and legibility (size and colour of print coupled with the colour and quality of the paper).

(5) A set of terms should be user-friendly and should use "we" and "you". Bulletin 3 sets out the whole of the British Fuel (Oils) Ltd's contract of domestic gas supply as a model of clear and helpful drafting. Here is one clause in that contract:

If we cannot supply you with gas for some reason which is beyond our control, for example damage to the pipeline system, then you will not be able to claim that we are in breach of our arrangement with you but we will take all steps that are reasonably practicable to secure the supply of gas to you.

In virtually all cases the central factor is one of knowledge (or lack of it). The number of consumers who know and understand what they are signing is minute. In an address given in 1997 Pat Edwards (who was then Director of Legal Affairs at the OFT) referred to the serious problem of tackling the "impenetrable jargon" in some consumer contracts but she then proceeded to sound a note of cautious optimism. She said:

"One of the most encouraging aspects . . . has been the willingness of suppliers— in the end—to rewrite their contracts totally and in plain intelligible language . . . It seems likely that the use of plain language, and the dropping of substantial unfairness, tend to go hand in hand. Doubtless, once terms are seen in the cold light of ordinary language, unfairnesses which were decently veiled by jargon and complexity stand out as the excrescences they are and the scales fall from the suppliers' eyes" (Bulletin 4, p.26).

Many examples can be found in the OFT Bulletins and in para.19 of the OFT Unfair Contract Terms Guidance. This was published in 2001 and can be downloaded from the OFT website at *www.oft.gov.uk*.

Choice of law evasion

A seller or supplier may seek to avoid the Regulations (or the Directive) by **9.21** a clause which applies, or purports to apply, the law of a non-Member State. Regulation 9 makes it clear that this is not possible if the contract has a close connection with the territory of the Member States.

9. Effect of Unfairness

Where a contract between a seller or supplier and a consumer contains an **9.22** unfair term, that term shall not be binding on the consumer (see reg.8(1)). The contract will then continue to exist without the unfair term if this is possible (see reg.8(2)).

10. Complaints and Enforcement

The 1999 Regulations beef up the enforcement powers contained in the **9.23** 1994 Regulations. They do this by (1) extending those powers beyond the OFT to a number of "qualifying bodies" and (2) conferring a number of ancillary powers to make the enforcement process easier and more effective. The statutory provisions are to be found in regs. 10–15 and Sch.1 (as amended).

Who are the "qualifying bodies" having enforcement powers?

9.24 Schedule 1 contains a list of mainly public bodies. It was amended by the Unfair Terms in Consumer Contracts (Amendment) Regulations 2001 to reflect some changes to the structure of the public bodies and to add the Financial Services Authority to the list of qualifying bodies. The list now reads as follows:

> The Information Commissioner
>
> Northern Ireland Authority Utility Regulator
>
> Ofgem
>
> Ofcom
>
> Ofwat
>
> The Rail Regulator
>
> Every weights and measures authority in Great Britain
>
> The Department of Enterprise, Trade and Investment in Northern Ireland
>
> The Financial Services Authority
>
> The Consumers' Association (Which?)

Which? is in a special position. It has power to apply for an injunction under reg.12 but no power to require production of documents or information under reg.13 and no duty to consider complaints under reg.11.

Duty to consider complaints (regs 10 and 11)

9.25 A person who alleges that a term in a contract drawn up for general use is unfair can make a complaint to the OFT and/or to a qualifying body. The OFT must consider a complaint unless (a) it appears to be frivolous or vexatious or (b) a qualifying body notifies the OFT in writing that it agrees to consider it—in which case that body must do so. In either case the OFT or the qualifying body must give reasons for a decision to apply, or not to apply for an injunction. Further (and this is of great importance in practice) in arriving at that decision the OFT or qualifying body can take into account any undertaking that has been given.

Application for injunctions (reg.12)

9.26 The OFT or any qualifying body can apply to the High Court[22] or to a county court for an injunction against any person appearing to the OFT or that body to be using or recommending an unfair term drawn up for general use in consumer contracts. This is subject to one qualification; a qualifying body

---

[22] See *Office of Fair Trading v Foxtons Ltd* [2009] EWCA Civ 288.

can only apply if it gives to the OFT not less that 14 days' written notice of its intention to do so (or such shorter period as the OFT may agree). When the matter comes to court it can grant the injunction on such terms as it thinks fit. Further, to prevent a party seeking to sidestep the injunction reg.12(4) is widely drawn. It provides that:

> An injunction may relate not only to the use of a particular contract term drawn up for general use but to any similar term, or a term having like effect, used or recommended for use by any person.

Breach of an injunction, or breach of an undertaking given to the court, will be punishable as contempt of court.

Power to obtain information and documents (reg.13)

The powers conferred by reg.13 are clearly valuable in (1) considering what **9.27** action, if any, to take on a complaint and (2) ascertaining whether there has been a breach of an undertaking or court order. For these purposes the OFT and a qualifying body can require any person to supply

(a) a copy of any document which that person has used or recommended for use, at the time the notice referred to in para.(4) below is given, as a pre-formulated standard contract in dealings with consumers;

(b) information about the use, or recommendation for use, by that person of that document or any other such document in dealings with consumers.

The power set out above is to be exercised by a notice in writing which may specify the way in which, and the time within which, it is to be complied with; it can be varied or revoked by a subsequent notice. Note that a qualifying body can only invoke (2) above where it has obtained the necessary undertaking or court order. If a party fails to comply with a reg.13 request the court can make an order to remedy the default and this can include a costs penalty against the person in default or any of its officers.

Duty of qualifying bodies to notify OFT (reg.14)

With the statutory enforcement powers widely dispersed as set out above, it **9.28** is clearly important for the information as to undertakings and court orders to be centralised and reg.14 requires qualifying bodies to notify the OFT of undertakings, court orders and applications to enforce previous court orders.

Publication, information and advice (reg.15)

Regulation 15 is largely self-explanatory and is of considerable practical **9.29** importance. It reads as follows:

> (1) The OFT shall arrange for the publication in such form and manner as it considers appropriate of:

    (a) details of any undertaking or order that are notified to it under regulation 14;
    (b) details of any undertaking given to it by or on behalf of any person as to the continued use of a term which the OFT considers to be unfair in contracts concluded with consumers;
    (c) details of any application made by it under regulation 12 and of the terms of any undertaking given to, or order made by, the court;
    (d) details of any application made by the OFT to enforce a previous order of the court.

(2) The OFT shall inform any person on request whether a particular term to which these Regulations apply has been—

    (a) the subject of any undertaking given to the OFT or notified to it by a qualifying body; or
    (b) the subject of any order of the court made upon application to it or notified to it by a qualifying body

and shall give that person details of the undertaking or a copy of the order, as the case may be, together with a copy of any amendment which the person giving the undertaking has agreed to make to the term in question.

(3) The OFT may arrange for the dissemination, in such form and manner as it considers appropriate, of such information and advice concerning the operation of these Regulations as may appear to it to be expedient to give to the public and to all persons likely to be affected by these Regulations.

Acting under this Regulation the OFT used to publish regular Bulletins setting out (1) some of the current OFT thinking and policy in exercising their enforcement powers and (2) details of action taken by the OFT (and other qualifying bodies) against named firms in relation to potentially unfair terms. This practice has ceased, but other OFT publications contain a mine of information. They can all be downloaded from the OFT website at *www. oft.gov.uk*.

11. POLICY AND PRACTICE OF THE OFT

9.30   Very few cases under the Regulations reach the courts but many thousands of clauses have been, and are still being, considered by the OFT. Thus, to take a random example, Bulletins 21 and 22 reveal that in the six months from July to December 2002 no less than 765 clauses were amended or abandoned as the result of enforcement action by the OFT under reg.10 (in the same period a further 38 clauses were revised in the light of enforcement action by other qualifying bodies—principally weights and measures authorities).

    If they consider that a complaint reveals a potentially unfair term they will adopt a three-pronged approach:

    (1) They will first open a dialogue with the firm, inviting them to modify or delete a term which, in their opinion, is unfair.

    (2) If this proves unsuccessful and unconstructive, they will seek an undertaking.

    (3) Finally, as a last resort, they will seek an injunction under reg.12.

In a Press release (33/2000) they pointed out that their success in achieving alteration to potentially unfair terms without litigation in more than 4,800 cases has saved hundreds of millions of pounds. However, in 1999 the OFT did launch proceedings against First National Bank in relation to a clause in a loan agreement which provided that contractual interest would continue to run even after judgment. The Court of Appeal held that the clause was indeed unfair but the House of Lords disagreed.[23] The litigation on bank charges is another example of the OFT's determination to curb unfair practices (above, para, 9.10).

12. CLAUSES WHICH MAY BE UNFAIR: SCHEDULE 2

As already stated (above, para.9.18), reg.5(5) provides that Sch.2 to these **9.31** Regulations contains an indicative and non-exhaustive list of the terms which may be regarded as unfair (the so-called "grey list"). The words "indicative and non-exhaustive" should be constantly borne in mind—Pt 18 of the OFT Unfair Contract Terms Guide (2001) gives examples of clauses which they consider as potentially unfair even though they are not mentioned in the Schedule.

The list in para.1 of Sch.2 comprises 17 examples lettered (a) to (q). We set them out below with a comment on each clause and, in some cases, an OFT example. The list opens with the words "Terms which have the object or effect of:" and then follow the 17 examples.

(a) excluding or limiting the legal liability of a seller or supplier in the event of **9.32** the death of a consumer or personal injury to the latter resulting from an act or omission of that seller or supplier;

Comment.   This situation is already largely covered by ss.2, 6 and 7 of UCTA—but the Regulations go beyond the Act by conferring the enforcement powers described above. Thus in one case the OFT achieved the deletion of the following clause:

The company does not accept responsibility for the failure of any fire protection equipment in the event of a fire.

In another case, a clause stated that persons using the equipment or facilities at a gymnasium did so at their own risk. It was amended so that it started with the words, "In the absence of any negligence or other breach of duty . . ."

(b) inappropriately excluding or limiting the legal rights of the consumer *vis-* **9.33** *à-vis* the seller or supplier or another party in the event of total or partial non-performance or inadequate performance by the seller or supplier of any of the contractual obligations, including the option of offsetting a debt owed to the seller or supplier against any claim which the consumer may have against him;

---

[23] *DGFT v First National Bank* [2001] UKHL 52.

Comment. The ground covered by this provision is similar to that covered by s.3(2) of UCTA in those cases where UCTA applies. It will be recalled that that section is not limited to cases of *breach* by the supplier; it could also catch a one-sided "force majeure" clause giving the supplier a right to suspend performance, or even to terminate the contract, if performance is prevented or delayed for reasons beyond the supplier's control. The reference to set-off[24] is not mirrored in UCTA and under the general law the position is as follows:

(1) Set-off is a procedural device which allows a defendant to put forward a claim (e.g. for damages for unsatisfactory quality) in reduction or extinction of the claimant's claim (e.g. for the price).

(2) If the supplier and the consumer have *liquidated* claims against each other, set-off is allowed.

(3) If the two claims arise out of the *same* transaction (a builder claims the invoice price and is met with a claim that his workmen caused damage to the consumer's house) set-off is allowed.

(4) In other cases, e.g. where the consumer claims damages for defective performance and the supplier seeks to set-off a debt due under an *earlier* transaction, set-off is not allowed.

9.34   The OFT has launched a campaign to ban "full payment in advance" terms in home improvement contracts, as these terms destroy the consumer's valuable right to set-off a claim for defective work against the price.

The following example of a para.(b) term relating to Microsoft software is a good illustration of a change in substance and in the use of plain intelligible language.

Before:

> LIMITED WARRANTY. MICROSOFT warrants that the support provided hereunder shall be substantially as described. THIS WARRANTY IS EXCLUSIVE AND IS IN LIEU OF ALL OTHER WARRANTIES AND MICROSOFT DISCLAIMS ALL OTHER WARRANTIES, EXPRESS OR IMPLIED, INCLUDING, BUT NOT LIMITED TO, WARRANTIES OF MERCHANTABILITY AND FITNESS FOR A PARTICULAR PURPOSE.

After:

> LIMITED WARRANTY. MICROSOFT warrants that it will provide Support with reasonable care, within a reasonable time and substantially as described in this Agreement. MICROSOFT does not make any other promises or warranties about Support service.

[24] *Barclays Bank v Kufner*, n.13.

This is a clear example of balancing the interests of supplier and consumer; the OFT acknowledges that the supplier also needs to protect his interests—but not to the extent provided by the original term. This group of potentially unfair terms is by far the largest section of the OFT illustrations; Bulletins 21 and 22 contain no fewer than 153 examples identified by the OFT in the six-month period (July–December 2002); they include terms excluding or limiting liability for defective performance, non-performance or delay, time limits, excluding or restricting set-off and using "guarantees" to restrict liability. We must once again stress two essential points which apply to every illustration; they merely represent the opinion of the OFT and not the opinion of a court, and each term under discussion must be considered in the context of the contract as a whole and not in isolation.

(c) making an agreement binding on the consumer whereas provision of services by the seller or supplier is subject to a condition whose realisation depends on his own will alone;   **9.35**

Comment.   This could catch a servicing agreement where the consumer was required to pay an annual fee even though the supplier might decide to discontinue carrying spare parts for that particular item (see OFT Bulletin No. 5 at p.76).

(d) permitting the seller or supplier to retain sums paid by the consumer where the latter decides not to conclude or perform the contract, without providing for the consumer to receive compensation of an equivalent amount from the seller or supplier where the latter is the party cancelling the contract;   **9.36**

Comment.   This highlights one of the key concepts of "unfairness", namely the one-sided nature of a particular provision. Essentially the clause covers three distinct situations, namely a term giving the seller or supplier the right to forfeit (1) a pre-contractual deposit, (2) a deposit liable to be forfeited if the consumer "cancels" and (3) a deposit liable to be forfeited if the consumer breaks the agreement. Under the general law (1) a pre-contractual deposit is recoverable by a consumer as of right if the contract does not happen, (2) a "cancellation" deposit is presumably forfeitable as of right as being the price paid by the consumer for a right not available to him or her under the general law and (3) a deposit payable on breach can be forfeited unless it amounts to a penalty. In all these cases a deposit (being a payment indicating that the consumer "means business") must be distinguished from a part-payment which the consumer can recover (subject to a set-off for damages) if the event giving rise to payment has not yet arrived.

The Regulations now provide that a deposit forfeiture clause may be unfair if it is not matched by a "reverse deposit"—a totally new concept. Here is an OFT illustration (omitting the company's name).

Before:

No order which has been accepted by (the Company) may be cancelled by (the Customer) except on terms that the Customer shall indemnify (the Company) in

> full against any losses and costs incurred by (them) as a result of cancellation.
> A MINIMUM CANCELLATION CHARGE of 25% OF THE CONTRACT
> PRICE WILL BE PAYABLE BY THE CUSTOMER IN THE EVENT THAT
> (THE COMPANY) ACCEPTS SUCH CANCELLATION.

After:

> You cannot cancel an order unless you . . . pay any losses and costs we suffer
> because of the cancellation. If we cancel the contract, we must pay you any losses
> or costs you suffer because of the cancellation.

Readers will be familiar with cases where a cancellation charge is imposed by
a hotel without any attempt by them to re-let the accommodation or to calculate
the costs saved by the cancellation. Such terms can now be open to challenge.

9.37   **(e)** requiring any consumer who fails to fulfil his obligation to pay a dispro-
portionately high sum in compensation;

Comment.   Under a loan agreement the *initial* rate of interest is a "core"
provision and therefore falls outside the Regulations if it is expressed in
plain, intelligible language (and it may well be that a reference to a "flat" rate
without a reference to the "true" rate based on the amount from time to time
outstanding could be attacked). Paragraph (e) relates to the rate of *default*
interest (which might be attacked under the general law as a penalty). The
word "disproportionate" must refer to the size of the transaction, the extent
of the default and to the loss that this causes to the other party. The OFT has
persuaded traders to reduce the amount of default interest on credit cards
and to replace a "termination" clause by a "suspension" clause.

9.38   **(f)** authorizing the seller or supplier to dissolve the contract on a discretionary
basis where the same facility is not granted to the consumer, or permitting
the seller or supplier to retain the sums paid for services not yet supplied to
him where it is the seller or supplier himself who dissolves the contract;

Comment.   This lack of mutuality as a key feature of unfairness has already
been mentioned in relation to para.(d). An obvious example would be a clause
in a policy of insurance giving the insurer (but not the insured) a discretionary
right to cancel the policy during the period of insurance. The OFT Bulletins
give a number of illustrations of one-sided termination rights covering a wide
variety of activities including blinds, computer systems, leases, football club
membership and satellite TV. In a widely publicised success story, the OFT
persuaded Sky TV to change its terms of business so that (1) Sky will have
no right to terminate during the "minimum period" unless the customer is in
breach and (2) more significantly, the customer will have a termination right
if, for example, Sky varies the conditions or withdraws one of the Channels
falling within the Option chosen by the customer.

9.39   **(g)** enabling the seller or supplier to terminate a contract of indeterminate
duration without reasonable notice except where there are serious grounds
for doing so.[25]

---

[25] But see below, para.9.42.

Comment. A contract of hire or storage or a contract for the provision of accommodation may give the supplier the right to terminate without notice. Clearly such a clause, which could put the consumer in great difficulty, is potentially unfair unless serious grounds exist for it. Examples of the latter would include the consumer becoming bankrupt or his cheques being dishonoured.

    (h) Automatically extending a contract of fixed duration where the consumer   **9.40**
    does not indicate otherwise, when the deadline fixed for the consumer to
    express this desire not to extend the contract is unreasonably early;

Comment. A contract of hire or a maintenance contract for one year might provide that "this contract will be automatically extended to three years unless the consumer informs the company in the first three months that he does not wish this to occur". In the vast majority of cases the consumer would be blissfully unaware of this provision until it is too late.

    (i) irrevocably binding the consumer to terms with which he had no real   **9.41**
    opportunity of becoming acquainted before the conclusion of the contract;

Comment. One obvious example would be a clause in a train ticket stating that "passengers are carried on our conditions of carriage which can be inspected at our Head Office" (see the *Thompson* case, above, para.8.09). Then again, terms not expressed in plain, intelligible language or put in minute print could be unfair under this provision. This can be regarded as one of the most important of the Sch.2 terms. In the words of the OFT (Bulletin 4, p.10):

> We interpret a 'real' opportunity as something more than the theoretical right to refer to a book held by the operator. While it is not practicable to put much information legibly on the back of a normal sized ticket, it is by no means impossible to take reasonable steps—for example by displaying posters in ticket offices—to alert consumers to, and summarise, significant provisions which they might not otherwise realise applied to them, and ignorance of which could cause them detriment.

One potential trap for consumers is the possibility that they may place an order by phone, fax or internet and then find themselves bound by conditions of sale of which they were unaware. There is a strong argument that, under general principles of contract law, the conditions will not bind the consumer because they were introduced too late (see paras 8.09–8.10, above). Quite apart from this, the OFT has persuaded a supplier to give the consumer a "money-back" seven-day cancellation right for unopened and unused goods if he does not agree to the hidden conditions.

In the context of leases the tenant may be required to observe the terms of a headlease or the terms of the landlord's insurance. The tenant will be unaware of those terms and accordingly the OFT has succeeded in obtaining deletion.

    (j) enabling the seller or supplier to alter the terms of the contract unilaterally   **9.42**
    without a valid reason which is specified in the contract[26];

---

[26] See below, para.9.44.

Comment. Under the general law neither party can vary the terms of a concluded contract, unless the contract itself gives such a right. The exercise of such a right (e.g. altering the duration of the contract or the time fixed for performance) would clearly undermine what the consumer expects and it may therefore be unfair.

The OFT attitude is that "any term in any kind of contract that effectively gives an unrestricted power to vary significant terms for captive consumers creates a contractual imbalance that is likely to be considered unfair." (Bulletin 5, p.10). This was written when criticising the terms of business of Northern Rock plc which (1) gave Northern Rock the right to restructure their customers' accounts (involving a reduction in the rates of interest) without notice to the customers and (2) prevented the customers from moving their money to another account without incurring a penalty. The OFT persuaded Northern Rock to change this policy. They also persuaded BSkyB to modify a "right to vary" clause and a ladies' health club to delete the following term:

> We reserve the right to alter hours of business if found necessary and change the annual membership system and/or price structure.

9.43   **(k)** enabling the seller or supplier to alter unilaterally without a valid reason any characteristic of the product or service to be provided;

Comment. If a building contract specifies the materials to be used, a clause giving the builder the right to substitute different materials may well be unfair.

A kitchen company was persuaded to restrict a substitution clause from "if for any reason the company is unable to supply a particular piece of furniture" to "if for any reason beyond the company's reasonable control . . ." The OFT also examined the following term in the conditions of a ferry company:

> The company accepts no liability for any inaccuracy in the information contained in this publication, which may be altered at any time without prior notice, and also reserves the right to alter, amend, or cancel any of the arrangements shown in this publication.

This was changed to:

> We reserve the right, **before you book**, to vary the services described in our brochures, including prices and departure dates, and to designate a different ferry for a particular journey.

9.44   **(l)** providing for the price of goods to be determined at the time of delivery or allowing a seller of goods or supplier of services to increase their price without in both cases giving the consumer the corresponding right to cancel the contract if the final price is too high in relation to the price agreed when the contract was concluded[27];

---

[27] See below, para.9.54.

Comment. It is common to find a price escalation clause as, for example, "the price quoted is the price prevailing at the date of the contract and the seller reserves the right to increase the price if this should prove necessary by reason of increases in the cost of work or materials". Similarly an order for a new car may contain a clause that the price will be the "price in the manufacturer's list at the date of delivery". Such clauses may be unfair, unless they give the consumer the option of pulling out.

The OFT has persuaded traders to modify price increase terms by (1) making the increases index linked (2) giving the customer a termination right if the price is increased or (3) improving that right. They also came across a term used by a trader with the improbable name of .0.0.0.0.0.0.1.A.A.A. Abbeyflow Ltd stating that "the quoted prices will be adjusted to meet any price variation in labour or materials occurring after the date of quotation". The term was deleted.

> **(m)** giving the seller or supplier the right to determine whether the goods or services supplied are in conformity with the contract, or giving him the exclusive right to interpret any term of the contract; **9.45**

Comment. In cases involving breach such a provision (e.g. "the certificate of the company's surveyor shall be conclusive") is already controlled by UCTA. Thus in relation to goods supplied to a consumer the clause would be void (see ss.6 and 7 read with s.13) while a corresponding clause relating to services would be controlled by the test of reasonableness (s.3 read with s.13). Such terms can easily mislead a consumer and the Regulations enable them to be modified or banned without the need for litigation. In another building case the clause gave the supplier the right to decide that defects had been rectified (so that he could obtain the release of money held by a third party). This was changed to a clause giving the consumer 21 days to give written confirmation of satisfaction.

> **(n)** limiting the seller's or supplier's liability to respect commitments undertaken by his agents or making his commitments subject to compliance with a particular formality; **9.46**

Comment. A clause might provide "we are not responsible for any statements made by our agents or employees in negotiating this contract unless authorised in writing by a director". Under the general law a clause limiting the authority of an agent is effective (see above, para.8.42, n.87) but in a consumer transaction the consumer is likely to rely heavily on the salesman and a "small print" clause of this type may well be unfair under the Regulations.

A common clause, which can operate unfairly, is the so-called "entire agreement" clause which effectively prevents the consumer from relying on any other document, letter or oral statement (especially promises made by an enthusiastic salesman). The matter is discussed in a five-page survey in the OFT Bulletin 2, p.14. An advertising company agreed to delete a clause which bluntly stated that "no verbal agreements will be honoured" and a security company agreed to the following plain-English variation. Before:

> All the terms of the Contract between the Company and the Customer are contained in the Contract and in these conditions and no oral or written arrangements . . . not contained in the Contract shall be in any way binding on the Company.

After:

> The Company intends to rely upon the written terms set out here and on the other side of this document. If you require any changes, please make sure that you ask for these to be put in writing. In this way we can avoid any problems surrounding what the Company and you the Customer is expected to do.

9.47   (o) obliging the consumer to fulfil all his obligations where the seller or supplier does not perform his;

Comment. The unfairness of such a provision (which overlaps with (c) above) is self-evident. In one case a clause bound ticketholders to the contract even where the supplier defaulted in supplying what was agreed at the time of ticket purchase. It was deleted.

9.48   (p) giving the seller or supplier the possibility of transferring his rights and obligations under the contract, where this may serve to reduce the guarantees for the consumer, without the latter's agreement;

Comment. Under the general law the burden of a contract cannot be assigned; the *assignor* remains liable to perform. If the contract does confer a right to assign obligations, the consumer might thereby lose the value of a long-term guarantee. The clause may therefore be unfair.

9.49   (q) excluding or hindering the consumer's right to take legal action or exercise any other legal remedy, particularly by requiring the consumer to take disputes exclusively to arbitration not covered by legal provisions, unduly restricting the evidence available to him or imposing on him a burden of proof which, according to the applicable law, should lie with another party to the contract;

Comment. This provision overlaps paragraph (m) above. The ground is already largely covered by s.13 of UCTA and by the Arbitration Act 1996 (see below, para.10.45).

Modifications

9.50 Para.2 of Sch.2 modifies three of the preceding provisions ((g), (j) and (l)); a clause which satisfies the modifying provisions is less likely to be unfair. However, it must be stressed that:

> any standard term will be seen as being unfair, whether or not it appears in (or is excluded from) the list if it fails the unfairness test . . . The purpose of the Schedule is to *illustrate this test* . . . Similarly, the restrictions to the scope of the Schedule found particularly in paragraph 2 . . . exemplify situations in which— despite their apparent similarity to what is included in the Schedule—certain

kinds of terms may nonetheless not produce "imbalance, detriment or lack of good faith". (OFT Bulletin 5, p.10.)

The modifications in para.2 are set out below.

(a) Paragraph 1(g) is without hindrance to terms by which a supplier of **9.51** financial services reserves the right to terminate unilaterally a contract of indeterminate duration without notice when there is a valid reason, provided that the supplier is required to inform the other contracting party or parties thereof immediately.

Comment.   The "valid reason" can be contrasted with "serious grounds" in para.(g). Presumably the reason is not limited to default or insolvency by the consumer but can include reasons personal to the lender (such as a decision to withdraw from house mortgage loans). Although the proviso is not expressed in plain, intelligible language, the spirit of the Regulations suggests that the reason must be set out as part of the termination terms.

(b) Paragraph 1(j) is without hindrance to terms under which a supplier of **9.52** financial services reserves the right to alter the rate of interest payable by the consumer or due to the latter, or the amount of other charges for financial services without notice where there is a valid reason, provided that the supplier is required to inform the other contracting party or parties thereof at the earliest opportunity and that the latter are free to dissolve the contract immediately.

Comment.   On a strict reading of this proviso (and the placing of the comma) the words "where there is a valid reason" appear to qualify the words "other charges" but not the words "rate of interest"; in other words a term that "the lender may by written notice increase the rate of interest payable to the lender or decrease the rate of interest payable to the borrower" would not be within para.(j) provided that it also allowed the consumer to respond to the notice by terminating the contract. This seems surprising and the French text (which omits the commas) points to a different conclusion.

Paragraph 1(j) is also without hindrance to terms under which a seller or **9.53** supplier reserves the right to alter unilaterally the conditions of a contract of indeterminate duration, provided that he is required to inform the consumer with reasonable notice and that the consumer is free to dissolve the contract.

Comment.   It will be recalled that a term may very well be unfair if it gives the supplier the right to alter the terms of the agreement and to hold the consumer to a bargain different from the one he originally made.

If the supplier finds it necessary to alter a term in a contract of indeterminate duration, this proviso allows him to insert a contractual term to that effect provided that the consumer is then given the option of walking away from the contract. This proviso is not limited to contracts for financial services.

(c) Paragraphs 1(g), (j) and (l) do not apply to: **9.54**
— transactions in transferable securities, financial instruments and other products or services where the price is linked to fluctuations in a stock

exchange quotation or index or a financial market rate that the seller or supplier does not control;
— contracts for the purchase or sale of foreign currency, traveller's cheques or international money orders denominated in foreign currency.

Comment. These two provisos permit sellers or suppliers to insert alteration/termination clauses in cases where the seller/supplier's calculations can go wildly wrong as a result of share or currency fluctuations beyond his control.

9.55   (d) Paragraph (l) is without hindrance to price-indexation clauses, where lawful, provided that the method by which prices vary is explicitly described.

Comment. A general price escalation clause may well be unfair under para. (l) above, but a clause for price adjustment by reference to (for example) the retail price index might not be caught.

Burden of Proof

9.56   The Regulations provide (reg. 5(4)) that the burden of proving that a term was individually negotiated is on the seller/supplier. It does not deal with the burden of proving that "Schedule 2" terms are fair. Although, as already stated, the Regulations merely state that these terms "may" be unfair, we consider it likely that a court (and especially a county court where most of these cases are likely to be litigated) would treat such clauses as potentially unfair and would look to the seller/supplier to prove that this is not so.

13. CONCLUSION

9.57   There is a Latin maxim *"ubi ius, ibi remedium"*[28] which broadly means that a right is valueless unless there is an effective remedy. A large part of this Chapter has dealt with enforcement by the OFT and qualifying bodies—but this is essentially machinery for protecting *future* consumers. Whether the rights of an individual consumer have any real value must depend on whether those rights can be enforced without too much hassle and expense. We shall consider this in the next two Chapters.

---

[28] Literally, "where a right, there a remedy."

CHAPTER TEN

"HOW DO I ENFORCE MY RIGHTS WITHOUT GOING TO COURT?"

In the previous chapters we have considered the consumer's rights and rem- **10.01** edies and attempts to exclude them or to cut them down. We come now to the all-important question—how can the rights be enforced? The lawyer tends to think immediately of court proceedings but in this branch of the law the courts should only be used as a last resort—if only because the cost of proceedings may exceed the amount in dispute.

Scheme of this chapter

A short introduction will be followed by an examination of codes of prac- **10.02** tice—one of the most important developments in the consumer field. Our discussion will then focus on the Ombudsman schemes which play an increasingly significant role in consumer redress. This will be followed by sections dealing with arbitration, alternative dispute resolution and legal assistance fees.

1. HOW TO START

The obvious first step is to contact the supplier. If the client himself does not **10.03** receive satisfaction he might call in to see his solicitor or a Citizen's Advice Bureau or contact the OFT helpline Consumer Direct. A letter, fax or email sent to the head office, or to the chief executive, might produce results. Alternatively, a member of the staff of the Trading Standards Department might make a telephone call or visit the shop to see what the shop has to say. These Departments are anxious to adopt a neutral role—to play the part of conciliator rather than advocate. They do, of course, compile lists of complaints and forward them from time to time to the OFT.

If the suppliers are not co-operative, the next step might be to contact their trade association. This is especially relevant if they are members of a trade association with a code of practice approved by the OFT. This is considered below.

Mention must also be made of the press, both local and national, radio and television. Many of these bodies have someone dealing with consumer matters and if they are satisfied that the consumer has had a raw deal, they may print or publish a story about it. Needless to say they will take great care to get their facts right because damages for defamation can be very high.

A consumer may want to know if other consumers have had similar experiences. Among the myriad of websites is one called *clik2complaints.co.uk*. The pages are headed "Empowering you the consumer" and "Do something about it." Consumers submit the problem; it is then published (edited if necessary) and the trader is given a right of reply.

2. CODES OF PRACTICE

A. INTRODUCTION

10.04   One method of improving standards of business practice across the board is to introduce legislation (with criminal sanctions) on such matters as safety and unfair commercial practices.[1]

Another method is to leave it to the different sectors of commerce to put their own houses in order by the introduction of voluntary codes of practice by the various trade associations. The development of voluntary codes can be regarded as one of the most significant contributions which the Fair Trading Act 1973 made to the protection of individual consumers and accordingly it may be useful to examine this topic in some detail. We shall see later that the regime introduced by the 1973 Act came to a halt in 2001 and has been replaced by the OFT's new approach under the Enterprise Act 2002.[2] Support for the existing codes was withdrawn on December 31, 2001.

Section 124(3) of the Fair Trading Act placed a duty upon the Director General to encourage associations "to prepare, and to disseminate to their members, codes of practice for guidance in safeguarding and promoting the interest of consumers". The OFT gave its support to 42 codes. These included cars, electrical appliances, travel, laundries and cleaners, mail order trading and double glazing. A list of the codes is given in the following table to show the wide range of sectors covered by this regime from 1974 to 2001.

10.05

Operative from	Code
1974	AMDEA (Association of Manufacturers of Domestic Electrical Appliances): Principles for Domestic Electrical Appliance Servicing.
1975	ABTA (Association of British Travel Agents): Codes of Conduct.
1975	VBRA (Vehicle Builders and Repairers Association): Code of Practice for Vehicle Body Repair (Motor Car and Caravan Sector).
1976	RMI (Retail Motor Industry Federation Ltd): SMTA (Scottish Motor Trade Association): SMMT (Society of Motor Manufacturers & Traders): Code of Practice for the Motor Industry.
1976	NAMSR (National Association of Multiple Shoe Repairers): Society of Master Shoe Repairers: Code of Practice for Shoe Repairs.
1976	TSA (Textile Services Association Ltd): Code of Practice for Domestic Laundry and Cleaning Services.

[1] See below, paras 15.01 and 17.25.
[2] Below, para.10.11.

1976	FDF (Footwear Distributors Federation): Code of Practice for Footwear.
1976	RETRA (Radio, Electrical and Television Retailers' Association (RETRA) Ltd): Code of Practice for the Selling and Servicing of Electrical and Electronic Appliances.
1978	MOTA (Mail Order Traders' Association): Catalogue Mail Order Code of Practice.
1979	Photographic Industry Code of Practice.
1980	DSA (Direct Selling Association Ltd): Direct Selling Code of Practice.
1981	GGF (Glass and Glazing Federation): Code of Ethical Practice.
1984	Motorcycle Code.
1987	FLA (Finance and Leasing Association): Code of Practice.
1988	CCTA (Consumer Credit Trade Association): Code of Practice.
1988	NCCF (National Consumer Credit Federation): Code of Practice.
1988	CCA (Consumer Credit Association of the United Kingdom): Code of Practice.
1989	LPFA (London Personal Finance Association Ltd): Code of Practice.
1989	British Holiday and Home Parks Association Ltd: National Caravan Council: Code of Practice for Letting Holiday Caravans. Code of Practice for Selling and Siting Holiday Caravans.
1989	SMMT (Society of Motor Manufacturers and Traders): Code of Practice for Mechanical Breakdown Insurance Schemes.
1989	BDMA (British Direct Marketing Association Ltd): Direct Marketing Code of Practice.
1991	CSA (Credit Services Association): Code of Practice.
1995	BVRLA (British Vehicle Rental and Leasing Association): Code of Conduct.
1995	BRC (British Retail Consortium): Code of Practice for Extended Warranties on Electrical Goods.
1996	ABIA (Association of British Introduction Agencies): Code of Practice for Introduction Agencies.
1997	STAR (Society of Ticket Agents and Retailers): Code of Practice.
1998	OEA (Ombudsman for Estate Agents Scheme): Code of Practice for Residential Estate Agents.
1998	NTDA (National Tyre Distributors Association): Code of Practice for Tyre and Fast Fit Trade.

Advantages?

Whether voluntary codes and self-regulation are to be preferred to legislation **10.06**
is a matter of debate. The advantage from the point of view of industry is

that traders are allowed to police themselves, but this in turn may be disadvantageous to the consumer. It is clear from the results of monitoring exercises undertaken by the OFT that, predictably, not every member of a trade association honours its code. More surprisingly, not every trade association checks to ensure that its members follow the code, which is such a serious failing as to prevent the code being approved under the new OFT regime (see below para.10.11).[3]

Another serious disadvantage of relying on voluntary methods is that, even if all members of an association comply with their obligations, the rogues in the trade may well not be members. This is particularly true of the motor trade. The OFT must then turn to other weapons in its armoury, e.g. an enforcement order under the Enterprise Act 2002[4] or refusing a credit brokerage licence under the Consumer Credit Act 1974.[5]

However, some advantages can be cited. (1) Legislation would necessarily be of a general nature and inappropriate for setting precise standards for a particular industry, for example, pre-delivery inspections of cars or service calls within three days for electrical appliances. (2) Businesses are more likely to comply with their own optional rules than with statutory obligations imposed against their will. (3) Codes can be improved by renegotiation; for example, the ABTA Code was amended after a year to include surcharges and overbooking, both common causes of complaint. (4) Codes go beyond the existing law, in recommending practices which impose on suppliers obligations or restrictions not otherwise attaching to them, and thus consumers' rights are enhanced.[6] (5) The opportunity for conciliation and arbitration affords a cheap and quick mode of resolving disputes instead of taking action in the courts.[7]

Sanctions for non-compliance

10.07   An increasingly important question is how codes of practice should be enforced. The most obvious way is for the trade association itself to deal with recalcitrant members. Some associations have very wide powers, including fines and expulsion, and are prepared to use them. However, many have no real sanctions and can do little more than apply the "club" threat of social ostracism by their peers. The existence of sanctions is a crucial factor, if a code is to become an OFT Approved code.

It has been suggested, optimistically in our view, that an individual consumer may enforce a code against a member of a trade association by claiming that a breach of contract occurs when a trader fails to comply with a practice, on the basis that the contract includes an implied term that the

---

[3] On monitoring and other aspects of codes see Woodroffe, "Government Monitored Codes of Practice in the United Kingdom" (1984) 7 *Journal of Consumer Policy* 171; Cranston, *Consumers and the Law* (2nd edn), pp.31–42.
[4] Below, para.17.18.
[5] Below, para.20.03.
[6] For examples, see Woodroffe, n.3, above.
[7] For an assessment of trade arbitrations, see *Simple Justice*, National Consumer Council (1979), especially pp.71–82.

trader will comply with the code. In view of the limitations placed by the courts on implied terms such a plea is unlikely to succeed.[8] Of course, it is possible for a consumer to incorporate a code expressly when making the contract, but it would be unrealistic to expect all but the most enthusiastic and well-informed consumers to remember to refer to the point in their conversation when ordering a carpet or taking a car in for a body repair.

In contrast the criminal law will sometimes provide a more effective route. **10.08** For example, the Consumer Protection from Unfair Trading Regulations 2008[9] contain a number of provisions about codes of conduct, e.g. Sch.1: "1. Claiming to be a signatory to a code of conduct when the trader is not".[10]

On the assumption that self-regulation was not as effective a method of controlling business suppliers as it should be, two solutions were canvassed to give teeth to the codes. The less ambitious proposal was to amend s.34 of the Fair Trading Act 1973[11] so as to extend the definition of "unfair" to include non-compliance with a code of practice supported by the OFT. The virtue of such a change would be that the codes would then be made to apply to *all* members of a particular trade. This very change was recommended by the National Consumer Council in 1997 in its report *Unfair Trading*.

Duty to trade fairly

A much more far-reaching proposal, embracing the extension of s.34, was **10.09** to impose on traders a statutory "duty to trade fairly". A suggestion to this effect was put forward by Lord Borrie, the then Director General of Fair Trading, in a lecture[12] discussing the self-regulatory system of advertising control:

> "The duty not to publish misleading advertisements could be seen as a precursor to a more general statutory duty to trade fairly in consumer transactions, a duty which would not be enforceable apart from sectoral or general retail codes of practice giving it practical expression. Such codes could be prepared by the DGFT after consultation with relevant trade associations and the codes would need to be given some form of ministerial or parliamentary approval before becoming effective."

The OFT floated the idea in March 1982 in *Home Improvements: A Discussion Paper* and followed this up in 1986 with a discussion paper, *A General Duty to Trade Fairly*. However, such a bold approach was not welcomed by industry in a period of free market economy. Indeed the Government's policy at the time can be discerned from the titles of two White Papers—*Lifting the Burden* and *Building Business . . . not Barriers*.[13] In the end the Director General reluctantly admitted in *Trading Malpractices*[14]

---

[8] The narrow "business efficacy" test in *The Moorcock* (1889) 14 P.D. 64.
[9] See below, para.17.25 and Appendix Four.
[10] See also Sch.1, para.3, and reg.5(3)
[11] Discussed in Ch.17, below, para.17.08.
[12] "Laws and Codes for Consumers" [1980] J.B.L. 315 at 324.
[13] Cmnd. 9571 (1985) and Cm. 9794 (1986) respectively.
[14] OFT (July 1990), para.1.5. The arguments for and against the general duty appear on p.21.

that "the original proposals were over-ambitious in aiming in one provision both to raise trading standards generally and to improve the prospects for consumer redress" and came down in favour of a complete overhaul of Pt III of the Fair Trading Act 1973. More than a decade later that happened when the Enterprise Act 2002 repealed Pt III.[15]

The idea of a duty to trade fairly, though, did not go away. New impetus came from the European Commission which on June 18, 2003 proposed a Directive on Unfair Commercial Practices.[16] The Directive was duly adopted on May 11, 2005 and is considered with the 2008 Regulations in Chapter Seventeen.

"Raising Standards"

10.10 The early optimism engendered by self-regulation and the proliferation of codes supported by the OFT subsided in the late 1990s. At the end of 1996 the OFT issued a consultation paper *Voluntary Codes of Practice*. This was followed in February 1998 with its report *Raising Standards of Consumer Care—Progressing beyond codes of practice*. The OFT's suggested change in policy was set out on p.5 of the report:

> The main change suggested is to introduce standards to replace codes, with a core standard applicable to all business and sectoral versions where necessary. A key element would be access to effective, low-cost independent redress, without recourse to the courts. The standards would be drawn up under the British Standards Institution, and all those with a direct interest would participate. To administer the new scheme, the OFT proposes the creation of a new approval body that would vet all applicants, monitor their behaviour and deal with complaints. Successful applicants would be required to agree to follow the relevant standard. In return, they would be able to use a new, cross-sectoral quality logo.

B. OFT APPROVED CODES OF PRACTICE

Modern markets: confident consumers

10.11 The DTI (now BIS) did not take up the proposal to introduce standards instead of codes when it published its important and extensive White Paper, *Modern markets: confident consumers* (Cm.4410) in July 1999. However, in its new approach to codes it accepted that effective redress was vital and that a logo to identify approved codes was desirable. Its support for codes was made clear in para.4.3.

> Codes of practice can play an important part in protecting consumers' rights and in offering a higher level of consumer protection and service than the basics set down in law. Consumers with a complaint to make overwhelmingly turn first, as they should, to the seller for a solution. Codes are a way for:

---

[15] Below, para.17.13.
[16] Directive concerning unfair business-to-consumer commercial practices in the internal market (COM (2003) 356 final).

- *business* to assure customers that they will get value and that, if there is a problem, there is an effective way to solve it. And for business to gain a marketing advantage by using a code's logo in their advertising.
- *consumers* to know that they are dealing with a reliable supplier, and that redress is accessible if something goes wrong.

In due course many of the proposals in the White Paper were implemented by the Enterprise Act 2002. Section 8(2) gives the OFT the power to approve consumer codes and s.8(3) imposes a duty to specify the criteria for approval. Section 8 provides as follows:

(1) The OFT has the function of promoting good practice in the carrying out of activities which may affect the economic interests of consumers in the United Kingdom.

(2) In carrying out that function the OFT may (without prejudice to the generality of subsection (1)) make arrangements for approving consumer codes and may, in accordance with the arrangements, give its approval to or withdraw its approval from any consumer code.

(3) Any such arrangements must specify the criteria to be applied by the OFT in determining whether to give approval to or withdraw approval from a consumer code.

(4) Any such arrangements may in particular—

(a) specify descriptions of consumer code which may be the subject of an application to the OFT for approval (and any such description may be framed by reference to any feature of a consumer code, including the persons who are, or are to be, subject to the code, the manner in which it is, or is to be, operated and the persons responsible for its operation); and

(b) provide for the use in accordance with the arrangements of an official symbol intended to signify that a consumer code is approved by the OFT.

(5) The OFT shall publish any arrangements under subsection (2) in such manner it considers appropriate.

(6) In this section "consumer code" means a code of practice or other document (however described) intended, with a view to safeguarding or promoting the interests of consumers, to regulate by any means the conduct of persons engaged in the supply of goods or services to consumers (or the conduct of their employees or representatives).

New approach

The OFT issued a consultation paper (OFT 331) in February 2001 on its **10.12** new approach and published its response in July 2001: *Consumer codes of practice: the OFT's response to the consultation* (OFT 344). It confirmed its view that "codes of practice should deliver benefits to consumers beyond the law". It set out the core criteria to form the basis of the new regime, which in amended form appear in Appendix Two of this book. It specified seven priority sectors:

Used cars
Car repair and servicing
Credit

Funerals
Travel
Estate Agents
Direct marketing.

Furniture and domestic appliance repair were added in December 2002. "Our prime targets in drawing up a list of priority sectors are high risk/cost transactions where consumers are most vulnerable" (para.3.19). So far disappointingly, only two have been approved: car repair and estate agents.

Two stages

10.13   A two stage approach has been adopted:

> *Stage One*   Code sponsors, such as trade associations, will develop codes which comply with the core criteria. If successful, they will be informed by the OFT that they have "achieved stage one status".
>
> *Stage Two*   They will then be invited to take part in Stage Two, when they must prove that they have fulfilled the promises made at Stage One. If successful the OFT will endorse and promote the code, which can then be used in the businesses' marketing by displaying the logo "OFT Approved code".

It is proving to be a thorough, but rather slow, process indicating a justified reluctance of the OFT to approve codes which do not meet its strict criteria precisely. Stage Two inevitably cannot be rushed, since the OFT require evidence to verify that the code sponsors' promises made at Stage One have been performed; so, for example, the OFT must monitor the monitoring carried out by the trade associations.

However, this painstaking scrutiny of codes is causing disappointment and frustration in some sectors where code sponsors, though initially keen to gain approval, are losing their enthusiasm for the new regime. It may become difficult for the OFT to encourage businesses to devote considerable time and resources to bringing their existing codes up to the standard required by the core criteria, when so few have surmounted the hurdles of Stages One and Two during the last eight years. An illustration of the time-consuming process is the Carpet Foundation's code. It was submitted to the OFT for assessment in October 2004, completed Stage One in August 2005 and became an approved code in January 2007—27 months for a simple sector of business. SafeBuy has been stalled at Stage One for four years.

The three main elements causing lengthy negotiations appear to be that the codes must include (1) rights for consumers which go beyond their existing rights rather than merely state that members comply with the law; (2) real sanctions against members for non-compliance; (3) monitoring procedures to check compliance by members and consumer satisfaction.

So far nine codes have achieved full OFT approval by reaching Stage Two,   **10.14**
while four are en route at Stage One.

Stage One

    SafeBuy
    Renewable Energy Association
    Institute of Professional Willwriters
    Motor Codes Ltd (Service and Repair)

Stage Two

    Bosch Car Service
    The Carpet Foundation
    The Property Ombudsman Ltd (Sales)
    Direct Selling Association
    Motor Codes Ltd (New Car Code)
    Vehicle Builders and Repairers Association Ltd
    British Association of Removers
    Debt Managers Standards Association
    British Healthcare Trades Association

The Association of British Travel Agents (ABTA) also reached Stage Two
in September 2005 but withdrew from the scheme after a year because of
changes to its financial protection arrangements.

Core criteria

The "core principles" were outlined in the White Paper. These have been   **10.15**
translated in detail into the core criteria. In May 2002 the OFT published
*Core criteria for consumer codes of practice. Guidance for those drawing up
codes of practice* (OFT 390). It was updated in March 2008 and is available
on the OFT website at *www.oft.gov.uk/codes*. We comment now on some of
the criteria.

General Principles   **10.16**

The core criteria are preceded in the OFT *Guidance* by some general principles which "before reading the detail of the core criteria it is important to
understand". These principles are set out in paras 1.1 to1.7 of the *Guidance*
and appear along with the core criteria in Appendix Two of this book.

Content (para.3)   **10.17**

Various unrelated matters are contained in this section (paras 3a to 3l).
They include staff training, high-pressure selling, delivery dates, cancellation
rights, warranties and protection of prepayments.

Complaints (para.4)

10.18 Procedures must be "speedy, responsive, accessible and user friendly". This rubric applies to both complaints handling and redress schemes. Pre-contractual material must publicise access to the system. Conciliation should be available.

Low cost redress is probably the most important feature of all. Decisions must be binding on the business, but not on the consumer who may still go to court if dissatisfied. (This is similar to ombudsman schemes, but contrasts with normal arbitration where a decision is binding on both parties and blocks off access to the courts.) As the criterion states, it is "to act as an alternative to seeking court action *in the first instance*" (our emphasis).

10.19 *Monitoring (para.5)*

A vital feature is the development of performance indicators (e.g. mystery shopping) to measure the effectiveness of the code and consumer satisfaction.

The code sponsor must provide the OFT with a written report annually with information on complaints, conciliations and its redress scheme, and also on monitoring and its disciplinary process.

10.20 *Enforcement (para.6)*

There must be procedures for handling non-compliance by code members, including independent disciplinary procedures, and a range of sanctions for non-compliance, e.g. fines and expulsion.

Conciliation and arbitration

10.21 As we have just seen in para.10.18, the criteria for an Approved code require conciliation to be available and all the codes discussed below include it. We suggested in para.10.03 that dissatisfied customers should first bring their complaints to the attention of the manager of the business. If the complaint is not resolved, then it may be appropriate to seek the help of Consumer Direct or a Citizens' Advice Bureau. If the complaint relates to new goods, the customer may agree to the manufacturer being brought in. Where the dispute is still not settled and the trader is a member of a trade association, the customer should ask the association to conciliate. No charge is made for this service.

However, it should be remembered that the association may appear to the consumer, rightly or wrongly, to lack impartiality and to be prejudiced in favour of its own member.[17]

Where a code provides for arbitration[18] the customer is required to pay a small fee, often refundable where the claim is upheld: this is the limit of

---

[17] cf. Ombudsman schemes, where independence and impartiality are prerequisites to membership of BIOA (below, para.10.38).

[18] A NCC report on research into arbitration schemes, *Out of Court*, is discussed by Goriely in (1991) N.L.J. 535.

liability where the arbitration is on the basis of "documents only". The fee does not cover the full cost of arbitration, the balance being borne by the trade association. Normally the arbitration will be "documents only", for the expense of oral arbitrations is prohibitive.

Publicity and information

It is not enough to introduce legislation and codes of practice to bolster the **10.22** consumer in his perpetual confrontation with the business world. Such rights are useless unless he knows of them and can exercise them. To ensure that as far as possible the consumer is made aware of his rights the Enterprise Act 2002, s.6, provides that the OFT "has the function of"[19] giving information and advice to the public. The core criteria also require publicity by code sponsors.

It is difficult to know whether the effect of consumer legislation and the codes has been to improve the quality of goods and services. The statistics given in the OFT's Annual Reports show a fairly steady level of complaints running at about 600,000 a year during the 1970s and 1980s. The 1993 Annual Report revealed that 769,518 complaints were received by trading standards departments and Citizens Advice Bureaux in 1992–1993. This upward trend has continued and the OFT Annual Report for 2006 discloses that Consumer Direct, the help-line run by the OFT, recorded 963,684 complaints from February 2006 (when it became a national service) to December 2006. What is significant is that "research indicated that only about one per cent of people who felt they had a reason to complain about goods or services" sought the help of these agencies.[20] Clearly the reported figures are merely the tip of the iceberg.

The main culprits have regularly been motor vehicles, furniture and floor coverings, household appliances and electronic equipment, and clothing and footwear, with secondhand cars usually taking the gold or silver medal. One area giving an increasingly major headache to consumers, particularly in view of the large sums of money usually at risk, is that of home improvements (including double glazing); it continues to figure prominently in the top ten of this unenviable "top of the pops".

As we pointed out earlier,[21] the OFT withdrew support from the existing codes at the end of 2001 and we commented on them in some detail in the first six editions of this book. We now turn our attention to the nine OFT Approved codes.

C. NINE APPROVED CODES

New cars: Motor Codes Ltd

The Society of Motor Manufacturers and Traders was one of the first trade **10.23** associations to gain the support of the OFT to its code of practice in 1976. Its

---

[19] cf. the Consumer Credit Act 1974, s.4, which imposes a *duty* on the OFT to disseminate information and advice about the operation of the Act and the credit facilities available to the public.
[20] OFT Press Release, June 27, 1991.
[21] Para.10.04.

New Car Code of Practice was the first to receive OFT approval in September 2004. Motor Codes Ltd, a wholly-owned subsidiary of SMMT, was formed to administer the New Car Code from January 2009. It was relaunched in April 2009 as the Motor Industry Code of Practice for New Cars. It is more limited than the original code in that it covers only the sales of new cars and their warranties and imposes duties on manufacturers only (SMMT members) and not on car dealers. It is 19 pages long, though much is only advice to buyers, lists of legislation and illustrations.

Manufacturers' warranty

Transfers to subsequent owners should be allowed. The consumer may take the car to any franchised dealer in Europe for rectification work. An extension of the warranty period may be given when the car has been off the road for an extended period because of faults.

Spare parts

These will be readily available to authorised networks for a reasonable period after production of a model has ceased.

Complaints

The following procedure is laid down:

   (a) First refer the complaint to the dealer, addressing it to a senior executive, director or proprietor.

   (b) If the dealer does not resolve the matter, contact the manufacturer direct.

   (c) If no satisfactory solution is reached, contact the Code Advisory and Conciliation Service. It will try to effect a settlement between the consumer and its member.

   (d) If conciliation fails, it will arrange for arbitration. The arbitration will normally be "documents only".

Body repairs: VBRA

10.24   The Vehicle Builders and Repairers Association's Consumer Code of Practice has its origins in 1975 when the OFT first gave its support to it. It became an OFT Approved code in October 2004. It is concerned mainly with repairs to car bodies.

    It deals with estimates and quotations. Warranties for workmanship must last for at least 24 months or 24,000 miles, whichever occurs first.

    The complaints procedure follows the pattern outlined earlier. First complain to the trader. Then proceed to use the VBRA Conciliation Service. No fee is payable for conciliation.

    As a last resort arbitration is available. It is normally on a "documents only" basis.

Bosch Car Services: BCS

Robert Bosch Ltd is the first organisation to obtain OFT approval to a code **10.25** within the car repair and service sector. Members of the code are independent garages.

It deals with pre-contractual information, including completion times, and the offer of a detailed written estimate. It also covers guarantees and protection for pre-payments.

The usual complaints procedure is adopted—conciliation and arbitration. Monitoring and disciplinary provisions are included.

Direct selling: DSA

The Direct Selling Association Code of Practice for Consumers was drawn **10.26** up in 1980 by the Direct Selling Association in consultation with the OFT after an OFT study had identified consumer problems arising out of party plan selling. It became an Approved code in December 2004. Some detailed changes were made in March 2010 to comply with the CPR.

Cancellation and deposits

Members should not insist on payment in full when the order is placed. Customers are given a 14-day cancellation period; any deposit is then to be refunded. However, customers may now have a statutory right of cancellation by reason of the Doorstep Regulations 2008 (para.6.24).

Complaints

There is an unusual complaints procedure which is an improvement on the usual conciliation procedure. Initially a complaint may be referred to the Association. If it is not then resolved by the member company within 21 days, it passes to the Association's Code Administrator, a post created especially for this purpose. Unlike arbitration, however, if the customer is dissatisfied with the Administrator's adjudication, it is still open to him to seek redress in the county court.

Sanctions

The Code Administrator has various powers, where a member is in breach of the code, including an award of compensation of up to £5,000. He may "recommend" that the member appear before the Disciplinary Committee, which has a majority of independent members and can make a "recommendation" to the DSA council that the member be expelled (the most serious sanction). Are "recommendations" perhaps too weak, rather than "orders"?

Removals: BAR

The British Association of Removers (BAR) secured OFT approval for its **10.27** code in February 2008.

Cancellation

Among its many provisions one is worthy of note. If the remover cancels within 10 working days or less of the removal date, the customer will obtain a full refund plus 50 per cent. Such a late "cancellation" (a euphemism for an anticipatory breach of contract) may well cause a customer greater loss, e.g. in finding another, more expensive remover at short notice. Presumably this apparently generous clause is not intended to be an exemption clause in disguise, as the Code states "Nothing in this Code affects the contractual or statutory rights. . . of the Customer". Only a sceptic would wonder, though, whether it may mislead customers into believing that it is a cap on liability.

Complaints

The complaints procedure, as usual, includes conciliation and low-cost arbitration. However, arbitration is "subject to certain limits. . . available on request", a rather enigmatic statement which lacks transparency. There is an independent disciplinary panel to enforce the code.

Estate agents: Property Ombudsman

10.28 The Code of Practice of the Property Ombudsman is unique among the OFT codes in that it was prepared by an Ombudsman Scheme. It became an Approved code in September 2005. Initially it covered corporate estate agents only, e.g. the national agencies owned by building societies. The Ombudsman for Estate Agents (OEA) since 1998 has been open to independent residential estate agents who have chosen to join the OEA.

It changed its name to the Property Ombudsman in May 2009 and the code is now called the TPO Code of Practice for Residential Sales.

As well as being an Approved code it is one of the two codes so far approved by the OFT to run an estate agents redress scheme under the Consumer, Estate Agents and Redress Act 2007. This amended[22] the Estate Agents Act 1979 and made it compulsory for estate agents to join an approved redress scheme by October 2008. (The other approved redress scheme is the Surveyors Ombudsman Service (SOS) set up by the Royal Institution of Chartered Surveyors. The OFT is currently considering an application by a third organisation.)

The Code applies only to residential buildings sold with vacant possession. It protects the public against many malpractices hitherto rife in this sector. Of its many, detailed and valuable provisions we highlight the following.

10.29 *Instructions*

Agents must give their clients written details of their fees and terms of business. The fees will be due only if a purchaser exchanges contracts to buy the property, unless otherwise stated. Phrases such as "sole agency" must be explained in writing. They must not misrepresent the value of the property to gain instructions—asking prices must reflect market conditions.

---

[22] 2007 Act, s.53 and Sch.6.

Offers

They must tell clients quickly about all offers. When an offer is accepted subject to contract, they must ask the seller whether to withdraw it from the market; if it is not withdrawn, they must advise the buyer in writing.

Conflict of interest

The common malpractice of agents buying properties from their clients sur-reptitiously, perhaps through a nominee, is banned: they must inform the client and his solicitor in writing, before negotiations begin, of the conflict.

Complaints

As usual the first step is to use the member's in-house complaints procedure. If the complaint is not resolved, customers may go to the TPO provided they do so within six months of the "final view" given by the member. The virtue of this being an Ombudsman scheme is that the decision (including any award) is binding on the estate agent, but not on the customer who may reject it and go to court.

Disciplinary matters for non-compliance with the code are dealt with by the TPO Council from which the member may appeal to the Appeals Committee.

Carpets: Carpet Foundation

In January 2007 the OFT approved the Carpet Foundation Consumer Code **10.30** of Practice for exclusive use by Registered Specialist Retailers. It has two categories of members: manufacturers (owners of the "Quality Mark") and over 1,000 independent retailers known as "Registered Specialists". The code covers the sale and fitting of domestic carpets.

Terms of business

They must be written and include deposits, delivery, guarantees and quotations.

Quotations

"Estimates" are "the approximate costs" and "should be taken as a guide only". A "quotation" has "details of what is, and what is not, included", which presumably denotes a fixed price contract, and remains valid for at least 30 days.

Delivery

Where unreasonable delays occur, the consumer may be offered an alternative product and can cancel the order.

Deposits

In cases of liquidation other Carpet Foundation (CF) manufacturers will fulfil the order at the agreed price. The retailer will make a refund, where a customer cancels on reasonable grounds, e.g., divorce, serious illness.

Guarantees

There are four guarantees:

(1) two years for faults in a CF manufacturer's carpet;

(2) two years for pile reversal in a CF manufacturer's carpet;

(3) one year only for faults in a non-CF carpet;

(4) one year for installation faults by the retailer.

Complaints

As usual first complain to the retailer. The manufacturer will be brought in if it is a manufacturing fault. Next comes the CF Conciliation Service via their Technical Director. Finally arbitration by the British Carpet Technical Centre is available for £55 + VAT for each party—no subsidy by the retailer.

Sanctions

Non-compliance with the code may lead to referral by the CF to its Independent Non-Compliance Panel, which may expel members.

Debt management: DEMSA

10.31   The Debt Managers Standards Association (DEMSA) received OFT approval for its code in December 2008. It represents companies which, for a fee, act for debtors in negotiating with creditors to repay their debts. (A better route for debtors is to seek free advice from a CAB or money advice centre!)

Advertising

Members "must never" claim that their services are "free of charge" or an unrealistic, high rate of success in securing the writing off of debts.

OFT guidance

Members must comply with the OFT Debt Management Guidance Notes.

Information

They must give details of management fees, including the estimated total cost and duration of the contract. Customers will be given an opportunity to withdraw.

Complaints

The usual sequence is adopted: complain to the member, then to DEMSA which has a Code Administrator to deal with conciliation and disciplinary matters. If still dissatisfied customers may go to the Financial Ombudsman Service. DEMSA has an Independent Compliance and Disciplinary Panel with the usual sanctions.

IVAs

There is a detailed annex about Individual Voluntary Agreements.

Healthcare products: BHTA

The British Healthcare Trades Association (BHTA) has had an OFT   **10.32**
Approved code since September 2009. Its members supply various equipment
and other products, e.g. stair lifts, mobility vehicles, prosthetics. Such sales
often involve home visits.

The code runs to 21 pages and includes the following noteworthy provisions. (Section 14 applies only to "Commercial/Businesses Relationships"
and falls outside the Approved code.)

Contractual matters

A copy of the code must be provided on every home visit. If a deposit is not
refundable, this must be made clear when an order is placed.

A paradoxical provision states "All verbal [sic] claims or provisions. . .
must be put in writing". Presumably the ambiguous adjective "verbal" means
"oral" here. More importantly, does BHTA hope to exclude the liability of a
member with regard to an oral statement by a salesman, whether it would be
a misrepresentation or a contractual term? If a salesman intentionally or negligently misleads a customer, it is unlikely that he will prejuduce his employer
by later reducing the statement into writing. In any case, we consider the
clause to be ineffective if only because it is contradictory.

After-Sales service

A request for repair or service will be met with a home visit within three
working days.

Distance selling

Where a sale is initiated via the internet or mail order and the product is of
a type where an assessment is necessary to check whether it is appropriate to
the customer's needs, no purchase may occur unless a home visit and demonstration have taken place for that purpose.

Complaints

The customer must take the usual steps — first complain to the member,
then to the BHTA (itself called the "Code Administrator") and finally
resort to arbitration. Disciplinary matters are dealt with by the Disciplinary
Committee with an independent chairman.

3. PUBLIC UTILITIES—NEW CONSUMER COUNCILS

In September 1998 the Government published a consultation paper setting   **10.33**
out proposals for consumer councils for the energy, water and telecommuni-

cations sectors. Since then (1) a Consumer Council for the Gas and Electricity Industry has been set up under the Utilities Act 2000; (2) a Consumer Council for the Water Industry was set up in October 2005: Water Voice; and (3) the mammoth Communications Act 2003 required the regulator OFCOM to establish a Consumer Panel (membership to be approved by the Secretary of State) while ss.52–54 require public providers to establish independent dispute resolution procedures. The Consumers, Estate Agents and Redress Act 2007 made further changes by giving to the new National Consumer Council ("Consumer Focus") the functions of Postwatch and Energywatch.

These bodies assist consumers in three ways:

(a) they act as independent and influential consumer advocates with a voice at the heart of the regulatory system—advising utility regulators, utility companies and others on consumer issues;

(b) they have the specific task of handling consumer complaints against utility companies where they have not been resolved by the company concerned. They will be expected to mediate a satisfactory settlement wherever possible; if enforcement action is necessary they will pass the complaint to the relevant regulatory authority. They will also be expected to work with the utility companies to reduce the causes of complaints. Hopefully, the councils will succeed in resolving disputes without the need for litigation;

(c) they should provide consumers with good quality information and advice on how to get the best deal from the utility markets; influential councils and well-informed consumers can play a key part in driving standards up and prices down.

A former energy Minister John Battle told consumers to put behind them the traditional British reluctance to complain. He urged them to "expect and demand good service, remembering that you can take your business elsewhere. In the United Kingdom, the most open energy market in the world, it's cool to complain." (DTI Press Notice P/99/617).

4. OMBUDSMAN SCHEMES

Comparison with codes of practice

10.34   We have already suggested that from the consumer's point of view codes of practice suffer from the disadvantage that they do not appear to provide a completely impartial method of resolving disputes. However, the OFT's new approach to codes with its stringent core criteria for Approved codes will strengthen the consumer's position in those sectors where codes are ultimately approved.[23] As conciliation is often carried out by employees of the relevant trade association, there may be some justification for the scepticism of consumers in believing that he who pays the piper calls the tune.

---

[23] Above, para.10.11.

Of course, where a code of practice gives a complainant the opportunity of going to arbitration—and we have seen that not all codes do so—then without doubt the arbitrator will act independently and reach a fair and impartial conclusion. However, it should be remembered that although conciliation is free, the consumer must usually pay for arbitration. Then again a decision by an arbitrator is binding on the parties and final—the claimant cannot ignore it and later sue in the courts. None of these disadvantages is present in the ombudsmen schemes discussed below. All of the ombudsmen are independent and impartial. In every case the service is provided free of charge. If the complainant rejects the ombudsman's decision, litigation in the courts is almost always still available.

If then codes of practice have not provided consumers with suitable redress **10.35** procedures, are other routes of alternative dispute resolution (usually nowadays blessed with the acronym ADR) to be preferred? *Raising Standards*[24] came down firmly in favour of ombudsmen schemes in 1998:

> Use indicates that ombudsmen schemes are more popular with consumers than is trade-association-sponsored independent arbitration. There are a number of perceived benefits. They include: the fact that they are free to consumers; the ombudsman's ability to investigate cases as well as adjudicate on them; and the general perception (perhaps largely based on the objective stance perceived to have been taken by the better known operators in the financial services sector) that ombudsmen appear to be impartial. In response to the OFT's earlier consultation paper, some consumer bodies felt that arbitration was not suitable for consumer problems. Their view was that the nature of the process, with the element of legal confrontation, was off-putting. They also considered that successful arbitration required some semblance of equity in the knowledge and abilities of the parties, which is seldom present in consumer cases. Ombudsmen schemes also seem preferable from the OFT's perspective. (para.3.43)

This official support for ombudsmen was preceded by judicial support in the shape of Lord Woolf, whose proposed reforms of litigation—case management, practice, procedure, costs—came into force in April 1999. *Access to Justice*, his interim report to the Lord Chancellor in June 1995, recommended:

> 63. The retail sector should be encouraged to develop private ombudsman schemes to cover consumer complaints similar to those which now exist in relation to service industries; the government should facilitate this.
> 64. The relationship between ombudsmen and the courts should be broadened, enabling issues to be referred by the ombudsman to the courts and the courts to the ombudsman with the consent of those involved.

Background

The origins of ombudsman schemes can be found in the Nordic countries. **10.36** In the United Kingdom most of the schemes have been set up by statute and many, particularly the earlier schemes, are concerned with complaints about the activities of public bodies, including central and local government. Others,

[24] Above, para.10.10.

though, are voluntary and were set up at the expense of the businesses concerned to deal with complaints about particular sectors of the service industries. All the schemes have one thing in common, namely they exist to deal with complaints from members of the public about the way in which members of the schemes carry out their business, e.g. delay, carelessness, inefficiency or discourtesy. Ombudsmen must not be confused with regulators such as Ofcom or the Financial Services Authority, as the sole function of ombudsmen is to provide redress to individuals, not to control or supervise a business sector.

Ombudsman Association (BIOA)

10.37　The use of the term "Ombudsman" can be misleading in that it gives the impression that, whenever the word is used, the adjudicator will be impartial. It is a matter of regret that sometimes the term is used to describe someone who is concerned with handling complaints either on behalf of a trade association or even on behalf of a single organisation such as a newspaper or local authority; obviously in neither of these cases is the person independent.

To enable the public to identify genuine, independent ombudsmen the British and Irish Ombudsman Association was set up in 1993. Only those schemes are admitted to voting membership which satisfy its strict criteria, namely independence, effectiveness, fairness and public accountability. Of these four factors the crucial one is independence and it is this which distinguishes recognised ombudsmen schemes from other complaints procedures. (There are also many more associate members.)

BIOA members

10.38　The United Kingdom voting members cover the following sectors:

> Energy
> Estate agents
> Financial services
> Health services
> Housing
> Legal services
> Local government
> Parliamentary
> Pensions
> Police (Northern Ireland)
> Removals
> Surveyors
> Telecommunications
> Waterways

Details of the various schemes can be found at www.bioa.org.uk.

The largest scheme by far is the Financial Ombudsman Service created by the Financial Services and Markets Act 2000. It brought together eight different complaints handling organisations, not all of which were ombudsmen schemes; the best known were probably banking, building societies and insurance. The FOS jurisdiction was extended to cover consumer credit from April 6, 2007.[25]

Most ombudsmen are now creatures of statute with voluntary schemes becoming fewer—the Ombudsman for Estate Agents is a continuing example. The Funeral Ombudsman Scheme[26] was another voluntary scheme, but it died in 2002 after nine years when the two trade associations funding it—the Funeral Standards Council (mainly Co-ops) and the Society of Allied Independent Funeral Directors—withdrew financial support and left the scheme because they refused to pay 49p per funeral! It is to be hoped that no other ombudsman scheme will ever suffer this unique fate.

Jurisdiction and powers

The extent of the jurisdiction of a particular ombudsman depends on the **10.39** particular scheme. For example, the private sector schemes do not usually cover all members of the industry. Thus, the Ombudsman for Estate Agents was initially concerned only with the large chains of estate agents owned by banks, building societies and insurance companies and could not deal with complaints against independent estate agents.[27]

To discover the extent of the jurisdiction, powers and duties of a particular scheme the consumer adviser will normally need to peruse its terms of reference or rules which where appropriate will reflect the memorandum and articles of association of the company operating the scheme.

Usually complaints have to be brought within a specified time-limit and cannot be dealt with if the complainant has already issued court proceedings.

Procedures

Here again the adviser must look at the details of the particular scheme. **10.40** However, generally the ombudsman cannot consider a complaint until he is satisfied that the complainant has given the business concerned the opportunity to try to resolve the complaint by its own in-company complaints procedure. Once the ombudsman is satisfied that such procedures have been exhausted, he will then try to resolve the dispute by acting as a conciliator.

If conciliation fails, the ombudsman will commence his formal investigation and collect all the relevant evidence. Generally there will not be an oral hearing and the adjudication will be based on written evidence only. In reaching his decision the ombudsman will take into account such matters as the terms of the contract, codes of practice, previous decisions and in some schemes what is "fair and reasonable".

---

[25] Consumer Credit Act 2006, s.59.
[26] Geoffrey Woodroffe was the Funeral Ombudsman throughout its brief life.
[27] Now called the Property Ombudsman: para.10.28.

Remedies

10.41 One of the main aims of the ombudsman is to try to improve the quality of service in a particular organisation or industry. Thus if the ombudsman upholds a complaint, he may well make a recommendation that the business practices or procedures of the respondent organisation should be altered and improved to prevent a repetition of the problem. Sometimes an apology by the business will satisfy a complainant—it is strange how frequently an organisation, though at fault, will be absolutely certain that it has acted properly and efficiently and refuse to budge, while all the complainant desires is a formal apology that a mistake had been made. Often, though, the complainant will seek financial compensation. The maximum which can be awarded depends on the scheme; for example, the Financial Ombudsman Service may award up to £100,000. Failure by an organisation to carry out its services carefully and efficiently may cause distress to the complainant and some schemes contain express power for the ombudsman to award compensation for aggravation and distress. Often this has a maximum of £750.

Sanctions

10.42 Throughout this chapter we are concerned with the effectiveness of procedures. What can be done if a recommendation or award by an ombudsman is ignored by the respondent organisation? The answer depends on the particular scheme. In some a monetary award is legally binding on the organisation. In other schemes the recommendation and award by an ombudsman are not legally enforceable; but the business organisation with rare exceptions complies with the ombudsman's decision.

The ultimate sanction for non-compliance is publicity. Every ombudsman publishes an annual report, which will normally give examples of complaints made in the previous year and statistics on the number and type of complaints without naming the organisations involved. However, if an organisation were to fail to comply with a decision, in some schemes the ombudsman would have the power to name the culprit; it is the fear of the commercial effect of such adverse publicity which stimulates businesses into compliance.

5. ARBITRATION

Cheap, quick, informal?

10.43 Until 1971 the consumer, faced with a supplier who was not prepared to meet his proper obligations, had no choice but to abandon his complaint unless he was determined enough to launch himself upon the uncertain seas of litigation. The prospect of such action caused the consumer considerable anxiety for three principal reasons. First, it was likely to be expensive because of the level of legal fees. Secondly—and a related point—although he could save legal fees by conducting the case himself, he was put off playing the role of the litigant in person by the formality and complexity of court proceedings. Thirdly, he knew litigation to be a long-winded affair and was unhappy at having the doubtful outcome hanging over him like the sword of Damocles for years on end. Thus, the layman saw access to his legal rights guarded by a Cerberus whose three heads were expense, delay and formality.

These disadvantages were particularly identified in the 1960s and fully discussed in *Justice out of Reach*, the 1970 report by the Consumer Council. The report proposed a nationwide system of small claims courts, drawing partly upon experience in North America. (It is salutary to recall that the county courts were set up in 1846 to provide the sort of forum being ardently espoused a century and a quarter later.) The county court arbitration scheme was inaugurated in 1973. The small claims track now caters for court-based small claims.[28]

The consumer adviser must remember, however, that most of the codes **10.44** of practice discussed in this Chapter provide for low cost, documents only arbitration arranged by the relevant trade association. It must be stressed, though, that if consumers agree to their disputes being resolved by arbitration, they are normally bound by the arbitrator's decision. They cannot ignore it and then try the courts later in the hope that the district judge adopts a different attitude. This is the crucial distinction between arbitration and the ombudsman schemes.

The European dimension must not be overlooked. As the habit develops of consumers buying goods as well as services abroad, so the likelihood of trans-border disputes increases. The European Commission remarked in its 1993 Green Paper[29]:

> Access to justice is at once a human right and a prerequisite for an effective legal order.
>
> However, it follows from Article 7 of the Treaty that the national courts must be equally accessible to all individuals, without discrimination on grounds of nationality, and that the divergences between existing national procedures— which as such are quite legitimate—should not be such as to affect the equality of treatment of Community subjects in different countries who invoke respect of one and the same Community provision.
>
> It is up to the national courts to enforce Community law in the context of their powers and using their own procedures. But this means that if access to justice at national level is impeded, the effectiveness (and non-discriminatory application) of Community law is placed in jeopardy.

Consumer arbitration

The codes of practice approved by the OFT do not compel consumers to **10.45** take advantage of an arbitration scheme, if available, and point out that the complainant is free to take the alternative route of suing in the courts. This contrasts with the type of clause common in commercial contracts which

---

[28] See para.11.11.
[29] "Access of Consumers to Justice and Settlement of Consumers' Disputes in the Single Market" COM (93) 576.

makes arbitration a condition precedent to action in the courts (the so-called "*Scott v Avery*"[30] clause).

Such clauses can operate unfairly and legislation to control them has been in force since 1988. Under s.91 of the Arbitration Act 1996 a clause referring present or future disputes to arbitration is to be treated as "unfair" under the Unfair Terms in Consumer Contracts Regulations 1999 (which we discussed in Chapter Nine) where the value in dispute does not exceed a specified amount—currently £5,000 (SI 1996/3211).[31]

Two points can be made. First, the 1996 Act is wider than the Regulations because, by s.90, the term "consumer" includes a company or partnership. Secondly, it has been suggested that the £5,000 ceiling is a breach of EU law as it derogates from the Unfair Terms Directive (see, *Arbitration Law* published by Lloyd's of London, at para.1.47).

6. ALTERNATIVE DISPUTE RESOLUTION[32]

10.46   In Chapter Ten of our Fourth Edition we wrote that ADR was "increasingly in the news as the cost of legal aid continues to rise faster than general inflation". Much water has flowed under the bridge in the years since then as clients and the courts have sought to avoid the cost and delay of litigation. The Civil Procedure Rules, which are considered in the next Chapter, give the court wide powers to stay a case so that the parties can explore ADR; also, an unreasonable refusal to consider ADR (both before and after the start of proceedings) will be taken into account when the court awards costs. For small claims the cost of litigation is usually out of all proportion to the amount in dispute—hence the value of ADR. There are two main ADR organisations—namely the Centre for Dispute Resolution (CEDR) and ADR Group; the latter is probably more suitable for smaller cases. The Chartered Institute of Arbitrators also provides ADR services for consumers via its subsidiary IDRS Ltd—details can be found on their website.

The procedure varies from one mediation to another but essentially it involves getting the parties to reach their own agreement—rather than leaving it to a third person (the judge). A typical mediation will proceed as follows:

(1) Before the mediation starts the parties will be asked to prepare written position statements and to sign the mediation agreement; this confirms that anything said during the mediation is, and will remain, confidential.

(2) The parties will then come together and meet the mediator; he will ask each of them to make an opening statement.

---

[30] (1856) 5 H.L.C. 811.

[31] It was increased from £3,000 in order to mirror the small claims track under the new Civil Procedure Rules (SI 1999/2167).

[32] Many use "ADR" to mean any consumer redress system, including Ombudsmen and even codes of practice.

(3) The parties then retire to separate rooms and the mediator will shuttle between them—exploring the strength and weakness of each party's case in more detail and finding out what their main concerns are. In these separate discussions he will endeavour to get the parties to narrow their differences until an agreement emerges and this will then be recorded in writing.

ADR is under discussion in Brussels, as is evidenced by the Green Paper *on alternative dispute resolution in civil and commercial law*.[33] Another EU initiative is the European Extra Judicial Network (EEJ Net) which enables consumers in one EU country to contact ADR organisations in other countries.

7. LEGAL ASSISTANCE

A client faced with a consumer problem—perhaps a claim against a supplier **10.47** of goods, a builder, a valuer, a hospital or even (dare one say it) a solicitor— will need legal advice in the hope of disposing of the matter without having to go to court. As a first port of call the Community Legal Service website www.justask.org.uk has a great deal of information which may well point the consumer in the right direction. He may decide to seek help from a Law Centre or a Citizens Advice Bureau.

If the consumer consults a solicitor, r.2.03 of the Solicitors' Code of Conduct requires the solicitor to discuss funding options at the outset and to keep the client informed of the legal costs as the case progresses. There are at least three possibilities:

(1) The client may have "before the event" insurance covering legal assistance. Many house and motor policies provide for this.

(2) The client may enter into a conditional fee agreement with the solicitor. These are tightly controlled by statute but essentially they provide that (1) the solicitor will charge a reduced fee, or no fee, if the case is lost and (2) the solicitor will charge at his normal rate plus a "success fee" if the case is won. The central problem in most consumer cases relates to the small value of the claim—the legal costs may well be greater than the amount in dispute. If the claim is for £5,000 or less the other party is unlikely to pay any legal costs as part of a settlement and accordingly the costs will have to come out of, and may wipe out, any amount recovered. Accordingly solicitors will generally advise their clients that such arrangements will not be viable where the amount is small.

(3) A limited amount of help may be available from a solicitor who has obtained a contract from the Legal Services Commission. Under

---

[33] COM (2002) 196 final. See also draft Directive on certain aspects of mediation in civil and commercial matters (SEC (2004) 1314).

the scheme known as Legal Help a client must satisfy the solicitor that he or she qualifies financially and also satisfies the "sufficient benefit" test—i.e. that the matter is of sufficient benefit to the client in the light of all the circumstances (including the client's personal circumstances) to justify the work. This will usually involve considering whether a person of moderate means would be prepared to pay privately for the work. Once again the value of the amount in dispute will often be crucial. A solicitor instructed under the Legal Help scheme can do a limited amount of work for the client and this will be paid out of public funds.

CHAPTER ELEVEN

"WHAT HAPPENS IF I GO TO COURT?"

1. FUNDING THE ACTION

A. LEGAL AID

The Labour Government of 1945 introduced legal aid as part of its welfare **11.01** state programme. It was designed to enable, and it did enable, persons of limited means to take their case to court and to remove the old jibe that "the courts are available to rich and poor alike, just like the Ritz Hotel". While it greatly widened access to justice it was not without its critics who focused on (1) the lack of centralised control and (2) the soaring cost—civil legal aid totalled £680 million in 1990–1; this figure had risen to a staggering £1476 million by 1997. This led the present Labour Government to undertake a root-and-branch reform and to abolish it altogether in a number of areas. The key features of the new regime can be summarised as follows:

(1) Under the Access to Justice Act 1999 the responsibility for legal aid (both civil and criminal) has passed to a new body, the Legal Services Commission. This body provides funding for civil matters through the Community Legal Service which can fund information, advice and assistance with settlement. The geographical spread of legal aid is monitored by regional legal services committees.

(2) The provision of civil legal aid is confined to law firms and advice agencies which meet certain quality standards and have obtained a Special Quality Mark for specific areas of law (formerly known as franchise). A firm or agency seeking to provide legal services of a particular type in a particular geographical area will only be accepted if the regional Community Legal Service is satisfied that there is a need in their area for legal services of that type. The result is that the number of eligible firms has been drastically reduced and clients may well find it difficult to find an easily accessible lawyer (consumer law lawyers being a notable example). Quality control is achieved by regular audits.

(3) Apart from drastically limiting the number of providers, the other major cost-cutting aspect of the new regime has been the abolition of legal aid in a number of areas of work. In particular (and apart from a few exceptions such as clinical negligence) legal aid has been

withdrawn from personal injury litigation. Other excluded areas include boundary disputes, wills and trusts disputes, defamation, and most business disputes.

(4) A client seeking legal aid must qualify financially by satisfying the income and capital criteria in the Community Legal Service (Financial) Regulations 2000 as amended from time to time.

(5) The client must also pass a merits test. The Legal Services Commission Funding Code specifies six different prospects of success, namely very good (80 per cent) good (60 per cent) moderate (at least 50 per cent) poor (less than 50 per cent) borderline (not poor but uncertain due to difficult questions of law or fact) and unclear. This leads on to a cost-benefit analysis. The regional committee must be satisfied that (1) in very good cases the likely damages will exceed the likely costs (2) in "good" cases they will exceed the likely costs by 2:1 and (3) in "moderate" cases they will exceed the likely costs by 4:1.

(6) Cases which are likely to be allocated to the "small claims" track (see para.11.09 below) are excluded (this will shut out many consumer claims).

If the client clears all these hurdles and gets legal aid, the solicitor will be paid out of public funds. The solicitor must, however, draw the client's attention to the "charge" which can seriously affect the value of the claim to the client. If the costs payable by the Legal Services Commission exceed the assisted person's contribution and any costs recovered from the other side, the Legal Services Commission will have charge over any property recovered or preserved in the proceedings.

B. CONDITIONAL FEES

11.02 As previously explained (para.10.47 above), a solicitor can enter into a "conditional fee agreement" with his client under powers contained in the Courts and Legal Services Act 1990 and Orders made under that Act. The agreement will usually provide that (1) no costs are payable if the case is lost and (2) the solicitor can charge his usual hourly rate plus a success fee if the case is won. The amount of the success fee is a matter for agreement but it can be as high as 100 per cent of the usual charging rate. The widely used words "no win, no fee" are seriously misleading for two reasons. First, the agreement will normally be limited to the solicitor's own fees and will not normally include court fees and other outgoings such as experts' fees. Secondly, the client must realise that he may have to pay the other side's costs if he loses (although this is unlikely if the case is allocated to the small claims track as to which see para.11.11, below) and insurance is essential to cover this risk. Under the Access to Justice Act 1999 (many legal aid lawyers and their clients will wince at this title) both the success fee and the insurance premium will be recoverable from the other side if the case is won (but this will only be so if the court orders the loser to pay the winner's costs—and this will normally not be so in small claims track cases).

Under the conditional fee regime, the client's chances of legal representation will depend on the willingness of a solicitor to take the case and this will usually depend on finding an insurer who is prepared to do so.

A solicitor can agree to limit his client's liability for costs to the actual amount of costs recovered from the other side, so the client receives any compensation without deductions, but this might be difficult to negotiate for a consumer dispute.

2. PROCEDURE

Introduction

The Civil Procedure Rules have been in force since April 26, 1999. Designed **11.03** to eradicate the three evils of litigation at that time—delay, uncertainty and cost—they have succeeded on the first two but have been judged to have failed to deal effectively with the third. Costs greatly exceeding the value of matters being fought over are still a common occurrence. The appellate courts are continually counselling practitioners against such excesses and encouraging all the courts to monitor and control the level of costs by the use of costs estimates and cost-capping. In the meantime, court fees have also continued to rise as part of the move towards the civil courts becoming self-financing. At the same time, the reforms have led to a decrease in the number of cases and an increase in the number cases which settle at an earlier stage.

Although, since the inception of the Rules, there have been over 40 sets of regulations which have amended and updated them (together with a body of case law) most of them have been of a "tidying-up" nature rather than wholesale reform. The Rules themselves have proved fairly robust and Human Rights compliant. There have been some perceived areas of weakness, particularly with regard to service of proceedings (Pt 6) and they were changed in 2008 to make them less opaque and contradictory.

The following are the key distinguishing features of the Civil Procedure **11.04** Rules, namely:

(1) openness and "cards on the table"—no more last minute ambush;

(2) co-operation with the court and the other side and early disclosure of documents;

(3) proportionality;

(4) on-going attempts to settle—using the courts as a last resort;

(5) case management by the court; and

(6) pre-action protocols.

The overriding objective

11.05 The Rules are divided into Parts and many of them are supplemented by Practice Directions—a number of which are longer and more detailed than the Rules themselves. Part 1 sets out the overriding objective which must be constantly borne in mind both before and during the conduct of the case. It reads as follows:

> 1.1(1) These rules are a new procedural code with the overriding objective of enabling the court to deal with cases justly.
>
> (2) Dealing with a case justly includes, so far as is practicable:
>   (a) ensuring that the parties are on an equal footing;
>   (b) saving expense;
>   (c) dealing with the case in ways which are proportionate:
>   (i) to the amount of money involved;
>   (ii) to the importance of the case;
>   (iii) to the complexity of the issues; or
>   (iv) to the financial position of each party;
>   (d) ensuring that it is dealt with expeditiously and fairly; and
>   (e) allotting to it an appropriate share of the court's resources, while taking into account the need to allot resources to other cases.
>
> 1.2 The court must seek to give effect to the overriding objective when it:
>   (a) exercises any power given to it by the rules; or
>   (b) interprets any rule.
>
> 1.3 The parties are required to help the court to further the overriding objective.
>
> 1.4(1) The court must further the overriding objective by actively managing cases.
>
> (2) Active case management includes:—
>   (a) encouraging the parties to co-operate with each other in the conduct of the proceedings;
>   (b) identifying the issues at an early stage;
>   (c) deciding promptly which issues need full investigation and trial and accordingly disposing summarily of the others;
>   (d) deciding the order in which issues are to be resolved;
>   (e) encouraging the parties to use an alternative dispute resolution procedure if the court considers this appropriate and facilitating the use of such procedures;
>   (f) helping the parties to settle the whole or part of the case;
>   (g) fixing timetables or otherwise controlling the progress of the case;
>   (h) considering whether the likely benefit of taking a particular step justifies the cost of taking it;
>   (i) dealing with as many aspects of the case as it can on the same occasion;
>   (j) dealing with the case without the parties needing to attend at court;
>   (k) making use of technology; and
>   (l) giving directions to ensure that the trial of a case proceeds quickly and efficiently.

Two observations can be made. First, much of the necessary technology to assist the court in managing cases is now in place. Courts now have the benefit of recording equipment, computers for the judges, an electronic diary and a database system as well as templates for the production of word processed orders. Some courts also have video link facilities. The Rules have been amended to provide for telephone conferences to be the standard pattern for many interim and directions hearings for which suitable conference equipment has been installed in judges' chambers. Secondly, these management powers are supplemented by Pt 3 which contains sanctions for non-compliance with a court order or direction; these include striking out a claim or defence or ordering a defaulting party to pay money into court.

Pre-action Protocols

There are now at least nine Pre-action Protocols (PAPs), including Construction **11.06** and Engineering, Defamation, Personal Injury, Clinical Disputes, Professional Negligence, Judicial Review, Disease and Illness, Housing Disrepair and Rent Arrears. They have been structured with one central aim—to encourage the early settlement of cases. If we take the personal injury protocol as an example, we can pick out five points:

(1) The claimant must send two copies of a letter of claim to the defendant as soon as sufficient information is available to substantiate a realistic claim and before questions of quantum are addressed in detail.

(2) The defendant must reply and identify his insurer within 21 days.

(3) The insurer must reply within three months stating whether liability is denied and, if so, giving reasons.

(4) If the defendant denies liability his denial must be accompanied by any documents in his possession which are relevant to the issues.

(5) Part 36 of the Rules enables either party to make an offer to settle and there may be serious costs consequences if the matter comes to court and it is found that a party has unreasonably failed to make or to accept an offer.

New PAP

There is now a new "catch-all" PAP the aim of which is said to be as **11.07** follows:

"Aims

    1 The aims of this Practice Direction are to –
        (1) enable parties to settle the issue between them without the need to start proceedings (that is, a court claim); and
        (2) support the efficient management by the court and the parties of proceedings that cannot be avoided.

    2 These aims are to be achieved by encouraging the parties to –
        (1) exchange information about the issue, and
        (2) consider using a form of Alternative Dispute Resolution ('ADR')"

The new provisions make it clear that the court will expect the parties to have complied with this Practice Direction or any relevant pre-action protocol. The court may ask the parties to explain what steps were taken to comply prior to the start of the claim. Where there has been a failure of compliance by a party the court may ask that party to provide an explanation.

The court may decide that there has been a failure of compliance by a party because, for example, that party has—

(1) not provided sufficient information to enable the other party to understand the issues;

(2) not acted within a time limit set out in a relevant pre-action protocol, or, where no specific time limit applies, within a reasonable period;

(3) unreasonably refused to consider ADR; or

(4) without good reason, not disclosed documents requested to be disclosed.

If, in the opinion of the court, there has been non-compliance, the sanctions which the court may impose include—

(1) staying (that is suspending) the proceedings until steps which ought to have been taken have been taken;

(2) an order that the party at fault pays the costs, or part of the costs, of the other party or parties (this may include an order under r.27.14(2) (g) in cases allocated to the small claims track);

(3) an order that the party at fault pays those costs on an indemnity basis (r.44.4(3) sets out the definition of the assessment of costs on an indemnity basis);

(4) if the party at fault is the claimant in whose favour an order for the payment of a sum of money is subsequently made, an order that the claimant is deprived of interest on all or part of that sum, and/or that interest is awarded at a lower rate than would otherwise have been awarded;

(5) if the party at fault is a defendant, and an order for the payment of a sum of money is subsequently made in favour of the claimant, an order that the defendant pay interest on all or part of that sum at a higher rate, not exceeding 10 per cent above base rate, than would otherwise have been awarded.

The principles that should govern the conduct of the parties are that, unless the circumstances make it inappropriate, before starting proceedings the parties should—

(1) exchange sufficient information about the matter to allow them to understand each other's position and make informed decisions about settlement and how to proceed;

(2) make appropriate attempts to resolve the matter without starting proceedings, and in particular consider the use of an appropriate form of ADR in order to do so.

Further, the parties should act in a reasonable and proportionate manner in all dealings with one another. In particular, the costs incurred in complying should be proportionate to the complexity of the matter and any money at stake. The parties must not use the PAP Practice Direction as a tactical device to secure an unfair advantage for one party or to generate unnecessary costs.

ADR

The directions contain clear encouragement to the parties to settle rather **11.08** than litigate. The Practice Note to the Pre-action Protocols suggests some of the ways in which matters might be resolved without litigation, including:

* Discussion and negotiation.

* Early neutral evaluation by an independent third party (for example, a lawyer experienced in that field or an individual experienced in the subject matter of the claim).

* Mediation—a form of facilitated negotiation assisted by an independent neutral party (see above, para.10.46).

The Legal Services Commission has published a booklet on "Alternatives to Court", CLS Direct Information Leaflet 23 (*www.clsdirect.org.uk*), which lists a number of organisations that provide alternative dispute resolution services. Some county courts are already starting to offer such services and litigants are reminded at various stages of the benefits of compromise over uncertain and costly litigation.

It is expressly recognised that no party can or should be forced to mediate or enter into any form of Alternative Dispute Resolution. At the same time, the cases show that a party who unreasonably fails to mediate can incur a costs penalty.

Costs

Strictly speaking, there are no costs within the pre-action protocols them- **11.09** selves except on a retrospective basis, i.e. if proceedings do not settle and litigation ensues, the court can consider any costs incurred as part of the pre-action process. The rules provide for costs-only proceedings to be issued where all other matters have been resolved. These proceedings may, however, be defeated by a defendant filing an acknowledgement disputing the use of such proceedings. Thereafter the claimant has to issue proceedings for the *whole* of the claim and not just the costs.

What happens next?

11.10 If court proceedings become necessary the next stages are as follows:

(1) The claimant will file a "claim form" at the appropriate court. He can file in the county court regardless of value. A case can be issued in the High Court if the value of the claim is not less than £25,000 (or £50,000 in personal injury cases) but straightforward cases so issued are likely to be transferred out at some point to a convenient local county court for hearing.

(2) The particulars of claim can form part of the claim form or they can be served separately. They will contain details of such matters as the defects in the goods and the loss or damage sustained by the claimant. Both the claim form and any separate particulars must be verified by a "statement of truth".

(3) The court will issue the claim form (on payment of the appropriate fee) and will serve it on the defendant (unless the claimant wishes to serve it himself).

(4) Within 14 days of service of the particulars the defendant must file:

    (a) an admission; or
    (b) a defence; or
    (c) an acknowledgement of service (giving him a further 14 days to file a defence).

Failure to take steps (b) or (c) can lead to a default judgment.

(5) As soon as a defence is filed, the court will send to the parties a detailed allocation questionnaire. This must be completed and returned by a specified date not earlier than 14 days after service— and the possibility of applying for summary judgment should be considered at this stage before allocation has taken place.

(6) Part 26 of the Rules deals with the vital question of allocation. The procedural judge will consider the claim form, the defence and the completed questionnaires and will then allocate the case into one of the three tracks—small claims, fast or multi. For consumers and their advisers the small claims track will be the most important one; this is the normal track where the amount in dispute is £5,000 or less. The fast track (and fast is the operative word) is for cases where the amount in dispute is between £5,001 and £25,000 and the hearing will not last more than one day. The multi track is for cases (1) over £25,000 or (2) cases in the fast track band which will take more than one day. The claim form must indicate the band into which the claim falls and Pt 26 sets out the matters which must be taken into account. Note that the value of the claim is not the only relevant factor; thus, for example, a "small" claim may be allocated to a different track if it involves the construction of an exemption clause which will affect many other cases.

Money claims can now be issued and responded to online. See *www.hmcourts-service.gov.uk*.

In the remainder of this Chapter we will look in some detail at the small claims track and then briefly at the fast and multi tracks.

Small claims track (Part 27)

The emphasis is on informality and costs limitation—so that a person with a **11.11** small claim can bring it to the court without the need to instruct a solicitor.

To achieve the object set out above, Pt 27 of the Civil Procedure Rules contains the following provisions:

(1) A number of the rules which apply elsewhere will not apply in the small claims track. They include (a) disclosure of documents, (b) the strict rules of evidence, (c) most of the rules about experts, (d) most of the rules about hearings and (e) the provisions of Pt 36 relating to offers to settle and payment into court (these have costs consequences which are not appropriate to small track cases).

(2) At the allocation stage the procedural judge may:

  (a) give "standard directions" in the Notice of Allocation and fix a date for hearing;

  (b) give "special directions" in the Notice of Allocation and fix a date for hearing;

  (c) fix a date for a preliminary hearing (if, for example he feels that the claim or the defence has no reasonable chance of success); or

  (d) give notice that he proposes to decide the case on the papers without a hearing and invite the parties to notify the court by a specified date if they agree.

  "Standard directions" will include a direction that each party shall, at least fourteen days before the hearing, file and serve on each other party copies of all documents (including experts' reports) on which he intends to rely. The term "special directions" covers such matters as the inspection of documents, experts, witness statements and video evidence; it also covers directions appropriate to the type of case which have been provided for by Practice Directions including road traffic cases, vehicle repairs, holiday and wedding claims—see Appendix A to Practice Direction 27, para.2.2 for further detail. The standard form of directions used by many courts requires the parties to send copies of documents on which they intend to rely to the other party at least 14 days before the hearing. The list includes "experts' reports" but the standard form does not make it clear that such reports may only be relied upon if permission is given by the court.

(3) The case will normally (but not invariably) be heard by a district judge in his room; the general rule is that hearings should be open to

the public but this will not not be so if (a) the hearing is held away from the court or (b) the judge orders a hearing in private—he can do this if the parties agree or on certain other grounds listed in Pt 39.

11.12   (4) A party can present his case personally, or by a lawyer or lay representative (if the party is present).

(5) As stated above, the strict rules of evidence do not apply. Thus, for example, evidence need not be on oath and a party can rely on a witness statement even though the witness is not present—although the statement must be verified by a statement of truth. Expert evidence can only be used if the court has granted permission—and this will usually be limited to a written report from a single expert jointly instructed.

(6) The judge can adopt any method of proceeding that he considers fair and can limit cross-examination. Judges have traditionally taken a very pro-active role in small claims cases (especially as many of the claimants will not have a lawyer to present their case) and the rules reflect this (see r.27.8 and Practice Direction 27, para.4.3).

(7) If a party is unable or unwilling to attend the hearing, he can, at least seven days before the hearing, give written notice to the court that he will not be attending and asking the court to decide the case in his absence. A failure to send this notice is likely to lead to the case being struck out—although the rules allow the absent party to apply within fourteen days to have a judgment set aside if he can show a good reason for non-attendance and a reasonable chance of success at the hearing.

(8) Appeals from a small claims decision are the same as for any other appeal from a final decision of a court. First, permission to appeal is required from the trial judge or the appellate judge. This permission will only be given where the court considers that the appeal stands a real chance of success or there are some other compelling reasons why the appeal should be heard. Second, an appeal can only be brought on the basis that the appealed decision was wrong or unjust or because of a serious or other irregularity.

(9) A person with a small claim may be reluctant to use the courts for two reasons—fear of the complexity and fear of having to pay the other side's costs if he loses. The rules seek to overcome both of these fears. We have already dealt with informality; we must now mention that the general power to award costs to the winner is heavily circumscribed in the small claims track. Under r.27.14 the court can order a party to pay to the other party:

    (a) fixed costs on issue of proceedings (see Pt 45);

    (b) any sum paid for legal advice but only in injunction or specific performance proceedings;

    (c) court fees paid by the other party;

(d) reasonable witness expenses (including that of the litigant) for travelling or other expenses involved in staying away from home to attend a hearing;

(e) loss of earnings for a litigant or witness limited to £50 per day;

(f) £200 for court approved expert;

(g) such further costs as the court may summarily assess to be paid by a party who has behaved unreasonably, e.g. by their misconduct of the action, failing to attend a hearing, unreasonably failing to settle.

When a claim is allocated to the small claims track by consent, the small **11.13** claims costs provisions will apply unless the parties agree otherwise. It is important for parties to consider this before agreeing that the matter be dealt with on the lower track.

Costs on a successful appeal are limited in exactly the same way as the costs at first instance. In the small claims track they are limited to the fixed costs of issue, court fees, witness expenses, loss of earnings, experts' fees and (rarely used) the fixed costs of obtaining an injunction. The only escape from the rigours of the fixed costs regime would be for the successful party to convince the circuit judge hearing the appeal that the unsuccessful party has behaved unreasonably; if he succeeds on this point the circuit judge can summarily assess the costs without the small claims limitation.

This general inability to recover costs from the other side, and the need to balance the value of the claim against the cost of enforcing it, are key issues for solicitors consulted in small claims cases (the problems are much less acute if the client has legal expenses insurance). The solicitor may feel that he or she should take a "behind the scenes" advisory role, perhaps drafting the letter of claim and/or the claim form. This division of functions is known in the USA as "unbundling" and it will be interesting to see whether it takes off here (see an article by Suzanne Burn in *Busy Solicitors' Digest*, July 1999).

The fast track (Part 28)

The need to reduce delay is one of the central aims of the Civil Procedure **11.14** Rules and the fast track is a prime example. This is the normal track for cases where:

(1) the value of the amount in dispute is between £5,001 and £25,000;

(2) the trial is likely to last for no longer than one day; and

(3) oral expert evidence at the trial (where allowed) will be limited to (a) one expert per party in any expert field and (b) expert evidence in two expert fields.

Once a case has been allocated to the fast track (see para.11.06, above) the district judge will consider whether further details of the claim or defence are necessary, whether the case can be disposed of summarily and whether a preliminary hearing is necessary. Subject to this, he will make an order for directions which is likely to include a strict (and largely immovable) time-table; this will be geared to a fixed trial date not more than 30 weeks from service of the directions.

There are detailed rules as to disclosure of documents, exchange of witness statements, exchange of experts' reports, a "pre-trial checklist" and the preparation of a "trial bundle" limited to those documents which are really required. Also (and this is of great importance) the court will have an on-going power to control the cost of litigation; the rules require the parties to prepare costs estimates (present and future) on every court appearance.

It is also important to appreciate that under Pt 46 an award of costs for the trial advocate is severely limited—£485 for claims up to £3,000, £690 for claims from £3,001 to £10,000, £1,035 for claims from £10,001 to £15,000 and a mere £1,650 for claims above £15,000. Also, if the case is not finished in one day (and a day is normally limited to five hours), there is no scope for increasing the figures set out above. Bearing in mind how difficult it will be to move the trial date, it is vital that the timetable is adhered to as closely as possible in order to avoid difficulties as the trial date approaches.

The multi-track (Part 29)

11.15 This is the normal track for (a) claims in excess of £25,000 and (b) claims within the fast track band where the case is likely to last for more than one day or where the rules relating to expert evidence (see above) are not satisfied. Although the cases in this track are not subject to the severe time constraints of the fast track the court will nevertheless strive to fix a trial date at as early a stage as possible, such date being as immovable as the trial date for fast track. There may be two occasions on which the judge will meet the parties' lawyers (and in many cases the clients will also be present) to plan the conduct of the case. The first of these meetings is the Case Management Conference at which the judge is likely to give directions—this can involve approving directions which the parties have agreed between themselves. The second meeting is known as the Pre-Trial Review and it may take place after completion of a pre-trial checklist. The trial advocates will meet the trial judge about 8–10 weeks before the hearing date (a) to explore the possibility of settlement before the full trial costs are incurred and (b) if settlement is not possible, to prepare an agenda for the trial. At both of these meetings (neither of which is compulsory) the judge will be fully prepared and he will expect the same of the lawyers. In moving the case forward at these meetings the r.1 overriding objective must be constantly borne in mind by all concerned.

3. PRECEDENTS

For a selection of county court precedents in consumer cases see Appendix One.

Part II

THE CONSUMER AND THE CRIMINAL LAW

CHAPTER TWELVE

INTRODUCTION

In Part I we have examined the position of consumers as far as the civil law **12.01** is concerned. We saw that it is not enough for them to show that they have a right of action, for example, for breach of contract or negligence. Their main problem is how to enforce that right. The proportion of complainants who are prepared to sue to enforce their rights is small. This encourages traders to assume that they can adopt careless and sloppy practices with impunity. If they can get away with providing shoddy goods and incompetent service, traders will be tempted to lower their standards by the prospect of increased profitability. Not only is this clearly contrary to the interests of consumers; it is equally unfair to the honest trader who endeavours to maintain high standards and at the same time to compete with the rogues operating in the same line of business.

In pursuing its twofold aim—to protect consumers and to ensure that honest traders are able to make a living on equal terms without the need to resort to the malpractices of their dishonest competitors—Parliament has increasingly turned to the sanctions of the criminal law in its search for control. This approach has the significant advantage for the consumer that the expensive and time-consuming process of regulating the rogue is entrusted to public officials who usually have a duty to enforce its provisions. If the provisions of the criminal law also enable consumers to obtain compensation,[1] it will be unnecessary for them to rely on the rights explained in Part I: they will be superfluous.

The full range of criminal controls is very extensive. The following exam- **12.02** ples show some of their ambit.

(1) The Food Safety Act 1990[2] controls the quality of food. Section 14 prohibits the sale of "any food which is not of the nature or substance or quality demanded by the purchaser", for example, containing maggots, mould or metal.

(2) The Weights and Measures Act 1985 empowers trading standards inspectors to test weighing and measuring equipment, and also makes it an offence to deliver short weight when goods are sold by weight, number or other measurement.

---

[1] Below, para.16.03.
[2] Repealing most of the Food Act 1984.

(3) The Consumer Credit Act 1974 creates a large number of criminal offences, e.g. carrying on a consumer credit business without a licence.[3]

(4) The General Product Safety Regulations 2005 impose a general safety requirement prohibiting the supply of unsafe goods.[4]

(5) The Consumer Protection from Unfair Trading Regulations 2008 (the CPRs) regulate a wide range of commercial activities,[5] many of them previously controlled by the Trade Descriptions Act 1968 and the Consumer Protection Act 1987, Pt III.

12.03 The most important provisions of the Trade Descriptions Act 1968 and all of Pt III of the 1987 Act were repealed by the CPRs from May 26, 2008. We shall discuss them in Chapters Thirteen and Fourteen respectively in view of their historical importance—they were in force until May 26, 2008—and the continuation in force of some provisions of the 1968 Act. (Readers will find a much more detailed analysis of the 1968 Act in earlier editions of this book.)

Next in Chapter Fifteen we survey those statutory provisions which protect the consumer against unsafe goods, now to be found in Pt II of the 1987 Act and the 2005 Regulations.

Finally in Chapter Sixteen we consider the important question of compensation for the victims of criminal offences; how can they obtain financial redress for any loss which they may have suffered as a result of the convicted person's failure to comply with the criminal law? Two aspects are examined—orders for compensation under the Powers of Criminal Courts (Sentencing) Act 2000 and the right to bring civil proceedings for breach of statutory duty.

[3] See para.20.07 below.
[4] See para.15.25 below.
[5] See para.17.25 below.

Chapter Thirteen

"THE DESCRIPTION MISLED ME"

1. Introduction

This Chapter is concerned almost entirely with the Trade Descriptions Act **13.01**
1968. Some of its provisions continue in force and are discussed later, but the
two main offences—false descriptions of goods and services—disappeared
on May 26, 2008 with the repeal of sections 1 and 14 by the Consumer
Protection from Unfair Trading Regulations 2008 (CPRs) (SI 2008/1277).
Instead the CPRs will now protect consumers, in particular by reg.5 on "misleading actions" with its detailed list of matters in reg.5(4) and (5) and by the
black list of prohibited practices in Sch.1.

Why was the whole of the 1968 Act not repealed? Two reasons can be discerned. First, two practices fall outside the EU Unfair Commercial Practices
Directive (discussed in Chapter 17) which the CPRs implemented. They
concern false representations as to royal approval in s.12 and false trade
descriptions on imported goods in s.16 (see paras 13.13 and 13.14). Secondly,
the provisions as to offences, defences and enforcement in ss.18–20, 23–31,
33–36 and 38–39 had to be retained because other legislation refers to them,
e.g. the Trade Marks Act 1994, s.93.

Originally the 1968 Act also contained the provisions relating to misleading prices, but they became separately controlled by the Consumer Protection
Act 1987, Pt III,[1] until its repeal too by the CPRs.

Historical background

As early as 1423 an Act was passed regulating the marking of silver plate. **13.02**
Others dealt with the marking of gold and other precious metals, cutlery
and linen. The first statute to cover goods in general was the Merchandise
Marks Act 1862 which was replaced in 1887 by an Act of the same name.
This was added to by later statutes culminating in the Merchandise Marks
Act 1953.

Apart from these statutes dealing specifically with marking, there are
related Acts dealing with other aspects of the supply of goods. For example,
the Weights and Measures Act 1985 is particularly concerned with the *quantity* of goods being sold, e.g. coal and petrol, whereas the Trade Descriptions
Act 1968 is also concerned with *quality*. There is one major similarity between
the two Acts, namely, that their provisions are enforced by trading standards

---

[1] See Ch. Fourteen.

officers[2] (formerly known as inspectors of weights and measures) employed by local authorities. Whilst the above legislation has the effect of protecting the consumer, most of the legislation, like that relating to patents and trade marks, was passed with the intention of protecting one trader or manufacturer against unfair competition from another.

The position with regard to trade descriptions generally was looked into by the Committee on Consumer Protection, generally known as the Molony Committee, which published its Final Report in 1962.[3] It paid particular attention to the working of the Merchandise Marks Acts and highlighted a number of defects:

(a) The Acts were limited in their scope since they were relevant only where a description had been "applied" to goods, i.e. where goods had been physically marked with labels, dies, blocks, etc. Thus oral statements and many advertisements were not covered.

(b) Whatever the merits of the Acts, they were not generally enforced. The Acts of 1891 and 1894 gave the Board of Trade and Ministry of Agriculture, Fisheries and Food respectively the *power* to enforce the regulations; the Local Government Act 1933 gave a similar power to local authorities. Yet nobody was under a *duty* to enforce them.

13.03 These defects were cured by the passing of the Trade Descriptions Act 1968. The preamble to the Act discloses the two main offences:

(a) applying a false trade description to *goods* or supplying goods with such a description (section 1);

(b) making a false statement as to the provision of *services*, accommodation or facilities. (section 14)

Before considering these offences, two important general features of the Act need to be grasped. First, the Act operates in the criminal area only: Secondly, it applies only to suppliers in the course of a trade or business, i.e. not to private suppliers.

2. Goods

13.04 Section 1(1) prohibited false trade descriptions of goods until its repeal in 2008:

Any person who, in the course of a trade or business—

(a) applies a false trade description to any goods; or
(b) supplies or offers to supply any goods to which a false trade description is applied;

shall, subject to the provisions of this Act, be guilty of an offence.

---

[2] See below, para.13.25.
[3] Cmnd.1781.

Strict liability

The offences created by s.1 were offences of strict liability. Although charges **13.05** under these provisions often involved an element of dishonesty, as was pointed out by the Divisional Court in *Alec Norman Garages Ltd v Phillips*,[4] it was not necessary for the prosecution to prove dishonesty.

Section 1 covered two different offences: first, the application of a false trade description to goods; secondly, the supply of goods to which such a description had already been applied. Thus the first offence would be committed by a manufacturer incorrectly labelling goods, while the second offence would occur when a retailer displays or sells those same goods.

Applying a trade description:

The offences under s.1 and s.16 (see below, para.13.14) occur when a person **13.06** applies a false trade description to goods. A wide meaning is given by s.4 to the word "applies":

It covers:

(i) markings on the goods themselves, e.g. labels;

(ii) markings on anything in which the goods are supplied, e.g. packaging;

(iii) markings on anything in which the goods are placed, e.g. display units, vending machines, point-of-sale material;

(iv) oral statements, specifically mentioned in s.4(2).

Meaning of trade description

Section 2(1) defines a trade description as "an indication" of any of the **13.07** matters exhaustively listed in its 10 paragraphs:

(1) A trade description is an indication, direct or indirect, and by whatever means given, of any of the following matters with respect to any goods or parts of goods, that is to say—

(a) quantity, size or gauge;
(b) method of manufacture, production, processing or reconditioning;
(c) composition;
(d) fitness for purpose, strength, performance, behaviour or accuracy;
(e) any physical characteristics not included in the preceding paragraphs;
(f) testing by any person and results thereof;
(g) approval by any person or conformity with a type approved by any person;
(h) place or date of manufacture, production, processing or reconditioning;
(i) person by whom manufactured, produced, processed or reconditioned;
(j) other history, including previous ownership or use.

---

[4] [1985] R.T.R. 164.

Examples

13.08 The following examples may assist readers; the lettering follows that in s.2(1):

    (a) size of shoes, shirts, dresses or other clothing;

    (b) Axminster or Wilton carpet;

    (c) shirt labelled "65% polyester, 35% cotton";

    (d) "maximum speed 102 mph, 38 mpg";

    (e) car equipped with "five-tone horn playing 'Colonel Bogey' ";

    (f) "tested by the Road Research Laboratory";

    (g) tennis racket "as used by Sampras";

    (h) 1985 Audi Quattro;

    (i) "tuned by High Performance Motors Ltd";

    (j) "only one private owner; 46,000 miles".

Is it false?

13.09 Let us assume that there is a trade description within the meaning of s.2.

    The next question to consider is whether the trade description is a false trade description. Section 3(1) states simply and clearly that "a false trade description is a trade description which is false to a material degree."

3. SERVICES

13.10 An area not covered by the Merchandise Marks Act was services. This novel extension of criminal liability from goods to services doubtless accounted for a more tentative approach in section 14 as compared with section 1. The offence of making false or misleading statements about services, accommodation or facilities was not an offence of strict liability, as can be seen from the wording of s.14(1):

> It shall be an offence for any person in the course of any trade or business—
>
>   (a) to make a statement which he knows to be false; or
>   (b) recklessly to make a statement which is false;

This is the other important offence repealed by the CPRs.

4. PROPERTY

13.11 Section 14 of the 1968 Act included statements about "accommodation", such as holiday hotels, and "services" covered services relating to building, e.g. by an architect or builder. However, although some aspects of building and sale were covered, the 1968 Act did not apply to general statements about properties for sale such as their location or characteristics.

Eventually the Property Misdescriptions Act 1991 was passed: a Private Member's Bill advocated by the Consumers' Association. It remains in force, as the EU Unfair Commercial Practices Directive, though it is a maximum Directive, allows Member States to "impose requirements which are more restrictive or prescriptive" in relation to immovable property (art.4.9).

Section 1(1), provides:

> Where a false or misleading statement about a prescribed matter is made in the course of an estate agency business or a property development business, otherwise than in providing conveyancing services, the person by whom the business is carried on shall be guilty of an offence under this section.

The main impact is upon estate agents. It is intended to dissuade them from indulging in their previous practice of giving extravagant descriptions which often at best were half-truths—"the pretty cottage adjoining farmland" which turns out to be a one-up, one-down terraced house with open country at the front, but a noisy car exhaust and tyre fitting centre overlooking the back garden.

Its ambit also extends to a "property development business". Section 1(5) (f) provides that a statement is caught in this case only if the business is concerned with "the development of land" *and* the statement is made "with a view to disposing of an interest in a building or part of a building, constructed or renovated in the course of a business".

An offence is committed where the statement relates to "a prescribed matter", i.e. prescribed in an order made by the Secretary of State (s.1(5) (d)).

The Property Misdescriptions (Specified Matters) Order 1992[5] contains a long list of prescribed matters, e.g. location, view, fixtures and fittings, accommodation, surveys, treatments, history, council tax, easements.

The defences, enforcement and penalties are similar to those relating to the 1968 Act discussed below. Thus the familiar "due diligence" defence is available (s.2). However, on conviction the defendant may be fined, but not imprisoned (s.1(3)).

5. TWO CONTINUING OFFENCES

As we mentioned earlier, although ss.1 and 14 on misdescriptions of goods and services have been repealed, two offences are extant. **13.12**

Royal approval

Section 12 makes it an offence for a trader (1) to give a false indication that his goods or services are of a kind supplied to or approved by any member of **13.13**

---

[5] SI 1992/2834.

the Royal Family, or (2) to use an emblem signifying the Queen's Award to Industry without the authority of Her Majesty.

A new s.12(3) is added by the CPRs[6] excluding anything that is a commercial practice, as defined by the CPRs, unless it is unfair.

BIS (formerly DTI) consider that displaying such a flag or banner over a business building would be outside the CPRs and an offence under the 1968 Act.

Imported goods

13.14 Section 16 prohibits the import of goods into the UK where a false trade description is applied to them outside the UK and it relates to the place of manufacture, production, processing or reconditioning. This would apply, for example, to knives made in Korea or clothes made in China and labelled "Sheffield England" or "Made in Italy" respectively.

6. DEFENCES

As we pointed out in para.13.01, the provisions about defences and offences were not repealed by the CPRs.

The general defence

13.15 The defence provided by s.24(1) reads as follows:

> In any proceedings for an offence under this Act it shall, subject to subsection (2) of this section, be a defence for the person charged to prove—
>
> (a) that the commission of the offence was due to a mistake or to reliance on information supplied to him or to the act or default of another person, an accident or some other cause beyond his control; and
> (b) that he took all reasonable precautions and exercised all due diligence to avoid the commission of such an offence by himself or any person under his control.

It may be split into five defences. The defendant must prove that the commission of the offence was due to any one of the following causes:

(i) a mistake;

(ii) reliance on information supplied to him;

(iii) the act or default of another person;

(iv) an accident;

(v) some other cause beyond his control.

As Lord Templeman pointed out in *Wings Ltd v Ellis*,[7] where the company failed to invoke s.24, "Good intentions and mistake do not by themselves

---

6 Sch.2, Pt 1, para.10.
7 [1984] 3 All E.R. 577 at 594.

constitute a defence. The accused must plead and prove the circumstances specified in section 24."

Mistake

As far as mistake is concerned this is available only where the mistake is of **13.16** the defendant himself; it cannot be used where someone else's mistake is involved (e.g. an employer pleading the mistake of an employee).[8]

Act or default of another person

The defence most frequently relied upon is that the offence was due to the **13.17** "act or default of another person". When an employer is charged, he may rely on the default of an employee. However, when the employer is a company, it is necessary to distinguish between those employees who are the *alter ego* of the company, when their defaults are the company's defaults, and those employees who are not thus identified with the company which can then claim that the defaults are those of "another person". The difficulty was fully discussed by the House of Lords in *Tesco Supermarkets v Nattrass*,[9] a case involving s.11 (now repealed):

> Soap powder was advertised in a supermarket "Radiant 1 shilling off giant size 2/11d". This was intended to apply only to "flash packs" which were marked "1 shilling off recommended price". As the supermarket had run out of these packs, ordinary packs were on display. A customer was charged the full price of 3/11d for one of these.

Their Lordships held that where the person charged is a limited company, **13.18** the only persons who can be identified with the controlling mind and will of the company are the board of directors, the managing director and any other superior officer[10] to whom the board has delegated full discretion to act independently from the board. Thus, though a general manager may be the company's *alter ego*, the supermarket manager was not. Accordingly, since the offence was caused by his failure to ensure that sufficient flash-packs were available, Tesco were able to rely on his default.

To establish this defence the defendants must not merely produce the list of staff who might have been at fault; they must at least try to identify the actual person responsible by carefully investigating the circumstances to discover how the offences occurred.[11] Further, to rely on this defence s.24(2) requires the defendants at least seven clear days before the hearing to serve on the prosecutor a written notice giving such information as they have to identify the other person.[12] The reason for this provision is to enable the prosecution

---

[8] *Birkenhead & District Co-operative Society Ltd v Roberts* [1970] 1 W.L.R. 1497.
[9] [1972] A.C. 153.
[10] By s.20 such officers may be prosecuted too, where the offence has been committed with their consent or connivance.
[11] *McGuire v Sittingbourne Co-operative Society Ltd* [1976] Crim.L.R. 268.
[12] See *Birkenhead & District Co-operative Society Ltd v Roberts*, above, n.8.

to consider whether to proceed directly against the other person either for one of the main offences or under the by-pass provision in s.23.[13]

Due diligence defence

13.19 It is not enough for the defendant to prove one of the five defences in s.24(1) (a). He must also prove that he falls within what is now popularly known as the "due diligence defence", a defence frequently found in consumer protection legislation, namely "that he took all reasonable precautions and exercised all due diligence to avoid the commission of such an offence by himself or any person under his control."[14] These factors have generally been considered by the courts in relation to the default defence, particularly with regard to its application in the areas of vicarious liability, odometers and sampling.

Vicarious liability

13.20 Where an employer is charged with an offence because of the conduct of an employee and endeavours to rid himself of this vicarious liability by showing that the offence was due to the act or default of the employee, broadly the employer will be acquitted if he can show that he is personally blameless. Obviously, when this defence is used somebody is to blame. The question is whether the offence occurred in spite of the precautions and diligence of the employer.

Sampling

13.21 Suppliers dealing with large quantities of goods and relying on sampling must show that they have been taking reasonable precautions and been duly diligent. In *Rotherham Metropolitan BC v Raysun (UK) Ltd*[15]:

> The defendants, large-scale importers of Far East products, imported once a year about 100,000 packets of children's wax crayons from Hong Kong. Their agents there had samples analysed and had to send back only adverse reports: none was received. The defendants tested in England a single packet. They sold the crayons as "poisonless". The black crayons contained excessive amounts of toxic material.

The Divisional Court rejected their defence under s.24(1). They had not checked that the Hong Kong analyses were in fact taking place and their sample in England was "very moderate".

The by-pass provision

13.22 Although the so-called "by-pass provision" in s.23 is not a defence, it is appropriate to deal with it at this point in view of its close interaction with the defence in s.24(1). Section 23 states:

---

[13] See para.13.22.
[14] s.24(1)(b).
[15] *The Times*, April 27, 1988. See also *Amos v Melcon (Frozen Foods)* (1985) 149 J.P. 712, DC: "rump steak" was really silverside of beef; insufficient evidence of sampling; no defence.

Where the commission by any person of an offence under this Act is due to the act or default of some other person that other person shall be guilty of the offence, and a person may be charged with and convicted of the offence by virtue of this section whether or not proceedings are taken against the first-mentioned person.

Thus where X commits an offence, but the real culprit is Y, Y may be prosecuted for the offence committed by X. It is irrelevant whether or not proceedings have been taken against X. The corollary is that if no offence is committed by X, Y cannot be prosecuted under s.23.[16]

It can result in an offence being committed by a private person who cannot otherwise be charged, because he is not acting "in the course of a trade or business". Thus even if Y were a private person, he could be charged under s.23.[17]

Advertisements

Section 25 affords a special defence in the case of advertisements. In any proceedings for an offence relating to the publication of an advertisement the defendant is free from liability if he can prove that (a) the advertisement was received and published in the course of a business involving such publication, and (b) he did not know and had no reason to know that the publication would amount to an offence under the Act. The defence protects not only the publishers themselves, e.g. of newspapers and magazines, but also those who arrange for the publication of advertisements, e.g. advertising agencies. **13.23**

7. ENFORCEMENT

One of the major defects of the Merchandise Marks Acts was the absence of anybody with a duty to enforce their provisions. Section 26(1) clearly places the obligation of prosecution on trading standards officers in the following unequivocal terms: "It shall be the duty of every local weights and measures authority to enforce within their area the provisions of this Act." **13.24**

To assist the inspectors in carrying out their duties s.27 gives them the power to check compliance with the Act by making test purchases.

Section 28 of the Act enables them to enter premises to make spot checks and, if reasonable cause for suspicion of an offence exists, to require production[18] of the books and documents of the business.

Before instituting proceedings the local authority must give notice to BIS. Such liaison helps to prevent numerous prosecutions in different areas for the same offence, for example, for goods or services advertised and supplied nationally. However, multiple prosecutions do sometimes occur. **13.25**

---

[16] *Cottee v Douglas Seaton (Used Cars) Ltd* [1972] 1 W.L.R. 1408.
[17] *Olgeirsson v Kitching* [1986] 1 W.L.R. 304, DC.
[18] "Produce" does not mean "hand over and allow to take away": *Barge v British Gas Corp* (1983) 81 L.G.R. 53, DC.

A prosecution must be brought within three years of the commission of an offence or one year from its discovery, whichever is the earlier.[19]

8. PENALTIES

13.26 If proceedings are brought summarily, a fine not exceeding £5,000 may be levied in respect of each offence. If the defendant is convicted on indictment, not only may the fine be unlimited but imprisonment of up to two years may be imposed—both penalties may be meted out.[20] Occasionally prison sentences are imposed but the Divisional Court stated in *R. v Haesler*[21] that imprisonment is normally reserved for cases involving dishonesty.

---

[19] s.19(1). But see also s.19(2) and (4).
[20] s.18.
[21] [1973] Crim.L.R. 586.

CHAPTER FOURTEEN

"THE PRICE WAS WRONG"

1. HISTORICAL BACKGROUND

For the last forty years various statutory attempts have been made to control **14.01** misleading price claims. Some have adopted a very detailed approach, others a broad-brush approach. As with all very specific regulations businesses and their legal advisers spend (or waste?) long hours seeking and exploiting loopholes in their battle with consumer protection agencies. Hence the Government has resorted to "principles based" regulation exemplified by the Consumer Protection from Unfair Trading Regulations 2008 (the CPRs) (discussed generally in Chapter 17) which repealed the Consumer Protection Act 1987, Pt III.

The CPRs have particular provisions about price on which we comment later in this chapter. Before doing so we shall briefly explain the earlier approaches to the problem of misleading prices which may help to put the current statutory solutions into perspective. (Previous editions of this book examine the earlier legislation in some detail.)

Trade Descriptions Act 1968

The Molony Committee in 1961 recommended[1] that the problem should be **14.02** tackled by including in the definition of trade description "the former or usual price of any goods". However, instead the Trade Descriptions Act 1968 endeavoured to deal with the mischief with separate price provisions contained in s.11. It created three offences: (1) false comparisons with a recommended price; (2) false comparisons with the trader's own previous price; (3) an indication that the price is less than that actually being charged.

Recommended prices[2]

The first offence caused little difficulty inasmuch as it was easy to prove from manufacturers' lists whether or not an offence had been committed. However, the Act had no deterrent effect on the practice of manufacturers setting unrealistically high recommended prices (so-called "sky prices") to enable retailers to offer an apparent bargain to their customers by discounting.

---

[1] Para.636.
[2] The Resale Prices Act 1976 makes it unlawful to impose minimum resale prices (resale price maintenance or RPM) on distributors.

Previous prices

The second offence was similar to the first offence except that the false indication related to the price at which the supplier previously offered the goods.

Overcharging

The third offence was expressed in very wide terms and covered situations where the customer was charged a higher price than he would have expected to pay in view of the indications as to price given to him by the supplier.

Bargain Offers

14.03 The Director General's original intention was to refer bargain offers to the Consumer Protection Advisory Committee under Part II of the Fair Trading Act 1973, but it appeared that it might be difficult to provide evidence that the practice adversely affected the economic interests of consumers. Accordingly, early in 1978 he made his first recommendations to the Secretary of State under s.2(3) of the 1973 Act. The Secretary of State used a regulation-making power under the Prices Act 1974 to introduce the Price Marking (Bargain Offers) Order 1979.[3]

The Order was complex and not a model of clarity. It well illustrates the difficult task of attempting by detailed regulations to block up numerous, distinct business malpractices. The severe criticism of the Order from both sides of the fence—business suppliers and trading standards departments—resulted in 1987 in the replacement of both the Order and s.11 of the 1968 Act with new primary legislation.

Consumer Protection Act 1987, Pt III

14.04 The purpose of Pt III of the Consumer Protection Act 1987 was to adopt a much more flexible approach than the previous legislation in the hope that this would cope with the constantly changing commercial practices and marketing techniques of the modern world. This more general approach could be found in the main offence created by s.20(1) of giving a misleading price indication. The offence covered "any goods, services, accommodation or facilities". This broad approach is not unique in the field of consumer protection. Indeed, it can be found elsewhere in the 1987 Act in that s.10 introduced the "general safety requirement" as an umbrella to cover areas not dealt with in specific regulations.[4] Similarly Pt III contained a general umbrella offence. This was complemented by s.26 giving power to make regulations to be activated when particular practices required specific provisions.[5]

---

[3] SI 1979/364, as amended by SI 1979/633.
[4] Below, para.15.06.
[5] Below, para.14.05.

Bureaux de Change

The only regulations made under s.26 and preserved by the CPRs are the Price **14.05**
Indications (Bureaux de Change) (No.2) Regulations 1992.[6] Their purpose is
obvious from their title: they are concerned with transparency and information for consumers. Any traveller will have seen the effect of these regulations
when obtaining foreign currency. For example, the selling, buying and commission rates must be stated. If the rates for travellers' cheques and notes are
different, that must be shown. This information must be given "clearly and
prominently" and must be visible to consumers as they either approach or
enter the bureau de change.

2. THE CPRs

As we have seen, the CPRs[7] repealed the Consumer Protection Act 1987, Pt **14.06**
III, leaving as its only trace the Order discussed in para.14.05.

The regulation of prices now falls within the CPRs, of which a number of
provisions are aimed specifically at prices.

Reg.5 is concerned with "misleading actions", which we discuss more generally in para.17.28. Here we draw attention only to reg.5(2)(a). With reference to a commercial practice which "contains false information", it directs
attention to reg.5(4). This contains a list lettered (a) to (k) of relevant matters:
two are important on pricing—

(g) the price or the manner in which the price is calculated;

(h) the existence of a specific price advantage.

The black list of unfair practices in Sch.1 also needs to be considered. Paras 5
and 6 are both concerned with prices and the malpractices of bait advertising
and bait and switch respectively. Paragraph 20 deals with "gratis", "free" and
"without charge" offers which are not really so.

3. PRICE MARKING

We complete our survey of consumer protection measures about prices with **14.07**
a comment on the Price Marking Order 2004 (SI 2004/102). It implements
EU Directive 98/6/EC on consumer protection in the indication of prices of
products offered to consumers.

Article 4 requires a trader who indicates that a product is for sale to indicate its sale price in sterling. There are exceptions, e.g. in art.(3): auctions,
works of art and antiques. Advertisements for products are also exempt if
they are aural, on television, shown at a cinema or inside a small shop (280
square metres or less: art.1(2)).[8]

---

[6] SI 1992/737. See CPR Sch.3, para.5.
[7] SI 2008/1277
[8] art.5(3) and Sch. 2.

There are special provisions about sales at reduced prices (art.9) and precious metals (art.10).

Where a trader sells products from bulk and certain pre-packaged goods, he must indicate the unit price (art.5). Sch.1 contains a long list of the relevant unit of quantity for specified products ranging from coffee to coal and pies to pipe tobacco.

CHAPTER FIFTEEN

"THE GOODS AREN'T SAFE"

1. INTRODUCTION

In Chapter Five we considered Pt I of the Consumer Protection Act 1987   **15.01**
which imposes *civil* liability on *producers* of unsafe goods. In this chapter
we turn to Pt II of the 1987 Act and the General Product Safety Regulations
2005[1] which impose *criminal* sanctions on *producers and suppliers* of unsafe
goods (and only *consumer* goods in relation to the general safety requirements). First this recent legislation will be placed in its historical context by
briefly reviewing its legislative predecessors.

We have seen in earlier chapters that often consumer protection legislation
is concerned as much with shoddy, poor quality goods as with dangerous
goods. However, in many statutes a different approach is adopted where death
or personal injury is concerned: provisions are likely to be more stringent or
restrictive than in cases where only financial or economic loss results. Thus,
under the Unfair Contract Terms Act 1977, s.2, a clause excluding liability for
negligence is void in the case of death or personal injury, but valid if reasonable
in the case of other loss or damage, e.g. damage to property.[2] In other areas the
same emphasis is placed on ensuring that the individual is protected against
death or injury. For example, the Health and Safety at Work, etc. Act 1974, s.6,
ensures that articles for use at work are safe when properly used.

Concern for safety at home should be as serious as concern for safety in the   **15.02**
work place. The Foreword to *Consumer Safety. A Consultative Document*[3]
provided ample evidence.

> About 7,000 people in Great Britain die each year from accidents in the home,
> over a tenth of them from fires. This is comparable to the number killed on the
> roads. In addition over 100,000 receive hospital in-patient treatment for home
> accident injuries. No central statistics are kept for those not admitted to hospi-
> tal, but it is estimated that in England and Wales 650,000 receive out-patient care
> in hospitals and 500,000 attend their general practitioner for treatment.
> Apart from the toll of human suffering which these figures represent, there are
> substantial economic costs, both direct—through damage to property, as in the
> case of the 50,000 or so fires in the home each year—and indirect—*e.g.* the cost
> of medical treatment and hours lost from work.
> This Consultative Document is concerned with ways of reducing the cost and

---

[1] SI 2005/1803 implementing the 2001 EC General Product Safety Directive, below,
para.15.25.
[2] Above, para.8.28.
[3] Cmnd.6398, (1976).

suffering caused by home accidents. It considers how information, publicity and education on causes of home accidents and means of avoiding them can be improved; and in particular it discusses how the law can best ensure that goods which reach consumers are as safe to use as the public may reasonably expect.

As the last paragraph states, the Green Paper paid particular attention to the way in which the law could be improved with a view to ensuring that goods used by the consumer are safe. At that time this branch of the law was regulated by the Consumer Protection Acts 1961 and 1971. Several of the proposals contained in the paper for improving the legal protective framework were incorporated in the Consumer Safety Act 1978.

Consumer Safety Act 1978

15.03 Its main purpose was to prevent dangerous goods reaching the market or, if they had done so, to prohibit their further sale. The most important changes effected by the Act were these:

(1) It gave any Secretary of State much more flexible powers to make regulations to ensure that goods are safe and to prohibit the supply of unsafe goods.[4]

(2) It enabled quick action to be taken to ban the supply of dangerous goods by the use of "prohibition orders"[5] and "prohibition notices".

(3) It provided power by the service of a "notice to warn" to require manufacturers and distributors of goods, which were found to be dangerous only after they had been sold, to publish notices warning the public of the danger.[6]

(4) It imposed an enforcement duty on local authorities.[7]

These improvements are retained in the 1987 Act.

Consumer Safety (Amendment) Act 1986

15.04 Less than six years after the 1978 Act came into force the Government published a White Paper, *The Safety of Goods*,[8] setting out the Government's conclusions with regard to the effectiveness of the consumer products safety legislation. It contained proposals for amending the 1978 Act with a view to strengthening its provisions. One example mentioned in the White Paper illustrated the difficulties. In 1981 over a hundred types of electrical hair-curling brushes were imported in large numbers, mostly from the Far East. They failed to satisfy the regulations on matters such as insulation, but this hazard

---

[4] s.1.
[5] s.3(1). Prohibition orders are no longer available: below, para.15.14.
[6] ibid.
[7] s.5(1).
[8] Cmnd.9302, (1984).

did not become apparent until they had reached the shops and market stalls, been sold and were in use. It proved to be an expensive, time-consuming exercise to track down the unsafe appliances and have them removed from sale. In the interval, a death or serious injury could easily have occurred.

The purpose of the recommendations was to introduce preventative measures to assist in identifying and halting the supply of unsafe goods before they reached the shops; to enable enforcement officers to suspend the supply of apparently unsafe goods; and to introduce a general safety duty on all suppliers.

The 1986 Act added the first two of those new weapons to the armoury of the enforcement authorities. They both reappear in the 1987 Act:

(1) Customs officers were given power to detain imported goods for two days and to pass on information to trading standards officers, who would thus be given time to activate their other procedures.

(2) Trading standards officers were empowered to serve suspension notices to prohibit supplies of goods for up to six months, and to apply to the court for an order that goods be forfeited and destroyed. Related compensation provisions were also enacted.

2. CONSUMER PROTECTION ACT 1987, PT II

The proposal that there should be a general statutory duty on suppliers to supply safe consumer goods was first put forward in the consultative document *Consumer Safety*.[9] The absence of this duty on suppliers of consumer goods contrasted with the duty on suppliers of articles for use at work imposed by the Health and Safety at Work, etc. Act 1974. The Government's policy remained consistent and was reiterated in para.34 of the White Paper[10]: **15.05**

> The Government accepts that there is a case for widening the scope of the Act to place a general obligation on the suppliers of consumer goods to achieve an acceptable standard of safety where it is reasonable to expect them to anticipate and reduce risks arising from those goods. This would induce a greater sense of responsibility on the part of those suppliers who currently regard themselves as unaffected by legislation (and who may not be adequately deterred by the common law duty of care). At the same time it would provide wider scope for swift remedial action by enforcement authorities in the case of newly identified dangerous products.

This "general safety requirement" (GSR) was the novel feature of the 1987 Act but it has been repealed and replaced by the GSR contained in the General Product Safety Regulations 2005.[11] Otherwise the 1987 Act is in the main a consolidating statute bringing together in Pt II the provisions of the 1978 and 1986 Acts. **15.06**

---

[9] Above, n.3.
[10] Above, n.8.
[11] Below, para.15.29.

The regulatory regime now consists of the following measures which we shall consider below.

(1) Safety regulations impose specific requirements in relation to a particular type of product.

(2) Prohibition notices, notices to warn and suspension notices provide back-up powers to control particular traders dealing in unsafe goods.

(3) The GSR in the 2005 Regulations prohibits producers from placing unsafe consumer products on the market and imposes on distributors a duty of care in this respect. These Regulations are considered in a separate section at the end of this chapter.

As a preliminary it is necessary to look at some key words defined in the 1987 Act.

Key definitions

15.07 The definitions are found in various places. Those definitions relating to the Act as a whole are found in ss.45 and 46 (some of these have already been discussed in Chapter Five in relation to Pt I); those relating only to Pt II appear in s.19; and a few of more limited importance are given in the relevant section itself.

Safe

15.08 This is the core of Pt II—it is essentially concerned with dangerous, unsafe goods, not with shoddy goods of poor quality (this is true of Pt I too). Section 19(1) gives this meaning to the word "safe":

> 'safe', in relation to any goods, means such that there is no risk, or no risk apart from one reduced to a minimum, that any of the following will (whether immediately or after a definite or indefinite period) cause the death of, or any personal injury to, any person whatsoever, that is to say—
>
> (a) the goods;
> (b) the keeping, use or consumption of the goods[12];
> (c) the assembly of any of the goods which are, or are to be, supplied unassembled;
> (d) any emission or leakage from the goods or, as a result of the keeping, use or consumption of the goods, from anything else; or
> (e) reliance on the accuracy of any measurement, calculation or other reading made by or by means of the goods,
>
> and 'safer' and 'unsafe' shall be construed accordingly.

It can be seen that goods do not have to be absolutely safe, but the risk at worst must be "reduced to a minimum". This is a commonsense approach,

---

[12] s.19(2) amplifies this aspect.

since otherwise some products would be outlawed, e.g. motor vehicles, lawn mowers, power saws.

It is enough to refer to some of the regulations made under the 1961 and 1978 Acts[13] to find examples of unsafe goods: unstable carry-cot stands or prams; anorak hoods causing strangulation; explosive oil heaters or lamps; toys with sharp edges or spikes or loose doll's eyes; flammable nightdresses; retreaded motor tyres.

Electrical appliances provide frequent examples; here faulty insulation brings with it the hazard of electrocution—electric blankets, hair-curling brushes, vacuum cleaners and electric razors.

The importance of (b) lies in making regulations relating to the effectiveness **15.09** of safety equipment, e.g. life jackets, buoyancy rafts, fire extinguishers; for the risk arises not from the product itself but from the fact that, when circumstances occur in which the equipment is in "use", it is found at that late, critical stage to be unsuitable and thus to expose the user to risk. The significance of the word "keeping" can be seen in relation to labelling requirements on goods which create a hazard if not safely stored, e.g. garden pesticides.

Examples of the other factors in the list may be helpful:

(c) flat pack furniture, unassembled bicycles;

(d) household cleaning fluids, pressure cookers, gas cylinders;

(e) tyre pressure gauges, speedometers.

Goods

The definition of "goods" in s.45(1) is very wide and is not confined to con-   **15.10** sumer goods:

'goods' includes substances, growing crops and things comprised in land by virtue of being attached to it and any ship, aircraft or vehicle.

However, safety regulations may not be made in respect of crops, water, food, feeding stuff, fertilisers, mains gas, drugs and medicines.[14]

Supply

A supply is caught only if made "in the course of carrying on a business   **15.11** (whether or not a business of dealing in the goods in question[15]) and as principal or agent."[16] The business supply is covered; the private supply is not.

What types of transaction are "supplies"? The definition provides a detailed answer.

---

[13] These regulations continue in force until replaced by new regulations.
[14] s.11(7).
[15] s.46(5). These clarifying words do not appear in the equivalent provision of the 1961 Act. But in *Southwark LBC v Charlesworth* [1983] C.L.Y. 3311 the Divisional Court reached the same conclusion: a shoe repairer who sold an unsafe electric fire through his shop breached the Electrical Equipment (Safety) Regulations 1975 (SI 1975/1366).
[16] s.46(1).

  (i) Sale.

  (ii) Hire or loan.

  (iii) Hire-purchase.

15.12   Section 45(2) provides that in the case of hire, hire-purchase, credit sale or conditional sale agreements, "the supplier" is not the provider of the credit (the "ostensible supplier") but "the effective supplier" who is enabled to provide the goods by virtue of such financial facility.

Example

> D wishes to acquire on credit terms a car owned by a dealer S. S sells the car to a finance house C. C lets the goods on hire-purchase to D. S is "the supplier" under the 1987 Act. (To use Consumer Credit Act jargon, the credit-broker S (not the creditor C) is the supplier.)

  (iv) Work and materials.

  (v) Exchange, e.g. for trading stamps.

  (vi) Provision under a statutory function, e.g. the NHS.

  (vii) Gift, e.g. a prize.

Safety regulations

15.13   Safety regulations are an old feature of this area of consumer protection. Indeed, regulations under the Acts of 1961 and 1978 continue in force. The current offences for contravention of safety regulations are to be found in s.12, e.g. supplying goods prohibited by regulations. It is s.11 which contains the regulation-making power:

> (1) The Secretary of State may by regulations under this section ("safety regulations") make such provision as he considers appropriate for the purposes of section 10(3) above and for the purpose of securing—
>
> (a) that goods to which this section applies are safe;
> (b) that goods to which this section applies which are unsafe, or would be unsafe in the hands of persons of a particular description, are not made available to persons generally or, as the case may be, to persons of that description; and
> (c) that appropriate information is, and inappropriate information is not, provided in relation to goods to which this section applies.

Thus regulations may cover not only the goods, but also information about them. Further, s.11(1)(b) makes it clear that they may relate to the supply of goods to certain groups only, a doubtful point in earlier legislation, e.g. fireworks not to be sold to children.

The possible contents of regulations are illustrated by a list set out in s.11(2). They include provisions relating to:

  (i) composition or contents, design, construction, finish or packing;

  (ii) standards to be approved, e.g. British Standards;

(iii) testing or inspection, e.g. manufacturers' quality control procedures to prevent faulty batches of aerosol cans from reaching the market;

(iv) marks, warnings, instructions or other information on goods, e.g. warning symbols, first-aid instructions, lists of ingredients in cosmetics; or prohibiting the giving of "inappropriate information", e.g. misleading marks or insignia.

The regulations may also prohibit the supply of goods or components which are unsafe or do not satisfy the requirements of the regulations. Thus a permanent ban may be imposed on dangerous products which the Secretary of State considers to be inherently unsafe irrespective of design or construction, e.g. oral snuff, imitation dummies.

Emergency procedures

Extensive consultation is required by s.11(5) before the making of regulations. As many months may elapse in this way, the 1978 Act contained power for the Minister to make prohibition orders to by-pass the normal regulation-making procedures as a temporary measure in an emergency.[17]   **15.14**

Prohibition orders have now disappeared and been replaced by the expedited procedure set out in s.11(5). The Secretary of State may make regulations without consultation for a 12 months maximum where "the need to protect the public requires that regulations should be made without delay".[18]

Notices

The Act contains various powers to stop the distribution, or further distribution, of unsafe goods.   **15.15**

Suspension notice[19]

If an enforcement authority reasonably suspects that a trader is supplying goods in contravention of a safety provision, it may serve a "suspension notice" on him. This will prevent him disposing of his stock for a maximum of six months. The authority may have to pay compensation, if there was no contravention after all. A separate, but sometimes related, route is to apply to the court for forfeiture of the goods, which usually involves their destruction.[20] In neither of these cases is a conviction of the trader a prerequisite; only a "contravention" is needed.   **15.16**

Prohibition notice[21]

Like the suspension notice, the "prohibition notice" is aimed at a particular trader. It is served by the Secretary of State and prohibits the supply of   **15.17**

---

[17] See 2nd edn of this book, pp.238–240, for an explanation of this procedure.
[18] E.g. Fireworks Regulations 2003 (SI 2003/3085).
[19] s.14(1).
[20] s.16.
[21] s.13(1)(a).

unsafe goods. This is a useful follow-up to the local authority's suspension notice.

The power is rarely used. No such notice had been issued since 1992, until the banning in April 2003 of "yo-balls"—toy balls made of a jelly like material attached by an elastic strap to a finger loop. They could pose a risk of strangulation to children and so did not meet the requirements of the Toys (Safety) Regulations 1995.[22] The DTI served prohibition notices on three English and two Scottish companies.

Notice to warn[23]

15.18 Prohibition notices are appropriate where goods are still in the hands of the suppliers. What can be done if the goods have already reached the public and are in daily use? Prior to the Act the most that the Department of Trade and Industry could do was to ask manufacturers to publish a warning or itself to issue a press notice. Responsible manufacturers and importers readily do so. The motor industry is a good example; as soon as any apparent defect reveals itself as a danger, e.g. brakes, the producer gives it widespread publicity and advises owners to take in their vehicles to be checked.

Now it is possible for the Secretary of State to serve a "notice to warn" on any trader requiring him to publish a specified warning about unsafe goods at his own expense.

Recall

15.19 A major defect in the 1987 Act was that no one had the power to order manufacturers to recall dangerous products, although in practice they do recall such goods to avoid being sued under Pt I of the 1987 Act or for negligence.[24]

However, the General Product Safety Regulations 2005[25] (revoking the 1994 GPS Regulations) at long last give enforcement authorities the power to require the recall of dangerous products.[26]

General safety requirement (GSR)

15.20 The wide-ranging GSR imposed on suppliers by s.10 of the 1987 Act was the linch-pin of United Kingdom safety legislation until its virtual replacement by the GSR originally imposed by the 1994 Regulations and its ultimate repeal by the 2005 Regulations, reg.46. Accordingly our discussion of the 1987 Act GSR will be brief.[27]

No longer was it necessary to bring in regulations piecemeal when particular products proved to be dangerous. This was the difficulty faced by the enforcement authorities before the 1987 Act, when the closing of various

---

[22] SI 1995/204, made under the 1987 Act, s.11.
[23] s.13(1)(b).
[24] See Ch. 5.
[25] Below, para.15.25.
[26] Below, para.15.42.
[27] See the 3rd edn of this book, pp. 249–251, for a more detailed analysis.

specific loopholes by regulations was no help when tackling another type of unsafe product when it appeared on the market.

Section 10(1) contained the GSR offence: **15.21**

> A person shall be guilty of an offence if he—
>
> (a) supplies any consumer goods which fail to comply with the general safety requirement;
> (b) offers or agrees to supply any such goods; or
> (c) exposes or possesses any such goods for supply.

Unlike the safety regulations made under Pt II and the product liability provisions of Pt I of the 1987 Act, it was confined to *consumer* goods, i.e. "ordinarily intended for private use or consumption".[28]

Defences and penalties

The familiar defence is available that the accused "took all reasonable steps   **15.22**
and exercised all due diligence[29] to avoid committing the offence", with the usual duty to notify the prosecutor of the identity of any one else who is being blamed.[30]

The penalty for any of the offences is the same—on summary conviction a maximum fine of £5,000 and up to six months' imprisonment.[31]

Enforcement

Although the 1961 Act merely gave a discretionary power to trading stand-   **15.23**
ards inspectors, s.27(1) makes it their duty to enforce the provisions creating the offences explained above. Whether with the limited resources available to them local authorities are managing to cope with their ever-increasing responsibilities—the Consumer Credit Act 1974 is also their problem—is debatable. Nevertheless this duty is one which they must do their best to fulfil, unless the Secretary of State exercises the power given to him by s.27(2) to transfer the duty elsewhere. Sections 28 and 29 give the authorities the usual related powers of purchase, entry and seizure, testing, etc., and s.30 enables a customs officer to detain imported goods for two days.

Civil remedy

In the following chapter breach of statutory duty is examined.[32] The Acts   **15.24**
of 1961 to 1987 stand alone among the criminal statutes concerned with consumer protection in expressly affording the victim a civil remedy. Section 41(1) offers the remedy and s.41(4) prevents it being snatched away by invalidating any exclusion clause. Further, any contractual rights of the victim

---

[28] s.10(7).
[29] *Balding v Lew-Ways Ltd* [1995] Crim.L.R. 878: non-compliance with Toys (Safety) Regulations 1989 (SI 1989/1275); not "due diligence" to rely on analyst's report that toy complied with British Standard.
[30] s.39(1) and (2). See *Riley v Webb* [1987] Crim.L.R. 477.
[31] e.g. s.12(5).
[32] Below, para.16.11.

remain untouched.[33] However, this civil remedy applies only to breach of the safety regulations, not of the GSR. In practice it is rarely, if ever, used.

3. GENERAL PRODUCT SAFETY REGULATIONS 2005

1992 EU General Product Safety[34] Directive

15.25 We have just seen that the policy of ensuring that the consumer is protected from dangerous goods had been implemented in the United Kingdom by taking two complementary routes, First, legislation was introduced enabling regulations to be passed to regulate particular kinds of products which were inherently hazardous.[35] Such "vertical legislation" copes only with narrow sectoral problems which are attacked piecemeal, leaving the holes in the dyke to be plugged as and when they appear. So the second route was taken of introducing "horizontal legislation" with the imposition of a general safety requirement (GSR) by the Consumer Protection Act 1987.[36]

Of course, such problems exist at the European level too and can be met with similar solutions. The importance of safety was emphasised in point 72 of the 1985 EU White Paper *Completing the Internal Market* which stated that the health and safety of workers and consumers were interests which should be taken into account in the 1992 programme. This very same point was referred to in July 1985 when the European Commission submitted to the European Council a Communication concerning a *New Impetus for a Consumer Protection Policy*. This Communication gave a special priority to consumer safety and was followed in May 1987 by another Communication on *Safety of Consumers in Relation to Consumer Products*, which ended with the promise: "The Commission shortly intends to submit to the Council a proposal for a general Directive on consumer safety in relation to consumer products."

15.26 This ambition was not realised until June 1989 when the EU Commission submitted its proposal for a Directive on General Product Safety. Horizontal legislation already existed in such other influential countries as France and Germany. Indeed, in this area as in others there was a marked distinction between the approach adopted by the northern Member States and the southern or Mediterranean Member States whose legislation on product safety was much less stringent. These anomalies are highlighted in the Preamble to the 1992 Directive:

> Whereas some Member States have adopted horizontal legislation on product safety, imposing, in particular, a general obligation on economic operators to market only safe products; whereas those legislations differ in the level of protection afforded to persons; whereas such disparities and the absence of horizontal legislation in other Member States are liable to create barriers to trade and distortions of competition within the internal market.

[33] s.41(3).
[34] 92/59/EEC.
[35] Above, para.15.13.
[36] Above, para.15.20.

One difficulty was how to dovetail specific EU or national rules relating to particular products or product sectors into the general safety duty at the core of the Directive. Should the specific and general duties be mutually exclusive or should they overlap? The Directive comes down firmly on the former solution—no overlap.

Another hotly debated issue was whether the Directive should cover all products or only consumer products. The original plan was to include only consumer products. Although as the debate continued the scope of the draft directive was widened to encompass all products (whether manufactured or agricultural, new or used), the Directive in its final form was watered down again: it applies only to consumer goods and excludes some second-hand goods.

The Directive on General Product Safety was finally adopted on June 29, 1992 and was supposed to come into force within two years. In the event the Government's consultation process was rather protracted and the implementation of the GPS Directive within the United Kingdom was delayed until October 3, 1994. This was the date when the General Product Safety Regulations 1994 took effect.[37]

2001 EU General Product Safety Directive[38]

On December 3, 2001 an amended GPS Directive was adopted and **15.27** came into force on January 15, 2002. Its purpose, stated in the preamble, is "to complete, reinforce and clarify some of the [1992 Directive's] provisions in the light of experience as well as new and relevant developments on consumer product safety". It mainly re-enacts the provisions of its predecessor, which was repealed from January 15, 2004. Member States should have transposed the Directive into national law by that date, but once again the UK Government was late with an implementation date of October 1, 2005.

There is one major innovation—art.8(f) entitles Member States to order the recall of a dangerous product from consumers.

Relationship to 1987 Act

We saw in the previous section that the United Kingdom already had in place **15.28** a GSR introduced by the 1987 Act. Its virtual existence was limited to seven years as the main effect of the 1994 Regulations was to make the GSR in s.10 redundant; it has been repealed now by the 2005 Regulations.[39]

2005 GSR

The essence of the Regulations appears in reg.5:   **15.29**

> (1) No producer shall place a product on the market unless the product is a safe product.

---

[37] SI 1994/2328.
[38] 2001/95/EC.
[39] Reg.46

(2) No producer shall offer or agree to place a product on the market or expose or possess a product for placing on the market unless the product is a safe product.

(3) No producer shall offer or agree to supply a product or expose or possess a product for supply unless the product is a safe product.

(4) No producer shall supply a product unless the product is a safe product.

15.30 Unlike the GSR in the 1987 Act this is limited to a producer. However, it is backed up by a complementary provision in reg.8 aimed at distributors:

(1) A distributor shall act with due care in order to help ensure compliance with the applicable safety requirements and in particular he—

(a) shall not expose or possess for supply or offer or agree to supply, or supply, a product to any person which he knows or should have presumed, on the basis of the information in his possession and as a professional, is a dangerous product; and

(b) shall, within the limits of his activities, participate in monitoring the safety of a product placed on the market, in particular by—

(i) passing on information on the risks posed by the product,

(ii) keeping the documentation necessary for tracing the origin of the product,

(iii) producing the documentation necessary for tracing the origin of the product, and cooperating in action taken by a producer or an enforcement authority to avoid the risks.

(2) Within the limits of his activities, a distributor shall take measures enabling him to cooperate efficiently in the action referred to in paragraph (1) (b)(iii).

It can be seen that the producer is more in peril in that reg.5 creates an offence of strict liability, whereas the distributor's offence depends on his actual or presumed knowledge that the products are dangerous. Regulation 8(1)(b)(ii) imposes an additional traceability duty on distributors compared with the 1994 Regulations. Contraventions of regs. 5 or 8(1)(a) are the most serious offences (see below, para.15.43).

Both offences involve the supply of dangerous products to consumers. To discover the precise meaning of these words we need to look closely at some key definitions in reg.2.

Key definitions: reg.2

Product

15.31 "Product" is defined as follows:

'product' means a product which is intended for consumers or likely, under reasonably foreseeable conditions, to be used by consumers even if not intended for them and which is supplied or made available, whether for consideration or not, in the course of a commercial activity and whether it is new, used or reconditioned and includes a product that is supplied or made available to consumers for their own use in the context of providing a service. 'product' does not include equipment used by service providers themselves to supply a service to consumers, in particular equipment on which consumers ride or travel which is operated by a service provider;

A few comments need to be made.

(1) Although the wording does not state so expressly, clearly the Regulations apply only to goods and not to services themselves, like the Product Liability Directive.[40]

(2) The supply must be in the course of a "commercial activity". Thus a private sale by a consumer is not caught.

(3) Consumer goods fall within the Regulations.[41] A product will be caught **15.32** if it is "intended for consumers"; presumably it is the producer's intention which matters here. For example, if a producer makes a chain saw intending it to be sold to and used only by trained foresters, this would fall outside these words of the definition even if occasionally one of the saws was sold on by a trade customer to a member of the public, perhaps in a garden centre.

More problematical are the words "likely, under reasonably foreseeable conditions, to be used by consumers". Suppose that in the above case the producer discovered that his saws were frequently being sold on to consumers, perhaps in contravention of his terms of sale to the trade. Arguably once the producer discovers this, it can be said that his products are covered by the Regulations. Such difficulties will clearly arise in the case of building or gardening equipment hired out by the day, e.g. cement mixers, scaffolding, rotavators. The same is true of vans; large numbers of these are hired to consumers on a short-term basis to move house, etc., although the proportion of vans sold by producers to van and car rental companies is small compared to the sales to businesses which use the vans for their own transport purposes.

One further comment needs to be made on the definition by looking at its last sentence. Its purpose is to take outside the Regulations products which are actually being used by a trade or business even though such a product might equally be available for purchase by consumers. For example, if a hair dryer is used by a hairdresser in her salon, the equipment will fall outside the Regulations, whereas if the customer were to buy the same thing from the hairdresser, it would be covered. Taxis and private hire cars are clearly excluded too.

(4) It does not matter whether the product has been sold or given away in view of the words "whether for consideration or not".

(5) Unlike the GSR in the 1987 Act, second-hand goods are not excluded. **15.33** Indeed, the definition expressly states that a product may be "new, used or reconditioned".

However, two related exceptions appear in regs 4 and 30. A supplier of goods to be reconditioned or repaired or of antiques will not be caught provided he informed the consumer of the special facts.

Antiques are not defined. Presumably a judge would take into account whether the price reflected merely its utilitarian value or whether it took account of the age and perhaps rarity of the artefact.

The second exception will apply only where the supplier "informs" the consumer that the second-hand product is to be repaired or reconditioned before use (see reg.4). From the point of view of the supplier it will provide valuable evidence, if the sale note states this specifically.

---

[40] Above, para.5.15.
[41] Contrast the 1987 Act; above, para.15.10.

Producer

15.34 The definition is as follows:

'producer' means

(a) the manufacturer of a product, when he is established in a Member State and any other person presenting himself as the manufacturer by affixing to the product his name, trade mark or other distinctive mark, or the person who reconditions the product;

(b) when the manufacturer is not established in a Member State—
  (i) if he has a representative established in a Member State, the representative,
  (ii) in any other case, the importer of the product from a state that is not a Member State into a Member State;

(c) other professionals in the supply chain, insofar as their activities may affect the safety properties of a product;

This definition bears a close resemblance to the definition of producer given in the Product Liability Directive.[42] The definition includes businesses which are not "producers" in the ordinary sense of the word.

(1) The manufacturer himself is obviously included, but only if his business operates within the EU.

(2) Even though the producer may not be the actual manufacturer, if he gives the impression that he is the manufacturer ("presenting himself") by the way in which the goods are marked, he is treated as the producer.

(3) A business which reconditions its products is a producer, for example, a retailer taking goods in part-exchange and reselling after putting them in working order.

(4) Where there is no EU manufacturer, his representative carries the responsibility instead—presumably that means his agent. If there is no agent, the importer of the product into the EU is treated as the producer.

(5) Other businesses are also caught, even though they are merely distributors, if their "activities" may affect the product's safety. Examples would include a motor dealer conducting a pre-delivery inspection or a tyre distributor fitting replacement tyres.

Distributor

15.35 Distributor means:

a professional in the supply chain whose activity does not affect the safety properties of a product.[43]

A "distributor" is someone whose activities do not affect the product's safety; if they do so, he will fall within the meaning of "producer" (see (5) above). Such a business may also be a producer because of "own labelling", reconditioning or being the EU importer (see (2), (3) and (4) above).

---

[42] Above, para.5.24.
[43] Reg.2

Dangerous and safe products

A "dangerous product" is "a product other than a safe product". The latter   **15.36**
is defined in the following way:

'safe product' means a product which, under normal or reasonably foreseeable
conditions of use including duration and, where applicable, putting into service,
installation and maintenance requirements, does not present any risk or only
the minimum risks compatible with the product's use, considered to be acceptable and consistent with a high level of protection for the safety and health of
persons. In determining the foregoing, the following shall be taken into account
in particular—

> (a) the characteristics of the product, including its composition, packaging,
>   instructions for assembly and, where applicable, instructions for installa-
>   tion and maintenance,
> (b) the effect of the product on other products, where it is reasonably foresee-
>   able that it will be used with other products,
> (c) the presentation of the product, the labelling, any warnings and instruc-
>   tions for its use and disposal and any other indication or information
>   regarding the product, and
> (d) the categories of consumers at risk when using the product, in particular
>   children and the elderly.

The feasibility of obtaining higher levels of safety or the availability of other
products presenting a lesser degree of risk shall not constitute grounds for
considering a product to be a dangerous product;

Although the wording is not exactly the same, many of the factors appearing
in this definition are reminiscent of the factors mentioned in the definition of
"defect" in the Product Liability Directive and also in s.3 of the 1987 Act.[44]
Again, instructions are important and here they are spelt out to include
assembly, maintenance, use and disposal. One important feature is (d), high-
lighting particular categories such as children who might be at serious risk.

Another similarity appears in the sentence at the end about other products   **15.37**
being less risky. In the 1987 Act, s.3, the words are aimed at later products
being safer than the product in question, whereas in these Regulations the
comparison is between other products currently available. The Regulations
also acknowledge that "higher levels of safety may be obtained".

Clearly the definition is not imposing on producers a duty to place on the
market only perfectly safe goods. No product can be absolutely safe, so that
the broad test is whether the risk has been reduced to an acceptable level. The
beginning of the definition indicates as much by stating that a safe product is
one which "does not present any risk or only the minimum risks compatible
with the product's use, considered to be acceptable and consistent with a high
level of protection for the safety and health of persons". However, although a
product may be safe in spite of there being "minimum risks", the emphasis on
"a high level" of safety shows that producers should not be chary of spending a few pounds on introducing new safety features which will not price the
goods out of the reach of the average consumer.

---

[44] Above, para.5.17.

It should be noted, and we have made this vital point elsewhere, that the Regulations are not concerned at all with products which are shoddy and of poor quality. Their aim is simply to ensure that goods are not dangerous.

Information and monitoring

15.38 The GSR imposed on producers by reg.5 and the duty on distributors by reg.8 are intended to fulfil that aim, i.e. to prevent dangerous goods being supplied to consumers. However, even manufacturers with high standards and excellent quality control may make mistakes and place a product on the market which has unexpected and dangerous features. As a matter of self-interest manufacturers usually monitor the use of their products and react quickly, if the products turn out to be unsafe; otherwise they might be sued in tort or prosecuted. That self-interest is bolstered by the statutory requirements in regs 7 and 8(2).

15.39 Regulation 7 is addressed to producers:

> (1) Within the limits of his activities, a producer shall provide consumers with the relevant information to enable them—
> > (a) to assess the risks inherent in a product throughout the normal or reasonably foreseeable period of its use, where such risks are not immediately obvious without adequate warnings, and
> > (b) to take precautions against those risks.
> (2) The presence of warnings does not exempt any person from compliance with the other requirements of these Regulations.
> (3) Within the limits of his activities, a producer shall adopt measures commensurate with the characteristics of the products which he supplies to enable him to—
> > (a) be informed of the risks which the products might pose, and
> > (b) take appropriate action including, where necessary to avoid such risks, withdrawal, adequately and effectively warning consumers as to the risks or, as a last resort, recall.
> (4) The measures referred to in paragraph (3) include—
> > (a) except where it is not reasonable to do so, an indication by means of the product or its packaging of—
> > > (i) the name and address of the producer, and
> > > (ii) the product reference or where applicable the batch of products to which it belongs; and
> > (b) where and to the extent that it is reasonable to do so—
> > > (i) sample testing of marketed products,
> > > (ii) investigating and if necessary keeping a register of complaints concerning the safety of the product, and
> > > (iii) keeping distributors informed of the results of such monitoring where a product presents a risk or may present a risk.

Regulation 8(1)(b) and (2) is addressed to distributors and is set out above in para.15.30.

These Regulations are concerned with ensuring that the consumer is informed of potential risks and dangers and so can take precautions to prevent being harmed. The second aspect of the information provisions is concerned with monitoring the products while in use, so that the producer can withdraw the product from the market, if necessary. These monitoring provisions appear in reg.7(3), backed up by the possible measures listed in reg.7(4) and coupled with the distributor's duties specified in reg.8(1)(b) and (2).

Where, probably as a result of monitoring, a producer or distributor knows that a product on the market is dangerous, reg.9 compels them to notify an enforcement authority in writing.

Compliance with EU rules

The policy adopted by the Directive and so by the Regulations, where there **15.40** might be an overlap between the GSR and specific EU or United Kingdom rules, is to disapply the GSR in such cases. In deciding whether a product is covered by the Regulations or not the following sequence is suggested.

(1) First, consider reg.3. If *all* aspects of safety fall within specific EU rules, the Regulations do not apply at all.

(2) In contrast where such specific EU rules deal with only *some* aspects of safety, the GSR will apply to all other aspects. Regulation 3 deals with this possibility too.

(3) Where there are no EU rules one turns to reg.6(1). It provides that where a "product conforms to the specific rules of the law of part of the United Kingdom. . . the product shall be deemed safe . . .". This is self-explanatory.

(4) In the absence of the above rules the GSR applies. Regulations 6(2) and (3) give a list of factors to be taken into account in assessing whether the product conforms to the GSR, e.g. voluntary UK standards, codes of good practice and the state of the art.

Enforcement

Enforcement, as usual, is placed in the busy hands of local authority trading **15.41** standards services.[45] They are given substantial powers to serve various "safety notices":

(1) "a suspension notice" to prohibit temporarily the placing of a product on the market while they organise safety checks, etc (reg.11);

(2) "a requirement to mark" dangerous products with warnings (reg.12);

(3) "a requirement to warn" the public of risks (reg.13);

(4) "a withdrawal notice" prohibiting the placing of a product on the market (reg.14);

(5) "a recall notice" (reg.15). This is discussed below (para.15.42).

Regulations 16 and 17 contain a number of supplementary provisions about safety notices and details of appeals procedures. As a final resort

---

[45] Reg.10.

enforcement authorities may apply to the court for a forfeiture order, which will usually result in the dangerous products being destroyed (reg.18).

Recall

15.42　We have commented in early editions on the inability of public authorities to order the recall of unsafe products which have already reached the public. We consider the most important reform introduced by the 2001 Directive and the 2005 Regulations is the power to serve a recall notice given by reg.15. Such a procedure is expensive for business, since the cost of contacting customers who have the unsafe products can be enormous—advertisements in the press and, where the current ownership is known (cars are the best example), direct postal contact too. Regulation 15 is inevitably very detailed to ensure that the interests of business as well as of consumers are taken into account. Thus, a recall notice may not be served where other action would suffice (reg.15(4)). (The recall in 2010 by Toyota of 190,000 cars with defective accelerators was voluntary.)

Offences and Penalties

15.43　The offences are listed in reg.20. The most serious are contraventions of the GSR in regs.5 and 8(1)(a).[46]

The penalties, also in reg.20, are most severe for those two contraventions: a maximum of twelve months' imprisonment and a fine of £20,000, if convicted on indictment. For lesser offences the figures are three months and £5,000.

The usual "due diligence" defence is provided by reg.29.

Civil liability

15.44　The question for consumers is whether the Regulations enable a civil action to be brought. The answer is an unambiguous "no", given by reg.42. The consumer's right of action in the civil courts will be based on the contractual position discussed in Chapter Four or the tortious position under the Consumer Protection Act 1987 analysed in Chapter Five.

RAPEX and monitoring

15.45　In the previous pages we discussed the transposition into the law of the United Kingdom of those Articles of the Directive which are concerned with the responsibilities of producers and distributors. The 2005 Regulations are not confined to those matters. The Directive has a broader scope and deals, in the Articles and the Annex, with the duty of public authorities to monitor compliance with its provisions and to ensure that, if dangerous products reach the market, action is taken by the appropriate Member State to have them withdrawn from the market.[47]

The onus lies on the Member States to make appropriate monitoring

---

[46] Above, para.15.30.
[47] art.6.

arrangements and to establish or nominate appropriate authorities to effect compliance by suppliers with the GSR.[48] Regulations 32 to 39 deal with the interrelation between BIS, the European Commission and enforcement authorities and with market surveillance and public information.

Emergency procedures are specially built into the Directive. Where there is a "serious and immediate risk", the Member State must ensure that there is a "rapid exchange of information" between its own authorities. If the grave risk is not merely local, it must immediately inform the Commission.[49] RAPEX (the Community System of Rapid Exchange of Information) was originally introduced in 1984 by a Council decision. BIS is the central contact point for RAPEX in the UK.

In limited circumstances the Commission may take the initiative[50]—there was some anxiety in a number of countries that the Brussels bureaucracy, as they saw it, would be too keen to interfere. The Commission will be assisted by a new Committee on Product Safety Emergencies.

Safety of services

Neither the EU Directives nor home grown UK legislation extend beyond the safety of goods to cover services too. Recently, however, there has been some activity in Brussels on this important topic. The European Commission published a consultation paper *"Safety of Services"* in August 2002 suggesting a number of options such as data collection to monitor the safety of service activities. The most significant proposal was a general safety obligation on service providers similar to the GSR in the GPS Directive. It appears from the EC Commission's report to the Council and Parliament in June 2003 that lack of evidence of specific internal market problems makes it difficult to justify substantive Community action. Even so, six months later the ball was gently played back to the Commission by a Council Resolution[51] asking the Commission to consider how far safety might be improved by adopting European standards on services and to bring forward proposals for action by October 2004. We still await developments with interest, but probably not in the immediate future.

15.46

---

[48] art.6.
[49] Reg.33(5); art.12.
[50] art.13. See reg.35.
[51] O.J./C299/1, 2003.

CHAPTER SIXTEEN

"CRIME AND COMPENSATION"

1. INTRODUCTION

A commonly held view of the consumer protection lobby is that it is a waste **16.01**
of effort for Parliament and the courts to amend and improve upon the long-
standing rights of consumers, e.g. under the Sale of Goods Act 1979, and to
launch assaults across a broad front on attempts to rob the consumer of those
rights, e.g. under the Unfair Contract Terms Act 1977. In both the above
examples the consumers clearly have a right of action for breach of contract,
but of what benefit are their rights unless machinery exists to enable them to
be enforced without difficulty? The immediate need is for reform to be concentrated upon the enforcement of existing rights rather than the creation of
new ones and for information and education to ensure that consumers are
aware of those rights.

We discussed in Chapter Ten enforcement under the civil law. We saw that **16.02**
frequently the consumer has no alternative to suing the recalcitrant trader
in the county court; for there is often no ombudsman scheme in a particular
sector nor even a trade association able or prepared to bring about a settlement of the complaint by conciliation or to discipline the trader for falling
below the standards set out in a code of practice. In such circumstances
there are clearly considerable advantages to consumers if they can reap some
benefit from the fact that the trader has committed a criminal offence in addition to having broken one of its civil obligations. However, it should be borne
in mind that criminal offences are not created for the purpose of providing
consumers with compensation, as was pointed out in the 1976 Review of the
Trade Descriptions Act 1968, para.281:

> We believe that compensation is primarily a matter for the civil law, and that an
> award of compensation under the Powers of the Criminal Courts Act should be
> regarded as a windfall rather than a right which itself justified prosecution under
> the Act.

It is proposed in this chapter to deal with two aspects of recovery arising out of
the criminal law. First, we shall look at the power of the courts on conviction
to award compensation under the Powers of Criminal Courts (Sentencing)
Act 2000. Secondly, we shall consider the circumstances in which it is possible
to sue for breach of statutory duty.[1]

---

[1] See below, para.16.11

2. POWERS OF CRIMINAL COURTS (SENTENCING) ACT 2000

16.03 The recommendations of the 1970 Widgery Report with regard to the remedies available under the criminal law for compensating victims of crime were broadly carried into effect by the Criminal Justice Act 1972. The particular provision which now concerns us was replaced by s.130 of the Powers of Criminal Courts (Sentencing) Act 2000.[2]

In essence it enables the court to order a convicted person to pay compensation for any damage resulting from the offence. The section states:

> A court by or before which a person is convicted of an offence, instead of or in addition to dealing with him in any other way, may, on application or otherwise, make an order (in this Act referred to as "a compensation order") requiring him (a) to pay compensation for any personal injury, loss or damage resulting from that offence or any other offence which is taken into consideration by the court in determining sentence.

This discretionary power is available whenever there has been a conviction in any court, including a magistrates' court. It is especially valuable in cases where the loss may be too small to justify the cost of civil litigation.

Maximum

16.04 The amount of compensation where the conviction is on indictment in the Crown Court is unlimited. In the magistrates' court it is limited to £5,000.[3] This limit relates to each offence of which the accused is convicted; so if a supplier is convicted of four offences, the order may reach £20,000.

Special care must be taken when the accused asks for other offences to be taken into consideration for which he has not been prosecuted. No additional sums may be awarded in respect of such t.i.c. offences.[4]

Example

16.05 A tour operator publishes a brochure containing false statements in contravention of reg.5 of the Package Travel Regulations 1992.[5] Forty people from different parts of the United Kingdom book holidays in reliance on the brochure. The tour operator, when prosecuted in one area, asks for the 39 other offences to be taken into consideration. The magistrates' order for the 40 offences cannot exceed £5,000 in total.

From the point of view of the victims in this example it would be preferable for separate charges to be brought in each area, so that altogether the orders would have a ceiling of £200,000.

---

[2] Itself replacing the Powers of Criminal Courts Act 1973.
[3] 2000 Act, s.131.
[4] See H. Street, "Compensation Orders and the Trade Descriptions Act" [1974] Crim.L.R. 345.
[5] See para.6.55.

Type of loss

The compensation may relate to "any personal injury, loss or damage". **16.06**
Thus claims for breach of contract or for the tort of negligence are covered.
Further, the Act is wide enough for an order to be made in respect of loss for
which no civil remedy is available: in such a case in the absence of a successful
prosecution the victim has no remedy.[6]

Assessment

As the assessment of compensation will commonly be made by lay magis- **16.07**
trates, it is inappropriate for the power to be exercised in complicated cases,
e.g. where the principles of remoteness of damage need to be understood and
applied. An order will be made only in straightforward cases. Lawton L.J.
explained the court's approach in *R. v Thomson Holidays Ltd*[7]:

> "Parliament, we are sure, never intended to introduce into the criminal law the
> concepts of causation which apply to the assessment of damages under the law
> of contract or tort. . . . [The court] must do what it can to make a just order on
> such information as it has. Whenever the making of an order for compensation
> is appropriate, the court must ask itself whether loss or damage can fairly be
> said to have resulted to anyone from the offence for which the accused has been
> convicted."[8]

The defendants were convicted under s.14 of the Trade Descriptions Act 1968
for making a false statement in their brochure that a hotel had a night club
and swimming and paddling pools. Compensation of £50 was awarded to the
complainant.

A separate point to bear in mind is that the victim must show that the
defendant is liable for the amount claimed. In *R. v Vivian*[9] the Court of
Appeal quashed an order in respect of damage to a car alleged to have been
done by a thief in a collision, as there was no proof that he was responsible
for all the damage: further, the appellant claimed that the sole estimate given
for the repairs was excessive. Talbot J. said[10] that the view of the court was
that "no order for compensation should be made unless the sum claimed by
way of compensation is either agreed or has been proved." This appears to
leave a large loophole for defendants and certainly makes it necessary in this
type of case for victims to be less perfunctory in preparing claims, e.g. by
obtaining more than one estimate.

Situations where it would be appropriate to make an order include misde- **16.08**
scribed goods, e.g. clocked or misdescribed cars, where the reduction in value
or cost of repair can be easily proved, and holiday cases where part of the cost
can be refunded to take account of inconvenience and loss of enjoyment.

---

[6] See *R. v Chappel* [1984] Crim.L.R. 574.
[7] [1974] Q.B. 592 at 599.
[8] See also *R. v Daly* [1974] 1 All E.R. 290; *R. v Kneeshaw* [1974] 1 All E.R. 896: the machinery
is intended "for clear and simple cases" (per Lord Widgery C.J.).
[9] [1979] 1 All E.R. 48.
[10] ibid. at 50.

In determining whether to make an order and, if so, for what amount, the court must take into account the defendant's means[11] and generally limits the award to a sum which he can manage to pay over two or three years. Thus in *R. v McIntosh*[12] the Court of Appeal revoked a £90 order against a burglar on the grounds that he had no means and would find it hard to obtain employment on his release from prison because of his wooden leg—surprisingly not an impediment to the nefarious activities of this Long John McSilver in a trade where one would expect agility to be a sine qua non! Similarly it is not generally appropriate to make an order where the defendant is sentenced to a significant period of imprisonment, unless he has assets in hand to pay the compensation.[13]

How to apply

16.09 No procedure is laid down for making the application for compensation. Generally it is enough for the victim to forewarn the clerk or prosecutor before the trial commences, so that the application may be brought to the notice of the court after conviction and the victim then heard. Alternatively the court may act of its initiative without an application. Although it is customary for the prosecution to pass on a request for compensation, they are not under a duty to conduct an inquiry into the defendant's means.[14]

An order is enforceable in the same ways as a fine. Thus the court may impose a term of imprisonment in default.

Interrelation with civil claims

16.10 Generally the trial of the criminal charge will be held some time before any civil proceedings reach that stage. In the subsequent civil proceedings two points must be borne in mind. First, the conviction may be used in evidence.[15] Secondly, when awarding damages the court must take into account sums paid under the order.[16]

If exceptionally the civil proceedings have already come to an end, whether by judgment or settlement, no order can be made even though the victim can still show loss. In *Hammertons Cars Ltd v London Borough of Redbridge*[17]:

> The complainant bought a car described as "in perfect condition". It was not. He settled an action against the sellers on the basis that he paid his own legal costs of £170 and expert's fee of £25. When the sellers were convicted under the Trade Descriptions Act he was awarded £195 compensation by the justices. The dealer successfully appealed against the order to the Divisional Court.

Lord Widgery C.J., doubting whether in any case the section would cover such legal costs, said:

[11] s.35(4).
[12] [1973] Crim.L.R. 378.
[13] *R. v McCullough* (1982) 4 Cr.App.R.(S.) 98 CA; *R. v Morgan* (1982) 4 Cr.App.R.(S.) 358, CA.
[14] *R. v Johnstone* (1982) 4 Cr.App.R.(S.) 141.
[15] Civil Evidence Act 1968, s.11.
[16] s.134(2).
[17] [1974] 2 All E.R. 216.

"It seems to me to be abundantly clear that if the victim brings civil proceedings, and those civil proceedings are brought to an end, then they should be regarded as quite independent of the criminal proceedings and no compensation order should be made in respect of liabilities which arose, or might have arisen, in the civil proceedings."

3. BREACH OF STATUTORY DUTY

As has been seen earlier, frequently a consumer who has suffered loss will **16.11** have a remedy flowing directly or indirectly from the civil or criminal law. As far as the civil law is concerned, the remedy may be for breach of contract, e.g. against a supplier of goods or services who has not fulfilled obligations imposed upon him by statute or the common law, or in tort for negligence or under the Consumer Protection Act 1987, e.g. against a manufacturer. Alternatively or additionally, where the supplier's activities involve a criminal offence resulting in a successful prosecution, the consumer may seek compensation under the 2000 Act discussed above.

However, a hiatus exists where the supplier has not broken a contract with the consumer, maybe because they are not in a contractual relationship; nor has he been negligent; nor does the Consumer Protection Act 1987, Pt I, apply, perhaps because the damage is too small; nor has the consumer recovered compensation, even though the supplier has committed a criminal offence, e.g. because no prosecution was brought. In such circumstances the consumer's last resort is to try to show that the supplier is liable in tort for breach of statutory duty.

If it were possible for such an action to be brought in every case where a supplier has failed to comply with his statutory duties, the consumer's position would be much more straightforward. In the absence of an award of compensation under the 2000 Act, he would be able to institute civil proceedings on this basis without concerning himself with such questions as privity of contract with the supplier.

However, the courts when construing statutes have been reluctant to **16.12** imply into them civil rights for the victim. The rationale seems to be that the legislation is for the protection of the public generally and is not intended to afford a civil remedy to individual members of the public. The reasoning is unconvincing. To draw an analogy from the contractual principles of offer and acceptance, where an offer is made to the world at large, contracts are formed only with those individuals who accept the offer; similarly where a duty is imposed on suppliers for the benefit of the public at large, it should be possible for those particular members of the public who suffer loss as a result of a breach of that duty to come forward and claim damages in a civil action founded upon that statutory duty.

Yet generally the courts are content to leave consumers to their separate civil rights. Thus in *Square v Model Farm Dairies (Bournemouth) Ltd*,[18] where the plaintiff alleged that contaminated milk sold in breach of the food

---

[18] [1939] 2 K.B. 365.

legislation had made his family ill with typhoid fever, the Court of Appeal rejected his claim because he had a remedy under the Sale of Goods Act. A comparable case is *Buckley v La Réserve*[19] where an action failed against a restaurant which, in contravention of the Food and Drugs Act 1955, sold food unfit for human consumption (the food was snails: legal symmetry would have been attained had the contamination of the snails resulted from ginger beer[20]). It is important to note that on the particular facts the plaintiff's civil rights would not have given him a remedy unless he could prove negligence, as he was taken to the restaurant as a guest, and had no contractual claim against the restaurant: nevertheless the court adopted the same stance as in the *Square* case.

16.13   Two cases involving defective cars also illustrate the courts' unhelpful attitude to consumers. In *Phillips v Britannia Hygienic Laundry Co*[21] the plaintiff failed to recover for injuries resulting from the defendants' breach of duties imposed by the antecedents to the Motor Vehicles (Construction and Use) Regulations.[22] Similarly a seller was not liable to a victim injured by a vehicle which the seller delivered in such a condition that its use on the road was unlawful, although he thereby committed an offence under the Road Traffic Act.[23]

The courts' restrictive interpretation leads to this principle in the consumer field: an action for breach of statutory duty has a chance of success only if the statute expressly states that a breach of the duty is actionable, e.g. the Consumer Protection Act 1987, s.41(1)[24]:

> An obligation imposed by safety regulations shall be a duty owed to any person who may be affected by a contravention of the obligation and, subject to any provision to the contrary in the regulations and to the defences and other incidents applying to actions for breach of statutory duty, a contravention of any such obligation shall be actionable accordingly.

Where a statute states the opposite, the position is equally clear. Where a statute is silent on the point, the presumption is that it gives no civil remedy. Such a presumption is strengthened where the statute expressly preserves other civil remedies, following the reasoning in *Square v Model Farm Dairies (Bournemouth) Ltd*,[25] for then Parliament is implicitly leaving the public to their general civil rights.

---

[19] [1959] Crim.L.R. 451.
[20] See *Donoghue v Stevenson*, para.5.40.
[21] [1923] 2 K.B. 832.
[22] SI 1986/1078.
[23] *Badham v Lambs Ltd* [1946] K.B. 45.
[24] Above, para.15.24. For another example, see Consumer Credit Act 1974, s.92(3): entry to premises to recover possession of goods or land, below, para.25.08.
[25] Above, para.16.12.

Part III

ADMINISTRATIVE CONTROL

Chapter Seventeen

"THEY'RE TRADING UNFAIRLY"

The civil and criminal sanctions discussed earlier in this book do a great deal **17.01** to protect the consumer, but by themselves they are not enough. In particular:

(1) Industry is never static for long and the enterprising trader is likely to come up with new business practices. Some of these, while within the law, may be harmful to consumers and swift action may be needed to curtail them.

(2) There may be a number of dishonest or inefficient traders who may make large profits, e.g. by the delivery of shoddy goods. They may not be deterred by the occasional fine or award of compensation. What the consumer really needs is a system whereby such traders can be restrained from trading altogether unless they mend their ways.

(3) The standards set by the law are minimum standards and the consumer can benefit if traders can be persuaded to undertake additional voluntary obligations.

(4) Neither the civil nor the criminal law achieves one of the most important aims of consumer protection—making the consumer aware of his rights.

It is at this point that we meet the third weapon of consumer protection—administrative control. This involves a public body charged with the task of keeping the consumer scene under permanent review. The principal weapons of administrative control are to be found in the Enterprise Act 2002 (replacing the Fair Trading Act 1973), the Consumer Credit Act 1974 (see Chapters Eighteen to Twenty-Seven) and the Consumer Protection from Unfair Trading Regulations 2008 (the CPRs) (see below, para.17.25). For a further example of administrative control see Chapter Nine.

The scheme of this chapter is as follows: **17.02**

(1) The Fair Trading Act 1973 will be considered first to put the current regime in historical perspective.

(2) Stop Now Orders will be briefly discussed, as their life was brief—from 2001 to 2003.

(3) The Enterprise Act 2002 will then be considered with its new regime dealing with both domestic and European Union infringements of the law.

(4) The Unfair Commercial Practices Directive 2005 and the CPRs, which will have a massive impact on consumer protection, follow next.

(5) The Business Protection from Misleading Marketing Regulations 2008, another province of the OFT, will be discussed in the last section.

1. THE FAIR TRADING ACT 1973

17.03 The Fair Trading Act 1973 appeared out of the blue with no warning or consultation in the form of Green or White Papers.

Most of the Act did not break new ground inasmuch as broadly it consolidated, with some changes and improvements, the pre-existing law relating to competition. It gave the Director General of Fair Trading power to initiate subordinate legislation to protect the consumer by banning undesirable trade practices as and when they appeared (Pt II). It also enabled the Director General to bring into line individual rogue traders who regularly flouted their legal obligations (Pt III).

The essential difference between Pts II and III of the Fair Trading Act was that Pt II was concerned with undesirable *practices*, whereas Pt III was concerned with undesirable *traders*.

Part II—Adverse Consumer Trade Practices[1]

17.04 The point of Pt II was to refer consumer trade practices to the Consumer Protection Advisory Committee. A reference under s.14 could be made by the Director General or any Minister. The CPAC considered "whether a consumer trade practice specified in the reference adversely affects the economic interest of consumers".

The real punch in Pt II lay in s.17, which provided that references by the Director General might include proposals for action by the Secretary of State. The practice had to fall within one of the four paragraphs of s.17(2). The common flavour of these paragraphs was of misleading or confusing consumers or pressurising them to enter into unfair transactions.

The Secretary of State could make an order by statutory instrument giving effect to the proposals. The intention and expectation was that it would be possible to identify new abuses at an early stage, to recommend and quickly to put into effect prohibitive measures and thus to squash the practice before it mushroomed.

Three Orders

17.05 Only three orders were made and then Pt II was repealed by the Enterprise Act 2000.

(1) The Consumer Transactions (Restrictions on Statements) Order 1976 (SI 1976/1813) attacked the continuing use of void exemption clauses (e.g. "No money back on sale goods"). It also compelled

---

[1] See previous editions of this book for a detailed analysis of Pts II and III.

retailers and manufacturers who chose to give guarantees or warranties with their goods to state that these did not affect the buyers' statutory rights.

(2) The Mail Order Transactions (Information) Order 1976 (SI 1976/1812) concerned suppliers requiring prepayment or deposits without specifying, or keeping to, delivery dates. This was revoked and its provisions incorporated in the Consumer Protection (Distance Selling) Regulations 2000 (SI 2000/2334) discussed in Chapter Six.

(3) The Business Advertisements (Disclosure) Order 1977 (SI 1977/1918) required business sellers to make it clear, in their advertisements to consumers, that they were traders to prevent them masquerading as private sellers.

Their replacements

The Orders in (1) and (3) above remained in force until they were revoked by the CPRs on May 26, 2008. However, the malpractices which they attacked continue to be offences.   **17.06**

The Order in (1) above has been partly replaced by an amendment to the Sale and Supply of Goods to Consumers Regulations 2002: reg.15(2A) deals with the guarantee aspect (see para.5.06).[2] The other aspect of this Order is covered by the CPRs, reg.5(2)(a) and (4)(k): a misleading action includes false information about "the consumer's rights". This is discussed in para.17.28.

The Order in (3) above has also been replaced by the CPRs. The black list of unfair practices in Sch.1 includes para.22:   **17.07**

> Falsely claiming or creating the impression that the trader is not acting for purposes relating to his trade, business, craft or profession, or falsely representing oneself as a consumer.

This is an offence under reg.12.

Part III—Persistently Unfair Traders

During its 30 years' existence, until the repeal of Pt III by the Enterprise Act 2002, hundreds of assurances were obtained covering diverse activities. Used car dealers, home improvement firms, sellers of electrical goods and mail order businesses figured most prominently.   **17.08**

The first assurance in 1974 was typical in so far as it covered three improper practices, namely, Trade Descriptions Act offences, breaches of the Sale of Goods Act implied conditions and the non-delivery of goods paid for in advance.

Section 34(1) required the Director General to try to obtain an assurance where a person had "persisted in a course of conduct" which was "unfair to consumers". Successive Director Generals stressed the difficulty of proving

---

[2] CPRs, Sch.2, para.97.

persistence. In the 1994 DTI consultation paper, *Reform of Part III of the Fair Trading Act* 1973, it was suggested that the words "persisted in" should be replaced by "carried on" to ease the task of the OFT.

Conduct was not to be regarded as "unfair" unless it was one of the two types specified in the Act: either contravention of an enactment imposing duties, prohibitions or restrictions enforceable by *criminal* proceedings or breaches of contract or other wrongs enforceable by *civil* proceedings.

Proposals for reform

17.09 Because the procedure was so long and complex the 1994 DTI consultation paper proposed that the DGFT should be empowered to issue "warning notices" requiring rogue traders to discontinue their malpractices at once. The OFT too in its 1996 consultation paper *Consumer Affairs Strategy* stated that it had "long argued for reform" of Pt III because its effectiveness was "widely recognised to be limited, as a result of both the time which it may take to conclude cases, and of the relatively weak sanctions available" (para.7.15).

Finally in July 1999 the DTI published its wide-ranging White Paper, *Modern Markets: confident consumers* (Cm. 4410). It stated (para.7.5):

- The level of criminal sanctions, and the risk of civil action by consumers, do not deter determined rogues who continue to carry on unlawful conduct where the profits outweigh the occasional judicial setback and where they can live with an adverse effect on their reputation. This problem is compounded by the time it takes to enforce some of the existing legislative provisions. This enables the rogue trader to keep ahead of the authorities.
- There is no means of preventing a rogue trader from continuing to pose a threat to consumers by moving from one dishonest practice to another.

It proposed to amend the 1973 Act by empowering the courts "to grant injunctions against specific practices carried out by specific traders" and by extending to trading standards departments the powers under Pt III hitherto exercised by the OFT only. These reforms were effected by the Enterprise Act 2002.

2. STOP NOW ORDERS (SNORS)

17.10 Before the Government had found Parliamentary time to bring in its proposed reforms to Pt III of the Fair Trading Act 1973 Brussels intervened in the shape of Directive 98/27/EC on Injunctions for the protection of consumers' interests (the Injunctions Directive), which had to be transposed into UK law by January 1, 2001. It was implemented late by the Stop Now Orders (E.C. Directive) Regulations 2001,[3] which came into force on June 1, 2001.

---

[3] SI 2001/1422 (known as SNORs).

Injunctions Directive

The Directive and the Regulations were concerned only with EU legisla- **17.11**
tion (as implemented by the Member States). Thus in the UK two separate
systems ran in parallel until both were replaced by the Enterprise Act 2002—
Stop Now Orders for "Community infringements" and Pt III for domestic
infringements of "home grown" UK law.

Its purpose is clearly explained in the DTI Consultation Paper (February
2000) on its implementation:

> The purpose of the Directive is to permit consumer protection bodies to apply to
> the courts or competent administrative authorities both in their own and in other
> Member States for orders to stop traders infringing the legislation implementing
> nine specific consumer protection directives where these infringements harm the
> collective interests of consumers. It is not intended as a means of seeking redress
> for individual consumers.

The Directive listed nine Directives, but the Regulations added a tenth
adopted after the Directive. Others have been added since. They cover the
following areas:

Doorstep selling

Consumer credit

Television broadcasting

Package travel

Medicines

Unfair terms

Timeshare

Distance selling

Sale of consumer goods and guarantees.

Electronic commerce

Air travel

Unfair commercial practices

Enforcement

For Community infringements the Pt III regime was replaced by new pro- **17.12**
visions set out in Sch.2 to the Regulations. The new procedures formed
the model for those now in force under the Enterprise Act 2002 discussed
below.

One major change was that enforcement was (and is) no longer limited
to the OFT. "Qualified entities", both public bodies and others, could do
so. The "public UK qualified entities" were specified in Sch.3 and included

trading standards departments and statutory regulators (e.g. gas, water, rail) following the approach adopted by the Unfair Terms in Consumer Contracts Regulations 1999. The "lead body" to coordinate enforcement was the OFT.

In addition "other UK qualified entities" could be designated by the DTI. As the Directive is concerned with enforcement throughout Europe, "Community qualified entities" could also bring proceedings in any Member State: they are listed in the Official Journal under art.4.3 of the Directive.

For businesses (and maybe enforcers too) two separate systems aimed at rectifying similar conduct by similar traders were confusing and onerous, even though SNORs applied only to UK legislation with an EU provenance. As *Consumer reforms*,[4] an OFT consultation paper on the Enterprise Bill, stated, "Part 8 of the Enterprise Bill simplifies this structure by establishing a more consistent enforcement regime. This will enable injunctive action to be taken against traders who infringe a wider range of consumer protection legislation". We now turn to that regime.

3. THE ENTERPRISE ACT 2002

17.13 The Enterprise Act 2002 is an immense piece of legislation covering both competition law (Competition Appeal Tribunal, mergers, market investigation references, cartels) and consumer law enforcement. We are concerned with the last item which is contained in Pt 8 of the Act and came into force on June 20, 2003. (In Chapter one we dealt with another important change made by the Act with its restructuring of the OFT.)

We pointed out in para.17.12 that the new enforcement regime put in place by the 2002 Act is based on SNORs. However, with the repeal of Pt III of the Fair Trading Act 1973[5] a similar framework applies to all UK legislation whether or not it emanated from Brussels.

There are inevitably some detailed differences, since the enforcement of EU infringements must comply with the Injunctions Directive, whereas the control of domestic infringements is not subject to such limitations.

Domestic infringements

17.14 A domestic infringement is defined by s.211 as follows:

(1) In this Part a domestic infringement is an act or omission which—

(a) is done or made by a person in the course of a business,
(b) falls within subsection (2), and
(c) harms the collective interests of consumers in the United Kingdom.

(2) An act or omission falls within this subsection if it is of a description specified by the Secretary of State by order and consists of any of the following—

(a) a contravention of an enactment which imposes a duty, prohibition or restriction enforceable by criminal proceedings;

---

[4] OFT 502 (August 2002).
[5] Sch.26.

(b) an act done or omission made in breach of contract;
(c) an act done or omission made in breach of a non-contractual duty owed to a person by virtue of an enactment or rule of law and enforceable by civil proceedings;
(d) an act or omission in respect of which an enactment provides for a remedy or sanction enforceable by civil proceedings;
(e) an act done or omission made by a person supplying or seeking to supply goods or services as a result of which an agreement or security relating to the supply is void or unenforceable to any extent;
(f) an act or omission by which a person supplying or seeking to supply goods or services purports or attempts to exercise a right or remedy relating to the supply in circumstances where the exercise of the right or remedy is restricted or excluded under or by virtue of an enactment;
(g) an act or omission by which a person supplying or seeking to supply goods or services purports or attempts to avoid (to any extent) liability relating to the supply in circumstances where such avoidance is restricted or prevented under an enactment.

There are three requirements:

(1) The act or omission must be "in the course of a business", defined by s.210(8) to include a profession and undertaking "for gain or reward" or "otherwise than free of charge".

(2) It harms the collective interests of UK consumers. A "consumer", as defined by s.210(2), (3) and (4), is an individual to whom goods or services are (or are sought to be) supplied by a business. The individual must not be a business customer, although he may be setting up in business but not yet trading ("with a view to carrying on. . .").[6]

(3) It falls within the exhaustive list in s.211(2). For example, (a) covers safety offences,[7] (b) a breach of the implied terms of the Sale of Goods Act 1979 and (c) tortious liability under the Consumer Protection Act 1987, Pt I. Section 211(2) also requires the conduct to be "of a description specified by the Secretary of State by order". The specified list is a long one[8] and, in addition to more than fifty pieces of primary and secondary legislation, includes common law breaches too. This was to be expected, in view of the references to "breach of contract" and "enactment or rule of law" in s.211(2)(b) and (c).

Community infringements

Community infringements may result in enforcement in the UK or in another state in the European Economic Area (EEA). As far as the UK is concerned, they are defined by s.212.   **17.15**

(1) In this Part a Community infringement is an act or omission which harms the collective interests of consumers and which—

---

[6] s.210(4)(b).
[7] See Ch. Fifteen.
[8] Enterprise Act 2002 (Pt 8 Domestic Infringements) Order 2003 (SI 2003/1593).

(a) contravenes a listed Directive as given effect by the laws, regulations or administrative provisions of an EEA State, or

(b) contravenes such laws, regulations or administrative provisions which provide additional permitted protections.

(2) The laws, regulations or administrative provisions of an EEA State which give effect to a listed Directive provide additional permitted protections if—

(a) they provide protection for consumers which is in addition to the minimum protection required by the Directive concerned, and

(b) such additional protection is permitted by that Directive.

(3) The Secretary of State may by order specify for the purposes of this section the law in the United Kingdom which—

(a) gives effect to the listed Directives;

(b) provides additional permitted protections.

"Consumer" in this context has a different meaning from that in s.211, for by s.210(6) it means "a person who is a consumer for the purposes of (a) the Injunctions Directive, and (b) the listed Directive concerned". A listed Directive is an EU Directive specified, wholly or partly, in Sch.13 to the 2002 Act. Consequently each Directive must be checked to see whether in a particular case "the collective interest of" such consumers is harmed.

Enforcers

17.16 We saw that enforcement of the SNORs was in hands of three types of "entitities".[9] This pattern is repeated, though their names are changed to "enforcers" and the three types are differently constituted. Section 213 creates the new structure. A fourth type—CPC enforcers—was added in 2006.

General enforcers

There are three categories: the OFT, every trading standards department in Great Britain (called a "weights and measures authority") and the Department of Enterprise, Trade and Investment in Northern Ireland.

Designated enforcers

The Secretary of State may designate a body by order, if he thinks that it "has as one of its purposes the protection of the collective interests of consumers". If that general precondition is satisfied, then he may choose "a public body only if he is satisfied that it is independent" or any other (private) body which "satisfies such criteria as [he] specifies by order".[10]

So far he has designated only public bodies as enforcers. They are the Civil Aviation Authority, the Information Commissioner, the Office of the

---

[9] Above, para.17.12.

[10] See s.213(2), (3) and (4). An order may designate an enforcer for all or only some infringements (s.213 (6)). Cf. the "super-complaints" procedure for consumer bodies designated under s.11(5) to make a complaint to the OFT; e.g. the National Consumer Council, Which?, Citizens Advice, CAMRA.

Rail Regulator, the Gas and Electricity Markets Authority and the Director Generals of Telecommunications, of Water Services and of Gas and of Electricity Supply for Northern Ireland.[11] He has also issued guidance on the criteria for private bodies.

Community enforcers

A Community enforcer is a "qualified entity" for the purposes of the Injunctions Directive as listed in the Official Journal under Art.4.3, but not a general or designated enforcer, so only enforcers from other EEA states may be such.[12]

CPC enforcers

The EU Regulation on Consumer Protection Cooperation (Reg. (EC) No.2006/2004 as amended by the UCPD) requires the creation of a network of enforcement bodies across the EU to stamp out cross border infringements. A new section 215 (5A) has been added by the Enterprise Act 2002 (Amendment) Regulations 2006 (SI 2006/3363) designating the CPC enforcers. They include the CAA, FSA, Ofcom, PhonepayPlus and all the general enforcers (see above).

What can they enforce?

General enforcers can apply for an enforcement order in respect of any infringement, domestic or Community. Designated enforcers are limited to infringements to which their designation relates. Community and CPC enforcers may act only in respect of a Community infringement.[13]

Enforcement procedure

Coordination by OFT

Because of the range of enforcers there is a danger of overlap and duplica-   **17.17**
tion of proceedings. By s.216 the OFT is given the lead role of coordinator. It may direct that only itself or a specified enforcer may apply for an enforcement order. This power, though, does not extend to controlling Community enforcers. (SNORs had similar provisions.)

Consultation and undertakings

Another replication of SNORs appears in s.214. Before applying for an order an enforcer must consult the business and the OFT to try to ensure that the infringement ceases and is not repeated. The consultation period is normally 14 days, but seven days suffice in the case of an interim order and consultation may be dispensed with altogether, if the OFT thinks that there should be no delay in applying to the court.

[11] SI 2003/1399.
[12] Above, para.17.12, s.213(5).
[13] s.215(2), (3), (4) and (4A).

As action in the courts is intended to be used as a last resort, under s.219 enforcers may accept an undertaking that the business will not "continue or repeat the conduct" or "engage in such conduct in the course of his business or another business".[14] The last two words are to prevent the culprit from carrying on his malpractices by setting up or moving to a different business. If the business complies with the undertaking, that will be the end of the matter. The enforcer must notify the OFT of the undertaking, so that monitoring may take place. If the undertaking is broken, the courts are the next step.

Applications to the court

17.18   Applications for an enforcement order—the expression "Stop Now Orders" is obsolete—are made to the High Court or county court (or Court of Session or sheriff in Scotland).[15] Section 217 empowers the court to make an enforcement order.

> (1) This section applies if an application for an enforcement order is made under section 215 and the court finds that the person named in the application has engaged in conduct which constitutes the infringement.
> (2) This section also applies if such an application is made in relation to a Community infringement and the court finds that the person named in the application is likely to engage in conduct which constitutes the infringement.
> (3) If this section applies the court may make an enforcement order against the person.
> (4) In considering whether to make an enforcement order the court must have regard to whether the person named in the application—
>
> > (a) has given an undertaking under section 219 in respect of conduct such as is mentioned in subsection (3) of that section;
> > (b) has failed to comply with the undertaking."

It can be seen from s.217(1) and (2) that an odd distinction is made between Community infringements and domestic ones. For a domestic infringement, which falls within s.217(1), the court must find that the defendant "has engaged" in the conduct. For a Community infringement, which falls within s.217(1) and (2), it is enough if the defendant "is likely" to do so. (This distinction also appears elsewhere in Pt 8.) The reason, it seems, is that the Government thought that the wording of the Injunctions Directive covered not merely past and present infringements but also future ones in that art.2.1(a) talks of "requiring the cessation *or prohibition* of any infringement" (emphasis supplied). We are not convinced, as the preamble and other Articles do not suggest such a wide interpretation. In any case, for the sake of conformity, why not make domestic infringements all-embracing too? In practice, where no infringement has already taken place, it may be an impossible task for enforcers to find convincing evidence to prove this "likelihood".

Where "it is expedient that the conduct is prohibited or prevented . . . immediately", s.218 enables the court to make an interim order.

---

[14] s.219(4).
[15] s.215(5).

Finally, instead of making an order, the court may accept an undertaking.[16] What happens if a business fails to comply with an enforcement order or an undertaking given to the court? The usual sanction for such bold conduct ensues—it is contempt of court, so prison could be the culprit's resting place.

Companies and accessories

There are complex provisions in ss. 222 and 223 where the business is a "body corporate". They enable the court to make orders against "accessories" such as directors and managers and against members of a group of companies where, for example, two companies are subsidiaries of the same parent company. A "controller" may also be sanctioned, e.g. someone with at least a third of the voting power at any general meeting either personally or with "associates" (a broad list including "the spouse of a relative of the individual's spouse" and a business partner).[17] This should obviate the rogue's ruse of putting his business apparently in the hands of others, while in reality running it himself.

Information and guidance

The OFT has always taken seriously its role of providing information to consumers and business. Section 229(1) continues the practice by imposing on the OFT a duty to publish advice and information "to explain the provisions" of Pt 8 and to indicate "how the OFT expects such provisions to operate".[18]   **17.19**

We end this section by recommending one of its many publications: *Enforcement of consumer protection legislation. Guidance on Part 8 of the Enterprise Act* (June 2003). It includes a summary of the legislation specified under ss.211 and 212. Like all such guidance it states, "It should not be regarded as a definitive interpretation of the Pt 8 provisions".

4. UNFAIR COMMERCIAL PRACTICES DIRECTIVE

Background to the Directive

We have already mentioned the EU Unfair Commercial Practices Directive[19] earlier in this chapter. The general principle of a "duty to trade fairly", though it can be found in a number of European and other jurisdictions, has hitherto had no place in English law. We noted in Chapter Ten the proposal floated by Lord Borrie in 1980 that a "general statutory duty to trade fairly in consumer transactions" should be introduced via codes of practice and saw   **17.20**

---

[16] s.217(9) and s.218(10).
[17] s.222(3), (4), (10), (11) and (12).
[18] s.6 also permits the OFT to publish educational materials and support others providing information or advice.
[19] Directive 2005/29/EC of May 11, 2005.

that the OFT's support for that proposal was reluctantly removed in 1990 as "over-ambitious".[20]

We observed that, though the UK initiatives came to nought, the European Commission had picked up the torch in June 2003 with a proposed Directive on Unfair Commercial Practices. Within two years the proposal had been adopted as Directive 2005/29/EC "concerning unfair business-to-consumer practices in the internal market" (the Unfair Commercial Practices Directive or UCPD, as we shall call it).

Before considering the Consumer Protection from Unfair Trading Regulations 2008 (the CPRs), which transpose the UCPD into UK law, we shall make some preliminary points on the UCPD to explain the provenance and approach of the CPRs and comment upon the DTI's approach to implementation.

Purpose

17.21   The 25 Preambles to the UCPD explain its general purposes and the reasons for the particular articles. Preambles (3), (4) and (6) focus on generalities:

> (3) The laws of the Member States relating to unfair commercial practices show marked differences which can generate appreciable distortions of competition and obstacles to the smooth functioning of the internal market. In the field of advertising, Council Directive 84/450/EEC of 10 September 1984 concerning misleading and comparative advertising establishes minimum criteria for harmonising legislation on misleading advertising, but does not prevent the Member States from retaining or adopting measures which provide more extensive protection for consumers. As a result, Member States' provisions on misleading advertising diverge significantly.
>
> (4) These disparities cause uncertainty as to which national rules apply to unfair commercial practices harming consumers' economic interests and create many barriers affecting business and consumers. These barriers increase the cost to business of exercising internal market freedoms, in particular when businesses wish to engage in cross border marketing, advertising campaigns and sales promotions. Such barriers also make consumers uncertain of their rights and undermine their confidence in the internal market.
>
> (6) This Directive therefore approximates the laws of the Member States on unfair commercial practices, including unfair advertising, which directly harm consumers' economic interests and thereby indirectly harm the economic interests of legitimate competitors. In line with the principle of proportionality, this Directive protects consumers from the consequences of such unfair commercial practices where they are material but recognises that in some cases the impact on consumers may be negligible. It neither covers nor affects the national laws on unfair commercial practices which harm only competitors' economic interests or which relate to a transaction between traders; taking full account of the principle of subsidiarity, Member States will continue to be able to regulate such practices, in conformity with Community law, if they choose to do so. Nor does this Directive cover or affect the provisions of Directive 84/450/EEC on advertising which misleads business but which is not misleading for consumers and on comparative advertising. Further, this Directive does not affect accepted advertising and marketing practices, such as legitimate product placement, brand differentiation or the offering of incentives which may legitimately affect con-

---

[20] See above, para.10.09.

sumers' perceptions of products and influence their behaviour without impairing the consumer's ability to make an informed decision.

It can be seen from the above that the UCPD is not confined to the harmonisation of the law on unfair commercial practices, but also amends the 1984 Directive on Misleading and Comparative Advertising. This was replaced by Directive 2006/114/EC which we shall consider in section 6 of this chapter.

A number of points may be gleaned from the Preambles: **17.22**

(1) The UCPD aims to eliminate distortions of the internal market caused by different laws on unfair trading.

(2) It is concerned with practices which "directly harm consumers' economic interests" (Preambles (4) and (6)) rather than "only competitors' economic interests" (Preamble (6)). Preamble 7 elaborates this point by stating that the UCPD "addresses commercial practices directly related to consumers' transactional decisions in relation to products".

(3) This is a framework directive creating—to use that vogue expression—principles-based legislation, so that practices are regulated where "the consequences . . . are material", not merely "negligible" (Preamble (6)). We shall see this moderate approach when we consider the DTI's proposals on enforcement.

(4) Another important result of the framework approach is that it will simplify matters for consumers and businesses alike. As Preamble (12) puts it, they "will be able to rely on a single regulatory framework based on clearly defined legal concepts regulating all aspects of unfair commercial practices across the EU". Thus "it is necessary to replace Member States' existing, divergent general clauses and legal principles" (Preamble (13)).

DTI's consultation programme

The DTI accepted that the UCPD would probably involve the repeal of exist-   **17.23**
ing UK law in its *Consultation on a draft EU Directive* (July 2003, p.39):

> Transposition of the framework Directive in the UK may present an opportunity to deregulate some of the existing body of UK regulations . . . Domestic legislation which implements existing EU directives may remain, but other sectoral provisions that go beyond or conflict with the provisions of the framework Directive may need to be removed.

In December 2005 it issued a consultation paper on the implementation of the UCPD and published a Summary of Responses in June 2006. *The Government Response to the Consultation Paper on Implementing the Unfair Commercial Practices Directive* ("the *Government Response*") was issued in December 2006. It acknowledged that it "committed itself to simplifying existing laws wherever sensible and appropriate in order to establish a modern and robust fair trading framework." The full list of the laws affected is set out in the CPRs, Schs 2, 3 and 4; the most notable statutes to disappear were most of the Trade Descriptions Act 1968 and the Consumer Protection Act 1987, Pt III.

UK implementation

17.24 Article 19 gives the deadlines to which Member States must adhere. They must "adopt and publish" the necessary regulations by June 12, 2007 and bring them into force by December 12, 2007. Not for the first time the DTI failed to meet its obligations on time. The CPRs came into force on May 26, 2008.

Before commenting on the Articles, we cannot but quote the conclusion reached in the DTI's December 2006 consultation paper (p.3):

> The coming into force of the UCPD will mark a new era in UK fair trading history. The UCPD will allow enforcers to tackle those practices that are unfair but not currently unlawful, taking either civil or criminal enforcement action as appropriate. Simplification and modernisation of the existing framework will also make the law easier for its users—business, consumers and enforcers—to understand and apply. The Government is confident that the wide-ranging changes set out below will help it meet its objective of raising the UK's consumer protection regime to the level of the best in the world.[21]

We earnestly hope that such an ambitious objective can be attained. Certainly the UCPD is a major step on that journey.

5. THE CONSUMER PROTECTION REGULATIONS

Introduction

17.25 The UCPD was implemented by the Consumer Protection from Unfair Trading Regulations 2008 (SI 2008/1277). The CPRs broadly adopt a "copy out" approach making it unlikely that the EU Commission will bring proceedings in the ECJ claiming (as they did, unsuccessfully, in relation to the Product Liability Directive: para.5.35) that the transposition into UK law is inaccurate.

The OFT have published two guides to the CPRs on their website. The better, more detailed one is *Guidance on the Consumer Protection from Unfair Trading Regulations* (May 2008, 84pp). It states that it is "principally intended to help traders to comply" with the CPRs and contains many useful examples of the types of commercial practices which may be unfair or permissible. The other one, described as a *Basic Guide for Business* (Aug 2008), is

---

[21] In 2003 with that same "best in the world" aim, the DTI commissioned a study from Brunel University (Geoffrey Woodroffe and Dimitrios Giannoulopoulos) comparing the consumer protection laws and organisations of the G7 Countries, Australia, Canada and Norway (including the duty to trade fairly).

just that: its 22 pages are in large print, contain many illustrations and deal mainly with the black list in Sch.1.

Before turning to the various regulations which control commercial malpractices, we draw attention to reg.2 (the interpretation provision) which contains the definitions of the essential words and phrases, e.g. average consumer, commercial practice, consumer, product, professional diligence and transactional decision.

When is a practice unfair?

The attack on "unfair commercial practices" is launched succinctly by   **17.26** reg.3(1): they "are prohibited". They may be divided into six categories:

(1) the general prohibition: reg.3(3);

(2) promotion by a code owner: reg.4;

(3) misleading actions: reg.5;

(4) misleading omissions: reg.6;

(5) aggressive practices: reg.7;

(6) the black list in Sch.1.

What is a "commercial practice"? It is widely defined in reg.2(1) and means "any act, omission, course of conduct, representation or commercial communication (including advertising or marketing)". It must be directly connected with the supply of a product "to or from" consumers, whether occurring before, during or after a transaction. Thus it will apply where a consumer, who is selling a solid gold necklace to a cash-for-gold firm[22], is told that it is only gold plated and so receives a very low price.

(1) General prohibition

Reg. 3(3) is as follows:

> A commercial practice is unfair if—
>
> (a) it contravenes the requirements of professional diligence; and
> (b) it materially distorts or is likely to materially distort the economic behaviour of the average consumer with regard to the product.

This is a general "catch-all" provision in contrast to the other five varieties which are specific types with detailed lists of matters or factors to be taken into account.

(a) "Professional diligence" is defined as "the standard of special skill and care which a trader may reasonably be expected to exercise towards consumers", commensurate with honest market practice and good faith. The meaning is essentially similar to the duty imposed on suppliers of

---

[22] See *Which?* (February 2010): "Cash for Your Gold".

services under English law,[23] though here the regulation relates to the supply of a "product" meaning "any goods or service and includes immovable property".

(b) Who is the "average consumer"? "Consumer" has the usual meaning to be found in recent EU legislation: any "individual . . . . acting for purposes which are outside his business": so companies are excluded, as are all traders of any type. What does "average" add? "Average consumer" is defined by reg.2(2) as "reasonably well informed, reasonably observant and circumspect".

This objective test is modified by reg.2(4) where "the practice is directed to a particular group", when the "average consumer shall be read as referring to the average member of that group". It is also modified by reg.2(5) where the group comprises "particularly vulnerable" consumers "because of their mental or physical infirmity, age or credulity in a way which the trader could be reasonably be expected to foresee". The supply of wheelchairs or stair lifts comes to mind, or the repair of roofs or front drives where unsuspecting elderly people are preyed upon by itinerant rogues.

(2) Promotion by code owners

17.27 Codes of conduct are given special treatment by the CPRs . Reg.4 states:

> The promotion of any unfair commercial practice by a code owner in a code of conduct is prohibited.

Clearly OFT Approved codes, which we discussed in Chapter 10, will not contain such material. However, one can imagine some traders masquerading as "professional" people—some funeral directors and used car dealers fit this category—and getting together to form an association with a code of practice: this will be of dubious value to consumers if it contains provisions such as exemption clauses which, though unreasonable and unfair, consumers believe to be valid merely because they appear in a code.

(3) Misleading actions[24]

17.28 Misleading practices fall into two categories—misleading actions (reg.5) and misleading omissions (reg.6). As we saw in para.17.27, another type of unfair practice is an aggressive one (reg.7).

The common feature of all three varieties is that they cause the consumer "to take a transactional decision he would not have taken otherwise". A "transactional decision" is defined in reg.2(1); e.g. whether or on what terms to purchase, pay for or dispose of a product.

Would the consumer have made a different decision if not misled or pressured?

---

[23] Above, para.6.44.
[24] Regs 5–7 are reproduced in Appendix Four to this book.

A commercial practice is a "misleading action" within reg.5(1) if it satisfies the conditions in para.5(2), i.e. "it contains false information and is therefore untruthful" or deceives or is likely to deceive the average consumer" in relation to a list (a) to (k) set out in reg.5(4). This is so "even if the information is factually correct".

The list in reg.5(4) includes:

(b) the main characteristics of the product;

(e) the nature of the sales process;

(f) a statement or symbol about sponsorship or approval of the trader or product;

(g) the price;

(i) service, repair etc;

(j) the nature, attributes and rights of the trader; and

(k) the consumer's rights or risks.

The "main characteristics" in para.4(b) are defined in reg.5(5) which contains another non-exhaustive long list (a) to (r) including:

(a) availability;

(e) composition;

(f) accessories;

(i) method and date of manufacture;

(k) delivery;

(l) fitness for purpose;

(n) quantity;

(o) specification; and

(p) geographical origin.

Readers familiar with the Trade Descriptions Act 1968 will recollect that almost all of the ten matters specified in the 1968 Act, s.2(1) (which defined a "trade description" of goods) appear in the more extensive lists mentioned above.

Paragraph 4 (j) ("nature, attributes. . .") is elaborated in reg.5 (6) with yet another list (a) to (h) including identity, qualifications, affiliations and awards.

The list in reg.5 (4) contains a third matter where a cross-reference is necessary, although para.4 (k) does not specifically mention this. Regulation 5 (7) amplifies the meaning of "consumer rights": these "include rights the consumer may have under Part 5A of the Sale of Goods Act 1979 and Part 1B of the Supply of Goods and Services Act 1982", i.e. the "new" rights (discussed in para.7.16 et seq.) such as repair and replacement. Presumably the "old" rights (discussed in para.7.24 et seq.) such as rejection are also covered, as reg. 5(7) states that consumer rights "*include* rights. . . .. under Part 5A" (emphasis supplied), i.e. they are not limited to such rights. Thus it will continue to be an offence for a trader to state "No refunds", "No money back on sale goods" or "No exchanges, credit notes only".

Our last comment on reg.5 concerns two different types of misleading action set out in reg.5(3)(a) and (b). The first concerns marketing which creates confusion with a competitor's products or trade marks. The second is another code of conduct provision: it concerns a trader's failure to comply with a firm and verifiable commitment in a code by which he is bound.

(4) Misleading omissions

17.29 Regulation 6 deals with "misleading omissions" and is concerned with the omission or hiding of "material information" rather than giving false information.

"Material information" means by reg.6(3) information which the average consumer needs to take an informed decision. Information which is unclear or unintelligible may be treated as misleading, so as with the Unfair Terms Regulations (see para.9.19) plain and intelligible language is crucial for suppliers.

Special requirements are set out in reg.6(4) where the supplier makes an "invitation to purchase", e.g. name and address of the trader, price, delivery charges, cancellation rights. "Invitation to purchase" means a commercial communication which indicates characteristics of the product and the price appropriately and enables the consumer to make a purchase. What is "appropriate" will depend on the type of transaction, e.g. goods in a window or on a shelf of a shop, internet supplies of goods or services such as travel. The expression presumably has its usual contractual meaning as something leading to an offer (see para.6.15): i.e. an invitation to treat.

(5) Aggressive practices

17.30 Regulation 7 deals with "aggressive commercial practices". The question here is whether freedom of choice is impaired by "harassment, coercion or undue influence". Regulation 7(2) lists various factors to be taken into account in relation to harassment etc. For example, "timing, location, nature or persistence" are relevant; so pushy evening telephone calls from utilities or telecommunications companies can be controlled. The exploitation of misfortune or grave circumstances impairing the consumer's judgment are relevant too, e.g. pressuring the recently redundant or bereaved.

(6) Schedule 1 black list

17.31 Regulation 3(4)(d) states that a practice is unfair, if "it is listed in Schedule 1". Preamble (17) to the UCPD emphasised that it is "the full list . . . and those are the only" practices deemed to be unfair. In case the point has been missed, Sch.1 itself is headed "COMMERCIAL PRACTICES WHICH ARE IN

ALL CIRCUMSTANCES CONSIDERED UNFAIR". This contrasts with the "grey list" approach adopted by the Unfair Terms Regulations where Sch.2 contains an "Indicative and non-exhaustive list of terms which may be regarded as unfair" (see para.9.31).

Schedule 1 consists of 31 practices. We mention a few examples, following the numbering in the schedule.

1 and 3: false claims about codes of conduct;
5: bait advertising;
6: bait and switch;
12: inaccurate claims about risk to personal security;
14: pyramid schemes;
15: closing down sales;
17: false claims about curing illnesses;
20: "free" products;
21: invoices for unordered goods;
26: persistent cold calling by telephone, fax, e-mail etc;
28: advertisements aimed at children; and
31: winning prizes.

Offences and defences

Regulation 8 applies to the general prohibition under reg.3(3). This is not a strict liability offence. Does the defendant "knowingly or recklessly" engage in the practice?   **17.32**

Regulations 9 to 12 impose strict liability: "A trader is guilty of an offence if he engages . . ." They apply to offences under regs 5 to 7 and Sch.1. There are two exceptions. Regulation 9 does not apply to reg.5(3)(b) (codes) and reg.12 does not apply to Sch.1, paras 11 and 28 (advertisements). Although no offences are committed in these exceptional cases, enforcement proceedings may be brought under the Enterprise Act 2002, Pt 8, which we discussed earlier in this chapter.

Regulations 13 to 18 are similar to the equivalent provisions of the Trade Descriptions Act 1968 which have not been repealed. Readers are referred to the explanation of these in Chapter Thirteen:

Regulation 13 the usual penalties: fines and prison.
Regulation 14: time limits for prosecution.
Regulation 15: offences by bodies corporate.
Regulation 16: act or default of another person.
Regulation 17: the due diligence defence.
Regulation 18: the defence of innocent publication of advertisements.

Enforcement

Again readers are referred to Chapter Thirteen for an explanation.   **17.33**

Regulation 19 imposes a duty of enforcement on every "enforcement officer" (defined in reg.2(1)).

Regulations 20–25 cover related matters, e.g. powers to make test purchases and powers of entry.

Regulations 26 and 27 concern amendments to the Enterprise Act 2002. Regulation 27 is included to comply with the UCPD, art.12(a), and adds s.218A to the 2002 Act. Where an application is made for an enforcement order in respect of a Community infringement in relation to the UCPD, the court may require evidence to substantiate the accuracy of a factual claim.

The Schedules

17.34   Schedule 1

This contains the black list of banned practices.

Schedule 2

This contains amendments to Acts (Pt 1) and Regulations and Orders (Pt 2). (All of the changes mentioned below are dealt with in detail elsewhere in this book.)

Part 1 includes the repeal of most of the Trade Descriptions Act 1968 (including ss.1 and 14). The Consumer Protection Act 1987, Pt III, is also repealed; pricing is now covered by reg.5(4)(g). The Enterprise Act 2002, s.10(2), is repealed too taking with it the two remaining orders made under the Fair Trading Act 1973, Pt II: the Consumer Transactions (Restrictions on Statements) Order 1976 (SI 1976/1813) and the Business Advertisements (Disclosure) Order 1977 (SI 1977/1918) are unnecessary in view of reg.5(4)(k) and 5(7) and Sch.2, para.97, and Sch.1, para.22, respectively.

Part 2 comprises revocations of and amendments to Regulations and Orders. These include the Control of Misleading Advertisements Regulations 1988 (SI 1988/915).

Schedule 3

This contains "Transitional and Saving Provisions". For example, para.5 preserves the Price Indication (Bureaux de Change) (No.2) Regulations 1992 despite the repeal of the Consumer Protection Act 1987, Pt III (see para.14.05).

Schedule 4

This contains a list of all the "Repeals and Revocations".

6. MISLEADING ADVERTISEMENTS

Changing of the guard

17.35   The CPRs discussed in the last section introduced a new regime for the regulation of misleading advertisements. Previously the enforcement powers of the

OFT emanated from the Control of Misleading Advertisement Regulations 1988[25] which implemented the 1984 EU Misleading Advertising Directive[26]; in their amended form they covered comparative advertising too.

Business Protection Regulations

The 1988 Regulations were revoked by the CPRs[27] and replaced by the Business Protection from Misleading Marketing Regulations 2008[28] (the BPRs) which came into force on May 26, 2008 (the same day as the CPRs). They consolidate the 1988 Regulations and their various amendments and so deal with both misleading and comparative advertising.

There is one major difference between the old and the new regulations: as the title of the BPRs indicates, they are for the protection of business only, not of consumers. This can be seen from reg.3(2)(a) which states that advertising is misleading which deceives "*the traders* to whom it is addressed" (emphasis supplied) whereas the CPRs, reg.5(2)(a), refer to "the average consumer". Regulation 3(2)(b) underlines the business limitation by requiring the advertising "to injure a competitor". There is, though, one significant similarity between the CPRs, reg.5,[29] and the BPRs, reg.3: the lists of relevant matters are almost identical.

In view of their application to business-to-business transactions only we shall confine ourselves to those few remarks on the BPRs, although readers may find it helpful to consult earlier editions of this book which discuss the similar 1988 Regulations more fully.

The CPRs

Following the revocation of the 1988 Regulations and the repeal of other legislation which dealt with advertising such as the Trade Descriptions Act 1968 and the pricing provisions of the Consumer Protection Act 1987, Part III, the statutory control of advertising to consumers depends upon the CPRs.

We discussed the CPRs in the previous section, but highlight below some of the points already covered which relate to advertising:

(1) The definition of "commercial practice" specifically includes "advertising and marketing".

(2) "Misleading actions" and "misleading omissions" in regs.5(1) and 6(1) clearly cover advertising as they both refer initially to "a commercial practice".

(3) The same is true of "aggressive commercial practices" in reg.7(1).

---

[25] SI 1988/915, amended by SI 2000/914.
[26] 84/450 O.J. L250/17.
[27] Sch.2, para.81.
[28] SI 2008/1276.
[29] Para.17.28.

(4) Many of the banned practices in Sch.1 inevitably involve advertisements in that they talk about "claiming", "falsely stating", "promoting", "falsely claiming" etc. Two practices are noteworthy in the list:
11. "Using editorial content. . .."(advertorial).
28. "Including in an advertisement. . .."

ASA and self-regulation

17.36   The Advertising Standards Authority has made it clear that, in dealing with complaints, it will have regard to the CPRs. How does self-regulation fit into the regulatory framework?

The Advertising Standards Authority (ASA) was established in 1962 to provide independent supervision of the industry's self-regulatory arrangements through a monitoring programme and investigation of complaints. The first Code was published in 1961 and modelled on the 1937 International Code of Advertising Practice. It is kept under continuous review and amendment by the Committee of Advertising Practice (CAP). The Code applies to advertisements in newspapers, magazines, posters, brochures, leaflets and other printed publications, for the public, cinema commercials and viewdata services. The most recent code, effective from March 4, 2003, is called the "British Code of Advertising, Sales Promotion and Direct Marketing" and takes account of new media advertising such as email.

A separate system operates in relation to broadcasting. The Broadcasting Act 1990 imposed a duty on the Independent Television Commission and the Radio Authority to draw up and enforce codes governing standards and practice in advertising and programme sponsorship. In December 2003 the regulatory regime changed when Ofcom (the Office of Communications) took over the functions of these bodies under the Communications Act 2003.

In 2004 Ofcom contracted out its day-to-day monitoring functions to the ASA.[30] This "co-regulation" has simplified matters for complainants and advertisers alike, since the ASA is now responsible for ensuring that both non-broadcast advertisements and broadcast advertisements comply with the relevant codes. The Broadcasting Committee of Advertising Practice (BCAP) writes and keeps under review the broadcast codes: the BCAP Radio Advertising Standards Code and the BCAP Television Advertising Standards Code.[31]

---

[30] The Contracting Out (Functions Relating to Broadcast Advertising) and Specification of Relevant Functions Order 2004 (SI 2004/1975).
[31] All the codes can be accessed at *www.cap.org.uk/cap/codes*.

Part IV

CREDIT TRANSACTIONS

CHAPTER EIGHTEEN

THE BACKGROUND TO CONSUMER CREDIT

1. INTRODUCTION

There has been a dramatic increase in consumer credit in the last fifty **18.01** years—both in this country and in other Western industrialised countries. By far the greatest area is house purchase but there are many others including furniture, electrical appliances, clothing, vehicles, holidays and home repairs and improvements. The Crowther Report on Consumer Credit revealed that in 1966 the amount of medium and long-term credit extended totalled £3,692,000,000 (house purchase credit accounted for approximately 45 per cent of this figure). At the end of the year the total outstanding was £9,684,000,000, of which some 80 per cent was attributable to houses and flats. Forty years later, a staggering £1.25 trillion was outstanding at the end 2006.

The Crowther Committee clearly realised that:

> The use of consumer credit . . . enables individuals to enjoy the services of consumer durable goods sooner than they otherwise would and in a period of inflation offers them a real prospect of acquiring them more cheaply. Consumers in general are able to obtain a more satisfying 'basket' of goods and services with the same income. Thus consumer credit may be said to enhance consumer satisfaction. Furthermore, some individuals, who lack the self-discipline to save up for the purchase of a durable consumer good but are nevertheless unlikely to break their contract with a creditor, are able to buy a durable consumer good which might otherwise never be theirs.[1]

One need only add that this reason applies, a fortiori, to house purchase. **18.02**

The situation described above (a highly topical issue as we go to press) has its corresponding dangers and these are two-fold. First, borrowers may be tempted to overstretch their resources—either through bad economic planning or because they do not appreciate the full extent of their obligations. Secondly, some lenders might be tempted to "cash in" on the attractions of consumer credit by inducing borrowers (some of whom may already be under severe financial stress) to sign agreements which are one-sided and impose unduly onerous obligations. Research commissioned by the government and carried out between March and May 2002 found that the majority of households use credit modestly (and a number of credit facilities are underused) but a small minority are heavy credit users. Thus five per cent of households were

---

[1] Cmnd.4596, p.118.

spending a quarter of their gross income on consumer credit repayments and seven per cent had four or more credit commitments. A more worrying picture emerges from more recent research carried out by Leeds University Business School. They reported in October 2003 that the amount of debt being chased by bailiffs had risen by 70 per cent to £5 billion in the past two years and that arrears amounted to £60 billion, £2,000 per household.

Until the passing of the Consumer Credit Act 1974 the law developed in a fragmentary and piecemeal fashion—following rather than leading, checking abuses *after* they had come to light rather than laying down ground rules in advance. Thus:

(1) The Bills of Sale Acts 1878 to 1882 were passed to deal with (inter alia) mortgages of personal property where the borrower retained possession.

(2) The Moneylenders Acts 1900 to 1927 were passed to regulate the activities of certain moneylenders (but not, e.g. banks).

(3) The Pawnbrokers Acts 1872 to 1960 regulated the activities of pawnbrokers.

(4) The Hire-Purchase Act 1965 regulated hire-purchase agreements where the hire-purchase price did not exceed £2,000 and where the hirer was not a body corporate. (This limit was increased to £7,500 in 1983.)

18.03   The unsatisfactory nature of this fragmentary approach can be seen by looking at money-lending. If the lender happened to be a bank, the Moneylenders Acts did not apply at all, even though the borrower may have been an inexperienced private individual and the contract may have been a harsh one on the particular facts. On the other hand, if the lender was within the provisions of the Act the full rigours of the Act were applied, even though the borrower was a large public company well able to look after itself. Again, as new forms of credit developed (e.g. credit cards) the absence of any regulatory machinery meant that there was virtually no effective control at all. All this was changed by the Consumer Credit Act 1974 which is probably the most comprehensive and sophisticated Act of its kind in the Western world.

The Act was designed to sweep away the piecemeal controls listed above and to replace them with a single code governing all forms of lending. The only pieces of legislation which remain unrepealed are the Bills of Sale Acts 1878 to 1882—the reason is that the Consumer Credit Act does not regulate mortgages of personal property. A suggestion made by the Crowther Committee that the Government should introduce a Lending and Security Act has not so far been implemented.

2. Consumer Credit Act 2006

18.04   Government concern at over-indebtedness, indicated by research such as that mentioned in para.18.02 above, led to the creation of an "over-indebtedness task force" and to the publication jointly by the DTI and DWP of a paper *Tackling Over-indebtedness—Action Plan 2004*.

In July 2001 it had announced a review of the 1974 Act focussing on the financial limit, licensing, information disclosure, early settlement, consumer redress and, last but not least, unfair credit transactions. This led to the publication in December 2003 of the White Paper *Fair, Clear and Competitive— The Consumer Credit Market in the 21ˢᵗ Century.*

Those areas not requiring primary legislation—e.g. advertising, precontractual disclosure, early settlement calculations—were immediately reformed in 2004 by a series of statutory instruments. However, primary legislation was needed for the reform of the other areas—financial limit, licensing, unfair credit relationships and consumer redress—and in due course the Consumer Credit Act 2006 was passed. It received Royal Assent on March 30, 2006 and came into force gradually as ordered by statutory instruments under s.71.

Finally before turning to an analysis of the Consumer Credit Act 1974 one point must be stressed. The 2006 Act is not a free standing statute: its principal effect is to *amend* the 1974 Act. In Part IV of this book a reference to "the Act" is a reference to the 1974 Act (as amended) and a reference to a section is to that section in the Act.

3. CONSUMER CREDIT ACT 1974—TEN PRELIMINARY POINTS

The scope and effect of the Consumer Credit Act will be examined in detail in the next eight chapters. In the remainder of this chapter it is proposed to deal with ten preliminary matters.   **18.05**

(1) The Act contains no definition of the word "consumer". We have already seen that under the Unfair Contract Terms Act 1977 the term "consumer" means a private consumer as opposed to a business consumer, and the Enterprise Act 2002 adopts a similar approach. *The Consumer Credit Act 1974 is not limited in this way.* In the two major types of agreement—consumer credit and consumer hire—the Act provides control where the debtor or hirer is an "individual" but the definition of this term is not what one might expect. The original definition has been narrowed by the 2006 Act, s.1, and took effect on April 6, 2007.[2] Section 189(1) now reads:

'individual' includes—

   (a) a partnership consisting of two or three persons not all of whom are bodies corporate; and
   (b) an unincorporated body of persons which does not consist entirely of bodies corporate and is not a partnership;

This is a major change made by the 2006 Act, for now only partnerships of two or three people are protected whereas before there was no limit on their size. As before, sole proprietors of a business are covered but not companies. Thus some small traders are still protected just as much as the private individual.

Conversely, the Act regulates (at least in part) agreements where the credi-

---

[2] Consumer Credit-Credit Act 2006 (Commencement No. 2 and Transitional Provisions and Savings) Order 2007 (SI 2007/123).

tor or owner is *not* acting in the course of a business.[3] Indeed, in one section of the Act, the term "consumer" refers only to a partnership and other unincorporated bodies (s.158 (as amended) below, para.26.03).

(2) Another change, and even more drastic, is the abolition of the financial limit (previously £25,000).

18.06　(3) Section 189 adopts the very helpful practice of drawing together all the definitions which appear throughout the Act. Section 189(1) contains no less than 177 definitions. Some are defined in the section itself (e.g. the term "individual"). In other cases s.189 refers to the section where the definition is to be found, e.g.:

> 'exempt agreement' means an agreement specified in or under section 16.

It is vitally important to refer constantly to s.189 because words are often used in unexpected ways. Thus, for example, the definition of the word "surety" is wide enough to include the principal debtor (unless the context otherwise requires).

(4) Another helpful innovation[4] (not so far copied by the draftsman of the annual Finance Act) is Sch.2 which contains 24 worked examples showing the use of the new terminology. Section 188(3), however, provides that:

> In the case of conflict between Schedule 2 and any other provision of this Act that other provision shall prevail.

(5) Although the Act is a long one, a very large part of the detail is contained in regulations. They cover such matters as the total charge for credit, regulated and exempt agreements, documentation and rebate for early settlement.

18.07　(6) The control provided by the Act is twofold:

(a) Control of business activity—notably through the licensing system administered by the OFT.[5]

(b) Control of individual agreements.

(7) The Act provides various civil and criminal sanctions, as well as the administrative sanctions in ss.29 and 32 (non-renewal, suspension and revocation of a licence). The criminal sanctions are usefully collected together in Sch.1. Section 170(1) provides that:

> A breach of any requirement made (otherwise than by any court) by or under this Act shall incur no civil or criminal sanction as being such a breach except to the extent (if any) expressly provided for under this Act.

---

[3] See below, para. 19.10.
[4] The Government has recently introduced another helpful practice under which all Government Bills are accompanied by explanatory notes. They are available for the 2006 Act.
[5] See Ch.Twenty, below, para.20.02.

Thus s.48 makes it an offence to canvass certain types of agreement (e.g. personal loans) off trade premises. If a person borrows money in a case where the lender has contravened s.48, he cannot avoid liability under that contract by pleading that it is illegal. Nor could he bring an action for breach of statutory duty. Such claims or defences are shut out by s.170(1). Presumably the criminal court would still be able to award compensation under the Powers of Criminal Courts (Sentencing) Act 2000.[6] The section does not affect the power of the court to grant an injunction (s.170(3)).

(8) As one might expect, the statutory rights enjoyed by the debtor, the hirer, a surety or a relative[7] cannot in any way be cut down or fettered by the agreement.[8]

(9) One of the features of the Act is that certain steps can only be taken if the court or the OFT makes an order to that effect. An example of the former is the enforcement of an agreement which has not been properly executed.[9] An example of the latter is the enforcement of an agreement made by a creditor or owner while he was unlicensed. In either case s.173(3) provides that consent of the debtor or hirer "given at that time" shall be as effective as an order. The words "given at that time" presumably refer to the time of enforcement so that a provision for consent in the contract would not be effective. Clearly the court would examine the facts very carefully to ensure that there was a true consent.

(10) It may be useful to end this chapter by setting out a few important definitions which will be met from time to time in the next eight chapters.

Hire-purchase agreement

A hire-purchase agreement is defined as an agreement under which goods are **18.08** bailed[10] in return for periodical payments by the bailee and the property in the goods will pass to the bailee if the terms of the agreement are complied with and one or more of the following occur:

    (i) the exercise of an option to purchase by the bailee; or

    (ii) the doing of any other specified act by any party to the agreement; or

    (iii) the happening of any other specified event.

Conditional and credit sale agreements

A *conditional sale* agreement is an agreement for the sale of goods or land **18.09** under which the purchase price or part of it is payable by instalments and the property in the goods or land is to remain with the seller (notwithstanding

---

[6] Above, para.16.03.
[7] As to which see below, para.18.10.
[8] See s.173(1) and (2).
[9] Below, para.21.02.
[10] Goods are "bailed" if one person ("the bailor") transfers possession to another ("the bailee") for a specific purpose.

that the buyer is to be in possession of the goods or land) until such conditions as to the payment of instalments or likewise as may be specified in the agreement are fulfilled.

If, however, there is a straight sale of goods on credit terms the property will usually pass to the buyer immediately under s.18, r.1 of the Sale of Goods Act 1979 and the agreement will be a *credit sale* agreement, *not* a conditional sale agreement.

Thus the crucial difference is whether the property passes to the buyer when the contract is made (credit sale) or at a later stage (conditional sale).

The term "property" is used to mean ownership.

18.10 *Relative*

Relative means husband, wife, brother, sister, uncle, aunt, nephew, niece, lineal ancestor or lineal descendant. Relationship by marriage is also included and the reference to "husband or wife" includes a former or a reputed spouse.

Associate

18.11 The associate of an individual means (i) a relative, and (ii) a partner, or the relative of a partner, of that individual.

"Restricted-use" and "unrestricted-use"

18.12 These terms are defined in s.11 and are largely self-explanatory. If the debtor can actually use the credit in any way he wishes the agreement will be an "unrestricted-use" agreement, even though certain uses would constitute a breach of contract. Thus a loan paid by the lender to the borrower would be an unrestricted-use agreement. On the other hand, a hire-purchase agreement, a sale on deferred terms or a loan where the money goes straight from the lender to a third party (e.g. the supplier of goods or services) would be a restricted-use agreement. We shall meet the distinction at several points in the following chapters.

4. THE CONSUMER CREDIT DIRECTIVE

Introduction

18.13 After more than 30 years of calm with comparatively few changes the 1974 Act is passing through a period of change, improving consumer protection but making business more complex for lenders and consumer advisers alike. Having come to grips with the amendments made by the 2006 Act (discussed at various points in Chapters Eighteen to Twenty-Five) they must now apply their minds to Directive 2008/48/EC "on credit agreements for consumers and repealing Council directive 87/102/EEC" (the Consumer Credit Directive or CCD, as it is known). (As its title shows, it repeals Directive 87/102/EEC.)

Preamble to the CCD

The justification for Brussel's intervention again in this area is set out in the **18.14** Preambles to the Directive. Preamble (3) points to "substantial differences between the laws of Member States". This situation "in some cases leads to distortions of competition among creditors in the Community" (Preamble (4)). Preamble (6) asserts:

> "The development of a more transparent and efficient credit market within the area without internal frontiers is vital in order to promote the development of cross-border activities".

This is a maximum Directive for the reasons given in Preamble (9):

> "Full harmonisation is necessary in order to ensure that all consumers in the Community enjoy a high and equivalent level of protection of their interests and to create a genuine internal market. Member States should therefore not be allowed to maintain or introduce national provisions other than those laid down in this Directive. However, such restriction should only apply where there are provisions harmonised in this Directive. Where no such harmonised provisions exist, Member States should remain free to maintain or introduce national legislation".

It follows that, though many believe that the Act (as amended and as elaborated by copious regulations) provides adequate protection for consumer debtors, amendments to the Act are inevitable and to some extent protection will be reduced. That perhaps is a pessimistic view, for there will be some new provisions which will be of value to consumers, e.g.

- art. 5.6: explanations to consumers;

- art.8: creditor's assessment of creditworthiness:

- art.9: information on credit reference agency reports;

- art.13: termination rights;

- art.14: 14 day cancellation rights;

- art.16: partial early repayment; and

- art.21 : disclosure of fees by intermediaries.

Some CCD Articles

Member States are meant to publish and bring into force legislation **18.15** implementing the CCD by May 12, 2010. BIS (BERR) issued a useful consultation document "Consultation on Proposals for Implementing the Consumer Credit Directive" (125pp.) in April 2008 setting out its proposals. So far the UK regulations have not been published, although they are expected soon. Meanwhile we shall comment briefly on some of the articles of the CCD.

Art.2: Scope

A list of 12 exceptions appears in art.2.1, some of which are currently regulated by the Act, e.g. second mortgages, hire and hire-purchase agreements. BIS propose to leave untouched the existing legislation on hire agreements. Art 2.2(c) exempts agreements for a total amount of credit exceeding EUR 75,000, though the 1974 Act upper limit has now been abolished (with some exceptions) (para.18.05).

Art.3: Definitions

Amongst the 14 definitions is (a) "consumer": "a natural person. . ...acting for purposes which are outside his trade, business or profession" in contrast to the 1974 Act where "individual" includes some businesses (para.18.05). "Credit intermediary" in (f) is used for what we would call a credit broker.

Art. 5: Pre-contractual information

A list of 19 items appears in art.5.1. It includes all the obvious matters and is similar to current UK regulations. The most novel is the requirement by art. 5(1) to provide the information "by means of the Standard European Consumer Credit Information Form" set out in Annex II.

An additional duty is imposed on creditors by art. 5.6 to "provide adequate explanations to the consumer" to enable him to assess whether the proposal is "adapted to his needs and to his financial situation" and by explaining various matters, e.g. the pre-contractual information, the consequences of default.

Art. 8: Creditworthiness

The above explanation ties in neatly with art.8. The creditor must assess the consumer's creditworthiness on information from the consumer, a database or elsewhere. These provisions together may well prevent people borrowing beyond their means, as they have in recent years with self-certification of income and the lending of 100 per cent of the value of buildings, and may lead to more debtors themselves becoming responsible borrowers.

Art. 9: Database access

A new right for debtors is given by art.9.2. If a creditor rejects an application for credit, it must inform the consumer "immediately and without charge of the result" of any database search, e.g. of a credit reference agency.

Art. 10: Information in agreements

Art.10.2 contains a list of 21 pieces of information to be included in the agreements themselves. (Overdrafts are treated separately in art.10.5.) The provisions are less prescriptive and detailed than those of the Act explained in Chapter Twenty-One, e.g. no boxes for signature.

Art. 13: Open-end agreements

An "open-end" credit agreement is not defined and seems to be an indefinite **18.16** one with no fixed term, e.g. credit or store cards. Art.13.1 gives consumers a new right to terminate such an agreement by at most one month's notice. Where the creditor has a contractual right to terminate, he must give at least two months' notice.

Art. 14: Withdrawal

Although the Act gives a five day cancellation right in limited circumstances (para.22.05), art.14.1 allows a debtor "to withdraw from the credit agreement without giving any reason" within 14 days.

Art. 16: Early repayment

The difference between the early settlement provisions in s.94 of the Act (para.25.12) and art.16.1 is that the CCD permits partial early repayment. BIS proposes to use the same formula as at present.

Art.19: APR

The calculation of the APR is dealt with by art.19 and the formula is set out in Annex I.

Art. 21: Intermediaries

By art.21 intermediaries must (a) in advertising indicate whether they are independent or work exclusively for one or more creditors and (b) disclose the fee payable for their services.

Summary

As we mentioned earlier, some of the changes enhance consumer protection, but perhaps at the cost of excessive complexity. We await the overdue regulations with bated breath.

CHAPTER NINETEEN

"WHAT AGREEMENTS ARE CAUGHT BY THE ACT?"

We have already seen that the scope of the Act is very wide. In this chapter **19.01** it is proposed to work through the very intricate provisions of the Act and Regulations to find out the precise extent of control. The scheme of this chapter is as follows:

1. Regulated agreements
2. Partially regulated agreements
3. Exempt agreements
4. Linked transactions

1. REGULATED AGREEMENTS

Most of the statutory controls only apply to a "regulated agreement". In **19.02** order to find out whether an agreement is regulated it is necessary to proceed in two stages:

(1) Does the agreement come within the definition of "consumer credit agreement" in s.8 or "consumer hire agreement" in s.15? If the answer is "no", the agreement cannot be a regulated agreement.

(2) If the answer to (1) above is "yes", then by ss.8(3) and 15(2) any such agreement *is* a regulated agreement unless it is an exempt agreement. The concept of "exempt agreement", which depends on s.16 and the Regulations, is dealt with later in this chapter.[1]

Consumer credit agreement

Let us start by listing the many types of agreement which can come within **19.03** this term. They include:

(a) Hire-Purchase.
(b) Conditional Sale.
(c) Credit sale.
(d) Personal loan.
(e) Overdraft.

---

[1] Below, para.19.12.

(f) Loan secured by land mortgage.

(g) Credit card.

(h) Pledges.

(i) Store cards.

Section 8(2) (as amended) defines a consumer credit agreement as an agreement whereby one person (the creditor) provides an individual (the debtor) with credit of any amount. Five points are worthy of note:

(i) There must be an "agreement". Thus where a sale is for cash and on delivery of the goods the buyer asks for time to pay, the granting of "credit" would not amount to an "agreement" unless it formed part of a separate bargain—as, for example, where the borrower agrees to pay interest on the outstanding amount.

(ii) The creditor can be an "individual" or a body corporate, but the debtor must be an "individual".[2]

(iii) The Act draws a sharp distinction between the "credit" and the "total charge for credit." The term *"credit"* includes a cash loan and any form of financial accommodation[3] and clearly refers to the loan, etc., itself. The term "total charge for credit" refers to interest and other charges.[4] Section 9(4) provides that:

> An item entering into the total charge for credit shall not be treated as credit even though time is allowed for payment.

19.04   (iv) As an illustration of the above principles s.9(3) defines the "credit" in a hire-purchase agreement as the total price of the goods less (a) the deposit (if any), and (b) the total charge for credit.

Example

> A finance house C agrees to let a Porsche car on hire-purchase to D (an individual). The total price is £27,000; this includes a down payment of £5,000 and a total charge for credit of £3,000. When these two items are deducted from the price (£27,000–£8,000) one is left with credit of £19,000.[5]

(v) With the removal of the statutory ceiling of £25,000 it is usually unnecessary to calculate the "credit" to decide whether an agreement with a consumer is regulated. However, there is still such a ceiling for business debtors and hirers (below, para.19.15).

---

[2] See above, para.18.05.
[3] s.9(3). For a recent example, see *Dimond v Lovell* at para.7.58 above. Some 40,000 road traffic cases were stayed while this case made its slow progress through the courts.
[4] Below, para.19.16.
[5] See *Humberside Finance v Thompson* [1997] C.C.L.R. 23 where the debtor paid a "payment waiver premium" under a clause extinguishing his liability if he died. The finance company claimed that this payment brought the "credit" above the statutory ceiling. The claim was rejected; the premium formed part of the "total charge for credit" and was not part of the "credit".

Three further examples

The distinction between "credit" and "the total charge for credit" can be **19.05** crucial for the creditor. If the credit figure in the agreement wrongly includes an item which forms part of the total charge for credit, the agreement will be "not properly executed" and unenforceable by the creditor. The point has arisen in three recent cases; in two of them the creditor came to grief.

In *Wilson v First County Ltd (No.2)*[6] Mrs Wilson agreed to pay a £250 document fee as part of a credit transaction. The agreement included this item as part of the credit but the Court of Appeal ruled that it formed part of the total charge for credit. The agreement was therefore unenforceable.

In *Watchtower Investments Ltd v Payne*[7] the creditor paid over an amount after deducting a sum which was used to clear arrears under an earlier mortgage. This was one of the objects of the transaction and on that basis the deducted amount formed part of the credit.

In *McGinn v Grangewood Securities*[8] the facts were similar to those in *Watchtower*, except that the clearance of the arrears was not one of the objects of the transaction. Accordingly the Court of Appeal distinguished the earlier case and held that the agreement had wrongly included the deducted amount in the "credit"—with the same result as in *Wilson* (above).

Fixed and running-account credit

The term "consumer credit agreement" is subdivided into "fixed-sum credit" **19.06** and "running-account credit"—the distinction is important in deciding whether an agreement is regulated or exempt[9] and for certain other purposes. Section 10(1)(a) tells us that:

> running-account credit is a facility under a personal credit agreement whereby the debtor is enabled to receive from time to time (whether in his own person or by another person) from the creditor or a third party cash, goods and services (or any of them) to an amount or value such that, taking into account payments made by or to the credit of the debtor, the credit limit (if any) is not at any time exceeded.

Perhaps the two most common examples of running-account credit are bank overdrafts and store cards.

Debtor-creditor-supplier (D-C-S) agreements and debtor-creditor (D-C) agreements

These terms are defined in ss.12 and 13. It is necessary to mention them **19.07** at this point because a knowledge of them is vital when considering the all important question of whether the agreement is *regulated* or *exempt*.[10] The distinction between D-C-S and D-C turns on the relationship between the

---

[6] [2001] EWCA Civ 663. Followed in *Southern Pacific Personal Loans Ltd v Walker* [2009] EWCA Civ 1218: broker's fee part of total charge for credit.
[7] [2001] EWCA Civ 1159. See also *Southern Pacific Mortgage Ltd v Heath*, [2009] EWCA Civ 1135.
[8] [2002] EWCA Civ 522.
[9] See below, para.19.13, subpara(6).
[10] Below, para.19.12.

supplier of the credit and the supplier of the land, goods or services. The effect of ss.12 and 13 can be summarised as follows:

(i) If the supplier of the credit and the supplier of the goods, etc., is *the same person*, then it is D-C-S. Examples include hire-purchase, credit sale, and sale of land where the seller agrees to leave the price outstanding. This can be referred to as "two-party D-C-S".

(ii) If the supplier of credit and the supplier of the goods, etc., are *different* but work together under *"arrangements"*, then again it is D-C-S. Thus, a credit card company has "arrangements" with its approved suppliers and a finance company might have "arrangements" with a car dealer whereby they would provide loans to finance sales made by him to customers. In both these cases the credit contract would be a D-C-S agreement. This can be referred to as "three-party D-C-S".

(iii) If there are no such arrangements, the agreement is a D-C agreement. Thus if a customer borrows £4,000 from his bank to pay for central heating or a holiday or to finance his business, this is a D-C agreement.

(iv) If an agreement is made to refinance an existing indebtedness, whether to the creditor or any other person, then again it is D-C.

As already stated the distinction is critical on the "regulated or exempt" point—we shall see that under a D-C-S agreement the critical factor is the number of instalments, whereas under a D-C agreement the critical factor is the annual percentage rate of charge for credit. The distinction is also important for other purposes, including joint responsibility of supplier and creditor in cancellation cases[11] and under s.75.[12]

Consumer hire agreement

19.08 The second type of agreement to which the Act applies is a consumer hire agreement. Clearly, this type of agreement is less important than the consumer credit agreement, but it is worth remembering that it covers not only the domestic hiring of, e.g. a television set, but also the commercial hiring of, e.g. equipment. Section 15 makes it clear that there are six elements:

(a) a bailment of goods

(b) by one person (the owner)

(c) to an individual (the hirer), provided that

(d) it is not hire-purchase, and

(e) it is capable of lasting for more than three months[13] and

(f) it does not require the hirer to make payments[14] in excess of £25,000.

---

[11] Below, para.22.10.
[12] Below, para.23.05. This is a vital provision in relation to credit cards.
[13] The critical period is the duration of the bailment and not the duration of the payment obligation: *Clark v Ardington Electrical Services* [2002] EWCA Civ 510.
[14] Inclusive of VAT: *Apollo Leasing Ltd v Scott* [1986] C.C.L.R. 1. If the bailee does not have to pay anything, s.15 does not apply: *TRM Copy Centres (UK) Ltd v Lanwall Services Ltd* [2009] UKHL 35.

The financial ceiling is now irrelevant except for business hirers (s.16B, below, para.19.15). In deciding on how much the business hirer is *required* to pay one must look at his minimum contractual liability, having regard to any contractual right to terminate. Thus, if a three-year hiring (with no break clause) required the hirer to pay a rental of £9,000 per annum, this would bring the total to £27,000 and it would *not* be a regulated agreement (see Sch. 2, Example 20). The position would be different if, for example, the hirer had a right to terminate, without further payment, at the end of the second year.

2. PARTIALLY REGULATED AGREEMENTS

As already stated, the all important distinction is between *regulated* and *exempt* agreements. Before considering the nature of exempt agreements it might be useful to mention two types of agreement which are regulated in part only. **19.09**

Non-commercial agreements

By section 189 a non-commercial agreement is an agreement not made by the creditor or owner in the course of a business carried on by him. It is important to notice the words "*a* business." If, for example, a manufacturer made loans to his employees to enable them to buy season tickets or houses, the loans *would* be made in the course of *a* business (even though it was not a consumer credit or consumer hire business) and accordingly it would not be "non-commercial." If, however, the agreement is non-commercial then a number of specific provisions do not apply. The most important area is formalities and cancellation.[15] **19.10**

Small agreements

A small agreement is defined in s.17 as either; **19.11**

    (a) a regulated consumer credit agreement for credit not exceeding £50,[16] other than a hire-purchase or conditional sale agreement[17]; or

    (b) a regulated consumer hire agreement which does not require the hirer to make payments exceeding £50.

There is a further condition, namely, that the agreement is unsecured or secured by a guarantee or indemnity only. Not surprisingly, s.17(3) blocks attempts to split up a transaction into a series of small agreements (at one time encyclopaedia salesmen were notorious for this) by providing that in such a case each small agreement shall be treated as a regulated non-small agreement.

---

[15] See s.74(1)(a) and ss.77–79.
[16] The figure is reduced to £35 if it comes within the Cancellation of Contracts made in a Consumer's Home or Place of Work etc. Regulations 2008, Sch.1. See above, para.6.25.
[17] See above, paras 18.08–18.09.

Small debtor-creditor-supplier agreements for restricted-use credit are exempt from most of the provisions relating to formalities and cancellation.[18]

3. EXEMPT AGREEMENTS

19.12 Having decided that an agreement is a consumer credit or consumer hire agreement, we must now decide whether it is taken out of control by one of the exemptions. These are to be found in ss.16, 16A and 16B and in the Consumer Credit (Exempt Agreements) Orders 1989 (as amended) and 2007. The first four of them relate to land. The last two were introduced by the 2006 Act.

(1) A debtor-creditor-supplier agreement is exempt if (a) the creditor is a local authority or a body named in the regulations, and (b) the agreement finances (i) the purchase of land, or (ii) the provision of dwellings on any land, and in either case is secured by a mortgage of *that* land.[19]

(2) A debtor-creditor agreement is exempt if (a) the lender is a local authority, and (b) the agreement is secured by a mortgage of land. It will be apparent that in this case the purpose of the loan is immaterial.[20]

(3) A debtor-creditor agreement is exempt if (a) the lender is a body named in the regulations, (b) the agreement is secured by a mortgage of land, and (c) the agreement is to finance the purchase of land, the provision of dwellings or business premises on land and certain ancillary purposes.[21]

The bodies named in the Regulations include a large number of insurance companies, friendly societies and charities. Also included are certain public bodies (e.g. development corporations), but there the exemption only applies to a more limited class of purpose which is set out opposite to their names in Pt II of the Schedule to the Regulations.

Building Societies originally enjoyed blanket exemption but with the widening of their powers under the Building Societies Act 1986 this was abolished. Instead, any Building Society authorised under that Act will enjoy exemption if and only if the relevant agreement is exempt under the 1989 Order. For example, a Building Society loan not linked to house purchase, etc., would be regulated. Mortgages are now regulated under the Financial Services and Markets Act 2000.

(4) Even if an agreement to finance the purchase of land is not exempt under (1) to (3) above (e.g. because the lender is not one of the specified bodies) a further exemption is to be found in art.3(1)(b) which exempts a debtor-creditor-supplier agreement to finance the purchase of land, if the number of payments to be made by the debtor does not exceed four. There are further exemptions covering agreements to finance a premium under a contract of insurance relating to land.

19.13 (5) A debtor-creditor-supplier agreement is exempt under art.3(1)(a)(i) if (a) it is not hire-purchase or conditional sale, (b) it is for fixed-sum credit,

---

[18] See below, paras 21.06 and 22.04.
[19] s.16(2)(a).
[20] ibid.
[21] ibid.

(c) the number of payments to be made by the debtor *in respect of the credit* does not exceed four, and (d) they must be paid *within* 12 months of the date of the agreement. This exempts (inter alia) normal trade credit (e.g. payment within 30 days of invoice).

The word "within" has proved a tripwire for creditors (and no doubt their advisers) in two recent road traffic cases cases.

In *Zoan v Rouamba*[22] an agreement for the hire of a car to a motorist (who had been involved in an accident causing damage to his own car) provided that the hire charge was to be paid not later than the date on which he recovered damages from the other motorist or "*the first anniversary of this agreement*" whichever was the earlier. Certain details were omitted from the agreement (making it "not properly executed") and the question arose as to whether the agreement was an "exempt agreement" within art.3(1)(a)(i). The Court of Appeal held that it was not. As a general rule a period running "from" a certain date will exclude that date. Accordingly the "anniversary" of a date will be *12 months and one day* from that date—one day outside the maximum permitted by art.3. The defective agreement was therefore a regulated agreement; since the creditor could not recover the hire charges from the hirer, the charges did not represent a "loss" to the hirer and could not be recovered from the other motorist who had caused the damage.

A similar result was reached in *Ketley v Gilbert.*[23] In this case the hire charge was payable "on the expiration of twelve months starting on the date of this agreement." It was held that the charge was payable *at the end of* (and not *within*) the 12-month period.

(6) A debtor-creditor-supplier agreement is exempt under art.3(1)(a)(ii) if **19.14** (a) it is not hire-purchase or conditional sale, (b) it is for running-account credit, and (c) the whole of the credit for a period is repayable by a single payment. This will exempt many store cards and certain *charge* card agreements, e.g. American Express and Diners Club.

(7) A further important exemption is to be found in art.4 and relates to debtor-creditor agreements where (a) it is offered to a class or classes of person (e.g. employees) and not to the public generally and (b) the only item in the "total charge for credit" is interest which cannot exceed one per cent above the highest of any base rates published by the English and Scottish Clearing Banks, being the latest rates in force 28 days before the making of the agreement.

In practice, many agreements seek to protect the creditor by including a term in the agreement whereby the debtor's liability fluctuates according to a specified formula (e.g. the retail price index or changes in Bank of England minimum lending rate). In deciding whether the "low interest exemption" applies to such a case it is necessary to distinguish sharply between *credit* and *the total charge for credit*. If the *credit* can fluctuate then exemption under reg.4 is destroyed. On the other hand, the fluctuation of the annual *rate* of charge is permissible and this will not destroy the exemption—provided that

---

[22] [1999] 1 W.L.R. 986.
[23] *The Times*, January 17, 2001, CA.

at the date of the agreement the rate did not exceed the statutory ceiling set out above.

Thus if the agreement provided for interest to be paid annually at "1 per cent above HSBC base rate for the time being" the agreement will be exempt if at the date of the agreement the base rate did not exceed the highest rate prevailing 28 days before the making of the agreement. An increase in the rate after the date of the agreement will not destroy the exemption.

19.15   (8) An odd new exemption appears in s.16A: "high net worth". It applies where the consumer is a "natural person", which presumably includes a sole proprietor of a business. The DTI's Explanatory Notes, para.18, state that a partnership is outside the exemption, though arguably a partner is a "natural person". The agreement must include a declaration that the debtor or hirer agrees to forgo the statutory protection and someone else must make a "statement of high net worth" about him.

The Consumer Credit (Exempt Agreements) Order 2007[24] defines this as net income of at least £150,000 or net assets of £500,000 during the previous financial year. The statement must be made by the creditor, owner or an accountant belonging to one of the bodies listed in art.4(2). The form and content of the declaration and statement appear in Schs 1 and 2.

The Order came into force on April 6, 2008.

(9) We have already pointed out that the £25,000 limit has been retained for consumer credit or hire agreements to business customers. Section 16B(1) exempts from regulation agreements exceeding that figure if they are "wholly or predominantly for the purpose of a business carried on" by him. So mixed use agreements are regulated where the business use is a subsidiary purpose, e.g. a hire-purchase agreement for a dentist's or doctor's car used occasionally for home visits.

If the agreement includes a declaration by the customer to that effect, it is presumed to be such; its form and content are set out in Sch.3 to the 2007 Order (see above).

Agreements exempt under ss.16A and 16B will nevertheless still fall within the unfair relationship provisions in ss.140A to 140C (below, para.25.32).

The total charge for credit

19.16   We have already met this term on several occasions and it is now necessary to examine it more closely. It is vitally important for a number of reasons, including the following:

(a) Any sum forming part of the total charge for credit does not form part of the credit[25].

(b) Under art.4[26] a debtor-creditor agreement is exempt if the annual percentage rate of charge (below, para.19.19) does not exceed the statutory maximum.

(c) One of the cardinal principles of the Act is to give the debtor

---

[24] SI 2007/1168.
[25] s.9(3) above, para.19.03.
[26] Above, para.19.14 subpara. (7).

information on various matters and one such matter is the "true cost of borrowing".[27] In the United States this is known as "truth in lending". One of the objects of the legislation is to give the debtor an opportunity of "shopping around" and comparing the cost of credit offered by different lenders. It is certainly debatable whether many debtors take advantage of this facility.

The total charge for credit is dealt with in the Consumer Credit (Total Charge for Credit) Regulations 1980 as amended by the Consumer Credit (Total Charge for Credit, Agreement and Advertisements) (Amendment) Regulations.[28] The object of these Regulations is three-fold, namely (a) to specify what items are to be included, (b) to specify what items are to be excluded, and (c) to require the charge to be calculated as an annual percentage rate.

Items included

Regulation 4 provides that there shall be included (a) the total of the interest   **19.17** payments, and (b) other charges at any time payable under the transaction by or on behalf of the debtor or a relative of his, whether to the creditor or to any other person. This would clearly cover the general costs incurred in setting up the agreement—survey fees, legal fees and stamp duty are obvious examples. It also includes any premium payable under a compulsory insurance policy whose sole object is to ensure payment to the creditor of the credit, and/or items forming part of the total charge for credit, in the event of the death, invalidity, illness or unemployment of the debtor.

Items excluded

The generality of reg. 4 is cut down by reg.5. Among items excluded are the   **19.18** following: (a) sums payable on default, (b) sums which would be payable in any event even if it were a cash transaction (e.g. installation charges), and (c) all premiums other than those set out above.

Annual percentage rate (APR)

To enable comparisons to be made, reg.7 requires the total charge to be   **19.19** stated as an annual percentage rate reflecting (a) annual compounding, and (b) the continuing repayment of credit. If a prospective borrower is told by a finance house that the rate of interest is 12 per cent this is seriously misleading, because it does not acknowledge that the *outstanding capital is reducing* all the time: the true rate of interest (APR) is about double the flat rate of 12 per cent.

In the Fifth Edition of this book we summarised the three methods of calculating the APR under regs.7–9 of the 1980 Regulations. In order to comply with an EU Directive all these methods have been abolished and replaced with a highly complex equation which takes in the credit, the instalments and the relevant outstanding periods. The creditor must work out the rate in a

[27] See s.20.
[28] SI 1999/3177.

way which will satisfy the equation. The amended regulations require the rate to be calculated to one decimal place—but on the basis of rounding up if the second decimal place is 5 or greater (so that a rate of 12.26 per cent becomes 12.3 per cent).

19.20   The above explanation presupposes that all the items are constant and known at the date of the agreement. In practice this may not be so and the regulations recognise this by making certain assumptions. For example, a provision giving the creditor the right to increase the charges must generally be disregarded.[29] Similarly, there may be a clause for the index linking of the total charge for credit; here again it is to be assumed that changes will not occur (reg.15). If, however, the amount of a particular item is unknown at the date of the agreement and is not covered by the assumptions, then it seems that the exemption for low cost credit[30] cannot be claimed. This could arise where, for example, the creditor's insurance company require the debtor to pay for the installation of a burglar alarm and the cost of this is not known at the date of the agreement.

4. LINKED TRANSACTIONS

19.21   Having examined the crucial distinction between regulated and exempt agreements, it is necessary to end this chapter with a brief mention of linked transactions, i.e. transactions which are linked to an actual or prospective regulated agreement. The term "linked transaction" is important for a variety of reasons, including withdrawal, cancellation, early settlement and unfair relationships. It is clear from s.19 that an agreement for security will not be a linked agreement but, subject to this, the following are included:

(1) A transaction entered into in compliance with a term of the principal agreement, e.g. "the debtor shall insure his life with XYZ insurance company and shall enter into a maintenance contract with Eezikleen Ltd".

(2) A transaction to be financed by a debtor-creditor-supplier agreement. Thus where the supplier of a car and the supplier of the credit have "arrangements", the sale of the car is "linked" to the loan contract, so that cancellation of the latter will also cancel the former.[31]

(3) A transaction entered into by the debtor, hirer or a relative at the suggestion of the creditor, owner, an associate of his[32] or a person negotiating the principal agreement. Thus a dealer might say to a prospective borrower "you would have a better chance of getting a loan from the finance company if you took out a life policy". Such tie-ins are now rendered unlawful by the Courts and Legal Services Act 1990, but many building societies offer discounted rates of interest—but with "strings" such as a house or contents insurance.

---

[29] reg.2(1)(d). This is subject to an exception in reg.15A (added by the 1999 Regulations) in the case of low-start land mortgages where an increase is certain to occur.
[30] See above, para.19.14 subpara.(7).
[31] s.69(1), below, para.22.10.
[32] Above, para.18.11.

Regulations have been made[33] whereby certain types of linked agreement **19.22** are excluded from the provisions of the Act relating to effectiveness,[34] cancellation and early settlement. The excepted classes are:

(1) Contracts of insurance.

(2) Guarantees of goods.

(3) Agreements for the operation of a deposit and/or current account.

---

[33] Consumer Credit (Linked Transactions) (Exemptions) Regulations 1983 (SI 1983/1560).
[34] In general a linked agreement is ineffective until the main agreement is made (s.19(3)).

CHAPTER TWENTY

CONTROL OF BUSINESS ACTIVITIES

We have already seen that the Consumer Credit Act controls business activi-   **20.01**
ties as well as individual agreements. It is clear that business control is of very
great benefit to the consumer. It should help to ensure that the other party to
the transaction is a reputable trader and that the consumer is not pressurised
into a transaction by misleading advertising or other undesirable business
practices. In this chapter it is proposed to consider this aspect of consumer
protection under three main headings, namely:

1. Licensing.

2. Advertising.

3. Canvassing.

1. LICENSING

The licensing system set out in ss.22 to 24 and ss.147 to 150 can be described   **20.02**
as the linch-pin of the whole Act. For the first time a centrally administered
licensing system enables the entire credit industry to be kept under close
scrutiny. There is little doubt that the threat of the refusal or revocation of a
licence (i.e. loss of livelihood) is by far the strongest sanction provided by the
Act. It is a perfect example of the administrative control mentioned earlier in
this book.

Who needs a licence?

The Act lists nine types of business for which a licence is required. The last   **20.03**
two[1] were added by the 2006 Act:

    (a) consumer credit;

    (b) consumer hire;

    (c) credit brokerage;

    (d) debt-adjusting;

    (e) debt-counselling;

    (f) debt-collecting;

---

[1] See the 2006 Act, ss.24 and 25.

(g) credit reference agency;

(h) debt administration; and

(i) credit information services.

A number of problems arise. The first one is "what is a business?" The Act merely tells us that it includes a profession or trade; presumably cases from other branches of the law (e.g. income tax) can offer some guidance. The key factors include (i) the frequency of the transactions, (ii) the manner of operation, and (iii) profit motive. The word "frequency" leads on naturally to s.189(2) which provides that:

> A person is not to be treated as carrying on a particular type of business merely because *occasionally* he enters into transactions belonging to a business of that type [italics supplied].

There will clearly be borderline cases. Thus s.189 defines "consumer credit business"[2] by reference to the crucial phrase "regulated agreement" which was considered in Chapter Eighteen. It provides that:

> 'consumer credit business' means any business being carried on by a person so far as it comprises or relates to—
>
> (a) the provision of credit by him, or
> (b) otherwise his being a creditor,
>
> under regulated consumer credit agreements.

20.04   Let us take an example. Suppose that John sells television sets. Most of his customers pay cash but from time to time he sells a set on credit. Such a sale will be a debtor-creditor-supplier agreement and will be regulated, unless the credit is repayable by four or fewer instalments. Whether John needs a licence will depend on whether the credit sales take place more than "occasionally". If they only took place at very long intervals, and if they formed a very small part of John's turnover, then no licence would be required.[3]

Even if there is a business, a licence will only be required if the trader makes *regulated* agreements. Thus, if a creditor only makes exempt agreements or if the debtors are all companies, no licence will be required.

The above remarks also apply, mutatis mutandis, to a consumer hire business.

When we turn to the seven other types of business defined in s.145 (the Act uses the term "*ancillary credit business*") we find that there is one significant difference—the concept of "regulated agreement" is not critical. Thus, for example, an estate agent who introduces clients to an insurance company will require a licence as a credit-broker, even though his clients make (a) agree-

---

[2] As amended by the 2006 Act, s.23.
[3] See *Hare v Schurek* [1993] C.C.L.R. 47, CA. Even if a licence is not required, the agreement may still be a "regulated agreement" and subject to control (e.g. the formality rules, below, paras21.02–21.07).

ments which are not consumer credit agreements at all or (b) agreements which are exempt under s.16.

A local authority does not require a licence[4] even though the agreements which it makes may be regulated by the Act.

Its duration and the wide powers of the OFT

A licence is personal and non-assignable.[5] A standard licence lasts indefi- **20.05** nitely whereas a group licence is for a limited period of five years.[6] The OFT may now charge for licences (s.28A inserted by the 2006 Act, s.35).

The onus is on the applicant to prove to the OFT that he is a fit person to engage in activities covered by the licence.[7] In considering the application the OFT must consider any circumstances appearing to it to be relevant.[8] Section 25 sets out a non-exhaustive list of relevant matters including skills, knowledge, experience, dishonesty, contravention of the Act or certain other legislation, sex and race discrimination and unfair business practices such as irresponsible lending. In all these cases the section refers not merely to the trader himself but also to his employees, agents and associates (past or present). It is important to appreciate that the conduct in question need not involve any breach of the law, e.g. certain types of high-pressure salesmanship. As an alternative to refusing a licence the OFT may limit the licence to specified activities.[9]

If the OFT is "minded to refuse" an application it must invite the applicant to make written representations and to give notice, if he thinks fit, that he wishes to make representations orally. Appeal against refusal lies to the Consumer Credit Appeals Tribunal.[10] Further appeal lies to the Court of Appeal on a point of law. The above procedure is also followed in cases involving variation, suspension and revocation.[11] It will be seen that these provisions provide a potent weapon for the consumer. If a licensed trader is guilty of breaches of the Sale of Goods Act or of offences under the CPRs, these matters may come to the attention of the OFT via trading standards inspectors or via the courts.[12] Even a letter from an individual consumer will be relevant in building up evidence against the trader and such evidence can, in appropriate cases, lead to refusal, suspension or revocation of the licence. The very existence of these provisions can have a salutary effect; thus they may induce the trader to alter his business practices before he applies for a licence.

---

[4] See s.21.
[5] See s.22(2).
[6] s.22(1C) and (1D): amendments made by 2006 Act, s.34. Five years is prescribed by the Consumer Credit (Information Requirements and Duration of Licences and Charges) Regulations 2007 (SI 2007/1167): in force April 6, 2008.
[7] s.25(1).
[8] s.25(2), (2A) and (2B).
[9] See s.23(2).
[10] See ss.40A and 41 and Sch.A1 and the Consumer Credit Appeals Tribunal Rules (SI 2008/668).
[11] See ss.31–33. See *Credit Default Register v Secretary of State* [1993] C.C.L.R. 59 (revocation for intimidatory conduct).
[12] See s.166.

Imposition of "requirements" on licensees

20.06   The OFT is given a new power by s.33A to impose "requirements" on licensees and, in the case of group licences, on the supervisory bodies. Where it is "dissatisfied" with the way in which a business is carried on, it may notify the licensee and "require him to do or not to do" anything—a wide power on which the OFT must publish guidance under s.33E. The OFT may impose a civil penalty of up to £50,000 for non-compliance. Now that standard licences continue indefinitely the OFT will need to monitor licensed businesses and s.1(1) is amended to add this to its duties (see 2006 Act, s.62)

Contracts by or through unlicensed traders

20.07   An unlicensed trader who engages in any activity for which a licence is required commits an offence for which the maximum fine on summary conviction is £2,000. If he is convicted on indictment the maximum penalty is two years' imprisonment or a fine or both.[13] It may well be, however, that the most effective sanction is the unenforceability of agreements. Thus by s.40 a regulated agreement made by an unlicensed trader is only enforceable if the OFT makes a validating order. The OFT must consider (inter alia) the extent to which debtors and hirers have been prejudiced, the degree of culpability and whether or not it would have granted a licence to the trader if he had applied for it. It can limit the order to specific agreements and conditions can be imposed.

These sanctions are a powerful deterrent against unlicensed trading. Section 149 goes one step further; in effect it places the creditor or owner under a duty to ensure that the credit-brokers with whom they do business are themselves licensed. The creditor or owner has a strong incentive to check on this; the section provides that a regulated agreement made by a debtor or hirer who, for the purpose of making that agreement, was introduced to the creditor or owner by an unlicensed credit-broker is only enforceable against the debtor or hirer if the OFT makes a validating order. Thus a finance company might be unable to enforce a hire-purchase agreement if the debtor was introduced to them by an unlicensed dealer.

Section 148 contains a similar "unenforceability" provision where an agreement is made for the services of an unlicensed person carrying on an ancillary credit business. Such a person can only enforce the agreement if the OFT makes a validating order. The wording of the section is not entirely clear. If we take the case of an estate agent whose business includes that of being a "credit-broker", does the unenforceability apply solely to an introduction fee payable to him by the borrower, or does it mean that he cannot sue the seller for his commission? On principle the former view should prevail—the sanctions imposed by the Act should be confined to his activities *qua* credit-broker and the words "agreement for the services of a person carrying on an ancillary credit business" should be construed accordingly.

---

[13] See Sch.1.

In considering these provisions it must be borne in mind that consent by the debtor or hirer is as effective as a validating order (see s.173(3)).

2. ADVERTISEMENTS AND QUOTATIONS

We have already seen that the very nature of credit carries the danger that **20.08** the consumer may over commit himself. The likelihood of this is greatly increased if the creditor is allowed to exhibit a misleading advertisement with words like "five years to pay" in bold type and a very high interest charge tucked away in the small print.

Advertising controls are clearly required and are contained in two sets of statutory provisions—ss.43 to 47, which include a number of enabling powers, and the Consumer Credit (Advertisement) Regulations 2004.[14]

Advertisements and the consumer

Before embarking on a brief examination of the scope and content of adver- **20.09** tisement regulation it may be relevant to consider what rights accrue to the consumer as a result of a defective advertisement. There are three overlapping possibilities:

(1) If he is induced by a misleading advertisement to make a contract with the advertiser, he may have a civil claim under the general law for misrepresentation or for negligence.[15]

(2) If an advertisement contravenes the Act, the regulations or other legislation, the criminal court can exercise its general power to award compensation.[16]

(3) There is the ever-present possibility of a complaint to the OFT which could, in the last resort, lead to the suspension or revocation of a licence.

Scope of advertisement control

The advertising provisions stand apart from the rest of the Act; in some **20.10** respects the controls are wider and in some narrower. Thus:

(1) The controls are not restricted to "regulated agreements" (above, para.19.02). On the other hand, the controls will not apply if the advertisement indicates that the credit is only available to a body corporate (see s.43(3)(b)).

(2) The effect of the Consumer Credit (Exempt Advertisements) Order

[14] SI 2004/1484, replacing the Consumer Credit (Advertisement) Regulations 1989 (SI 1989/1125). In force October 31, 2004.
[15] See Chs 3 and 7.
[16] See Ch.16.

1985 (SI 1985/621 (as amended)) is to take many—but not all—types of exempt agreements outside the advertising controls.

(3) When we turn to the Advertisement Regulations themselves, we find one of the few distinctions between private and business transactions. These Regulations will not apply to an advertisement which (1) expressly or by implication states that the credit or hire facilities are available for the purposes of a person's business, and (2) does not indicate that the facilities are available for non-business purposes (see reg.10).

The definitions

20.11   It is clear from s.189 that the concept of "advertisement" is extremely wide and is not confined to visual forms. It can therefore include anything from a catalogue or brochure to films, radio and television commercials and even sales patter. It is also important to note that "the advertiser" is not necessarily the person who causes the advertisement to be inserted; it is the person who is indicated in the advertisement as willing to provide the credit, hire or credit brokerage facilities.

False advertisements

20.12   By section 46 an offence is committed if an advertisement is false or misleading in a material respect. Thus an "APR nil" advertisement has been held to be false where the trader made a hidden charge by giving a lower part-exchange allowance to instalment buyers than to cash buyers.[17] Similarly, the Rover company was convicted when, in large print, they gave £595 as the price of a new Metro while adding (in very small print at the bottom) that an extra £480 was payable for twelve months' road tax, number plates and delivery to the dealer.[18]

The Advertising Regulations

20.13   The 1989 Regulations complicated matters by dividing advertisements into three types—simple, intermediate and full. The 2004 Regulations contain just one list of compulsory information for credit advertisements in Sch.2 and another list for hire advertisements in Sch.3.

The Regulations deal in considerable detail with the form and content of advertisements. Thus they must:

(a) use plain and intelligible language;

(b) be easily legible or clearly audible;

(c) specify the name of the advertiser (reg.3).

---

[17] *Metsoja v H Norman Pitt & Co Ltd* (1989) 153 J.P.N. 630.
[18] *Rover Group Ltd v Sumner* [1995] C.C.L.R. 1, Chester Crown Court.

Where the credit or hire is secured on property, the advertisement must contain one of five different "health warnings" in cases involving mortgages on the customers' homes or foreign currency mortgages or, where credit is available to pay debts due to other creditors, two of the five warnings (reg.7). The APR is dealt with in detail in reg.8 and Sch.1.[19]

Regulation 4 is concerned with the content of advertisements and provides that the items of information listed in Schs 2 and 3 "shall be given equal prominence and shall be shown together as a whole". The list in Sch.2 for credit advertisements includes the amount of credit, cash price, advance payment and frequency, number and amount of instalments.

The advertiser must study the Regulations carefully and then make sure that the advertisement does not contain either too little information or too much.

Quotations

As part of the policy of giving customers pre-contractual information the Act **20.14** enables quotation regulations to be made (see ss.52 and 152). Regulations came into force on February 1, 1990 (SI 1989/1126) but following a recommendation by the OFT they were revoked because they had failed in their purpose of encouraging prospective borrowers to make comparisons. The only regulations currently in force are the Consumer Credit (Content of Quotations) and Consumer Credit (Advertisements) (Amendment) Regulations 1999 (SI 1999/2725) (as amended by SI 2000/1797). They do not impose a duty on a creditor to submit a quotation on request. They merely provide that, if he does provide one, it must include an appropriate "health warning" for homes and foreign currency loans.

3. CANVASSING

Section 49 follows the precedent set by the Moneylenders Acts by prohibiting **20.15** the canvassing of debtor-creditor agreements (e.g. personal loans) off-trade premises.

When is an offence committed?

The canvasser must be an individual and must solicit the debtor into the making of a regulated agreement by making oral representations to the debtor, or to any other individual, during a visit by the canvasser to non-trade premises. The visit must have been for the purpose of making such oral representations, so that a crime is not committed if one individual makes representations to another individual while they are both guests at a party. On the other hand, a social visit can be caught if the underlying intention was to make representations leading to the debtor-creditor agreement.

---

[19] The Consumer Credit (Advertisement) (Amendment) Regulations 2007 (SI 2007/827) amend the 2004 Regs with a new definition of "typical APR".

Previous request

20.16   No offence is committed if the visit was in response to a request made on a previous occasion, provided that the request was in writing signed by or on behalf of the person making it.[20] Presumably the person making the request need not be the debtor.

Trade premises

20.17   For *this* purpose the term "trade premises" is defined[21] as any premises where a business is carried on (whether on a permanent or temporary basis) by (a) the creditor or owner, (b) the supplier, (c) the canvasser's employer, or (d) the debtor.

Overdrafts

20.18   The OFT has made a determination[22] which exempts the soliciting of an agreement enabling the debtor to overdraw on specified types of current account, provided that the debtor already keeps an account with the creditor. This could be relevant where a bank manager invites his customer, ostensibly for a meal or a game of golf, but in reality to offer him overdraft facilities.

Circulars to minors

20.19   Minors (persons under 18) are particularly vulnerable to blandishments of "easy credit" and accordingly s.50(1) makes it an offence for a person, with a view to financial gain, to send to a minor any document inviting him or her to (a) borrow money, (b) obtain goods on credit or hire, (c) obtain services on credit, or (d) apply for information or advice on borrowing money or otherwise obtaining credit or hiring goods.[23] A defence is available where the person sending the circular did not know and had no reasonable cause to suspect that the addressee was a minor (s.50(2)) but the following subsection makes this defence somewhat difficult to raise if the document is sent to a school! Any such offence will not invalidate any resulting agreement[24] and such an agreement will be governed by a combination of common law rules, the Minors Contracts Act 1987, s.3 of the Sale of Goods Act 1979 and the Act.

---

[20] s.48(1)(b) and 49(2).
[21] cf. cancellation, below, para.22.05.
[22] On June 1, 1977.
[23] For a recent unsuccessful prosecution, see *Alliance & Leicester Building Society v Babbs* [1993] C.C.L.R. 77, DC.
[24] s.170(1), above, para.18.07.

CHAPTER TWENTY-ONE

"I CAN'T REMEMBER WHAT I SIGNED"

In the previous chapter we examined vitally important provisions relating to **21.01** the control of business activities.

We now turn to the other main form of control—the regulation of individual agreements. The law is to be found in Pts V to IX of the Act and much of it is modelled on the previous hire-purchase legislation. This chapter is concerned with formalities and copies.[1] The object of the legislation is to make sure that the debtor or hirer is made aware of his rights and obligations and that he can obtain further information if, for example, he has failed to keep a record of his payments. Once again a large amount of the detail is contained in regulations.

Sanctions for non-compliance

The sanctions are potentially severe. If the creditor or owner fails to comply **21.02** with the various formalities, the agreement is said to be *"not properly executed"*. By s.65 the creditor or owner cannot enforce such an agreement against the debtor or hirer unless (a) the court makes an enforcement order,[2] or (b) the debtor or hirer consents to enforcement (s.173(3)).[3] What happens if the creditor or owner, in defiance of s.65, enforces the agreement by retaking the goods? If the repossession amounts to the tort of trespass or conversion, the creditor or owner will be liable for this. If, however, the repossession is only unlawful because it contravenes s.65, it seems that the only remedy of the debtor or hirer is to apply for a mandatory injunction to restore the status quo.[4] That leaves merely the administrative sanction of taking action which can put the licence of the creditor or owner in jeopardy.

The purpose of the sanctions is to put the creditor or owner at a disadvantage if they do not comply with the rules designed for the protection of the consumer. The agreement is not invalidated[5]: it becomes *unenforceable by the creditor or owner* without an order of the court.[6] From the point of view of the debtor or hirer it is still valid and fully enforceable. For example, if goods held under a hire-purchase agreement are defective, the debtor can bring a

---

[1] ss.58–65 and 77–80.
[2] Below, para.25.06.
[3] Above, para.18.07.
[4] ibid.
[5] *R. v Modupe* [1991] C.C.L.R. 29, CA (total price omitted; liability to repay continued, though unenforceable). See also *McGuffick v Royal Bank of Scotland* [2009] EWHC 2386 (Comm): the agreement is not void.
[6] The court has a wide discretion—see s.127, para.25.06 below.

claim under the Supply of Goods (Implied Terms) Act 1973 even though the agreement is "improperly executed". Further, a dishonest hirer can be prosecuted for seeking to evade an "existing liability", even though the "liability" is unenforceable without a court order under s.65.[7]

If the creditor applies for summary judgment under Pt 24 of the Civil Procedure Rules the debtor may say "this agreement is unenforceable because I never received a copy" (or words to that effect!). There is no need for him to *prove* this fact; he can defeat the claim for summary judgment by showing that there is a real prospect of the defence succeeding.[8]

Pre-contractual information

21.03 As part of the policy outlined above, s.55 enables regulations to be made whereby specified information must be disclosed to the prospective debtor or hirer before a regulated agreement is made. Such regulations came into force on May 31, 2005: the Consumer Credit (Disclosure of Information) Regulations 2004[9] state that the information is the same as that required in the agreement itself and specified in the 1983 Regulations discussed in para.21.06.

Consideration period in land mortgage cases

21.04 We have already seen that many land mortgage cases are outside the main control provisions because the agreements are exempted under s.16 or by regulations.[10] If, however, the agreement is a regulated agreement, s.58 lays down a special pre-contractual period of reflection and isolation; the reason for this is that the post-contractual cancellation provisions do not apply to any agreement secured on land.[11]

In two cases, however, the special reflection rules do not apply, namely (a) a restricted-use agreement to finance the purchase of the mortgaged land, and (b) an agreement for a bridging loan in connection with the purchase of the mortgaged land or other land. In these two cases the debtor will have neither reflection rights nor cancellation rights.

Let us suppose that John, a moneylender, is prepared to lend George £8,000 on the security of George's house. The reflection and isolation rules can be summarised as follows:

(1) At least seven days before sending the agreement for signature, John must give to George a copy of the agreement (and of any document referred to therein) containing a notice in the prescribed form indicating George's right to withdraw from the transaction.[12]

---

[7] *R. v Modupe*, above, n.5.
[8] *Anglo Leasing Plc v Pascoe* [1997] C.C.L.R. 69. The wording of r.24.2 strengthens the creditor's chances of success by weeding out weak defences.
[9] SI 2004/1481.
[10] See above, para.19.12.
[11] s.67, below, para.22.05.
[12] s.58(1) and 61(2). Thus a copy of the proposed mortgage would have to accompany the reflection copy which refers to it.

(2) When seven days have elapsed, John can post the agreement for signature unless he has received a notice of withdrawal.[13]

(3) John must not approach George in any way during the "*consideration period*" except at George's specific request. The consideration period begins when the "reflection copy" is sent[14] and ends seven days after the sending of the agreement for signature[15] or, if earlier, its return by George duly signed.

Regulations have now been made relating to the wording of the "reflection **21.05** copy". Thus the heading of a prospective credit agreement must be as follows:

> Copy of proposed credit agreement containing notice of your right to withdraw
> DO NOT sign or return this copy.

The document must also contain an explanatory box containing the following words:

YOUR RIGHT TO WITHDRAW

This is a copy of your proposed Credit agreement which is to be secured on land. It has been given to you now so that you may have at least a week to consider its terms before the actual agreement is sent to you for signature. You should read it carefully. If you do not understand it you may need to seek professional advice. If you do not wish to go ahead with it you need not do so.

If you decide NOT to go ahead with the agreement you should inform or, if you prefer, any supplier or broker involved in the negotiations. You can do this in writing or orally for example by telephone. If the agreement arrives for signature and you have decided NOT to go ahead DO NOT SIGN IT. Then you will not be legally bound by the agreement.

Finally the agreement itself must contain the following box:

YOUR RIGHTS

Under the Consumer Credit Act 1974 the creditor should have given you a copy of this agreement at least seven days ago to allow you time to consider whether to go ahead. If he did not, the agreement cannot be enforced without a court order.

The above requirements also apply to a regulated consumer hire agreement secured by land mortgage.

Formalities of the agreement itself

Sections 60 and 61 enable regulations to be made to ensure that the debtor or **21.06** hirer is made aware of his rights and duties, the amount and rate of the total charge for credit and the protection and remedies available to him under the Act. The detail is to be found in the Consumer Credit (Agreements) Regulations

---

[13] s.61(2) and (4).
[14] See (1) above.
[15] See (2) above.

1983 which specify the information which must be included, having regard to the particular type of agreement.[16] Thus the debtor under a hire-purchase agreement must be made aware of (inter alia) his right of termination,[17] and the restriction on the creditor's right to repossess protected goods.[18] The Regulations (not surprisingly) require that the information should be easily legible and of a colour which is easily distinguishable from the colour of the paper.[19] They also specify the prominence to be given to particular parts of the agreement, and the place where the debtor or hirer must sign and the words to be contained in the signature box. The financial and related particulars (description of goods, deposit, credit, cash price, APR, total charges, repayments, etc.) must be shown together as a whole and not interspersed with other information.

The Act itself lays down three broad requirements in s.61:

(a) a document in the prescribed form itself containing all the prescribed terms[20] and conforming to regulations under s.60(1) is signed in the prescribed manner both by the debtor or hirer and by or on behalf of the creditor or owner, and

(b) the document embodies all the terms of the agreement, other than implied terms, and

(c) the document is, when presented or sent to the debtor or hirer for signature, in such a state that all its terms are readily legible.

The wording of para.(a) makes it clear that the debtor or hirer must sign *personally*. It is also clear that a signature on a blank form, with the details filled in later, would not be sufficient.[21]

Copies

21.07 Sections 62 to 63 contain copy provisions which are similar, but not identical, to the provisions in the Hire-Purchase Act 1965. The basic rule is that the debtor or hirer is always entitled to at least one copy of the agreement; in many cases he is entitled to two copies.

The provisions are complex but they can be conveniently divided into (a) cases where the agreement is presented to the debtor or hirer for signature, (b) cases where it is sent to him for signature and (c) cases where it is neither presented nor sent.

---

[16] See SI 1983/1553, regs2–5. Amended from May 31, 2005 by the Consumer Credit (Agreements) (Amendment) Regulations 2004 (SI 2004/1482).

[17] Below, para.22.14.

[18] Below, para.25.25.

[19] reg.6(2).

[20] See reg.6 of and Sch.6 to the Agreements Regulations for the meaning of this term. See *Carey v HSBC Bank plc* for judicial guidance: para.21.14.

[21] Consider *Eastern Distributors v Goldring* [1957] Q.B. 600, a decision on a slightly different provision in the Hire-Purchase Act 1938.

(a) Agreement presented to debtor or hirer

In the vast majority of cases in practice the document which he signs **21.08** will be *"an unexecuted agreement"*, i.e. a document embodying the terms of a prospective regulated agreement. In other words, the document is an offer by the debtor or hirer and there will be no concluded agreement until the document is signed by the creditor or owner thus accepting the offer. In this situation one copy must be given to the debtor or hirer immediately after he has signed[22] and, in addition, a copy of the executed agreement must be delivered or sent to him within seven days after the making of the agreement.[23]

In the less likely situation where the creditor or owner has already signed, signature by the debtor or hirer will convert the document into an *"executed agreement"*, i.e. a contract; in that situation a copy of that agreement must be given to him there and then. In this situation no further copy is required.[24]

(b) Agreement sent to the debtor or hirer for signature

Here the position is somewhat similar to that mentioned above. In all cases **21.09** the agreement which is sent to the debtor or hirer for signature must be accompanied by a copy.[25] If the document becomes an "executed agreement" when he signs, no further copy need be sent to him.[26] Usually, however, the document which the debtor or hirer signs is an offer to the creditor or owner and will not become an "executed agreement" until a later date—i.e. until it is signed by the creditor or owner. In that situation a copy of the executed agreement must be delivered or sent to the debtor or hirer within seven days of the making of the agreement.

(c) Cases where the prospective agreement is neither delivered nor sent

The situations contemplated here are those where the debtor completes an **21.10** application form which he sees in a newspaper or which he picks up from a dispenser. In this situation the creditor or owner must deliver or send a copy of the executed agreement within seven days of the date on which it is made.[27]

(d) Cancellation cases

Special provisions apply in cancellation cases.[28]

(e) Form and contents of copies

This matter is dealt with in considerable detail in the Consumer Credit **21.11** (Cancellation Notices and Copies of Documents) Regulations 1983.[29] A

---

[22] s.62(1).
[23] s.63(2).
[24] s.63(1) and (2)(a).
[25] s.62(2).
[26] s.63(2)(b).
[27] s.63(2).
[28] Below, para.22.06.
[29] SI 1983/1557.

failure to comply with these formalities will mean that the agreement is "not properly executed" (see ss.62–65 read with s.182(2)) and the consequences for the creditor or owner can be very serious.[30]

(f) Other documents

21.12 The duty to supply a copy includes a duty to supply a copy of every other document referred to in the agreement. Read literally this would require the creditor or owner to supply a copy of the Consumer Credit Act merely because the agreement referred to it. Fortunately the Regulations make it clear that this is not necessary.[31]

Post-contractual information

Additional information on request

21.13 The copy provisions are supplemented by ss.77 to 79 which, as already stated, are designed to assist the debtor or hirer who has failed to keep a record of his payments (alternatively, he may have mislaid either or both of the copies referred to above). In each of these cases the debtor or hirer may make a written request and send the sum of £1. To ensure that the creditor or owner is not put to unreasonable trouble, the sections require him to send to the debtor or hirer, within the prescribed period,[32] a copy of the executed agreement and a signed statement containing certain particulars (e.g. as to sums paid, due and payable) "according to the information to which it is practicable for him to refer". Further, to prevent the creditor or owner from being inundated with such requests, the information need not be given at all if the request was made within one month of a previous request having been complied with.

Section 77 concerns fixed sum credit, s.78 running-account credit and s.79 hire agreements. In each case the creditor or owner "is not entitled, while the default continues, to enforce the agreement".

Hundreds of claims by creditors for arrears have been met by debtors, advised by claims management companies (often on a fishing expedition) and solicitors, with the argument that the agreements are void and the debts have ceased to exist because the creditor has not given the required copies under s.77 to the debtor. This defence depends on the meaning of "not entitled . . . to enforce ." (A similar problem arises where agreements are improperly executed and so under s.65(1) "enforceable. . ..on an order of the court only".) The County Court cases have been stayed while awaiting the decision on a test case by the Commercial Court: *McGuffick v Royal Bank of Scotland.*[33] The court decided unsurprisingly that the agreement was not void. It remained valid and the debt continued to exist. Thus although the

---

[30] See above, para.21.02 and below, para.25.06. See also *Carey*, para.21.14.
[31] SI 1983/1557, reg.11(e).
[32] Twelve working days (SI 1983/1569, reg.2).
[33] n.5.

bank could not enforce the agreement until it had given the relevant copy, it was proper for it to report the debtor's liability to a credit reference agency.

Another test case (decided the following month) where again hundreds of **21.14** County Court cases around the country were stayed pending its outcome is *Carey v HSBC Bank plc.*[34] Here the question was about copies of credit card agreements under s.78. Must they be copies such as photocopies of the original agreements or will something else suffice provided it contains the required information? The answer is the latter. Judge Waksman QC, in view of the general importance of the issues before him, helpfully took the view that "the purpose of this judgment is to give general guidance" (para.2). In para.234 he set out a Summary of Findings as follows:

"(1) A creditor can satisfy its duty under s.78 by providing a reconstituted version of the executed agreement which may be from sources other than the actual signed agreement itself;
(2) The s.78 copy must contain the name and address of the debtor as it was at the time of the execution of the agreement. But the creditor can provide the name and address from whatever source it has of those details. It does not have to take them from the executed agreement itself;
(3) The creditor need not, in complying with s.78, provide a document which would comply (if signed) with the requirements of the Consumer Credit (Agreements) Regulations 1983 as to form, as at the date the agreement was made;
(4) If an agreement has been varied by the creditor under a unilateral power of variation, the creditor must still provide a copy of the original agreement, as well as the varied terms."

Judge Waksman also had to consider issues about the form and content of credit agreements themselves under s.61(1)(a)[35] and again gave general guidance by stating in para.173 "Agreed Principles" with which all the parties agreed:

"(1) It is not sufficient for the piece of paper signed by the debtor merely to cross-refer to the Prescribed Terms without a copy of those terms being supplied to the debtor at the point of signature;
(2) A document need not be a single piece of paper;
(3) Whether several pieces of paper constitute one document is a question of substance not form. In particular a physical connection between several pieces of paper is not necessary in order for them to constitute one document;
(4) Additionally, a physical connection (or one or more physical connections) between several pieces of paper does not necessarily constitute them as one document;
(5) Accordingly, where the debtor's signature and the Prescribed Terms appear on separate pieces of paper, the question of whether those pieces of paper together constitute one document is a question of substance and not form."

Following these cases in November and December 2009, the OFT published draft guidance on the application of ss.77–79. In a press release of January 27, 2010 (05/10) the OFT said:

---

[34] [2009] EWHC 3417 (Q.B.).
[35] Para.21.06.

"There has been a great deal of confusion over the meaning of these sections with many borrowers being misled into thinking they can get their debt written off.

This guidance is to clarify the legal position and the OFT view on standards expected of the industry, and to make consumers aware that they may be at risk if they seek to use these sections to avoid paying legitimately owed debts."

We warmly support the OFT's comments in view of the questionable activities of some credit management companies, since they charge for the advice and conciliation which would be available free of charge from CABx, money advice centres and trade associations such as the Finance and Leasing Association and mislead consumers into believing that their financial commitments can easily (if not cheaply) be avoided or reduced.

Additional information without request

21.15 In the case of a running-account credit agreement, other than a small agreement,[36] the creditor must send to the debtor periodic statements at least once a year containing the information required by regulations.[37] Similar provisions in relation to fixed-sum credit agreements now appear in s.77A (added by the 2006 Act); the form and content of the statements are given in the Consumer Credit (Information Requirements and Duration of Charges) Regulations 2007 (SI 2007/1167).

Information as to the whereabouts of the goods

21.16 So far all the provisions have required information to be given *by* the creditor or owner, but s.80 is concerned with the reverse situation. It provides that where a regulated agreement requires the debtor or hirer to keep goods in his possession or control, he must, within seven working days after receiving a written request from the creditor or owner, tell the creditor or owner where the goods are. If the information is not given within 21 days of receiving the request the debtor or hirer commits an offence.

Guarantees

Formality and copy provisions also apply to guarantees of regulated agreements.[38]

Electronic agreements

The Consumer Credit (Electronic Communications) Order 2004[39] enables regulated agreements to be made electronically and notices, copies and statements to be given in the same way.

---

[36] Above, para.19.11.
[37] s.78(4) and SI 1983/1570 which deal with form, contents and time-limits (as amended by the 2006 Act: new s.78(4A)).
[38] See ss.105–110 and SI 1983/1556
[39] SI 2004/3236. In force May 31, 2005.

CHAPTER TWENTY-TWO

"CAN I GET OUT OF THE AGREEMENT?"

We have seen that a debtor or hirer may commit himself too heavily (perhaps **22.01** aided by an over-enthusiastic salesman). In this chapter we shall consider his right to resile from a regulated agreement and the financial consequences of his doing so. The subject will be considered under four headings, namely:

1. Withdrawal

2. Rescission and Repudiation

3. Cancellation

4. Termination

The above topics must be distinguished from the problem which arises where the consumer wants to perform the agreement ahead of time. Early settlement is considered in Chapter Twenty-Five (para.25.12).

1. WITHDRAWAL

On general contractual principles a prospective debtor or hirer can withdraw **22.02** from the transaction at any time before his offer has been accepted by revoking his offer. In the case of a regulated agreement his position is strengthened by s.59(1) which provides that an agreement is void if it binds a person to enter, as prospective debtor or hirer, into a prospective regulated agreement. This provision may, however, be cut down by regulations but the only regulations so far made are confined to certain types of business credit.[1]

Section 57, which deals with withdrawal, provides that no special form of wording is required[2] and the notice of withdrawal can be written or oral. Two important points should be noted:

(1) The list of persons to whom notice of withdrawal can be given is surprisingly wide. It includes not only the credit-broker or supplier but also "any person who, in the course of a business carried on by him, acts on behalf of the debtor or hirer in any negotiations for the agreement."[3] Thus if, for example, the prospective debtor had instructed a solicitor to negotiate on his behalf, a notice given by him to that solicitor would be sufficient. Such a

---

[1] See SI 1983/1552.
[2] s.57(2).
[3] s.57(3).

deemed agent is under a deemed contractual duty to transmit the notice to his deemed principal (the creditor or owner) forthwith.[4]

(2) Withdrawal has the same effect as cancellation. Thus, (a) the prospective debtor or hirer can recover all payments made by him to the creditor or owner (e.g. a pre-contract deposit, or a payment made for a survey of the house); (b) the withdrawal will also terminate any linked transaction[5] and sums paid under it become repayable; (c) under a three-party D-C-S agreement[6] the creditor and the supplier are jointly liable to repay the sums paid by the debtor; and (d) the prospective debtor or hirer will have a lien over the goods until sums repayable to him have been repaid.[7]

One final point: the Act does not cut down the general rule that the revocation of an offer must be communicated to the offeree before acceptance. Thus if the consumer uses the post he runs the risk that his letter of withdrawal will be lost in the post or will only reach the creditor or owner after their acceptance. In both of these cases the withdrawal is ineffective.

2. RESCISSION AND REPUDIATION

22.03 Again on general contractual principles a debtor or hirer may have a right to rescind an agreement for misrepresentation or to treat it as repudiated by a breach by the creditor or owner. One example of this is considered in the next chapter. The deemed agency provisions referred to above also apply to rescission.[8] The principal distinction between rescission and accepting a repudiation is that the former is retrospective and the innocent party is treated as if the agreement had never been made. In the latter case obligations arising before the acceptance of repudiation remain enforceable, although they can usually be reduced or extinguished by a claim for damages.

3. CANCELLATION

22.04 We have already seen that a "consumer" will have cancellation rights in cases covered by the Cancellation of Contracts made in a Consumer's Home or Place of Work etc. Regulations 2008[9] and also under the Distance Selling Regulations.[10] A somewhat similar cancellation right is available under ss.67 to 73 of the Act (for a somewhat wider class of "consumer") and this is considered below. The cancellation rights under the Regulations will not apply if the consumer has cancellation rights under the rules discussed below.

The object of the cancellation provisions in ss.67 to 73 is clear enough—to give the debtor or hirer a chance for second thoughts (i.e. a "cooling-off

---

[4] s.175.
[5] For the meaning of this term see above, para.19.21.
[6] Above, para.19.07.
[7] The consequences of cancellation are considered in more detail in paras 22.10–22.13.
[8] See s.102.
[9] Para.6.24.
[10] Para.6.35.

period") in a case where he may have been pressurised by a doorstep salesman into signing an agreement. The matter can be considered under the following headings:

(1) What agreements are cancellable?

(2) The copy provisions.

(3) The time for cancellation.

(4) How is cancellation effected?

(5) Effect of cancellation.

(6) Duty to return goods.

(7) The part-exchange allowance.

(1) What agreements are cancellable?

A regulated consumer credit or hire agreement is cancellable if two conditions **22.05**
are satisfied, namely, (a) oral representations were made by or on behalf of
the negotiator in the presence of the debtor or hirer[11]; *and* (b) the unexecuted
agreement was not signed by the debtor or hirer at premises where a business
was carried on by (i) the creditor or owner, (ii) any party to a linked transaction (other than the debtor or hirer or a relative of his), or (iii) the negotiator
in any antecedent negotiations.

Let us suppose that John, a trader, goes to a car dealer to buy a new car.
The transaction is financed by a loan from a finance company who require
John to take out a life policy with an insurance company. The car dealer (the
negotiator) makes oral representations in John's presence. If John signs the
agreement at the office of the dealer, finance company or insurance company,
he will have no right of cancellation. On the other hand, if he signs at his own
home, or at his own business premises, then cancellation is available. Thus,
the definition of business premises does *not* include the business premises of
the debtor or hirer.[12] The place where the representations were made is immaterial. They must, however, have been made in the *presence* of the debtor or
hirer. Representations made on the telephone would not give cancellation
rights. If no oral representations were made at all (e.g. a mail-order purchase)
there is no right of cancellation.

In the case of land transactions the concept of post-contractual cancellation can result in considerable administrative problems. Accordingly, the
cancellation provisions do not apply to (a) an agreement secured on land, (b)
a restricted-use agreement to finance the purchase of land, or (c) a bridging
loan in connection with the purchase of land. It will be recalled that in case
(a) above the prospective debtor or hirer will have a pre-contractual period
of reflection and isolation.

---

[11] See *Moorgate Services Ltd v Kabir, The Times,* April 25, 1995, CA.
[12] Contrast the canvassing rules, above, para.20.17.

Two other types of agreement are not cancellable. They are (a) a non-commercial agreement,[13] and (b) a "small" debtor-creditor-supplier agreement for restricted-use credit.[14]

> Let us suppose that a doorstep salesman induces Mrs Smith to buy a children's encyclopedia at a price of £45 payable by nine instalments of £5. Nothing is said about the passing of property. (i) This is a "small" agreement[15]; (ii) since the supplier of the goods and the supplier of the credit are the same person it is "debtor-creditor-supplier"; (iii) since Mrs Smith cannot get her hands on the credit it is "restricted-use"; (iv) therefore no cancellation is possible.

(2) The copy provisions

22.06   The basic rules in ss.62 and 63[16] are modified in three respects by s.64. Thus:

(a) each copy must contain a notice in the prescribed form indicating the right of cancellation, how and when it is exercisable and the name and address of a person to whom notice of cancellation may be given[17];

(b) in cases where a second copy is required it must be sent *by post*[18];

(c) in cases where a second copy is not required a notice, containing the information mentioned in (a) above, must be posted to the debtor or hirer within seven days of the making of the agreement.[19]

Exemptions

22.07   The OFT can grant exemption from the duty to send a cancellation notice in certain specified cases if satisfied that this requirement can be dispensed with without prejudicing the interests of debtors or hirers (see s.64(4) and the Consumer Credit (Notice of Cancellation Rights) (Exemptions) Regulations 1983).[20]

(3) The time for cancellation

22.08   The cancellation period starts when the debtor or hirer signs the unexecuted agreement and ends five days after the debtor or hirer *receives* the statutory second copy or notice.[21] Thus, if the second copy is received on a Friday the cancellation period runs out at midnight on the following Wednesday. If the second copy is delayed in the post the cancellation period will, to that extent,

---

[13] Above, para.19.10.
[14] s.74(2).
[15] Above, para.19.11.
[16] Above, para.21.07.
[17] s.64(1)(a) read with the Consumer Credit (Cancellation Notices and Copies of Documents) Regulations 1983 (SI 1983/1557).
[18] s.63(3).
[19] s.64(1)(b).
[20] SI 1983/1558.
[21] s.68.

be prolonged since the period only starts to melt away when the debtor or hirer *receives* the second copy.

What happens if the second copy is not received at all and the creditor or owner then sends a further copy? Alternatively, what happens if the second copy or notice is sent off more than seven days after the making of the agreement? The wording of the Act is ambiguous. If the third copy or the late copy could be regarded as given "under" s.63, then it would start the five-day period running. On the other hand it could be argued that a notice is only given "under" s.63 if it is posted within seven days; if this is correct then the effect of delay or non-receipt would be that the right of cancellation would remain permanently available. This seems so absurd that the court is likely to prefer the former view.

(4) How is cancellation effected?

By section 69 the agreement can be cancelled if the debtor or hirer serves a notice of cancellation on (a) the creditor or owner, (b) the person specified in the copy or notice or (c) the agent of the creditor or owner (including his deemed agent).[22] No special form of wording is required but it is clear from the definition of "notice"[23] that it must be in writing. If it is posted it takes effect as from the date of posting and the mere fact that it is not received by the creditor or owner is immaterial (this is in marked contrast to the second copy or notice which only triggers the count-down of the cancellation period when it is received).[24] The Regulations require that the second copy or the notice (see (2) above) must include a cancellation form which the debtor or hirer can use to cancel the agreement.[25]

22.09

(5) Effect of cancellation

Subject to two exceptions the general effect of cancellation is to treat the agreement, and most linked transactions,[26] as if it had never been made.[27] Thus the debtor or hirer can recover his payments and is discharged from liability to make further payments. In the case of a three-party D-C-S agreement[28] for restricted-use credit the creditor and supplier are jointly and severally liable to repay sums paid by the debtor or a relative. The debtor, hirer or relative has a lien over the goods until repayable sums are repaid to him. Thus, if Albert paid a £500 deposit to buy a £5,000 car and the remaining £4,500 was paid by a creditor who had "arrangements" with the seller, the effect of a cancellation of the loan agreement would be that (a) the sale contract, as a linked transaction, would also be cancelled, (b) the seller and

22.10

---

[22] See above, para.22.02.
[23] s.189.
[24] Notice of cancellation (effective when posted) can also be contrasted with notice of withdrawal—see above, para.22.02.
[25] SI.1983/1557, regs 5 and 6 and Sch., Pts IV and VI.
[26] By SI 1983/1560 certain linked transactions (insurance, guarantee of goods, deposit accounts and current accounts) will survive the cancellation of the main agreement.
[27] s.69(4).
[28] Above, para.19.07.

creditor would be jointly and severally liable to repay the £500 to Albert, and (c) if the £4,500 were paid direct to the supplier he would have to repay it to the creditor.[29]

Two exceptions

22.11   (1) The first exception is in s.70(2) and deals with a debtor-creditor-supplier agreement for restricted-use credit to finance (a) the doing of work or supply of goods to meet an emergency, or (b) the supply of goods which have become incorporated in any land or thing before service of the notice of cancellation. Since the debtor is unable to return the goods, it would clearly be wrong to allow him to avoid payment simply by serving a notice of cancellation. Accordingly, in this type of case the cancellation will wipe out the credit part of the agreement but the debtor will remain liable to pay the cash price for the goods or work.

(2) The second exception is to be found in s.71 and it deals with a case where the credit has already been advanced by the creditor before the expiry of the cancellation period. Here the strict application of the cancellation provisions would cause hardship. On the one hand, since the agreement is treated as never having been made, the creditor might be able to bring an action to recover money lent. On the other hand the debtor might try to avoid all liability in reliance on s.70(1)(b) which provides that any sum payable by the debtor or his relative shall cease to be payable. To deal with these problems s.71 starts by providing that cancellation of a regulated consumer credit agreement (other than a debtor-creditor-supplier agreement for restricted-use credit) shall not destroy the obligation to repay the credit and interest. The words in brackets are inserted because, as we have seen, this type of transaction does not raise the type of problem at which s.71 is aimed—the supplier merely repays the credit to the creditor. The section then goes on to provide a complex formula. First of all it provides that if the whole or part of the credit is repaid within one month of cancellation, or not later than the first instalment repayment date, no interest is chargeable on the amount repaid. In other words, the consumer will have had the use of the money interest-free. It then goes on to deal with credit which is repayable by instalments where any part of the credit is still outstanding after the first repayment date. In such a case the creditor must serve a notice[30] recalculating the instalments over a period starting when this notice is served and ending with the final contractual repayment date. This shortening of the repayment period will often mean larger instalments.

(6) Duty to return goods

22.12   Let us remind ourselves at this point of the distinction between debtor-creditor-supplier agreements and debtor-creditor agreements:

---

[29] s.70(1)(c).
[30] See SI 1983/1559 which sets out the form of the request.

(a) Where the debtor under a debtor-creditor agreement uses the credit to buy goods, the sale contract is *not* a linked transaction and is not affected by cancellation of the credit agreement.

(b) In the case of a debtor-creditor-supplier agreement the supply of the goods is either an integral part of the credit agreement itself (e.g. hire-purchase) or a linked transaction under s.19 which is cancelled along with the credit agreement. In either case the debtor will have to restore the goods to the other party under the rules set out below.

Section 72 deals with a case where a debtor-creditor-supplier agreement for restricted-use credit, a consumer hire agreement or a linked transaction (to which the debtor, hirer or a relative is a party) is cancelled after the debtor, hirer or relative has obtained possession. In such a case the possessor is under a duty to restore the goods to the person from whom he got them and in the meantime to retain possession and to take reasonable care. The duty to restore the goods is merely a duty to redeliver them at *his own* premises on receiving a written request from the other party. The duty is also discharged if the possessor delivers the goods (whether at his own premises or elsewhere) to any person to whom a notice of cancellation could have been sent other than the "deemed agent".[31] Alternatively, he can send the goods to such a person, but in this case he must take reasonable care to see that they are received by the other party and are not damaged in transit. The duty to take reasonable care comes to an end 21 days from cancellation, unless within that time the possessor has received a written request for redelivery and has unreasonably failed to comply with it.

There is, however, a sting in the tail. The duty to restore does not apply to emergency or incorporation cases where, as we have seen, the debtor remains liable to pay the price.[32] Nor does it apply to perishable goods, nor to goods which by their nature are consumed by use and were so consumed before cancellation—a classic case of having one's cake and not having to pay for it![33]

Any breach of s.72 is actionable as a breach of statutory duty.

(7) The part-exchange allowance

Section 73 deals with a case where, as part of a cancelled agreement, the **22.13** negotiator agreed to take goods in part exchange and those goods have been delivered to him. The effect of s.73(2) is to give the debtor or hirer a right to recover the part-exchange allowance from the negotiator, unless within 10 days of cancellation the goods were returned to the debtor or hirer in substantially the same condition. If the negotiator was the supplier in a three-party debtor-creditor-supplier agreement, the negotiator and the creditor are jointly and severally liable to repay the allowance, and the lien of the debtor

---

[31] See above, para.22.09.
[32] s.69(2)(b), above, para.22.11.
[33] Thus the hirer of a motor vehicle would not have to pay for petrol consumed before cancellation.

or hirer[34] extends to cover the return of the goods (during the 10-day period) or the part-exchange allowance.

4. TERMINATION

22.14   If there is no right of withdrawal, rescission or cancellation the final possibility (apart from any contractual right of termination) is a right of termination under ss.99 to 101. These are limited in scope; ss.99 and 100 only apply to regulated hire-purchase and conditional sale agreements while s.101 relates to regulated consumer hire agreements. In either case the statutory rights cannot be cut down by agreement; on the other hand if the agreement is *more* favourable to the debtor or hirer he can take advantage of it.

Hire-purchase and conditional sale

22.15   Sections 99 and 100 give debtors the right to terminate a hire-purchase or conditional sale agreement at any time before the last instalment falls due. It can be exercised by giving notice to any person who is entitled or authorised to receive payments. However, there are two cases in which the right to terminate is not available. The first is where, under a conditional sale agreement relating to land, title has passed to the buyer. The second is where, under a conditional sale of goods, the property has become vested in the buyer and has then been transferred to a third person, e.g. a sub-buyer.

Termination only operates for the future, so that sums which have *accrued due* remain payable.[35] The effect of termination may well be to leave the creditor with heavily depreciated goods. In order to provide some measure of compensation, s.100(1) requires the debtor to pay such further sum (if any) as will bring the total payments up to *one-half* of the total price. If, however, in any action the court is satisfied that a smaller sum is adequate to cover the creditor's loss, the court may order such smaller sum to be paid. This could clearly be relevant if, for example, a hirer acquired a car on hire-purchase and then wished to terminate the agreement after only a few weeks' use. He would presumably tender a sum falling far short of one-half, leaving it to the creditor to take court proceedings. The court has no discretion with regard to sums which have already accrued due.

The debtor may also have to pay damages if he is in breach of an obligation to take reasonable care of the goods[36] and he must allow the creditor to retake them.[37]

22.16   If the creditor agrees to carry out any installation and if the cost of the installation forms part of the total price, it is clearly reasonable that he should be paid for this in full. Accordingly, the reference to one-half is a reference to the installation charge in full and one-half of the balance.[38]

---

[34] Above, para.22.10.
[35] s.99(2).
[36] s.100(4).
[37] s.100(5).
[38] s.100(2).

Example

A television set is let out on hire-purchase at a price of £300, including a £30 installation charge. The debtor pays a £50 deposit and one instalment of £10 is outstanding. He now wishes to terminate the agreement. He must first of all pay the £10. Then (unless otherwise ordered) he must bring his payments up to one-half of the total price:

$$\text{one half} = £30 + \frac{270}{5} \qquad = \qquad £165$$

$$\text{less sums paid and due} \qquad = \qquad 60$$

$$\text{further sum payable}^{[39]} \qquad = \qquad \underline{£105}$$

Consumer hire

Section 101 gives the hirer a non-excludable right to terminate the agreement, **22.17** but the earliest termination date is 18 months after the making of the agreement (unless the contract provides for an earlier termination date).[40] Once again termination only operates for the future and sums which have accrued due are not affected. The hirer must give a termination notice equal to the shortest payment interval, or three months, whichever is less. Thus, if rentals are payable monthly, the hirer can end the agreement by giving one month's notice at the end of month 17.

The exercise of a right of termination can often cause financial problems to the owner, especially where the owner leases out commercial equipment. Accordingly, s.101(7) provides that in three cases the statutory right of termination is not available at all. These are:

(a) where the total payments (disregarding sums payable on breach) exceed £1,500 in any one year;

(b) where goods are let out for the hirer's business and were selected by the hirer and acquired by the owner, at the hirer's request, from a third party;

(c) any agreement where the hirer requires the goods to relet them in the course of a business.

Apart from these special cases the OFT has a general power to exclude the operation of s.101 from agreements made by a particular trader[41] or within a specified description[42]

The section does not mention damages for failure to take reasonable care but on principle the hirer owes a duty of reasonable care as a bailee at common law and will be liable to pay damages for breach of that duty.

---

[39] s.100(1).
[40] s.101(3).
[41] See s.101(8) as amended by the Consumer Credit (Increase of Monetary Amounts) Order 1983 (SI 1983/1571).
[42] s.101(8A): inserted by the 2006 Act, s.63.

CHAPTER TWENTY-THREE

"THE GOODS ARE DEFECTIVE"

In Part I of this book we considered the terms implied by ss.12 to 14 of the **23.01** Sale of Goods Act 1979, and we also dealt briefly with hire-purchase and hiring agreements. In this chapter we shall consider these problems again in the context of credit transactions. The basic point can be made very briefly at the outset—the differences between cash and credit transactions are very slight. It is proposed to consider this topic under five headings and for convenience the term "connected lender" will be used in preference to "creditor with whom the supplier had arrangements". The five headings are:

1. Cash sale—unconnected lender

2. Cash sale—connected lender

3. Credit sale and conditional sale

4. Hire-purchase

5. Hire

1. CASH SALE—UNCONNECTED LENDER

Let us suppose that Robert borrows money from his bank and uses it to buy **23.02** a car which proves to be defective. The loan is a debtor-creditor agreement and, as we have seen, the purchase of the car is not a linked transaction. As between seller and buyer, the position is governed by the Sale of Goods Act 1979. These matters have been fully discussed in Chapters Three, Four and Seven. Alternatively, if the seller was guilty of misrepresentation Robert may be entitled to rescind the contract or to claim damages.[1] As between Robert and his bank the bank are not affected by any breach of contract on the part of the seller. It follows that Robert will have to continue to repay the loan and his sole remedy is against the seller. If he cannot afford the repayments his only right as against the bank is to wait for an arrears notice and a notice of default[2] or for proceedings to enforce the loan agreement and then apply to the court for a time order.[3]

---

[1] Above, para.7.03.
[2] Below, paras 25.17 and 25.19.
[3] Below, para. 25.16.

2. CASH SALE—CONNECTED LENDER

23.03 Let us now suppose that the seller introduces Robert to a finance company with whom the seller has arrangements. The finance company makes a loan to Robert to finance the sale. This is a three-party debtor-creditor-supplier agreement. As between Robert and the seller, the position is exactly the same as in the previous example. As regards the position between Robert and the finance company there are two overlapping provisions of considerable practical importance which may enable Robert to hold the finance company responsible for the seller's default.

Section 56

23.04 The first provision is s.56 of the Consumer Credit Act which applies (inter alia) to antecedent negotiations with the debtor conducted by the supplier in relation to a transaction financed by a debtor-creditor-supplier agreement.[4] The key provision is s.56(2) which reads as follows:

> "Negotiations with the debtor . . . shall be deemed to be conducted by the negotiator in the capacity of agent of the creditor as well as in his actual capacity."

In other words, if the seller made a misrepresentation (e.g. as to credit terms or the quality of the goods), he will have made it as *agent* for the finance company. Thus Robert could bring proceedings against the finance company, or he could merely discontinue his payments, wait to be sued and then counterclaim. It remains to add that s.56(3) makes void a clause (a) purporting to make the negotiator the agent of the dealer, or (b) relieving a person from liability for acts or omissions of any person acting as, or on behalf of, a negotiator. This raises a problem in relation to a clause in a contract between creditor and debtor excluding liability for all misrepresentations, including those made by the dealer. Would such a clause automatically be void under s.56(3) or would it still be subject to the reasonableness test under s.3 of the Misrepresentation Act 1967?[5] It is felt that a carefully drafted clause should be given the latter construction—it would seem strange that the creditor should be in a worse position merely because the misrepresentation was made by the dealer rather than by the creditor himself or by some other agent.

Section 56 can be regarded as an exception to the general rule that the dealer is not an agent of the creditor—even if he carries a stock of the creditor's finance application forms.[6] It should also be noted that s.56 is not limited to defects in the goods but applies to all negotiations. Suppose that H takes a car on hire-purchase from F1. Before completing his payments he takes it to a dealer D and agrees to sell it to D in part exchange for another car owned by D. D sells the new car to a linked finance company

---

[4] s.56(1)(c).
[5] As redrafted by s.8 of the Unfair Contract Terms Act 1977, above, para.8.41.
[6] The leading case is *Branwhite v Worcester Works Finance Co* [1969] 1 A.C. 552. See also *Woodchester Equipment (Leasing) Ltd v British Association of Canned and Preserved Food Importers and Distributors* [1995] C.C.L.R. 51, CA.

F2 who then let it out to H. D promises H to pay off the balance owing to F1 but fails to do so and becomes insolvent. By s.56 the promise by D was made as agent of F2; accordingly if F1 sues he can claim an indemnity from F2.[7]

Section 75

The second provision affecting three-party debtor-creditor-supplier agreements is s.75. This is a vital provision of consumers, where a supplier of goods or services refuses to meet its obligations under the contract or becomes insolvent. In this situation it is provided that: **23.05**

> (1) if the debtor . . . has . . . any claim against the supplier in respect of a misrepresentation or breach of contract, he shall have a like claim against the creditor, who, with the supplier, shall accordingly be jointly and severally liable to the debtor.

Subsection (3)[8] lays down two limitations.

> Subsection (1) does not apply to a claim—
> (a) under a non-commercial agreement, or
> (b) so far as the claim relates to any single item to which the supplier has attached a cash price[9] not exceeding £100 or more than £30,000.

As already stated there is substantial overlap between ss.56 and 75. If the "negotiator" makes a misrepresentation, the buyer/borrower may well have a claim against the creditor under either section. In two respects, however, s.56 is wider; it is not limited to three-party D-C-S agreements and it is not subject to the s.75 upper and lower limits.[10]

The real importance of s.75(1) lies in the words "or breach of contract". It means that the creditor will be liable not merely for the misrepresentation or for breach of express terms but also for breach of the *implied* terms, e.g. under the Sale of Goods Act 1979.[11] This seems reasonable enough; finance companies who finance the transaction by letting the goods out on hire-purchase have been responsible for the quality of the goods ever since 1938. The effect of s.75 is to place them in basically the same position if they choose to finance the transaction by means of a connected loan. From the debtor's point of view the effect of s.75 can be very favourable. In an extreme case he might have a claim against a solvent finance company whereas a person buying with his own money, or with money borrowed from an unconnected lender, would only have had a claim against an insolvent seller. **23.06**

It will be appreciated that the amount of the claim can be far greater than

---

[7] *Forthright Finance v Ingate* [1997] C.C.L.R. 95, CA.
[8] As amended by the Consumer Credit (Increase of Monetary Limits) Order 1983 (SI 1983/1878).
[9] This is the cash price of the item, *not* the credit advanced.
[10] See above.
[11] See above, Chs Three and Four.

the amount of the credit. Nor is the creditor only secondarily liable—the liability is "joint and several", so that the debtor may pursue the creditor *before* the supplier if he wishes.

Unless the supplier is insolvent, the creditor will not be saddled with ultimate liability, for as between creditor and supplier the creditor is entitled to join the supplier as a party to the proceedings and to claim an indemnity from him.[12]

Credit cards

23.07   In the example above[13] we took the case of a car buyer, connected lender and dealer. Another situation where s.75 is highly relevant is in relation to buyer, credit card company and approved supplier. If goods bought with a credit card prove to be defective and cause enormous damage (e.g. death or personal injury or damage to property, including buildings), the buyer (or his personal representatives) will have a claim against the credit card company for the full amount of the damage.

The precise legal effect of a renewable credit card still remains to be decided—is it a standing offer or a single contract or a new contract at each renewal?[14] One further point has been decided: a credit card payment by the consumer gives him an absolute discharge and he cannot be made to pay again, if the credit card company becomes insolvent before it has paid the retailer.[15]

As a modern example of s.75 in operation, many holiday-makers used credit cards to book holidays with tour operators which went into liquidation before the holidays had been completed. The credit card companies wrongly resisted s.75 claims against them on the ground that the holiday-makers should look to the special fund set up by the tour operators. Similarly a buyer placing a deposit when ordering, say, furniture, curtains or domestic electrical equipment would be well advised to pay by credit card; then if the retailer goes bust, the buyer can recover the deposit from the credit card company.

Problems may arise when booking a package holiday through a travel agent. The OFT took the view in its paper, *Connected Lender Liability* (March 1994) that s.75 will apply even though the payment is made directly to the travel agent, where he is acting as agent for the tour operator.[16] While we support this view, we urge consumers to pay the tour operator itself; without doubt the tour operator will then be "the supplier" within the meaning of s.75(1).

23.08   As part of an aggressive sales campaign a credit card company C2 may persuade a customer of C1 to surrender his card and take a C2 card instead. This can raise a problem of timing. Consider the following scenario:

---

[12] s.75(2) and (5).
[13] Above, para.23.03.
[14] We prefer the third view.
[15] *Re Charge Card Services* [1988] 3 W.L.R. 764.
[16] He usually is: see above, para.6.50.

January	consumer with card company X orders goods and pays by card
February	consumer switches to card company Y
March	the goods are delivered and are defective.

On these facts, some companies in the position of X are refusing to pay a s.75 claim (see para.23.05 above) on the ground that the card has been surrendered. We believe that this argument can be successfully attacked; the use of the X card in January crystallised a potential claim against that company.

Credit cards abroad

A related matter is the use of a credit card abroad. We stated in previous editions that we agreed with the OFT that s.75 applies to overseas transactions by a UK-based cardholder.[17] This was disputed by (among others) Lloyds TSB and Tesco Personal Finance. The OFT sensibly thought it desirable to have the point tested in court and in *Office of Fair Trading v Lloyds TSB Bank Plc*[18] the House of Lords, unanimously affirming the decision of the Court of Appeal, decided the issue in the OFT's favour. **23.09**

One further point arises—which system of law will the English courts apply when the supply contract was made abroad? Suppose Sarah buys an expensive watch in Vietnam using Mastercard. On her return she discovers that it is faulty or, even worse, a pirated copy worth a few pounds. Her "like claim" against the creditor in England will presumably be based on Vietnamese law as the proper or applicable law of the contract, since "her claim against the supplier" for breach of contract would be governed by that law if she had brought her claim in Vietnam. This effect of s.75 appears not to have been decided by the courts. Regrettably for consumers, we consider that the English court would require expert evidence on Vietnamese law to learn whether her claim would have succeeded abroad. If the claim involved an EU country, the problem would be less complicated since the same rules about goods being in conformity with the contract and remedies apply by virtue of the EU Directive 1999/44/EC "on certain aspects of the sale of consumer goods and associated guarantees" (above para.7.12).

Some further points on s.75

Clearly s.75 is of great importance to consumers (even though in 1983 the lower cash limit in s.75(3) was raised from £30 to £100, thereby taking many credit transactions outside the s.75 protection). It must however be appreciated that s.75 can only be used by the consumer if the relevant credit agreement was a "regulated agreement" (above, para.19.02). If, for example, he books a holiday and pays with his American Express or Diner's Club **23.10**

---

[17] *Connected Lender Liability*, pp.26–28. See also *Connected Lender Liability—A Second Report* (OFT, May 1995).
[18] [2007] UKHL 48.

charge card, the credit agreement is within the "single repayment" exemption (above, para.19.14 subpara.(6)); accordingly it is not a regulated agreement and s.75 will not help the consumer. Debit cards are not covered either, as no credit is provided.

It is also important to note that a consumer who has a claim against the supplier has "a like claim" against the creditor. In a Scottish case[19] it was held that a breach of the sale contract gives the consumer a right to rescind not only that contract but also the connected loan contract. It is thought that this reasoning cannot be correct since the two claims are not identical. The court could have reached the same (and correct) result by a different route—namely by allowing the consumer to sue the supplier and the creditor for the return of the price of the goods which he had rejected.

The OFT has urged consumers to take full advantage of their legal rights by using credit cards when making substantial purchases of goods or services.

3. CREDIT SALE AND CONDITIONAL SALE

23.11   A dealer may sell goods and allow the customer to pay by instalments. If nothing is said about the passing of property, it will pass as soon as the contract is made[20] and the sale will be a credit sale. If, however, the passing of property is postponed it will be a conditional sale.[21] In either case the obligations of the seller with regard to the goods are to be found in the Sale of Goods Act 1979. It will be recalled that a notification of purpose to a credit-broker will be as effective as if it had been notified to the seller (see above, para.4.34).

There are just three further points. First, the relevant provisions of the Sale of Goods Act apply even though the agreement is outside the Consumer Credit Act (e.g. because it is a debtor-creditor-supplier agreement with four or fewer instalments). Secondly, a trader who buys goods on credit for his trade will not be "dealing as consumer" and therefore an exemption clause which satisfies the reasonableness test will be binding on him. Thirdly, s.11(4) of the Sale of Goods Act[22] does not apply to a "consumer" conditional sale agreement.

4. HIRE-PURCHASE

23.12   In the case of a hire-purchase agreement (*whether or not it is regulated* by the Consumer Credit Act) the implied obligations with regard to the goods are contained in the Supply of Goods (Implied Terms) Act 1973.[23] The terms are virtually identical to those for the sale of goods and they include notification of purpose to a credit-broker.[24]

---

[19] *U.D.T. v Taylor* (1980) S.L.T. (Sh.Ct.) 18.
[20] Above, para.2.11.
[21] Above, para.18.09.
[22] Above, para.7.48.
[23] Above, para.4.37.
[24] Above, para.4.37.

In practice, the dealer will frequently sell the goods to a finance company, which will then let the goods out on hire-purchase. If the hire-purchase agreement is a regulated agreement the dealer will be a "credit-broker" or "negotiator" and s.56[25] will apply. In other words, any representations made by the dealer are treated as made as agent for the finance company as well as in his personal capacity. Thus, the debtor has two concurrent remedies; he can bring a claim against the finance company which is bound by the dealer's representations. He can also bring a claim against the dealer, either in negligence[26] or on the basis of a collateral contract.[27]

5. HIRE

The statutory implied terms have already been considered[28] and the law is **23.13** not affected in any way by the Consumer Credit Act. Section 56[29] does not apply and there is no rule of law that the dealer is to be regarded as the agent of the finance company; in many cases this will not be so. If, however, the documentation used by the finance company misleads a consumer into thinking that he is dealing with the dealer, the finance company may be estopped from denying that the dealer's sales staff had authority to speak on its behalf. In such a case statements made by the sales staff will bind the finance company.[30]

---

[25] Above, para.23.04.
[26] *Hedley Byrne & Co Ltd v Heller and Partners Ltd*, above, para.3.05. There can also be liability without any statement under the general law of negligence which was discussed in Ch.Five.
[27] *Andrews v Hopkinson* [1957] 1 Q.B. 229. The dealer was also liable in negligence. See above, n.26.
[28] Above, para.4.40. See also Law Commission Report No.95.
[29] Above, para.23.04.
[30] *Lease Management Services v Purnell Secretarial Services, Canon (South West) Third Party*, *The Times*, April 1, 1994, CA.

CHAPTER TWENTY-FOUR

"I HAVE LOST MY CREDIT CARD"

The credit token, and especially the credit card, is of great importance as a **24.01** form of consumer credit and the 1974 Act brings them within the ambit of control.

The Act contains a number of provisions relating to "credit tokens" and "credit token agreements" and these provisions will be considered in this chapter.

What is a credit token?

The term is defined in s.14(1) as "a card, check, voucher, coupon, stamp, **24.02** form, booklet or other document or thing given to an individual by a person carrying on a consumer credit business who undertakes":

   (a) that on production of it (whether or not some other action is also required) he will supply cash, goods and services (or any of them) on credit, or

   (b) that where, on the production of it to a third party (whether or not any other action is also required), the third party supplies cash, goods and services (or any of them), he will pay the third party for them (whether or not deducting any discount or commission) in return for payment to him by the individual.

Thus the term clearly includes credit cards and trading checks used in a form of credit known as "check trading". It does *not* include a cheque card, because the bank issuing a cheque card merely promises to honour cheques. Debit or switch cards also fall outside the term, as the bank does not provide any credit. Nor does it cover trading stamps or free gift vouchers (e.g. on the back of a cereal packet), because the customer will not receive goods *on credit*.

Unsolicited credit tokens

The mass-mailing of Access cards provoked widespread criticism and now **24.03** s.51 makes it an offence "to give a person a credit token if he has not asked for it." The request must be in writing and signed by the person making it, unless (a) the credit token agreement is a small debtor-creditor-supplier agreement, or (b) the card is renewed.

This section also applies (in the opinion of the OFT) to an arrangement whereby a card is automatically replaced by another one. A Press Notice PN 128/03 dated October 8, 2003 reported that Marks & Spencer had sent letters to cardholders informing them that their existing storecards would be replaced by a new card called &more. The OFT intervened to persuade the company to modify this arrangement. Existing storecard holders would be told that if they wanted to keep their storecards they need take no action. If they wanted to change to the new card, they must take positive steps to achieve this (thus reducing the element of inertia selling).

What is a credit token agreement?

24.04 By s.14(2) (read with s.189) it is a regulated consumer credit agreement for the provision of credit in connection with the use of a credit token. Thus the term will not apply to an agreement where, for example, the debtor is a body corporate or the agreement is exempt. It will be recalled that agreements involving the use of Diner's Club or American Express charge cards are exempt agreements, because they are debtor-creditor-supplier agreements for running-account credit and the indebtedness over a period has to be discharged by a single payment.[1]

Modification of formalities

24.05 The formalities required for a regulated agreement were considered in Chapter Twenty. They are modified in two minor respects in the case of a credit token agreement. The first relates to the sending of the second copy; by s.63(4) it need not be given within seven days following the making of the agreement if it is given before or at the time when the credit token is given to the debtor. The second relates to the notice setting out cancellation rights; by s.64(2) it need not be posted within seven days following the making of the agreement if it is posted to the debtor before the credit token is given to him, or if it is sent by post with the credit token.

Additional copies

24.06 Where, under the credit token agreement, the creditor issues a new token to the debtor he must at the same time give the debtor a copy of the executed agreement (if any) and of any document referred to in it. Failure to do so has the usual consequences, i.e. the creditor cannot enforce the agreement while the default continues and, if it continues for one month, he commits an offence.[2] The section does not apply to a small agreement.[3]

Liability of debtor

24.07 We come now to the problem which is likely to be the most troublesome one in practice—the extent of the debtor's liability if the token is used by someone else without the debtor's authority. This matter is primarily governed by ss.66 and 84. By s.66 the debtor under a credit token agreement is not liable

---

[1] Above, para.19.14 subpara.(6).
[2] s.85.
[3] ibid.

for use made of the token by another person unless (a) the debtor had previously accepted the token, or (b) its use constituted an acceptance by him. The debtor accepts a credit token when he or a person authorised by him to use it under the terms of the agreement:

(a) signs it, or

(b) signs a receipt for it, or

(c) uses it.

If the token has been accepted under s.66 we can turn to s.84 to consider the debtor's liability for its misuse by someone else. The provisions of this section can be summarised as follows:

(1) The underlying principle is that the debtor should give notice of the loss or misuse as soon as possible. Accordingly, the credit token agreement must contain, in the prescribed manner,[4] particulars of the name, address and telephone number of a person to whom notice of loss, etc., can be given. If the agreement does not contain this information the debtor will not be liable for misuse at all.[5]

(2) The debtor is not liable for any loss arising after the creditor has been given written or oral notice that the token has been lost or stolen or is otherwise liable to misuse.[6] The notice takes effect when received, but if it is given orally the agreement may provide that it is not effective unless confirmed in writing within seven days.[7]

(3) Subject to (2) above, the debtor's liability depends on the person by whom the token was misused. If it was misused by a person who acquired possession of the token with the debtor's consent, he is liable *without limit*.[8] In other cases (e.g. loss or theft) his liability is limited to £50,[9] or the credit limit if lower, for misuse in a period beginning when the token ceased to be in the possession of an authorised person and ending when the token is once again in the possession of an authorised person.[10]

Thus the moral is clear: the onus is on the debtor to notify the loss to the creditor without delay.

Cancellation

If the debtor cancels a credit token agreement he can only recover a sum paid for the token, and he will only cease to be liable for such a sum, if the token has been returned to the creditor or surrendered to a supplier.[11] **24.08**

---

[4] i.e. prominently and so as to be easily legible (see Consumer Credit (Credit-Token Agreements) Regulations 1983 (SI 1983/1555, reg.2).
[5] s.84(4).
[6] s.84(3).
[7] s.84(5).
[8] s.84(2).
[9] See SI 1983/1571; the limit was formerly £30.
[10] s.84(1).
[11] s.70(5).

Some further points on misuse

24.09 There has been massive publicity concerning the enormous losses sustained by credit card companies through credit card frauds—although the companies have largely themselves to blame by agreeing to honour transactions where goods are ordered over the telephone without a signature by the customer. Consumers are urged to be very wary in giving their card number over the telephone. In any event the consumer should always check his statement carefully and immediately report any unauthorised transactions.

The use of "chip and pin" cards has led to a reduction in losses sustained by credit card fraud—this has certainly been the French experience too.

CHAPTER TWENTY-FIVE

"I CAN'T AFFORD TO PAY"

In practice there are two main areas where a debtor is likely to seek legal advice. The first is where he is dissatisfied with the goods. This has been considered in Pt I of this book and in Chapter Twenty-Two. The second is where, for one reason or another, he finds himself in difficulties with his payments. The legal adviser can approach the problem by asking a number of preliminary questions: **25.01**

(1) Is there a contract at all?

If, for example, the document signed by the debtor was merely an offer, revocation is possible before it has been accepted.[1] **25.02**

(2) Is the contract voidable for misrepresentation?

If so, it can be rescinded and money recovered, if it is not too late.[2] **25.03**

(3) Has the debtor a claim for breach of contract against the creditor?

If so, he may be able to treat the contract as repudiated, or he may have a claim for damages which he can set against the instalments.[3] **25.04**

(4) Is the agreement cancellable?

If so, the debtor may be able to serve a notice of cancellation under provisions which have already been discussed.[4] **25.05**

(5) Was the agreement "improperly executed"?

We have seen that if the creditor fails to comply with the statutory formalities as to contents, signature and copies (and pre-contractual reflection in certain land mortgage cases) the agreement can only be enforced against the debtor or hirer on an order of the court[5] or with the consent of the debtor or hirer given at the time.[6] **25.06**

One of the features of the legislation is the very wide power given to the

---

[1] See also s.57, above, para.22.02.
[2] See above, paras7.03–7.09.
[3] Above, para.7.51.
[4] Above, para.22.04.
[5] s.65.
[6] s.173(3).

court to rewrite the agreement or to postpone its enforcement. If the creditor or owner brings proceedings for an enforcement order, the court must consider the degree of culpability for the defect and the prejudice (if any) which it has caused to any person.[7] The court can then do any of the following things:

(a) it may make an enforcement order;

(b) it may make a "time order" under s.129[8];

(c) it may modify the agreement as set out below and then make an enforcement order relating to the agreement as modified; or

(d) it may dismiss the application—but only if it considers it just to do so having regard to the matters mentioned above.[9]

Power to modify agreement and enforcement orders

25.07   Section 127(2)[10] provides that:

> If it appears to the court just to do so, it may in an enforcement order reduce or discharge any sum payable by the debtor or hirer or any surety, so as to compensate him for prejudice suffered as a result of the contravention in question.

We must also consider ss.135 and 136 which are not confined to proceedings for an enforcement order but apply to any order made by the court in relation to a regulated agreement. By s.135(1) an order may include a provision:

> (a) making the operation of any term of the order conditional on the doing of specified acts by any party to the proceedings;
> (b) suspending the operation of any term of the order either—
>
> (i) until such time as the court subsequently directs, or
> (ii) until the occurrence of a specified act or omission.

Section 136 gives the court a wide power to alter the agreement in consequence of a term of an order made under the Act. This can include a reduction in the rate of interest.[11] These very wide powers cannot be used to suspend an order requiring a person to deliver up goods unless the court is satisfied that they are in that person's possession or control.[12] In the case of a consumer hire agreement the

---

[7] s.127(1).
[8] Below, para.25.16.
[9] s.127(1).
[10] s.127(3) to (5) provided that "the court shall not make an enforcement order" where certain provisions in ss.60–64 were not complied with. The 2006 Act, s.15, repeals ss.127(3) to (5) so that now the court *always* has discretion. In force April 6, 2007: Consumer Credit Act 2006 (Commencement No.2 and Transitional Provisions and Savings) Order 2007 (SI 2007/123). See early editions of this book for a discussion of the old law.
[11] *Southern and District Finance Plc v Barnes, The Times*, April 19, 1995, CA.
[12] s.135(2).

section cannot be used to extend the period for which the hirer is entitled to possession.[13]

We must also mention certain special powers available to the court in the case **25.08** of hire-purchase and conditional sale agreements. These are considered later.[14]

Finally, the court has a general power under s.136 to amend any agreement or security in consequence of a term of the order.

The cases show that, as forecast in the Third Edition of this book, these wide powers will only be exercised if the court feels that the debtor or hirer has been prejudiced by the failure to comply with the formalities. If the breach is only a technical one (e.g. the second copy sent a few days late) the court is likely to waive the breach entirely.[15]

What happens if the creditor or owner purports to terminate the agreement and repossesses the goods? If it involves entry on premises without the consent of the debtor or hirer there may be liability for breach of statutory duty.[16] Apart from this there may be very little that the debtor or hirer can do about it, because of the "no sanctions" rule in s.170.[17] The section does not however prevent the grant of an injunction[18] and it is just possible that a mandatory injunction could require the goods to be returned to the debtor or hirer. Apart from this, the only sanction is the ever-present administrative sanction of reporting the matter to the Office of Fair Trading.

Despite the unenforceability of the agreement for defective formalities (see **25.09** above) there is no doubt that the creditor or owner can sue the debtor or hirer in tort if, for example, the debtor or hirer wrongly disposes of the goods[19] or report the customer to a credit reference agency.[19a] Similarly the sanction of not allowing enforcement of "the agreement" would not apply where, for example, the agreement has expired by effluxion of time so that the creditor or owner has a common law right to repossess which he can, it is thought, enforce by action.

In this Chapter and elsewhere in Pt IV of this book there are numerous references to "the court". By s.141 any action by the creditor to enforce a regulated agreement must be brought in the county court. An attempt to gain an advantage by starting in the High Court may be struck out as an abuse of process.[20]

"The section infringes my human rights", says the finance company!

The Human Rights Act 1998 has spawned many ingenious arguments—but **25.10** few as remarkable as one involving consumer credit. In *Wilson v First County*

---

[13] s.135(3).
[14] Below, paras25.22 and 25.30.
[15] See *Nissan Finance UK v Lockhart* [1993] C.C.L.R. 39, CA, and contrast *National Guardian Mortgage Corp v Wilkes* [1993] C.C.L.R. 1: failure to supply the s.58 pre-contract copy (above, para.21.04); prejudice to borrower; court reduced interest by 40%.
[16] s.92(3), below, para.25.24.
[17] Above, para.18.03.
[18] s.170(3).
[19] See *Eastern Distributors Ltd v Goldring* [1957] 2 Q.B. 600.
[19a] *McGuffick v Royal Bank of Scotland*, para.21.13.
[20] *Barclays Bank v Brooks* [1997] C.C.L.R. 60, QBD.

Trust (No. 2)[21] a finance company sued a debtor who claimed that the agreement was "improperly executed" within s.61 and that by virtue of s.127(3) it was irredeemably unenforceable. The finance company boldly argued that this section violated their human rights and was therefore incompatible with the European Convention on Human Rights. They argued that (a) it denied them the right to a fair trial under art.6 and (b) it was an unlawful interference with their possessions under art.1 of the First Protocol. Amazingly these arguments succeeded in the Court of Appeal but the House of Lords disagreed. They ruled that (a) art.6 was solely concerned with procedural matters and s.127(3) was a matter of substance and (2) even if the section infringed art.1 of the First Protocol, it was justified as a reasonable and proportionate response to a genuine social problem. The significance of this case disappeared with the repeal of s.127(3).

(6) Can the debtor terminate the agreement?

25.11   This has already been considered. (See above, para.22.14.)

(7) Can the debtor settle early and obtain a rebate?

25.12   The debtor may be able to find another source of credit which is less expensive to him. In the case of hire-purchase the debtor may be better advised to settle early, become the owner of the goods and re-sell them.[22] Section 94 gives the debtor a non-excludable right to complete the agreement ahead of time on service of a notice on the creditor and on payment of all sums due, less any statutory rebate of the charge for credit.[23]

In calculating the total charge for credit the critical factor is the time during which the creditor will be kept out of his money. Accordingly, it is clearly reasonable to allow for a rebate where the debtor pays off early, because the creditor will be able to earn fresh interest on the repaid amount. Section 95 enables regulations to be made for the calculation of this rebate, which will apply in any case of early settlement—whether by reason of re-financing, breach or for any other reason. How then is the rebate to be calculated? Three principles must be borne in mind:

   (a) the total charge for credit should be spread actuarially over the repayment period and the debtor should get a rebate corresponding to the proportion of the total charge for credit which would have accrued after the settlement date;

   (b) where capital is being constantly repaid (as in the case of mortgages and hire-purchase agreements) the proportion will reflect the fact

---

[21] [2003] 3 W.L.R. 568, H.L. A number of cases where unmeritorious debtors benefitted from s.127(3) or (4) led to their repeal: n.10 above.

[22] If the finance company gives an incorrect settlement figure, it may be estopped from claiming the true amount due if their mistake has caused the hirer to alter his position: *Lombard North Central v Stobart* [1990] C.C.L.R. 53, CA.

[23] Where sums are due from a debtor who has made only a partial early payment, the creditor can get judgment for the (unrebated) sum due; but the debtor can claim the rebate when satisfying the judgment: *Forward Trust Ltd v Whymark* [1990] 2 Q.B. 670, CA.

that the interest payable at the beginning of the agreement is much greater than it is at a later stage when the outstanding capital is much lower;

(c) a completely even actuarial spread would be unfair to the creditor because certain one-off expenses are incurred at the beginning of the transaction (legal fees, survey fees, stamp duty, etc.).

The calculation of the rebate was originally governed by the Consumer Credit (Rebate on Early Settlement) Regulations 1983 (SI 1983/1562). These were heavily criticised by consumer bodies as being unfair to consumers, not least by their inclusion of the so-called "rule of 78". They have been replaced from May 31, 2005 by the Consumer Credit (Early Settlement) Regulations 2004 (SI 2004/1483). **25.13**

Regulation 4 incorporates an actuarial formula to be used in calculating the amount of the rebate, in place of different formulae provided for in the 1983 Regulations in relation to different cases. The Schedule contains examples which illustrate the application of the new formula.

The 1983 Regulations were very complex. The formula in the 2004 Regulations is no less mind boggling and requires an actuary, or at least an accountant, to understand its application. Regulation 4(1) is as follows:

The amount of the rebate is the difference between the total amount of the repayments of credit that would fall due for payment after the settlement date if early settlement did not take place and the amount given by the following formula— **25.14**

$$\sum_{i=1}^{m} A_i(1 + r)^{aj} - \sum_{i=1}^{n} B_j(1 + r)^{bj}$$

where:

A_i = the amount of the ith advance of credit,

B_j = the amount of the jth repayment of credit,

r = the periodic rate equivalent of the APR/100,

m = the number of advances of credit made before the settlement date,

n = the number of repayments of credit made before the settlement date,

a_i = the time between the ith advance of credit and the settlement date, expressed in periods,

b_j = the time between the jth repayment of credit and the settlement date, expressed in periods, and

Σ represents the sum of all the terms indicated.

Like the 1983 Regulations they reflect the principles set out above. Thus: **25.15**

(1) They seek to meet point (c) above by allowing the settlement date (on which the rebate calculation depends) to be notionally deferred by one month (see reg.6).

(2) The Regulations also assist the creditor by allowing him to exclude from the rebate calculations (a) taxes and duties, and (b) sums payable or paid under a linked transaction.

If a debtor is contemplating making an early settlement, he can in writing ask the creditor to give him a statement containing the settlement figure.[24] If the creditor fails to comply within seven working days the usual sanctions will follow.[25]

(8) Time orders

25.16 If the debtor or hirer is unable to withdraw, rescind, cancel, terminate or settle early, and if all the formalities have been complied with, the next possibility is to apply for a "time order". Apart from s.127[26] the debtor or hirer can apply for a time order (a) after he has been served with a notice of default,[27] or (b) where the creditor or owner brings proceedings to enforce a regulated agreement or any security or to recover possession of any goods or land to which a regulated agreement relates[28] or (c) where the debtor or hirer has been given a notice of sums in arrears (see below, para.25.17), 14 days have elapsed and they have notified the creditor or owner of their intention to apply together with a proposal.[29]

In *Southern and District Finance v Barnes*[30] the Court of Appeal laid down the following guidelines:

(1) The power to grant a time order only relates to "any sum owed"— but where a creditor brings a possession action the balance of the loan can be treated as "owed" and s.136 will apply to it.

(2) The court can only vary the terms of a regulated agreement under this section if:

(a) the proposed amendment is truly a consequence of the term of the order; and
(b) the making of the amendment is also just (see below).

(3) In any time order application the court must first consider whether it is just to make the order. This will involve a consideration of all the circumstances and the position of the creditor as well as that of the debtor.

(4) Any time order should normally be made for a stipulated period on account of temporary financial difficulty.

---

[24] s.97. The contents of the statement and the calculation of the settlement date are contained in the Consumer Credit (Settlement Information) Regulations 1983 (SI 1983/1564) as amended by the 2004 Regs.
[25] See above, para.21.02.
[26] Above, para.25.06.
[27] See County Court (Amendment) Rules 1985 (SI 1985/566), Ord.49, r.4(5).
[28] s.129. See *First National Bank v Syed* [1991] C.C.L.R. 37, CA (debtor proposed instalments which would not even cover interest accruing; order refused).
[29] s.129A inserted by the 2006 Act, s.16.
[30] [1995] C.C.L.R. 62, CA.

(5) The court must consider what instalments would be reasonable, both as regards amount and timing.

(6) If the rate of interest is altered, the court will bear in mind that (a) smaller instalments will result in a liability to pay interest on accumulated arrears and (b) the payment period will be extended.

(7) If the full amount is due, the order will clearly affect the term of the loan, or the rate of interest, or both.

(8) If justice requires the making of a time order, the court should suspend any possession order while the time order is complied with.

In a recent case[31] involving an allegedly unfair contract term the House of Lords considered that debtors undoubtedly suffered a detriment by the ability of the court to enter judgment without considering their powers under s.129. However, this was not caused by the disputed contractual term but by the drafting of the Act in not requiring the provisions of s.129 to be brought to the notice of debtors. This lacuna will no doubt be filled when "information sheets" have to be given with arrears statements, to which we now turn.

Sums in arrears notices and information sheets

The 2006 Act, ss.9 to 11, introduces new provisions to ensure that debtors **25.17** and hirers are reminded of the fact that they are in arrears and at the same time given information to help them. These are ss.86B, 86C and 86D of the 1974 Act which contain the requirements about the new "notices of sums in arrears".

Section 86B deals with fixed-sum credit and consumer hire agreements. The broad effect is that where the debtor or hirer is at least two payments in arrear, the creditor or owner must within 14 days give them an arrears notice. Section 86C imposes comparable requirements in respect of running-account credit agreements. Such notices must include "arrears information sheets". These are sheets which the OFT must prepare under s.86A and "include information to help debtors and hirers who receive" arrears notices (s.86A(2)).

Three final points should be noted. (1) The creditor or owner not complying with these requirements cannot enforce the agreement or claim interest during the period of non-compliance (s.86D). (2) Regulations[31a] contain the detail about the form and content of arrears notices and the information in information sheets, e.g. the legal consequences of non-payment, details of advice agencies. (3) Non-commercial agreements and small agreements fall outside these provisions.

---

[31] *Director General of Fair Trading v First National Bank* [2003] UKHL 52.
[31a] SI 2007/1167: para.21.15.

Notice of default sums and interest

25.18 Another new notice is introduced by the 2006 Act, s.12, and inserted into the 1974 Act as s.86E. Where a debtor or hirer incurs a "default sum", the creditor or owner must give them a notice in the form, with the contents and within the period prescribed by the regulations mentioned in para.21.15. "Default sum" is defined in a new s.187A (inserted by the 2006 Act, s.18) as "a sum other than interest payable in connection with a breach of the agreement by him".

The sanctions for non-compliance are similar to those in respect of arrears notices mentioned in para.25.08: the agreement is unenforceable and interest is not payable on the default sum, in this case for 28 days after the notice was given. Here again non-commercial and small agreements are not affected.

To prevent interest being charged as compound interest on default sums, a new s.86F is inserted by the 2006 Act, s.13: interest is payable only if it is simple interest.

Default notice

25.19 The agreement may provide that, on default by the debtor or hirer, the creditor or owner shall become entitled to take certain action, e.g. to terminate the agreement, or to demand early payment of any sum, or to recover possession of any goods or land, or to enforce any security, or to treat any right conferred on the debtor or hirer (e.g. an option to purchase in the case of a hire-purchase agreement) as terminated, restricted or deferred. The effect of s.87 is that such a provision will not be enforceable unless the creditor or owner first serves on the debtor or hirer a notice of default in the prescribed form.[32] The notice must contain the following information[33]:

(a) it must specify the breach;

(b) if the breach is capable of remedy (e.g. default in payment) the notice must indicate what action has to be taken to remedy it and the date before which it must be done;

(c) if the breach is incapable of remedy (e.g. causing permanent damage to the goods) what compensation (if any) is required and the date before which it is to be paid;

(d) the consequences of non-compliance;

(e) a default information sheet; and

---

[32] See Consumer Credit (Enforcement Default and Termination Notices) Regulations 1983 (SI 1983/1561). Note that if the notice claims a sum larger than the amount owed by the debtor or hirer the notice is invalid: *Woodchester Lease Management Services Ltd v Swain & Co* [1999] 1 W.L.R. 263, CA.

[33] s.88 as amended by the 2006 Act, s.14, inserting ss.(4A). Also "14" was previously "7" days. In force October 1, 2006: Consumer Credit Act 2006 (Commencement No.1) Order (SI 2006/1508).

(f) in appropriate cases the restrictions on the creditor's right to repossess "protected goods" (below, para.25.25).

The date in (b) and (c) above must be not earlier than 14 days after the service of the notice of default. Presumably, if the notice is posted on February 1 it can specify February 15 as the date before which the act must be done.

Effect of default notice

If, before the specified date the debtor or hirer takes the steps specified in the notice, the default is treated as never having taken place.[34] Alternatively, as already stated, the debtor or hirer can apply under s.129 for a "time order". Such an order may contain either or both of the following provisions:
    25.20

(a) that any sum owed by the debtor or hirer or any surety shall be payable at such times as the court, having regard to the means of the debtor or hirer and any surety, considers reasonable;

(b) that a breach by the debtor or hirer (other than the non-payment of money) shall be remedied within such period as the court may specify.

Effect of repossession

The Act does not specify what remedies are available if the creditor or owner repossesses the goods or land without a default notice. The section provides that the creditor or owner is not *entitled* to repossess, etc., without serving a notice of default. It may well be, therefore, that non-compliance could be actionable as trespass to goods or conversion or there might be a breach of the implied warranty for quiet possession. There may also be liability for breach of statutory duty if there is unauthorised entry on premises[35] and the "snatch-back" of protected goods[36] will lead to the severe sanctions set out in s.91.[37]
    25.21

(9) Additional protection in hire-purchase and conditional sale cases

The notice of default provisions are backed up by four other provisions aimed at what is known as "snatch-back"—the repossession of goods or land without an order of the court.
    25.22

Entry on premises

In the case of a regulated hire-purchase or conditional sale agreement the creditor or owner cannot enter any premises to repossess the goods without
    25.23

---

[34] s.89.
[35] Below, para.25.24.
[36] Below, para.25.25.
[37] ibid.

an order of the court.[38] Clearly, a contractual provision conferring such a right would be void[39] but a consent at the time of entry would be effective.[40]

Land

25.24   If the debtor is in breach under a conditional sale agreement relating to land the creditor cannot recover possession of the land from the debtor, nor from any person claiming under him, without an order of the court.[41] The point relating to the debtor's consent will be equally relevant here.

In both the above cases, s.92(3) does provide a sanction—any entry in contravention of either of these provisions is actionable as a breach of statutory duty.

Protected goods

25.25   In the case of hire-purchase and conditional sale it is clearly inequitable that the debtor, having paid a substantial part of the price, should have the goods snatched away (with no credit for his payments) merely because he gets into arrears. Accordingly, s.90 gives him protection if (a) he is in breach, (b) he has not terminated the agreement, (c) he has paid to the creditor one-third or more of the total price and (d) the property in the goods remains in the creditor. In such a case the goods are called *"protected goods"*. The creditor cannot recover possession of the goods from the debtor without an order of the court.

The Act imposes serious sanctions for contravention. By s.91 if goods are recovered by the creditor in contravention of s.90 the agreement, if not already terminated, will terminate, the debtor is released from all further liability and he can recover from the creditor all sums paid by him under the agreement. A number of points arise under this very important provision.

(a) Where the agreement requires the creditor to carry out any installation work and the cost of this work forms part of the total price, then the fraction of one-third is calculated by taking the installation charge in full and adding one-third of the balance.[42] Thus, if the price of £300 includes an installation charge of £30 the fraction of one-third will be:

$$£30 + \frac{270}{3} = £120$$

(b) A dealer might be tempted to avoid the "protected goods" provisions in one of two ways. First of all there might be an agreement for a television set with a price of £150, of which £60 has been paid. If the customer then comes in for a £300 music centre the dealer might say "let us cancel the original agreement and make a new one for both items (£450) with a credit for sums already paid (£60)." Secondly, if the original agreement (with payments

---

[38] s.92(1).
[39] s.173(1).
[40] s.173(3).
[41] s.92(2).
[42] s.90(2). Similar to s.100(2), above, para.22.16.

exceeding one-third) related to a telescope and a camera, he might suggest that the telescope should be treated as fully paid up and that a new agreement should be made relating solely to the camera. In both cases the debtor starts inside s.90 and would end up outside it—because he has not paid one-third under the new agreement. To prevent such avoidance the effect of s.90(3) is to bring the new agreement within the section, even though one-third has not been paid.

Where the agreement provides that on default the hirer must pay default interest in addition to the hire-purchase price, the hirer can appropriate any payment towards the price (so as to gain protection under s.90). If he fails to do so, the creditor can appropriate. In a recent case[43] the creditor issued proceedings for possession and the summons showed that just over one-third of the price had been paid. He then sought to amend the summons by earmarking a small amount towards default interest. It was held that it was too late for him to do so.

(c) Repossession of the goods from the debtor without a court order kills **25.26** the agreement. Thus, on the one hand, the debtor cannot claim the return of the goods[44] while on the other hand the creditor cannot breathe any fresh life into the agreement by returning the goods to the debtor.[45]

(d) Section 90 prohibits recovery of possession only "from the debtor". Thus, if the creditor seizes the goods which the debtor has abandoned the section is not infringed.[46] A similar principle would apply where the creditor seizes the goods from a third party to whom the debtor has purported to sell them.[47]

(e) A consent by the debtor given at the time is as effective as an order of the court[48] but the court is likely to examine the facts closely to make sure that there was a true and free consent.[49]

(f) If the debtor chooses to terminate under s.99,[50] the goods are not protected.

Relief against forfeiture

The court has a general power to grant relief against the forfeiture of a pro- **25.27** prietary or possessory right (which could be relevant where, for example, the finance company sought to repossess after the debtor had paid most of the instalments). Such a power will only be exercised in exceptional circumstances.[51]

---

[43] *Julian Hodge Bank Ltd v Hall* [1998] C.C.L.R. 14.
[44] *Carr v Broderick & Co Ltd* [1942] 2 K.B. 275.
[45] *Capital Finance Co Ltd v Bray* [1964] 1 W.L.R. 323.
[46] *Bentinck Ltd v Cromwell Engineering Co Ltd* [1971] 1 Q.B. 324.
[47] Consider *Eastern Distributors Ltd v Goldring* [1957] 2 Q.B. 600.
[48] s.173(3).
[49] The matter could be raised if the debtor took proceedings alleging a breach of s.90 and denying his consent to the repossession. See *Chartered Trust Plc v Pitcher* [1988] R.T.R. 72, CA.
[50] Above, para.22.14.
[51] *Transag Haulage Ltd v Leyland Daf* (1994) 13 Tr.L.R. 361.

Additional powers of the court[52]

25.28 In any proceedings for an enforcement order, or for a time order, or in proceedings by the creditor to recover possession, the court may (in addition to its other powers) make (a) a return order, or (b) a transfer order.[53] A return order, as the name implies, requires the debtor to return the goods to the creditor. A transfer order is, in effect, a "split" order, in that it orders the debtor to return some of the goods to the creditor and it vests in the debtor the creditor's title to the remainder. This is subject to a ceiling set out in s.133(3), namely, that the maximum transferable to the debtor is found by deducting from the sum paid one-third of the unpaid balance. Thus, if the debtor had paid £80 out of a total price of £200, the court can vest in the debtor goods to the value of:

$$£80 - \left[\frac{200 - 80}{3} \right] = £40$$

In practice, the court frequently makes a return order and then exercises its powers under s.135 to suspend the operation of the order on condition that the debtor pays the balance by instalments fixed by the court.

(10) Additional protection in consumer hire cases

25.29 A number of provisions which are relevant to consumer hire have already been considered earlier in this chapter. They include s.65 (improperly executed agreements), s.87 (notice of default), s.92 (no entry on premises without court order) and s.129 (time orders). In addition, s.132 provides that where the owner recovers possession otherwise than by action the hirer may apply to the court for an order (a) extinguishing any further liability to make payments in whole or in part, or (b) requiring the owner to repay sums paid by the hirer in whole or in part. The court can also include such a provision when it makes an order for delivery to the owner. Such a power could be exercised where, for example, the hirer has paid a year's rental in advance and then finds it necessary to terminate the hiring after only a few weeks or where the owner retakes the goods following the hirer's default.

A hirer can also argue, in appropriate cases, that the owner had no right to terminate at all. The right to terminate depends primarily on the terms of the contract; if the termination clause is very precise it may be construed as exhaustive and as excluding the general common law right to terminate if the hirer commits a repudiatory breach.[54]

It will be recalled that the general power to make a "suspended" order under s.135 cannot extend the period for which the hirer is entitled to possession.[55]

---

[52] The county court has exclusive jurisdiction over regulated agreements; see s.141 and *Sovereign Leasing v Ali* [1992] C.C.L.R. 1 (transfer of action started in High Court).
[53] s.133.
[54] *Eurocopy Rentals v McCann Fordyce* [1995] C.C.L.R. 4.
[55] Above, para.25.07.

(11) Appropriation of payments

A debtor or hirer may have two or more separate regulated agreements with **25.30** the same creditor or owner. If he finds himself unable to pay a sum to cover all the sums due and sends a smaller amount, s.81 allows him, on making the payment, to appropriate it to one or more of the agreements in such proportions as he thinks fit. If he fails to appropriate at the time of payment, then s.81(2) may come into play. It provides that where one or more of the agreements is a hire-purchase, conditional sale, consumer hire or secured agreement, the payment shall be appropriated in the proportion which the sums *due* bear to each other.

Example

> £20 is due under a hire-purchase agreement relating to a dishwasher and £10 is **25.31** due under a hire agreement relating to a television set. The debtor sends a cheque for £12. If he fails to appropriate at the time of payment, £8 will go towards the dishwasher and £4 towards the television set.

Finally, if the debtor fails to appropriate in a case to which s.81(2) does *not* apply (e.g. if he has two debtor-creditor agreements with the same creditor) the general law will apply and the creditor will have the right of appropriation.

(12) Unfair relationships

Background

At the beginning of Pt IV of this book we referred in para.18.04 to the 2003 **25.32** White Paper, *Fair, Clear and Competitive–the Consumer Credit Market in the 21ˢᵗ Century*. We noted that one of the areas of concern was unfair credit relationships, to which we now turn.

The Act attempted to solve the problems faced by debtors, who had been unable to cope with credit transactions which they alleged were unfair, by using the powers given by ss.137 to 140. These provisions had been drafted very narrowly, so that the courts could not interfere, unless the credit bargain was "extortionate", i.e. it involved "grossly exorbitant" payments or "grossly contravenes ordinary principles of fair dealing". The absence of the words "grossly" would have given the judges greater room to manoeuvre, but as it was they were in a straitjacket and forced to give a restricted meaning to the expressions in the Act. (Readers may refer to previous editions of this book for a more detailed analysis of the old law.)

Criticism of sections 137 to 140

The White Paper listed a number of factors which had contributed to the **25.33** ineffectiveness of the existing law:

> (a) few cases had reached the courts because the qualifying hurdles were very high;

    (b) the wording of the legislation was imprecise, resulting in a restrictive interpretation by the courts;

    (c) the courts had focussed on interest rates under the agreement, whereas other terms (such as the level of security required, default charges and lack of transparency) were equally likely to cause detriment to consumers; and

    (d) the courts had considered only the position as at the date of the agreement and had refused to take into account such matters as a power to vary the rate of interest from time to time.

Unfair relationships—the new test

25.34 The new s.140A of the Act enables the court to make an order under the new s.140B (see below) if it finds that the relationship between the creditor and the debtor arising out of a credit agreement, or that agreement taken with any related agreement, is unfair to the debtor. Such unfairness can result from one or more of the following factors:

    (a) any of the terms of the agreement or of any related agreement (onerous charges and restrictions on termination rights are obvious examples);

    (b) the way in which the creditor has exercised or enforced any of his rights under the agreement or any related agreement (heavy-handed enforcement comes to mind); and

    (c) any other thing done (or not done) by, or on behalf of, the creditor (either before or after the making of the agreement or any related agreement). The bracketed words highlight an important difference between the new provisions and those which they replace. Sections 137 to 140 were only concerned with "the bargain" and not post-contractual matters.

    In *Carey v HSBC Bank plc*[56] the claimant argued that an unfair relationship resulted from the creditor's failure to comply with s.78. The High Court decided that such a failure did not make the relationship unfair.

    The court can take into account all matters which it considers relevant, including acts done or not done by the creditor's associate or former associate. The debtor's age, financial circumstances, track record and business experience will no doubt be relevant—and so will any misleading statements and high-pressure sales techniques.

Powers of the court

25.35 The new s.140B (inserted by the 2006 Act, s.20) contains a wide range of orders which may:

---

[56] Para.21.14

(a) require the repayment of any sum paid by the debtor or a surety;

(b) require the creditor to do or not to do anything;

(c) reduce or discharge any sum payable;

(d) direct the return to a surety of any property provided as security;

(e) set aside any duty imposed on the debtor or surety;

(f) alter the terms of the agreement; and

(g) direct accounts to be taken.

The OFT and two-tier enforcement—publication of guidance

A debtor seeking to challenge an agreement (and the changes set out above **25.36** are designed to make this easier) can do so by (a) making an application to the county court or (b) raising the matter in enforcement proceedings brought by the creditor or in any other proceedings in which such a challenge is relevant. The OFT has no power to intervene in individual cases, but it has a general power under Pt 8 of the Enterprise Act 2002 to apply for an enforcement order where a trader commits a breach of duty which is harmful to the collective interests of consumers (a further example of this public/private enforcement dichotomy can be found in the Unfair Terms in Consumer Contracts Regulations 1999). The new s.140D of the Act requires the OFT to publish advice and information about the interaction of unfair relationships and Pt 8 of the Enterprise Act 2002. This material is not law, but advisers may find it helpful when considering a possible challenge under the new regime. The OFT has published some guidance notes on the new provisions which can be downloaded from *www.oft.gov.uk*.

Transitional provisions

These can be found in paras 14–16 of Sch.3 and can be summarised as **25.37** follows:

(a) To enable creditors to review their practices and documentation, and to get their house in order, the Schedule creates a "transitional period" starting on April 6, 2007 and running for one year.

(b) Subject to (c) below, the power to make an order under the new s.140B can only be exercised where the debtor (i) brings proceedings after the end of the transitional period or (ii) challenges the agreement in proceedings started after the end of that period.

(c) No such order can be made if the agreement became a "completed agreement" before April 6, 2007 or during the transitional period. An agreement is "completed" if no further payments are due under it.

(d) There are corresponding provisions preserving the operation of ss.137–140 of the Act for agreements which do not continue beyond the end of the transitional period.

(e) Para.16 of Sch.3 specifies transitional provisions for related agreements and security documents.

Summary

25.38 The finance industry has not welcomed with open arms the new, wide (and, they believe, vague and uncertain) provisions. That is not surprising, as it is certain that the courts will be able to intervene much more readily—that is the intention and effect of the changes.

CHAPTER TWENTY-SIX

"I WANT TO SEE MY CREDIT FILE"

At the beginning of Chapter Eighteen we drew attention to the explosion of **26.01** credit business. A credit transaction can, of course, cause problems at both ends. The consumer may overreach himself and may plunge into debt. The creditor may supply goods or services on credit terms and then suffer substantial financial loss if the consumer fails to pay the sums due.[1] To protect himself the creditor will frequently consult a credit reference agency[2] as to the financial standing of the prospective debtor. If the debtor then finds that his application for credit has been rejected, or has been granted on unfavourable terms, he may well suspect that the credit reference agency has passed on unfavourable information. The Act, as originally drafted, contained provisions—which stand apart from the remaining provisions of the Act—giving the debtor a right:

(1) to ask for details of any credit reference agency consulted by the creditor or credit-broker;

(2) to obtain a copy of his file from the agency; and

(3) to have errors corrected.

The limited right to seek information from a credit reference agency (see (2) above) has been replaced by the much wider right of an individual to access personal data under the Data Protection Act 1998 which replaced, with substantial amendments, the Data Protection Act 1984. The 1998 Act (which was passed to give effect to an EC Directive) is not limited to computerised data; it also covers data which is "recorded as part of a relevant filing system"—a term which leaves considerable room for debate.

It is now proposed to conclude this Part of the book by looking briefly at the three matters listed above. It can be said at the outset that a company which keeps its own credit records of customers would not of itself be a credit reference agency; the reason is that the statutory controls only apply where the activities of the credit reference agency are carried on as a business (see s.145(8)).

---

[1] In many cases the creditor will take security from the debtor or from a third party and Pt VIII of the Act contains provisions which regulate security arrangements. The term "security" includes a guarantee.

[2] Such an agency will require a licence under the Act—see s.145(1)(e).

Duty to disclose name and address of agency

26.02 Section 157(1) of the 1974 Act entitles the debtor or hirer to make a written request to the creditor, owner or negotiator asking for the name and address of any credit reference agency to which the creditor, owner or negotiator applied for information as to his financial standing at any time during the antecedent negotiations. The creditor, etc., must then give him notice containing this information within seven working days of receiving the request (see s.157(1) and the Consumer Credit (Credit Reference Agency) Regulations 2000, reg.3).[3] The debtor or hirer must, however, act quickly because the duty to supply him with the information does not arise where his request is received more than 28 days after the end of the antecedent negotiations (whether on the making of the regulated agreement or otherwise).[4]

In practice the consumer will often be dealing with a credit-broker (as for example with a car dealer who arranges to finance the transaction through the creditor). Accordingly any request is likely to come from the consumer to the credit-broker. The regulations seek to ensure that the credit-broker will be able to pass on to the consumer the names of the agency or agencies consulted by the creditor as well as the agencies which he himself consulted. Accordingly, they provide that the creditor must give this information to the credit-broker not later than the date on which he informs him that he is not willing to make a regulated agreement.[5] The credit-broker must then include this information in the s.157 notice which he gives to the debtor or hirer.[6]

A creditor, owner or negotiator who fails to give the notice within the seven-day period commits an offence (see s.157(3)).

Duty on agency to disclose filed information

26.03 We have seen that the information rights of an individual are now to be found in the Data Protection Act 1998. Accordingly, s.158 of the 1974 Act now only applies to a "consumer" which is defined, for this purpose only, as a partnership of two or three persons or other unincorporated association. A consumer who suspects that a credit reference agency has information on him can make a written request for that information ("the file") together with a fee of £2. On receipt of the request and fee and such particulars as the agency may reasonably require to identify the file the agency must within seven working days supply him with a copy of the file together with a statement in the prescribed form[7] informing him of his rights under s.159 (as to which see below). It may well be that the file is not readily intelligible

---

[3] SI 1977/329.
[4] See s.157(2).
[5] Consumer Credit (Conduct of Business) (Credit Reference Agencies) Regulations 1977 (SI 1977/330), reg.2.
[6] ibid. reg.3.
[7] Consumer Credit (Credit Reference Agency) Regulations 2000 (SI 2000/290), reg.4 and Schs1, 2 and 3.

(perhaps because it is computerised). In any such case the consumer's right to a "copy of the file" is a right to a transcript reduced into plain English (see s.158(3)).

It may be, of course, that the agency has no file on the consumer; in that case they must give him notice of that fact but they need not return any fee paid (see s.158(3)).

An agency which contravenes any provision of s.158[8] commits an offence.

Rights of individual to obtain information under the 1998 Act

Under ss.7–9 of the 1998 Act an individual who makes a request in writing **26.04** and pays the appropriate fee has the following rights:

(1) The data controller must inform him or her whether any data relating to him or her is being processed.

(2) The data controller must also give a description of:

    (a) any relevant personal data;
    (b) the purposes for which it is being processed; and
    (c) the recipients or class of recipients to whom it is, or may be, disclosed.

(3) There must be communicated to him or her in intelligible form:

    (a) the information constituting the personal data; and
    (b) any information available to the data controller as to the source of that information.

(4) Where data is processed by automatic means to evaluate matters relating to him or her (e.g. reliability), and where this is the sole basis of any decision significantly affecting him or her (e.g. the grant or refusal of credit), the data controller must inform him or her as to the logic involved in that decision taking.

Where compliance with the request would involve information relating to a third party the controller can refuse to comply with that request unless (a) the third party consents or (b) it is reasonable to comply with that request even without such consent.

Where the data controller is a credit reference agency, s.9 provides that (a) the individual may limit the request to personal data relating to his or her financial standing (and the request is to be treated as limited in this way unless it shows a contrary intention) and (b) where the data controller is processing the data, the information must include a statement as to the rights available under s.159 (see below).

---

[8] See also s.160 which lays down an alternative procedure for "business consumers".

Correction of wrong information under the 1974 Act

26.05 A consumer may realise that the information disclosed under s.158 or the 1998 Act contains an entry which is incorrect—perhaps that he is an undischarged bankrupt or that he has an outstanding unsatisfied judgment against him. If the consumer considers that an entry is incorrect and that he is likely to be prejudiced if it is not corrected, he may give notice to the agency requiring them to remove the offending entry or to amend it (s.159(1)). The agency must then, within 28 days, send the consumer a notice stating that they have (a) removed the entry, (b) amended it, or (c) taken no action (see s.159(2)). In case (b) above the notice must include a copy of the amended entry.

If the notice is given under (b) or (c) above (or is not given at all within the 28-day period) the consumer is given a further right under s.159(3). In any such case he can, within 28 days, serve a further notice on the agency requiring it (a) to add to the file an accompanying notice of correction, not exceeding 200 words, drawn up by himself, and (b) to include a copy of it when furnishing information included in or based on that entry. On receiving this further notice the agency has a choice. It can either (a) comply with it and inform the consumer that it has done so, or (b) apply to the Information Commissioner (formerly the Data Protection Commissioner) on the grounds that "it would be improper for it to publish a notice of correction because it is incorrect, or unjustly defames any person, or is frivolous or scandalous, or is for any other reason unsuitable" (s.159(5)). Conversely, the consumer may apply to the Information Commissioner[9] on the ground that he has not received a correction notice within 28 days of requesting it. The Commissioner, after considering the relevant facts and the documentation,[10] can make such order as he thinks fit.

The consumer may have one further problem; the correction of an erroneous entry may be all very well for the future but what about the past? What can be done to correct damage which he may already have suffered as the result of the erroneous information having been passed on to an enquirer? The Regulations deal with this problem.[11] If the agency agrees to remove or amend an entry, or if it is ordered to do so by the Commissioner, the agency must notify each person to whom it furnished information relevant to the financial standing of the consumer at any time within six months before it received a s.158 request, particulars and fee (see above, para.26.03). This must be done within 10 working days after the notice of removal or compliance or after the expiry of the compliance period specified by the Commissioner under s.159(5) (see above).

Further rights under the 1998 Act

26.06 The s.159 rights summarized above are supplemented by further rights under the 1998 Act. Thus:

---

[9] Form CC 314/77 must be used for such an application.
[10] See SI 2000/290 which sets out the procedure to be followed.
[11] SI 1977/330, reg.5.

(1) Section 10 allows the individual to serve a notice on the data controller requiring him not to process (or to cease processing) any data on the ground that it would cause him unwarranted damage or distress. The controller must then within 21 days give a written notice stating that (a) he has complied or intends to do so or (b) the extent to which he considers the request unjustified.

(2) By s.13 the individual can claim compensation for damage and distress (but not for distress on its own) if he suffers damage flowing from inaccuracy of the data or from unauthorised disclosure—subject in either case to a "reasonable care" defence.

(3) By s.14 the court can order rectification, erasure, destruction and notification to third parties.

CHAPTER TWENTY-SEVEN

THE EUROPEAN UNION DIMENSION

1. INTRODUCTION

In this chapter we shall deal only with the basis for European Union com-   **27.01**
petence in the field of consumer protection. Our discussion of particular
Directives that have already been implemented into United Kingdom law
appears in the relevant chapters elsewhere in the book. Examples can be
found in Chapter Five (Product Liability), Chapter Six (Distance Selling),
Chapter Seven (Sale and Supply of Goods to Consumers), Chapter Nine
(Unfair Terms in Consumer Contracts), Chapter Fifteen (Safety), Chapter
Seventeen (Unfair Commerical Practices) and Chapter Nineteen (APR). This
list highlights the massive inroads which the EU is making into domestic
consumer law.

2. TREATIES

To set the scene, the original EEC Treaty of Rome has been amended con-   **27.02**
siderably over the years, most importantly by the Single European Act of
1987, the Maastricht Treaty on European Union of 1992 and the Treaty of
Amsterdam of 1997.

As a result of the Treaty of Amsterdam, Articles for Treaty provisions were
re-numbered. The new numbering is referred to below but where appropriate
reference is also made to the old number.

Article 2 of the Treaty sets out in very broad terms the objectives of
the Community—to treat the Member States as one single market and to
promote the development of economic activities subject to environmental
considerations:

> The Community shall have as its task, by establishing a common market and
> an economic and monetary union and by implementing common policies . . . to
> promote throughout the Community a harmonious and balanced and sustain-
> able development of economic activities . . .

To achieve such objectives, art.3 sets out various key activities of the
Community. Article 3(h) specifies as one of these activities:

> the approximation of the laws of Member States to the extent required for the
> proper functioning of the Common Market.

A new art.3(t) expressly refers to:

a contribution to the strengthening of consumer protection.

We see in art.3(t) the first direct formal recognition of the importance of consumer protection. Before the Maastricht Treaty amendments, consumer protection initiatives were developed without a specific Treaty basis.

Institutional involvement

27.03　The original European Treaties established supra-national bodies to be involved in the workings of the European Community now referred to as the European Union. The following institutions are the most important ones from the viewpoint of consumer protection.

(i) The Commission

27.04　The Commission's role includes establishing EU wide policies and in that light to develop proposals for consideration by the legislative bodies of the EU. Within the Commission, major subject areas for developing policy and proposals for legislation are allocated to separate units called Directorates-General. There is now a new Council covering employment, social policy, health and consumer affairs, reflecting the increased importance of consumer affairs from the Commission perspective. The Commission consults widely before finalising proposals for legislation to present to the Council.[1]

(ii) The Council (of Ministers)

27.05　The Council is still the main legislative body, despite an increased role for the European Parliament. The Council usually acts on proposals from the Commission.[2] The Council issues Directives, instructions to Member States to legislate to achieve the parameters set out in the Directive. A time limit for achieving the national legislation (either by means of primary or secondary legislation) is set out in the Directive.

Failure to comply fully by the due date may result in the Commission bringing an action against the defaulting Member State under art.226 (formerly Art.169) before the European Court of Justice.

In future, compliance may also be achieved by the further development of *Francovich* damages.[3] Following the *Francovich* case and later case law, a Member State may be obliged to compensate any individual suffering loss as a result of a Member State's failure to implement or to implement correctly a directive by the due date.

---

[1] For a full discussion of the role of the institutions, see Craig & de Burca, *EU Law* (1998), Chs Two and Three.
[2] See n.1, above.
[3] See above, para.9.04 and MacArthur & Wilson, "EU Law: Compensating Consumers" (1996) *Consumer Policy Review*, Vol.6, No.4, pp.145–148.

Treaty basis for Community action—Articles 94 and 308 (formerly Articles 100 and 235)

Articles 94 and 308 of the Treaty on European Union form the basis of   **27.06**
Community action in the area of consumer protection.
Article 94 reads:

> The Council shall, acting unanimously on a proposal from the Commission and after consulting the European Parliament and the Economic and Social Committee, issue directives for the approximation of such laws, regulations or administrative provisions of the Member States as directly affect the establishment or function of the common market.

Article 94 has been the mainstay of the Commission in its Treaty justification for intervention in the consumer protection area. It may seem strange that the Treaty did not contain a specific legal basis for consumer legislation, but it should be remembered that it was drafted at a time when the consumer movement in Europe was in its infancy. An example of art.94 being used by way of justification is the Product Liability Directive mentioned above.

Article 308 can be brought into play where a proposal does not fit within the ambit of art.94. Article 308 reads:

> If action by the Community should prove necessary to attain, in the course of the operation of the common market, one of the objectives of the Community and this Treaty has not provided the necessary powers, the Council shall, acting unanimously on a proposal from the Commission and after consulting the European Parliament, take the appropriate measures.

It can be seen that this wide-ranging provision gives the Council power to take measures to attain an objective where the Treaty does not contain the power elsewhere.[4] Article 308 was approved as an appropriate legal basis by the Heads of State or of Government in 1972 when they gave the green light to the preparation of a consumer protection programme.

Article 94 provides the primary basis for the EC consumer protection   **27.07**
policy, but has the drawback that directives must be adopted unanimously. (For this reason the Product Liability Directive took more than a decade to see the light of day.) A crucial change made by the Single European Act was to permit the adoption of a proposal by a "qualified majority". The amendment appears in art.95 (formerly art.100A).

Under the qualified majority procedure in the Council, the votes of Member States are weighted to reflect in part differences in their populations. This means that use of the qualified majority procedure can lead to the adoption of more controversial directives despite the opposition of one or more Member States. It should be noted that the Council is obliged, under art.95, to consult the European Parliament and the Economic and Social Committee before adopting any proposal. Moreover, art.95 contains

---

[4] See Close, "The Legal Basis for the Consumer Protection Programme of the EEC and Priorities for Action", in Woodroffe (ed.), *Consumer Law in the EEC* (1984), Ch.I, where arts 94 and 308 are discussed as bases for the Programme.

an express reference to consumer protection and aims at "a high level of protection".

The importance of the qualified majority procedure can be gauged from the fact that the Directives on Unfair Terms in Consumer Contracts and on General Product Safety both relied on art.95 as their justification.

Maastricht

27.08   The Treaty of the European Union, signed at Maastricht in the Netherlands on February 7, 1992, inserted for the first time into the Treaty of Rome a separate Title XI, Consumer Protection. This was further amended by the Treaty of Amsterdam and now consists of art.153 (formerly art.129a):

> (1) In order to promote the interests of consumers and to ensure a high level of consumer protection, the Community shall contribute to protecting the health, safety and economic interests of consumers, as well as to promoting their right to information, education and to organise themselves in order to safeguard their interests.
>
> (2) Consumer protection requirements shall be taken into account in defining and implementing other Community policies and activities.

Article 153 also confirms the importance of art.95 in the area of consumer protection.

The Maastricht Treaty raises the status of consumer protection to that of an independent EU policy. In particular, art.153 provides the basis for the development of consumer policies which do not have to be justified on the basis of harmonisation or market integration.

General framework for EU activities in favour of consumers

27.09   In 1999 European consumer policy based on Art.153 was given a guaranteed long-term budget. Four priority areas were singled out as eligible for financial support: consumer health and safety; protection of economic interests of consumers; education and information of consumers; and promotion and representation of their interests.

The five year strategy 2007–2013

27.10   Acting under the powers set out above the Commission has produced a number of programmes and action plans and these have led to much of the legislation listed at the beginning of this chapter.

The future policy of the Commission is set out in a press release of February 27, 2007. We finish on that ambitious note.

> The Competitiveness dimension will be at the heart of the forthcoming consumer policy strategy 2007–2013. The three main objectives of the Strategy will be:
>
> • to **empower** Europe's consumers. This means creating the right market conditions for them to be able to make informed, considered and rational choices and equipping them with the tools to do so.

- to **enhance** the economic and non-economic welfare of Europe's consumers, in terms of price, choice, quality and affordability.
- to protect consumers **effectively**. Market failures for consumers fall into two categories – those that individuals cannot address and those that they should address themselves. It is more efficient for public policy to tackle the former problems.

Consumer Rights Directive

We mentioned at the beginning of this chapter a number of Directives which **27.11** form the basis of much of UK consumer protection legislation. After a review of the so-called "Consumer Acquis" the European Commission decided that, instead of the EU legislation being scattered, it was desirable to consolidate it into a single Directive and brought forward a proposal for a Directive on Consumer Rights (COM (2008) 614/3).

This proposal has not received unanimous support, particularly in the United Kingdom. It is a maximum Directive. One unpopular effect would be that what is perhaps the most valuable right for consumers of the many discussed in this book—the right of rejection for breach of condition when buying goods[5]—may be removed. It is the remedy of which consumers in the high street are more likely to be aware than the "new" rights introduced via Brussels in 2003 such as repair, replacement and rescission.[6]

Another and more fundamental reason for our lukewarm reaction to this latest proposal is a view that the legal structure of consumer protection with all its current complexity—the effects of the new Directives on Consumer Credit[7] and on Unfair Commercial Practices[8] have yet to be fully understood—should be given time to settle down. The question is whether it is desirable constantly to change the rules of consumer protection if the players in the game—consumers and business—cannot keep up with the changes. We close on that plea for stability.

---

[5] Paras 7.29–7.48.
[6] Paras 7.16–7.23
[7] Para.18.13.
[8] Para.17.20.

COUNTY COURT PRECEDENTS

In the Bigtown County Court   Case No.   **A1.01**

BETWEEN:

Robert Lowe   Claimant

and

New Antiques Ltd   Defendants

PARTICULARS OF CLAIM

1. By an oral agreement made between the Claimant and the Defendant on December 1, 2009 the Defendant sold to the Claimant a pair of antique vases for £1,400 and the Claimant paid that sum to the Defendant. Attached to these particulars is a copy of the receipt for purchase.

2. It was an implied condition of the sale that the Defendant had a right to sell the vases.

3. The Defendant was in breach of this implied condition because he had no right to sell. On or about January 3, 2010 the police seized the vases on the ground that they belonged to a Mr Jones and that they were stolen from him by an unknown person who had sold them to the Defendant.

4. The Defendant has refused to refund the £1,400 (or any part of it) to the Claimant.

5. By reason of the matters set out above the Claimant is entitled to the return of £1,400 as money paid for a consideration which has wholly failed.

6. The Claimant is also entitled to interest under section 69 of the County Courts Act 1984 at the rate of 8 per cent per annum from December 1, 2009 until today's date (£56) and further interest at the rate of 0.31p per day until judgment or earlier payment.

And the Claimant claims

(a) £1,400 and interest as set out above.

(b) Costs

[I believe] [the claimant believes] that the facts stated in [this claim form] [these particulars of claim] are true.

In the Bigtown County Court   Case No.   **A1.02**

BETWEEN:

Geoffrey Woodroffe   Claimant

and

Reliable Karsales Ltd   Defendant

PARTICULARS OF CLAIM

1. By an agreement made in writing dated November 1, 2009 the Defendant sold to the Claimant a second-hand Bonecrusher car registration number M123 ABC at a price of £5,000, a copy of the sales receipt being attached to these particulars.

2. During the negotiations for the sale the Claimant was informed by one Lowe, an employee of the Defendant, that the engine was "good as new" and had done only 3,000 miles. This statement was an express term of the contract. Alternatively it was a misrepresentation which induced the Claimant to enter into the contract.

3. It was an implied condition of the contract that the car was of satisfactory quality and reasonably fit for the Claimant's purpose.

4. On or about January 10, 2010 the Claimant took the car to a garage for repair and was then informed that the engine had done 30,000 miles and that it was worn out and that it would cost £1,000 to replace.

5. The Defendant is accordingly in breach of the representation in paragraph 2 above and the express and implied terms under paragraphs 2 and 3 above.

6. The Claimant then wrote to the Defendant rejecting the car by reason of the misrepresentation and/or the breaches of contract and claiming the return of his £5,000 but the Defendant refused and has continued to refuse to accept the rejection.

7. On February 10, 2010 the Claimant hired an alternative Screecher vehicle from Carhire Ltd and has paid a hire charge of £100 per week, a copy of the hire agreement being attached to these particulars.

8. The Claimant has not used the Bonecrusher car since giving notice of rejection and it has at all material times been available for collection by the Defendant.

9. The Claimant is entitled to rescind, and has rescinded, the contract by reason of the misrepresentation by the Defendant. Similarly the Claimant is entitled to treat, and has treated, the contract as discharged by the Defendant's breaches.

10. Alternatively, the Claimant is entitled to damages under section 2(1) of the Misrepresentation Act 1967 and/or under section 53 of the Sale of Goods Act 1979 in the sum of £3,000 (being the amount by which the price of £5,000 and the hire-charges of £2,000 exceed the current value of the car namely £4,000) plus further damages to cover additional hire charges of £100 per week until judgment or earlier payment.

11. Under section 69 of the County Courts Act 1984 the Claimant is also entitled to interest at such rate and for such period as the court thinks just.

And the claimant claims:

1. Under paragraph 9 £5,000;

2. Alternatively, under paragraph 10 damages for misrepresentation and/or for breach of contract;

3. Under paragraph 11 above interest under section 64 of the County Courts Act 1984.

4. Costs

[I believe] [the claimant believes] that the facts stated in [this claim form] [these particulars of claim] are true.

In the Bigtown County Court   Case No. **A1.03**

BETWEEN:

JOHN LOWE   Claimant

(A child, by ROBERT LOWE,
   his litigation friend)

and

TOY IMPORTERS LTD   Defendants

PARTICULARS OF CLAIM

1. On January 4, 2010 Robert Lowe the father and litigation friend of the Claimant bought a catapult for the Claimant (then aged eight) from Rundown Stores Ltd a company now in liquidation.

2. The said Robert Lowe has been informed by the liquidator that Rundown Stores Ltd purchased all their catapults from the Defendants who imported them from Taiwan. Accordingly under section 2(2)(c) of the Consumer Protection Act 1987 the Defendants are liable for damage under the Act.

3. The catapult was defective within section 3 of the 1987 Act and when it was first used by the Claimant it broke and a piece entered his left eye.

PARTICULARS OF DEFECT

The moulded plastic which formed the catapult frame was too weak to withstand normal use by a child.

4. By reason of the defect the Claimant has suffered damage within section 5 of the 1987 Act.

PARTICULARS OF DAMAGE

The Claimant was born on November 1, 2001 and is now aged eight years. He suffered acute pain and suffering and underwent two operations in an unsuccessful attempt to save the sight of his left eye. Full particulars are set out in the medical report served with these Particulars of Claim.

PARTICULARS OF PAST AND FUTURE EXPENSES AND LOSSES

Full particulars are set out in the statement which is served with these Particulars of Claim.

> 5. The Claimant is also entitled to interest under section 69 of the County Courts Act 1984 for such periods and at such rate as the court thinks just.

And the claimant claims:

> 1. Under paragraphs 3 and 4—damages in excess of £15,000;
>
> 2. Under paragraph 5—interest under section 69 of the County Courts Act 1984.
>
> 3. Costs

[I believe] [the claimant believes] that the facts stated in [this claim form] [these particulars of claim] are true.

In the Bigtown County Court   Case No. **A1.04**

BETWEEN:

Robert Lowe   Claimant

and

Ghastly Holidays Ltd (1)   Defendants
Eesipay Ltd (2)

PARTICULARS OF CLAIM

1. By an agreement in writing ("the agreement") dated January 10, 2010 the First Defendant agreed to provide a skiing holiday for the Claimant and his wife and son, a copy of the relevant page in the brochure being attached to these particulars of claim.

2. The Claimant paid the sum of £2,000 for the holiday by means of a credit card issued by the Second Defendant under arrangements made between the First and Second Defendants. The agreement between the Claimant and the Second Defendant was therefore a fixed sum restricted use debtor-creditor-supplier agreement falling within section 75 of the Consumer Credit Act 1974. A copy of the claimant's credit card account showing the payment made by the claimant through the second defendant to the first defendant is attached to these particulars of claim.

3. It was an express term of the contract between the Claimant and the First Defendant that the Claimant and his family would stay at the Ski Palace Hotel which was described in the First Defendant's brochure as a "first class luxury hotel".

4. In breach of the said term the Claimant and his family were unable to stay at the Ski Palace Hotel because it was still in the course of construction. They were compelled to accept accommodation at the Backstreet Mews Hotel which was not a first class luxury hotel.

PARTICULARS

1. There was no bar.
2. There was no lift.
3. The walls were peeling.
4. The Claimant and his family were unable to sleep because of the noise from a nearby discotheque.

5. In consequence of the said breach the Claimant's holiday was ruined and he and his family came home more tired than when the holiday started.

6. The Claimant is entitled to the return of the £2,000 as money paid on a total failure of consideration or alternatively as damages for loss of enjoyment and mental distress.

7. The Claimant is also entitled to interest under Section 69 of the County Courts Act 1984 at such rate and for such period as the court thinks fit.

And the Claimant claims against the First and Second Defendants jointly and severally:

1. Under paragraph 6 £2,000;

2. Under paragraph 7 interest under section 69 of the County Courts Act 1984.

3. Costs

[I believe] [the claimant believes] that the facts stated in [this claim form] [these particulars of claim] are true.

In the Bigtown County Court   Case No. **A1.05**

BETWEEN:

Rosemary Woodroffe   Claimant

and

Furnishings Ltd   Defendant

PARTICULARS OF CLAIMS

1. By a hire-purchase agreement ("the Agreement") in writing made on November 1, 2008 between the Claimant and the Defendant and bearing number 12345, a copy of which is attached to these Particulars, the Defendant supplied to the Claimant a suite of furniture at a hire-purchase price of £1,500. The Claimant signed the Agreement at the Defendant's store.

2. Under the terms of the agreement the Claimant paid a deposit of £300 and she agreed to pay the balance by twelve monthly instalments of £100 on the first day of each month. The agreement was a regulated consumer credit agreement within the Consumer Credit Act 1974 ("the Act").

3. The Claimant paid the first seven instalments and the goods became "protected" goods within section 90 of the Act. The total paid up sum is £1,000.

4. On June 20, 2009 the Claimant was made redundant and she failed to pay the instalment due on July 1, 2009.

5. On or about September 10, 2009 a driver employed by the Defendant knocked at the door of the Claimant's home and when the door was opened by the Claimant's husband the said driver and another man forced their way into the house and removed the suite. In doing so the Defendant was in breach of section 92(1) of the Act.

6. Under the Act the Claimant is entitled to damages for trespass and to the return of all her payments.

7. Under Section 69 of the County Courts Act 1984 the Claimant is also entitled to interest at such rate and of such period as the court thinks just.

And the Claimant claims against the Defendant:

1. Under Paragraph 6 £1,000 and damages for trespass not exceeding £5,000;

2. Under Paragraph 7 interest under section 69 of the County Courts Act 1984.

3. Costs

[I believe] [the claimant believes] that the facts stated in [this claim form] [these particulars of claim] are true.

OFT APPROVED CODES CORE CRITERIA

Introduction

1.1 Following consultation, the core criteria for the OFT's Consumer   **A2.01**
Codes Approval Scheme (CCAS) were published in July 2001.
Before reading the detail of the core criteria guidance it is important to understand some of the general principles relating to the
scheme and to code provisions. This guidance provides pointers,
not rigid rules, to help code sponsors develop their codes to meet
the core criteria. It does not provide advice on sector specific
issues.

Purpose of the CCAS

1.2 Codes will only be approved if we believe they will be effective in
protecting and promoting consumer interests. The CCAS does not
relieve businesses of their legal obligations. Nor should a code be
limited to ensuring adherence to the law – compliance with the law
is taken as read. Code sponsors should develop codes that offer
consumers benefits beyond the protection afforded by law.

Scope of the CCAS

1.3 The CCAS is committed to promoting business to consumer codes
of practice that meet our core criteria and have obtained OFT
approval. Codes that only cover business to business conduct cannot
be considered under the scheme. For the CCAS, a code sponsor is
defined as any body that administers voluntary business to consumer
codes (as opposed to statutory codes) and can influence and raise
standards within its sector. The Enterprise Act 2002 allows us to
consider applications from a wider range of organisations than previously.

Membership requirement

1.4 It is a requirement for the CCAS that all eligible members of a
code sponsor's organisation sign up to the code in order to ensure a
consistency of message to consumers. Consumer could be misled if
not all members are required to adhere to the code and yet can still
advertise their membership of the sponsoring organisation.

Preparing your code

1.5 The aim of the scheme is to put the 'self' back into self-regulation. Responsibility for drafting codes rests with code sponsors who have the necessary expertise in their sectors. We will not usually assist code sponsors in drafting their codes, but in exceptional cases we may do so.

1.6 The core criteria set out what we would expect to see in codes submitted to us for approval and what code sponsors' codes need to be able to demonstrate to get approval. We recognise elements of the core criteria may not be relevant to all sectors. We will always consider an alternative approach to meeting the core criteria if code sponsors put forward an acceptable case why the alternative proposed is more appropriate to their sector.

Presentation

1.7 Code sponsors must ensure the language and content of their codes and any other associated documentation, can be easily read and understood by consumers. Print size must be large enough to be easily read. We recommend that code sponsors seek accreditation from an appropriate body that their code is in plain English. Code sponsors may wish to consider producing two different publications of the code with the notes/guidance/annotation being targeted towards member businesses and consumers respectively.

The core criteria

A2.02   **1. Organisation**

1a Code sponsors should have a significant influence on the sector.

1b Codes shall include a provision that compliance with the code is mandatory. Code sponsors must be able to demonstrate that members are prepared to observe the code's provisions.

1c Code sponsors shall have adequate resources and funding to ensure the objectives of the code are not compromised.

A2.03   **2. Preparation**

2a Code sponsors shall be able to demonstrate that organisations representing consumers, enforcement bodies and advisory services have been adequately consulted throughout the preparation of the code.

2b. Code sponsors shall be able to demonstrate that organisations representing consumers, enforcement bodies and advisory services are being adequately consulted throughout the operation and monitoring of the code.

3. <u>Content</u>   A2.04

3a The code shall include measures directed at the removal or easing of consumer concerns and undesirable trade practices arising within the particular sector.

3b The code shall require that code members ensure that their relevant staff know about and meet the terms of the code as well as their legal responsibilities. Appropriate training is to be provided.

3c The code shall address clear and truthful marketing and advertising as appropriate to the sector.

3d The code shall address clear and accessible pre-contractual information as appropriate to the sector.

3e The code shall address high-pressure selling as appropriate to the sector.

3f The code shall address clear terms and conditions of supply and fair contracts as appropriate to the sector.

3g The code shall address delivery and completion dates as appropriate to the sector.

3h The code shall address cancellation rights as appropriate to the sector.

3i The code shall address guarantees and warranties as appropriate to the sector.

3j The code shall address protection of deposit or prepayments as appropriate to the sector.

3k The code shall address customer service provisions as appropriate to the sector.

3l The code shall address the additional effort/help to be provided to vulnerable consumers as appropriate to the sector.

4. <u>Complaints</u>   A2.05

4a The code shall include a requirement that code members shall have in place speedy, responsive, accessible and user friendly procedures for dealing with consumer complaints. A specific reasonable time limit for responding to complaints shall be prescribed.

4b The code shall include a requirement that code members will offer the same level of co-operation with local consumer advisers or any other intermediary acting on behalf of a consumer when making a complaint as they would to the complainant.

4c The code shall include procedures for dealing with complaints including the availability of conciliation services directed at arranging a decision acceptable to both parties.

4d The code shall include the availability of a low cost, speedy, responsive, accessible and user-friendly independent redress scheme to act as an alternative to seeking court action in the first instance.

The scheme shall be binding in respect of code members who shall not be able to refuse to allow a complaint to go before the scheme if a customer so chooses.

The code member shall be bound to accept a decision made under the scheme. Any such scheme shall be able to take into account possible breaches of the code where relevant to the complaint.

A2.06 5. Monitoring

5a The code sponsor shall develop performance indicators, e.g. mystery shopping exercises and independent compliance audits, to measure the effectiveness of the code.

5b The code sponsor shall implement the performance indicators and make available the results of their monitoring procedures and satisfaction surveys to demonstrate the effectiveness of the code.

5c The code sponsor shall provide a written report annually to the OFT on the operation of the code to include:

- changes to the code agreed with the OFT and implemented
- numbers and types of complaints including information on outcomes from the conciliation process and the independent redress scheme
- results from monitoring, satisfaction surveys and the disciplinary process.

It would be preferable if the report were compiled by an independent person or body with powers to recommend actions

5d The code sponsor shall provide copies of the annual reports to the OFT.

5e The code sponsor shall regularly review the code and update its provisions in the light of changing circumstances and expectations.

5f Consumer satisfaction shall be regularly assessed.

A2.07 6. Enforcement

6a Code sponsors shall establish a procedure for handling non-compliance by members with the code. The procedure shall include independent disciplinary procedures and reasonable timescales for action.

6b The code sponsor shall also set out a range of sanctions, e.g. warning letters, fines, termination of membership, for dealing with non-compliance.

7. Publicity

7a   Code sponsors and members shall ensure that their customers are   **A2.08**
     aware of the code.

7b   Code members are to make clear, e.g. in advertising, point of sale,
     their adherence to a code of practice.

7c   Copies of codes shall be available without charge to customers, to
     members, to local consumer advisors and to others with a legitimate
     interest.

7d   Copies of any code related publicity generated by the code sponsor
     shall be provided to the OFT in advance of publication.

7e   Code sponsors and members shall publicise the fact that the OFT
     has approved the code by using the CCAS logo in the prescribed
     manner.

7f   Code sponsors shall comply with the terms of the standard copyright
     licence, disseminate the terms to their members and monitor their
     members use of the CCAS logo. Appropriate action shall be taken
     by the code sponsor against a member for non-compliance with the
     copyright licence.

From publication OFT390, updated March 2008.

CONSUMER CREDIT DIRECTIVE 2008/48/EC

DIRECTIVES

Directive 2008/48/EC Of the European Parliament and of the Council of 23 April 2008

on credit agreements for consumers and repealing Council Directive 87/102/ EEC

NOTE

The Preamble and Annexes are not reproduced.

CHAPTER I

SUBJECT MATTER, SCOPE AND DEFINITIONS

Article 1

Subject matter

The purpose of this Directive is to harmonise certain aspects of the laws, regulations and administrative provisions of the Member States concerning agreements covering credit for consumers.

Article 2

Scope

1. This Directive shall apply to credit agreements.

2. This Directive shall not apply to the following:

(a)   credit agreements which are secured either by a mortgage or by another comparable security commonly used in a Member State on immovable property or secured by a right related to immovable property;

(b)   credit agreements the purpose of which is to acquire or retain property rights in land or in an existing or projected building;

(c)   credit agreements involving a total amount of credit less than EUR 200 or more than EUR 75000;

(d)   hiring or leasing agreements where an obligation to purchase the object of the agreement is not laid down either by the agreement itself or by any separate agreement; such an obligation shall be deemed to exist if it is so decided unilaterally by the creditor;

(e) credit agreements in the form of an overdraft facility and where the credit has to be repaid within one month;

(f) credit agreements where the credit is granted free of interest and without any other charges and credit agreements under the terms of which the credit has to be repaid within three months and only insignificant charges are payable;

(g) credit agreements where the credit is granted by an employer to his employees as a secondary activity free of interest or at annual percentage rates of charge lower than those prevailing on the market and which are not offered to the public generally;

(h) credit agreements which are concluded with investment firms as defined in Article 4(1) of Directive 2004/39/EC of the European Parliament and of the Council of 21 April 2004 on markets in financial instruments[1] or with credit institutions as defined in Article 4 of Directive 2006/48/EC for the purposes of allowing an investor to carry out a transaction relating to one or more of the instruments listed in Section C of Annex I to Directive 2004/39/EC, where the investment firm or credit institution granting the credit is involved in such transaction;

(i) credit agreements which are the outcome of a settlement reached in court or before another statutory authority;

(j) credit agreements which relate to the deferred payment, free of charge, of an existing debt;

(k) credit agreements upon the conclusion of which the consumer is requested to deposit an item as security in the creditor's safe-keeping and where the liability of the consumer is strictly limited to that pledged item;

(l) credit agreements which relate to loans granted to a restricted public under a statutory provision with a general interest purpose, and at lower interest rates than those prevailing on the market or free of interest or on other terms which are more favourable to the consumer than those prevailing on the market and at interest rates not higher than those prevailing on the market.

3. In the case of credit agreements in the form of an overdraft facility and where the credit has to be repaid on demand or within three months, only Articles 1 to 3, Article 4(1), Article 4(2)(a) to (c), Article 4(4), Articles 6 to 9, Article 10(1), Article 10(4), Article 10(5), Articles 12, 15, 17 and Articles 19 to 32 shall apply.

4. In the case of credit agreements in the form of overrunning, only Articles 1 to 3, 18, 20 and 22 to 32 shall apply.

[1] OJ L 145, 30.4.2004, p. 1. Directive as last amended by Directive 2008/10/EC (OJ L 76, 19.3.2008, p. 33).

5. Member States may determine that only Articles 1 to 4, 6, 7 and 9, Article 10(1), points (a) to (h) and (l) of Article 10(2), Article 10(4) and Articles 11, 13 and 16 to 32 shall apply to credit agreements which are concluded by an organisation which:

(a)   is established for the mutual benefit of its members;

(b)   does not make profits for any other person than its members;

(c)   fulfils a social purpose required by domestic legislation;

(d)   receives and manages the savings of, and provides sources of credit to, its members only; and

(e)   provides credit on the basis of an annual percentage rate of charge which is lower than that prevailing on the market or subject to a ceiling laid down by national law,

and whose membership is restricted to persons residing or employed in a particular location or employees and retired employees of a particular employer, or to persons meeting other qualifications laid down under national law as the basis for the existence of a common bond between the members.

Member States may exempt from the application of this Directive credit agreements concluded by such an organisation where the total value of all existing credit agreements entered into by the organisation is insignificant in relation to the total value of all existing credit agreements in the Member State in which the organisation is based and the total value of all existing credit agreements entered into by all such organisations in the Member State is less than 1 % of the total value of all existing credit agreements entered into in that Member State.

Member States shall each year review whether the conditions for the application of any such exemption continue to exist and shall take action to withdraw the exemption where they consider that the conditions are no longer met.

6. Member States may determine that only Articles 1 to 4, 6, 7, 9, Article 10(1), points (a) to (i), (l) and (r) of Article 10(2), Article 10(4), Articles 11, 13, 16 and Articles 18 to 32 shall apply to credit agreements which provide for arrangements to be agreed by the creditor and the consumer in respect of deferred payment or repayment methods, where the consumer is already in default on the initial credit agreement and where:

(a)   such arrangements would be likely to avert the possibility of legal proceedings concerning such default; and

(b)   the consumer would not thereby be subject to terms less favourable than those laid down in the initial credit agreement.

However, if the credit agreement falls within the scope of paragraph 3, only the provisions of that paragraph shall apply.

Article 3

Definitions

For the purposes of this Directive, the following definitions shall apply:

(a) "consumer" means a natural person who, in transactions covered by this Directive, is acting for purposes which are outside his trade, business or profession;

(b) "creditor" means a natural or legal person who grants or promises to grant credit in the course of his trade, business or profession;

(c) "credit agreement" means an agreement whereby a creditor grants or promises to grant to a consumer credit in the form of a deferred payment, loan or other similar financial accommodation, except for agreements for the provision on a continuing basis of services or for the supply of goods of the same kind, where the consumer pays for such services or goods for the duration of their provision by means of instalments;

(d) "overdraft facility" means an explicit credit agreement whereby a creditor makes available to a consumer funds which exceed the current balance in the consumer's current account;

(e) "overrunning" means a tacitly accepted overdraft whereby a creditor makes available to a consumer funds which exceed the current balance in the consumer's current account or the agreed overdraft facility;

(f) "credit intermediary" means a natural or legal person who is not acting as a creditor and who, in the course of his trade, business or profession, for a fee, which may take a pecuniary form or any other agreed form of financial consideration:

(i) presents or offers credit agreements to consumers;

(ii) assists consumers by undertaking preparatory work in respect of credit agreements other than as referred to in (i); or

(iii) concludes credit agreements with consumers on behalf of the creditor;

(g) "total cost of the credit to the consumer" means all the costs, including interest, commissions, taxes and any other kind of fees which the consumer is required to pay in connection with the credit agreement and which are known to the creditor, except for notarial costs; costs in respect of ancillary services relating to the credit agreement, in particular insurance premiums, are also included if, in addition, the conclusion of a service contract is compulsory in order to obtain the credit or to obtain it on the terms and conditions marketed;

(h) "total amount payable by the consumer" means the sum of the total amount of the credit and the total cost of the credit to the consumer;

(i) "annual percentage rate of charge" means the total cost of the credit to the consumer, expressed as an annual percentage of the total amount of credit, where applicable including the costs referred to in Article 19(2);

(j) "borrowing rate" means the interest rate expressed as a fixed or variable percentage applied on an annual basis to the amount of credit drawn down;

(k) "fixed borrowing rate" means that the creditor and the consumer agree in the credit agreement on one borrowing rate for the entire duration of the credit agreement or on several borrowing rates for partial periods using exclusively a fixed specific percentage. If not all borrowing rates are determined in the credit agreement, the borrowing rate shall be deemed to be fixed only for the partial periods for which the borrowing rates are determined exclusively by a fixed specific percentage agreed on the conclusion of the credit agreement;

(l) "total amount of credit" means the ceiling or the total sums made available under a credit agreement;

(m) "durable medium" means any instrument which enables the consumer to store information addressed personally to him in a way accessible for future reference for a period of time adequate for the purposes of the information and which allows the unchanged reproduction of the information stored;

(n) "linked credit agreement" means a credit agreement where

(i) the credit in question serves exclusively to finance an agreement for the supply of specific goods or the provision of a specific service, and

(ii) those two agreements form, from an objective point of view, a commercial unit; a commercial unit shall be deemed to exist where the supplier or service provider himself finances the credit for the consumer or, if it is financed by a third party, where the creditor uses the services of the supplier or service provider in connection with the conclusion or preparation of the credit agreement, or where the specific goods or the provision of a specific service are explicitly specified in the credit agreement.

CHAPTER II

INFORMATION AND PRACTICES PRELIMINARY TO THE CONCLUSION OF THE CREDIT AGREEMENT

Article 4

Standard information to be included in advertising

1. Any advertising concerning credit agreements which indicates an interest rate or any figures relating to the cost of the credit to the consumer shall include standard information in accordance with this Article.

This obligation shall not apply where national legislation requires the indication of the annual percentage rate of charge in advertising concerning credit agreements which does not indicate an interest rate or any figures relating to any cost of credit to the consumer within the meaning of the first subparagraph.

2. The standard information shall specify in a clear, concise and prominent way by means of a representative example:

(a) the borrowing rate, fixed or variable or both, together with particulars of any charges included in the total cost of the credit to the consumer;

(b) the total amount of credit;

(c) the annual percentage rate of charge; in the case of a credit agreement of the kind referred to in Article 2(3), Member States may decide that the annual percentage rate of charge need not be provided;

(d) if applicable, the duration of the credit agreement;

(e) in the case of a credit in the form of deferred payment for a specific good or service, the cash price and the amount of any advance payment; and

(f) if applicable, the total amount payable by the consumer and the amount of the instalments.

3. Where the conclusion of a contract regarding an ancillary service relating to the credit agreement, in particular insurance, is compulsory in order to obtain the credit or to obtain it on the terms and conditions marketed, and the cost of that service cannot be determined in advance, the obligation to enter into that contract shall also be stated in a clear, concise and prominent way, together with the annual percentage rate of charge.

4. This Article shall be without prejudice to Directive 2005/29/EC.

Article 5

Pre-contractual information

1. In good time before the consumer is bound by any credit agreement or offer, the creditor and, where applicable, the credit intermediary shall, on the basis of the credit terms and conditions offered by the creditor and, if applicable, the preferences expressed and information supplied by the consumer, provide the consumer with the infor-

mation needed to compare different offers in order to take an informed decision on whether to conclude a credit agreement. Such information, on paper or on another durable medium, shall be provided by means of the Standard European Consumer Credit Information form set out in Annex II. The creditor shall be deemed to have fulfilled the information requirements in this paragraph and in Article 3, paragraphs (1) and (2) of Directive 2002/65/EC if he has supplied the Standard European Consumer Credit Information.

The information in question shall specify:

(a) the type of credit;

(b) the identity and the geographical address of the creditor as well as, if applicable, the identity and geographical address of the credit intermediary involved;

(c) the total amount of credit and the conditions governing the drawdown;

(d) the duration of the credit agreement;

(e) in the case of a credit in the form of deferred payment for a specific good or service and linked credit agreements, that good or service and its cash price;

(f) the borrowing rate, the conditions governing the application of the borrowing rate and, where available, any index or reference rate applicable to

the initial borrowing rate, as well as the periods, conditions and procedure for changing the borrowing rate; if different borrowing rates apply in different circumstances, the abovementioned information on all the applicable rates;

(g) the annual percentage rate of charge and the total amount payable by the consumer, illustrated by means of a representative example mentioning all the assumptions used in order to calculate that rate; where the consumer has informed the creditor of one or more components of his preferred credit, such as the duration of the credit agreement and the total amount of credit, the creditor shall take those components into account; if a credit agreement provides different ways of drawdown with different charges or borrowing rates and the creditor uses the assumption set out in point (b) of Part II of Annex I, he shall indicate that other drawdown mechanisms for this type of credit agreement may result in higher annual percentage rates of charge;

(h) the amount, number and frequency of payments to be made by the consumer and, where appropriate, the order in which payments will be allocated to different outstanding balances charged at different borrowing rates for the purposes of reimbursement;

(i) where applicable, the charges for maintaining one or several accounts recording both payment transactions and drawdowns, unless the opening of an account is optional, together with the charges for using a means of payment for both payment transactions and drawdowns, any other charges deriving from the credit agreement and the conditions under which those charges may be changed;

(j) where applicable, the existence of costs payable by the consumer to a notary on conclusion of the credit agreement;

(k) the obligation, if any, to enter into an ancillary service contract relating to the credit agreement, in particular an insurance policy, where the conclusion of such a contract is compulsory in order to obtain the credit or to obtain it on the terms and conditions marketed;

(l) the interest rate applicable in the case of late payments and the arrangements for its adjustment, and, where applicable, any charges payable for default;

(m) a warning regarding the consequences of missing payments;

(n) where applicable, the sureties required;

(o) the existence or absence of a right of withdrawal;

(p) the right of early repayment, and, where applicable, information concerning the creditor's right to compensation and the way in which that compensation will be determined in accordance with Article 16;

(q) the consumer's right to be informed immediately and free of charge, pursuant to Article 9(2), of the result of a database consultation carried out for the purposes of assessing his creditworthiness;

(r) the consumer's right to be supplied, on request and free of charge, with a copy of the draft credit agreement. This provision shall not apply if the creditor is at the time of the request unwilling to proceed to the conclusion of the credit agreement with the consumer; and

(s) if applicable, the period of time during which the creditor is bound by the pre-contractual information.

Any additional information which the creditor may provide to the consumer shall be given in a separate document which may be annexed to the Standard European Consumer Credit Information form.

2. However, in the case of voice telephony communications, as referred to in Article 3(3) of Directive 2002/65/EC, the description of the main characteristics of the financial service to be provided pursuant to the second indent of Article 3(3)(b) of that Directive shall include at least the items referred to in points (c), (d), (e), (f) and (h) of paragraph (1) of this Article, together with the annual

percentage rate of charge illustrated by means of a representative example and the total amount payable by the consumer.

3. If the agreement has been concluded at the consumer's request using a means of distance communication which does not enable the information to be provided in accordance with paragraph 1, in particular in the case referred to in paragraph 2, the creditor shall provide the consumer with the full pre-contractual information using the Standard European Consumer Credit Information form immediately after the conclusion of the credit agreement.

4. Upon request, the consumer shall, in addition to receiving the Standard European Consumer Credit Information, be supplied free of charge with a copy of the draft credit agreement. This provision shall not apply if the creditor is at the time of the request unwilling to proceed to the conclusion of the credit agreement with the consumer.

5. In the case of a credit agreement under which payments made by the consumer do not give rise to an immediate corresponding amortisation of the total amount of credit, but are used to constitute capital during periods and under conditions laid down in the credit agreement or in an ancillary agreement, the pre-contractual information required under paragraph 1 shall include a clear and concise statement that such credit agreements do not provide for a guarantee of repayment of the total amount of credit drawn down under the credit agreement, unless such a guarantee is given.

6. Member States shall ensure that creditors and, where applicable, credit intermediaries provide adequate explanations to the consumer, in order to place the consumer in a position enabling him to assess whether the proposed credit agreement is adapted to his needs and to his financial situation, where appropriate by explaining the pre-contractual information to be provided in accordance with paragraph 1, the essential characteristics of the products proposed and the specific effects they may have on the consumer, including the consequences of default in payment by the consumer. Member States may adapt the manner by which and the extent to which such assistance is given, as well as by whom it is given, to the particular circumstances of the situation in which the credit agreement is offered, the person to whom it is offered and the type of credit offered.

Article 6

Pre-contractual information requirements for certain credit agreements in the form of an overdraft facility and for certain specific credit agreements

1. In good time before the consumer becomes bound by any credit agreement or offer concerning a credit agreement as referred to in Article 2(3), (5) or (6), the creditor and, where applicable, the credit intermediary shall, on the basis of the credit terms and conditions offered by the creditor and, if applicable, the preferences expressed and information supplied by the consumer, provide the consumer with the information needed to compare different offers

in order to take an informed decision on whether to conclude a credit agreement.

The information in question shall specify:

(a) the type of credit;

(b) the identity and geographical address of the creditor as well as, if applicable, the identity and geographical address of the credit intermediary involved;

(c) the total amount of credit;

(d) the duration of the credit agreement;

(e) the borrowing rate; the conditions governing the application of that rate, any index or reference rate applicable to the initial borrowing rate, the charges applicable from the time the credit agreement is concluded, and, where applicable, the conditions under which those charges may be changed;

(f) the annual percentage rate of charge, illustrated by means of representative examples mentioning all the assumptions used in order to calculate that rate;

(g) the conditions and procedure for terminating the credit agreement;

(h) in the case of credit agreements as referred to in Article 2(3), where applicable, an indication that the consumer may be requested to repay the amount of credit in full at any time;

(i) the interest rate applicable in the case of late payments and the arrangements for its adjustment, and, where applicable, any charges payable for default;

(j) the consumer's right to be informed immediately and free of charge, pursuant to Article 9(2), of the result of a database consultation carried out for the purposes of assessing his creditworthiness;

(k) in the case of credit agreements as referred to in Article 2(3), information about the charges applicable from the time such agreements are concluded and, if applicable, the conditions under which those charges may be changed;

(l) if applicable, the period of time during which the creditor is bound by the pre-contractual information.

Such information shall be provided on paper or on another durable medium and all information shall be equally prominent. It may be provided by means of the European Consumer Credit Information form set out in Annex III. The creditor shall be deemed to have fulfilled the information requirements in this paragraph and in Article 3(1) and (2) of Directive 2002/65/EC if he has supplied the European Consumer Credit Information.

2.   In the case of a credit agreement of the kind referred to in Article 2(3), Member States may decide that the annual percentage rate of charge need not be provided.

3.   In the case of a credit agreement as referred to in Article 2(5) and (6), the information provided to the consumer in accordance with paragraph 1 of this Article shall also include:

(a)   the amount, number and frequency of payments to be made by the consumer and, where appropriate, the order in which payments will be allocated to different outstanding balances charged at different borrowing rates for the purposes of reimbursement; and

(b)   the right of early repayment, and, where applicable, information concerning the creditor's right to compensation and the way in which that compensation will be determined.

However, if the credit agreement falls within the scope of Article 2(3), only the provisions of paragraph 1 of this Article shall apply.

4.   However, in the case of voice telephony communications and where the consumer requests that the overdraft facility be made available with immediate effect, the description of the main characteristics of the financial service shall include at least the items referred to in points (c), (e), (f) and (h) of paragraph 1. In addition, in credit agreements of the kind referred to in paragraph 3, the description of the main characteristics shall include a specification of the duration of the credit agreement.

5.   Notwithstanding the exclusion provided for in Article 2(2)(e), the Member States shall apply at least the requirements of the first sentence of paragraph 4 of this Article to credit agreements in the form of an overdraft facility and where the credit has to be repaid within one month.

6.   Upon request, the consumer shall, in addition to receiving the information referred to in paragraphs 1 to 4, be supplied free of charge with a copy of the draft credit agreement containing the contractual information provided for by Article 10 insofar as that Article is applicable. This provision shall not apply if the creditor is at the time of the request unwilling to proceed to the conclusion of the credit agreement with the consumer.

7.   If the agreement has been concluded at the consumer's request using a means of distance communication which does not enable the information to be provided in accordance with paragraphs 1 and 3, including in the cases referred to in paragraph 4, the creditor shall immediately after the conclusion of the credit agreement fulfil his obligations under paragraphs 1 and 3 by providing the contractual information pursuant to Article 10 insofar as that Article is applicable.

Article 7

Exemptions from the pre-contractual information requirements

Articles 5 and 6 shall not apply to suppliers of goods or services acting as credit intermediaries in an ancillary capacity. This is without prejudice to the creditor's obligation to ensure that the consumer receives the pre-contractual information referred to in those Articles.

Article 8

Obligation to assess the creditworthiness of the consumer

1.   Member States shall ensure that, before the conclusion of the credit agreement, the creditor assesses the consumer's creditworthiness on the basis of sufficient information, where appropriate obtained from the consumer and, where necessary, on the basis of a consultation of the relevant database. Member States whose legislation requires creditors to assess the creditworthiness of consumers on the basis of a consultation of the relevant database may retain this requirement.

2.   Member States shall ensure that, if the parties agree to change the total amount of credit after the conclusion of the credit agreement, the creditor updates the financial information at his disposal concerning the consumer and assesses the consumer's creditworthiness before any significant increase in the total amount of credit.

CHAPTER III

DATABASE ACCESS

Article 9

Database access

1.   Each Member State shall in the case of cross-border credit ensure access for creditors from other Member States to databases used in that Member State for assessing the creditworthiness of consumers. The conditions for access shall be non-discriminatory.

2.   If the credit application is rejected on the basis of consultation of a database, the creditor shall inform the consumer immediately and without charge of the result of such consultation and of the particulars of the database consulted.

3.   The information shall be provided unless the provision of such information is prohibited by other Community legislation or is contrary to objectives of public policy or public security.

4.   This Article shall be without prejudice to the application of Directive 95/46/EC of the European Parliament and of the Council of 24 October 1995 on the protection of individuals with regard to the processing of personal data and on the free movement of such data [1].

CHAPTER IV

INFORMATION AND RIGHTS CONCERNING CREDIT AGREEMENTS

Article 10

Information to be included in credit agreements

1.   Credit agreements shall be drawn up on paper or on another durable medium.

---

[1] OJ L 281, 23.11.1995, p. 31. Directive as amended by Regulation (EC) No 1882/2003 (OJ L 284, 31.10.2003, p. 1).

All the contracting parties shall receive a copy of the credit agreement. This Article shall be without prejudice to any national rules regarding the validity of the conclusion of credit agreements which are in conformity with Community law.

2. The credit agreement shall specify in a clear and concise manner:

(a) the type of credit;

(b) the identities and geographical addresses of the contracting parties as well as, if applicable, the identity and geographical address of the credit intermediary involved;

(c) the duration of the credit agreement;

(d) the total amount of credit and the conditions governing the drawdown;

(e) in case of a credit in the form of deferred payment for a specific good or service or in the case of linked credit agreements, that good or service and its cash price;

(f) the borrowing rate, the conditions governing the application of that rate and, where available, any index or reference rate applicable to the initial borrowing rate, as well as the periods, conditions and procedures for changing the borrowing rate and, if different borrowing rates apply in different circumstances, the abovementioned information in respect of all the applicable rates;

(g) the annual percentage rate of charge and the total amount payable by the consumer, calculated at the time the credit agreement is concluded; all the assumptions used in order to calculate that rate shall be mentioned;

(h) the amount, number and frequency of payments to be made by the consumer and, where appropriate, the order in which payments will be allocated to different outstanding balances charged at different borrowing rates for the purposes of reimbursement;

(i) where capital amortisation of a credit agreement with a fixed duration is involved, the right of the consumer to receive, on request and free of charge, at any time throughout the duration of the credit agreement, a statement of account in the form of an amortisation table.

The amortisation table shall indicate the payments owing and the periods and conditions relating to the payment of such amounts; the table shall contain a breakdown of each repayment showing capital amortisation, the interest calculated on the basis of the borrowing rate and, where applicable, any additional costs; where the interest rate is not fixed or the additional costs may be changed under the credit agreement, the amortisation table shall indicate, clearly and concisely, that the data contained in the table will remain valid only until such time as the borrowing rate or the additional costs are changed in accordance with the credit agreement;

(j)   if charges and interest are to be paid without capital amortisation, a statement showing the periods and conditions for the payment of the interest and of any associated recurrent and non-recurrent charges;

(k)   where applicable, the charges for maintaining one or several accounts recording both payment transactions and drawdowns, unless the opening of an account is optional, together with the charges for using a means of payment for both payment transactions and drawdowns, and any other charges deriving from the credit agreement and the conditions under which those charges may be changed;

(l)   the interest rate applicable in the case of late payments as applicable at the time of the conclusion of the credit agreement and the arrangements for its adjustment and, where applicable, any charges payable for default;

(m)   a warning regarding the consequences of missing payments;

(n)   where applicable, a statement, that notarial fees will be payable;

(o)   the sureties and insurance required, if any;

(p)   the existence or absence of a right of withdrawal, the period during which that right may be exercised and other conditions governing the exercise thereof, including information concerning the obligation of the consumer to pay the capital drawn down and the interest in accordance with Article 14(3)(b) and the amount of interest payable per day;

(q)   information concerning the rights resulting from Article 15 as well as the conditions for the exercise of those rights;

(r)   the right of early repayment, the procedure for early repayment, as well as, where applicable, information concerning the creditor's right to compensation and the way in which that compensation will be determined;

(s)   the procedure to be followed in exercising the right of termination of the credit agreement;

(t)   whether or not there is an out-of-court complaint and redress mechanism for the consumer and, if so, the methods for having access to it;

(u)   where applicable, other contractual terms and conditions;

(v)   where applicable, the name and address of the competent supervisory authority.

3. Where paragraph 2(i) applies, the creditor shall make available to

the consumer, free of charge and at any time throughout the duration of the credit agreement, a statement of account in the form of an amortisation table.

4. In the case of a credit agreement under which payments made by the consumer do not give rise to an immediate corresponding amortisation of the total amount of credit, but are used to constitute capital during periods and under conditions laid down in the credit agreement or in an ancillary agreement, the information required under paragraph 2 shall include a clear and concise statement that such credit agreements do not provide for a guarantee of repayment of the total amount of credit drawn down under the credit agreement, unless such a guarantee is given.

5. In the case of credit agreements in the form of overdraft facilities as referred to in Article 2(3), the following shall be specified in a clear and concise manner:

(a)   the type of credit;

(b)   the identities and geographical addresses of the contracting parties as well as, if applicable, the identity and geographical address of the credit intermediary involved;

(c)   the duration of the credit agreement;

(d)   the total amount of the credit and the conditions governing the drawdown;

(e)   the borrowing rate, the conditions governing the applica-

tion of the borrowing rate and, where available, any index or reference rate applicable to the initial borrowing rate, as well as the periods, conditions and procedure for changing the borrowing rate and, if different borrowing rates apply in different circumstances, the abovementioned information in respect of all the applicable rates;

(f)   the annual percentage rate of charge and the total cost of the credit to the consumer, calculated at the time the credit agreement is concluded; all the assumptions used in order to calculate that rate as referred to in Article 19(2) in conjunction with Article 3(g) and (i) shall be mentioned; Member States may decide that the annual percentage rate of charge need not be provided;

(g)   an indication that the consumer may be requested to repay the amount of credit in full on demand at any time;

(h)   conditions governing the exercise of the right of withdrawal from the credit agreement; and

(i)   information concerning the charges applicable from the time such agreements are concluded and, if applicable, the conditions under which those charges may be changed.

Article 11

Information concerning the borrowing rate

1. Where applicable, the consumer shall be informed of any change in the borrowing rate, on paper or another durable medium, before the change enters into force. The information shall state the amount of the payments to be made after the entry into force of the new borrowing rate and, if the number or frequency of the payments changes, particulars thereof.

2. However, the parties may agree in the credit agreement that the information referred to in paragraph 1 is to be given to the consumer periodically in cases where the change in the borrowing rate is caused by a change in a reference rate, the new reference rate is made publicly available by appropriate means and the information concerning the new reference rate is also kept available in the premises of the creditor.

Article 12

Obligations in connection with credit agreement in the form of an overdraft facility

1. Where a credit agreement covers credit in the form of an overdraft facility, the consumer shall be kept regularly informed by means of a statement of account, on paper or on another durable medium, containing the following particulars:

(a) the precise period to which the statement of account relates;

(b) the amounts and dates of drawdowns;

(c) the balance from the previous statement, and the date thereof;

(d) the new balance;

(e) the dates and amounts of payments made by the consumer;

(f) the borrowing rate applied;

(g) any charges that have been applied;

(h) where applicable, the minimum amount to be paid.

2. In addition, the consumer shall be informed on paper or another durable medium of increases in the borrowing rate, or in any charges payable, before the change in question enters into force.

However, the parties may agree in the credit agreement that information concerning changes in the borrowing rate is to be given in the manner provided for in paragraph 1 in cases where the change in the borrowing rate is caused by a change in a reference rate, the new reference rate is made publicly available by appropriate means and the information concerning the new reference rate is also kept available in the premises of the creditor.

Article 13

Open-end credit agreements

1. The consumer may effect standard termination of an open-end credit agreement free of charge at any time unless the parties have agreed on a period of notice. Such a period may not exceed one month.

If agreed in the credit agreement, the creditor may effect standard termination of an open-end credit agreement by giving the consumer at least two months' notice drawn up on paper or on another durable medium.

2. If agreed in the credit agreement, the creditor may, for objectively justified reasons, terminate the consumer's right to draw down on an open-end credit agreement. The creditor shall inform the consumer of the termination and the reasons for it on paper or on another durable medium, where possible before the termination and at the latest immediately thereafter, unless the provision of such information is prohibited by other Community legislation or is contrary to objectives of public policy or public security.

Article 14

Right of withdrawal

1. The consumer shall have a period of 14 calendar days in which to withdraw from the credit agreement without giving any reason.

That period of withdrawal shall begin

(a) either from the day of the conclusion of the credit agreement, or

(b) from the day on which the consumer receives the contractual terms and conditions and information in accordance with Article 10, if that day is later than the date referred to in point (a) of this subparagraph.

2. Where in the case of a linked credit agreement, as defined in Article 3(n), national legislation at the time of the entry into force of this Directive already provides that funds cannot be made available to the consumer before the expiry of a specific period, Member States may exceptionally provide that the period referred to in paragraph 1 of this Article may be reduced to this specific period at the explicit request of the consumer.

3. If the consumer exercises his right of withdrawal, he shall:

(a) in order to give effect to the withdrawal before the expiry of the deadline referred to in paragraph 1, notify this to the creditor in line with the information given by the creditor pursuant to Article 10(2)(p) by means which can be proven in accordance with national law. The deadline shall be deemed to have been met if that notification, if it is on paper or on another durable medium that is available and accessible to the creditor, is dispatched before the deadline expires; and

(b) pay to the creditor the capital and the interest accrued thereon from the date the credit was drawn down until the date the capital is repaid, without any undue delay and no later than 30 calendar days after the despatch by him to the creditor of notification of the withdrawal. The interest shall be calculated on the basis of the agreed borrowing rate.

The creditor shall not be entitled to any other compensation from the consumer in the event of withdrawal, except compensation for any non-returnable charges paid by the creditor to any public administrative body.

4. If an ancillary service relating to the credit agreement is provided by the creditor or by a third party on the basis of an agreement between the third party and the creditor, the consumer shall no longer be bound by the ancillary service contract if the consumer exercises his right of withdrawal from the credit agreement in accordance with this Article.

5. If the consumer has a right of withdrawal under paragraphs 1, 3 and 4, Articles 6 and 7 of Directive 2002/65/EC and Article 5 of Council Directive 85/577/EEC of 20 December 1985 to protect the consumer in respect of contracts negotiated away from business premises[1] shall not apply.

6. Member States may provide that paragraphs 1 to 4 of this Article shall not apply to credit agreements which by law are required to be concluded through the services of a notary, provided that the notary confirms that the consumer is guaranteed the rights provided for under Articles 5 and 10.

7. This Article shall be without prejudice to any rule of national law establishing a period of time during which the performance of the contract may not begin.

[1] OJ L 372, 31.12.1985, p. 31.

Article 15

Linked credit agreements

1. Where the consumer has exercised a right of withdrawal, based on Community law, concerning a contract for the supply of goods or services, he shall no longer be bound by a linked credit agreement.

2. Where the goods or services covered by a linked credit agreement are not supplied, or are supplied only in part, or are not in conformity with the contract for the supply thereof, the consumer shall have the right to pursue remedies against the creditor if the consumer has pursued his remedies against the supplier but has failed to obtain the satisfaction to which he is entitled according to the law or the contract for the supply of goods or services. Member States shall determine to what extent and under what conditions those remedies shall be exercisable.

3. This Article shall be without prejudice to any national rules rendering the creditor jointly and severally liable in respect of any claim which the consumer may have against the supplier where the purchase of goods or services from the supplier has been financed by a credit agreement.

Article 16

Early repayment

1. The consumer shall be entitled at any time to discharge fully or partially his obligations under a credit agreement. In such cases, he shall be entitled to a reduction in the total cost of the credit, such reduction consisting of the interest and the

costs for the remaining duration of the contract.

2. In the event of early repayment of credit the creditor shall be entitled to fair and objectively justified compensation for possible costs directly linked to early repayment of credit provided that the early repayment falls within a period for which the borrowing rate is fixed.

Such compensation may not exceed 1 % of the amount of credit repaid early, if the period of time between the early repayment and the agreed termination of the credit agreement exceeds one year. If the period does not exceed one year, the compensation may not exceed 0,5 % of the amount of credit repaid early.

3. Compensation for early repayment shall not be claimed:

(a) if the repayment has been made under an insurance contract intended to provide a credit repayment guarantee;

(b) in the case of overdraft facilities; or

(c) if the repayment falls within a period for which the borrowing rate is not fixed.

4. Member States may provide that:

(a) such compensation may be claimed by the creditor only on condition that the amount of the early repayment exceeds the threshold defined by national law. That threshold shall not exceed EUR 10000 within any period of 12 months;

(b) the creditor may exceptionally claim higher compensation if he can prove that the loss he suffered from early repayment exceeds the amount determined under paragraph 2.

If the compensation claimed by the creditor exceeds the loss actually suffered, the consumer may claim a corresponding reduction.

In this case, the loss shall consist of the difference between the initially agreed interest rate and the interest rate at which the creditor can lend out the amount repaid early on the market at the time of early repayment, and shall take into account the impact of early repayment on administrative costs.

5. Any compensation shall not exceed the amount of interest the consumer would have paid during the period between the early repayment and the agreed date of termination of the credit agreement.

Article 17

Assignment of rights

1. In the event of assignment to a third party of the creditor's rights under a credit agreement or the agreement itself, the consumer shall be entitled to plead against the assignee any defence which was available to him against the original creditor, including set-off where the latter is permitted in the Member State concerned.

2. The consumer shall be informed of the assignment referred to in paragraph 1 except where the original creditor, by agreement with the assignee, continues to service the credit vis-à-vis the consumer.

Article 18

Overrunning

1. In the case of an agreement to open a current account, where there is a possibility that the consumer is allowed an overrun, the agreement shall contain in addition the information referred to in Article 6(1) (e). The creditor shall in any case provide that information on paper or another durable medium on a regular basis.

2. In the event of a significant overrunning exceeding a period of one month, the creditor shall inform the consumer without delay, on paper or on another durable medium,

(a)   of the overrunning;

(b)   of the amount involved;

(c)   of the borrowing rate;

(d)   of any penalties, charges or interest on arrears applicable.

3. This Article shall be without prejudice to any rule of national law requiring the creditor to offer another kind of credit product when the duration of the overrunning is significant.

CHAPTER V

ANNUAL PERCENTAGE RATE OF CHARGE

Article 19

Calculation of the annual percentage rate of charge

1. The annual percentage rate of charge, equating, on an annual basis, to the present value of all commitments (drawdowns, repayments and charges), future or existing, agreed by the creditor and the consumer, shall be calculated in accordance with the mathematical formula set out in Part I of Annex I.

2. For the purpose of calculating the annual percentage rate of charge, the total cost of the credit to the consumer shall be determined, with the exception of any charges payable by the consumer for non-compliance with any of his commitments laid down in the credit agreement and charges other than the purchase price which, for purchases of goods or services, he is obliged to pay whether the transaction is effected in cash or on credit.

The costs of maintaining an account recording both payment transactions and drawdowns, the costs of using a means of payment for both payment transactions and drawdowns, and other costs relating to payment transactions shall be included in the total cost of credit to the consumer unless the opening of the account is optional and the costs of the account have been clearly and separately shown in the credit agreement or in any other agreement concluded with the consumer.

3. The calculation of the annual percentage rate of charge shall be based on the assumption that the credit agreement is to remain valid for the period agreed and that the creditor and the consumer will fulfil their obligations under the terms and by the dates specified in the credit agreement.

4. In the case of credit agreements containing clauses allowing variations in the borrowing rate and, where applicable, charges contained in the annual percentage rate of charge but unquantifiable at the time of calculation, the annual percentage rate of charge shall be calculated on the assumption that the borrowing rate and other charges will remain fixed in relation to the initial level and will remain applicable until the end of the credit agreement.

5. Where necessary, the additional assumptions set out in Annex I may be used in calculating the annual percentage rate of charge.

If the assumptions set out in this Article and in Part II of Annex I do not suffice to calculate the annual percentage rate of charge in a uniform manner or are not adapted any more to the commercial situation at the market, the Commission may determine the necessary additional assumptions for the calculation of the annual percentage rate of charge, or modify existing ones. These measures, designed to amend non-essential elements of this Directive, shall be adopted in accordance with the regulatory procedure with scrutiny referred to in Article 25(2).

CHAPTER VI

CREDITORS AND CREDIT INTERMEDIARIES

Article 20

Regulation of creditors

Member States shall ensure that creditors are supervised by a body or authority independent from financial institutions, or regulated. This shall be without prejudice to Directive 2006/48/EC.

Article 21

Certain obligations of credit intermediaries vis-à-vis consumers

Member States shall ensure that:

(a)   a credit intermediary indicates in advertising and documentation intended for consumers the extent of his powers, in particular whether he works exclusively with one or more creditors or as an independent broker;

(b)   the fee, if any, payable by the consumer to the credit intermediary for his services is disclosed to the consumer, and agreed between the consumer and the credit intermediary on paper or another durable medium before the conclusion of the credit agreement;

(c)   the fee, if any, payable by the consumer to the credit intermediary for his services is communicated to the creditor by the credit intermediary, for the purpose of calculation of the annual percentage rate of charge.

CHAPTER VII

IMPLEMENTING MEASURES

Article 22

Harmonisation and imperative nature of this Directive

1. Insofar as this Directive contains harmonised provisions, Member States may not maintain or introduce in their national law provisions diverging from those laid down in this Directive.

2. Member States shall ensure that consumers may not waive the rights conferred on them by the provisions of national law implementing or corresponding to this Directive.

3. Member States shall further ensure that the provisions they adopt in implementation of this Directive cannot be circumvented as a result of the way in which agreements are formulated, in particular by integrating drawdowns or credit agreements falling within the scope of this Directive into credit agreements the character or purpose of which would make it possible to avoid its application.

4. Member States shall take the necessary measures to ensure that consumers do not lose the protection granted by this Directive by virtue of the choice of the law of a third country as the law applicable to the credit agreement, if the credit agreement has a close link with the territory of one or more Member States.

Article 23

Penalties

Member States shall lay down the rules on penalties applicable to infringements of the national provisions adopted pursuant to this Directive and shall take all measures necessary to ensure that they are implemented. The penalties provided for must be effective, proportionate and dissuasive.

Article 24

Out-of-court dispute resolution

1. Member States shall ensure that adequate and effective out-of-court dispute resolution procedures for the settlement of consumer disputes concerning credit agreements are put in place, using existing bodies where appropriate.

2. Member States shall encourage those bodies to cooperate in order to also resolve cross-border disputes concerning credit agreements.

Article 25

Committee procedure

1. The Commission shall be assisted by a Committee.

2. Where reference is made to this paragraph, Article 5a(1) to (4) and Article 7 of Decision 1999/468/EC shall apply, having regard to the provisions of Article 8 thereof.

Article 26

Information to be supplied to the Commission

Where a Member State makes use of any of the regulatory choices referred to in Article 2(5) and 2(6), Article 4(1), Article 4(2)(c), Article 6(2), Article 10(1), Article 10(2)(g), Article 14(2) and Article 16(4), it shall inform the Commission thereof as well as of any subsequent changes. The Commission shall make that information public on a website or in another easily accessible way. Member States shall take the appropriate measures to diffuse that information amongst national creditors and consumers.

Article 27

Transposition

1. Before 12 May 2010 Member States shall adopt and publish the provisions necessary to comply with this Directive. They shall forthwith inform the Commission thereof.

They shall apply those provisions from 12 May 2010.

When Member States adopt these provisions, they shall contain a reference to this Directive or be accompanied by such reference on the occasion of their official publication. The methods of making such reference shall be laid down by Member States.

2. The Commission shall undertake, every five years and for the first time 12 May 2013, a review of the thresholds laid down in this Directive and its annexes and the percentages used to calculate the compensation payable in the event of early repayment, assessing them in the light of economic trends in the Community and the situation of the market concerned. The Commission shall also monitor the effect of the existence of the regulatory choices referred to in Article 2(5) and 2(6), Article 4(1), Article 4(2)(c), Article 6(2), Article 10(1), Article 10(2)(g), Article 14(2) and Article 16(4) on the internal market and consumers. The results shall be made known to the European Parliament and the Council, accompanied where appropriate by a proposal to modify the thresholds and percentages as well as the abovementioned regulatory choices accordingly.

Article 28

Conversion of amounts expressed in euro into national currency

1. For the purposes of this Directive, those Member States who convert the amounts expressed in euro into their national currency shall initially use in the conversion the exchange rate prevailing on the date of adoption of this Directive.

2. Member States may round off the amounts resulting from the conversion provided that such rounding off does not exceed EUR 10.

CHAPTER VIII

TRANSITIONAL AND FINAL PROVISIONS

Article 29

Repeal

Directive 87/102/EEC shall be repealed with effect from 12 May 2010.

Article 30

Transitional measures

1. This Directive shall not apply to credit agreements existing on the date when the national implementing measures enter into force.

2. However, Member States shall ensure that Articles 11, 12, 13 and 17, the second sentence of Article 18(1), and Article 18(2) are applied also to open-end credit agreements existing on the date when the national implementing measures enter into force.

Article 31

Entry into force

This Directive shall enter into force on the 20th day following its publication in the *Official Journal of the European Union.*

Article 32

Addressees

This Directive is addressed to the Member States.

Done at Strasbourg, 23 April 2008.

For the European Parliament	*For the Council*
The President	*The President*
H.-G. Pöttering	J. Lenarčič

APPENDIX FOUR

CONSUMER PROTECTION REGULATIONS

Read this Appendix with Chapter Seventeen, Section 4.

STATUTORY INSTRUMENTS

2008 No. 1277

CONSUMER PROTECTION

THE CONSUMER PROTECTION FROM UNFAIR TRADING
REGULATIONS 2008

Interpretation A4.01

2.—(1) In these Regulations—

"average consumer" shall be construed in accordance with paragraphs (2) to (6);

"business" includes a trade, craft or profession;

"code of conduct" means an agreement or set of rules (which is not imposed by legal or administrative requirements), which defines the behaviour of traders who undertake to be bound by it in relation to one or more commercial practices or business sectors;

"code owner" means a trader or a body responsible for—

(a)

the formulation and revision of a code of conduct; or

(b)

monitoring compliance with the code by those who have undertaken to be bound by it;

"commercial practice" means any act, omission, course of conduct, representation or commercial communication (including advertising and marketing) by a trader, which is directly connected with the promotion, sale or supply of a product to or from consumers, whether occurring before, during or after a commercial transaction (if any) in relation to a product;

"consumer" means any individual who in relation to a commercial practice is acting for purposes which are outside his business;

"enforcement authority" means the OFT, every local weights and measures authority in Great Britain (within the meaning of section 69 of the Weights and Measures Act 1985[1]) and the Department of Enterprise, Trade and Investment in Northern Ireland;

"goods" includes ships, aircraft, animals, things attached to land and growing crops;

"invitation to purchase" means a commercial communication which indicates characteristics of the product and the price in a way appropriate to the means of that commercial communication and thereby enables the consumer to make a purchase;

"materially distort the economic behaviour" means in relation to an average consumer, appreciably to impair the average consumer's ability to make an informed decision thereby causing him to take a transactional decision that he would not have taken otherwise;

"OFT" means the Office of Fair Trading;

"premises" includes any place and any stall, vehicle, ship or aircraft;

"product" means any goods or service and includes immovable property, rights and obligations;

"professional diligence" means the standard of special skill and care which a trader may reasonably be expected to exercise towards consumers which is commensurate with either—

(a)

honest market practice in the trader's field of activity, or

(b)

the general principle of good faith in the trader's field of activity;

"ship" includes any boat and any other description of vessel used in navigation;

"trader" means any person who in relation to a commercial practice is acting for purposes relating to his business, and anyone acting in the name of or on behalf of a trader;

"transactional decision" means any decision taken by a consumer, whether it is to act or to refrain from acting, concerning—

(a)

whether, how and on what terms to purchase, make payment in whole or in part for, retain or dispose of a product; or

(b)

whether, how and on what terms to exercise a contractual right in relation to a product.

(2) In determining the effect of a commercial practice on the average consumer where the practice reaches or is addressed to a consumer or consumers account shall be taken of the material characteristics of such an average consumer including his being reasonably well informed, reasonably observant and circumspect.

(3) Paragraphs (4) and (5) set out the circumstances in which a reference

---

[1] 1985 c.72; section 69 was amended by paragraph 75 of Schedule 16 to the Local Government (Wales) Act 1994 (c.19) and by paragraph 144 of Schedule 13 to the Local Government etc (Scotland) Act 1994 (c.39). Back [4]

to the average consumer shall be read as in addition referring to the average member of a particular group of consumers.

(4) In determining the effect of a commercial practice on the average consumer where the practice is directed to a particular group of consumers, a reference to the average consumer shall be read as referring to the average member of that group.

(5) In determining the effect of a commercial practice on the average consumer—

(a) where a clearly identifiable group of consumers is particularly vulnerable to the practice or the underlying product because of their mental or physical infirmity, age or credulity in a way which the trader could reasonably be expected to foresee, and

(b) where the practice is likely to materially distort the economic behaviour only of that group, a reference to the average consumer shall be read as referring to the average member of that group.

(6) Paragraph (5) is without prejudice to the common and legitimate advertising practice of making exaggerated statements which are not meant to be taken literally.

Misleading actions

5.—(1) A commercial practice is a misleading action if it satisfies the conditions in either paragraph (2) or paragraph (3). **A4.02**

(2) A commercial practice satisfies the conditions of this paragraph—

(a) if it contains false information and is therefore untruthful in relation to any of the matters in paragraph (4) or if it or its overall presentation in any way deceives or is likely to deceive the average consumer in relation to any of the matters in that paragraph, even if the information is factually correct; and

(b) it causes or is likely to cause the average consumer to take a transactional decision he would not have taken otherwise.

(3) A commercial practice satisfies the conditions of this paragraph if—

(a) it concerns any marketing of a product (including comparative advertising) which creates confusion with any products, trade marks, trade names or other distinguishing marks of a competitor; or

(b) it concerns any failure by a trader to comply with a commitment contained in a code of conduct which the trader has undertaken to comply with, if—

(i) the trader indicates in a commercial practice that he is bound by that code of conduct, and

(ii) the commitment is firm and capable of being verified and is not aspirational,

and it causes or is likely to cause the average consumer to take a transactional decision he would not have taken otherwise, taking account of its factual context and of all its features and circumstances.

(4) The matters referred to in paragraph (2)(a) are—

(a) the existence or nature of the product;

(b) the main characteristics of the product (as defined in paragraph 5);

(c) the extent of the trader's commitments;

(d) the motives for the commercial practice;

(e) the nature of the sales process;

(f) any statement or symbol relating to direct or indirect sponsorship or approval of the trader or the product;

(g) the price or the manner in which the price is calculated;

(h) the existence of a specific price advantage;

(i) the need for a service, part, replacement or repair;

(j) the nature, attributes and rights of the trader (as defined in paragraph 6);

(k) the consumer's rights or the risks he may face.

(5) In paragraph (4)(b), the "main characteristics of the product" include—

(a) availability of the product;

(b) benefits of the product;

(c) risks of the product;

(d) execution of the product;

(e) composition of the product;

(f) accessories of the product;

(g) after-sale customer assistance concerning the product;

(h) the handling of complaints about the product;

(i) the method and date of manufacture of the product;

(j) the method and date of provision of the product;

(k) delivery of the product;

(l) fitness for purpose of the product;

(m) usage of the product;

(n) quantity of the product;

(o) specification of the product;

(p) geographical or commercial origin of the product;

(q) results to be expected from use of the product; and

(r) results and material features of tests or checks carried out on the product.

(6) In paragraph (4)(j), the "nature, attributes and rights" as far as concern the trader include the trader's—

(a) identity;

(b) assets;

(c) qualifications;

(d) status;

(e) approval;

(f) affiliations or connections;

(g) ownership of industrial, commercial or intellectual property rights; and

(h) awards and distinctions.

(7) In paragraph (4)(k) "consumer's rights" include rights the consumer may have under Part 5A of the Sale of Goods Act 1979[2] or Part 1B of the Supply of Goods and Services Act 1982[3].

Misleading omissions

6.—(1) A commercial practice is a misleading omission if, in its factual **A4.03** context, taking account of the matters in paragraph (2)—
(a) the commercial practice omits material information,
(b) the commercial practice hides material information,
(c) the commercial practice provides material information in a manner which is unclear, unintelligible, ambiguous or untimely, or
(d) the commercial practice fails to identify its commercial intent, unless this is already apparent from the context,
and as a result it causes or is likely to cause the average consumer to take a transactional decision he would not have taken otherwise.

(2) The matters referred to in paragraph (1) are—
(a) all the features and circumstances of the commercial practice;
(b) the limitations of the medium used to communicate the commercial practice (including limitations of space or time); and
(c) where the medium used to communicate the commercial practice imposes limitations of space or time, any measures taken by the trader to make the information available to consumers by other means.

(3) In paragraph (1) "material information" means—
(a) the information which the average consumer needs, according to the context, to take an informed transactional decision; and
(b) any information requirement which applies in relation to a commercial communication as a result of a Community obligation.

(4) Where a commercial practice is an invitation to purchase, the following information will be material if not already apparent from the context in addition to any other information which is material information under paragraph (3)—
(a) the main characteristics of the product, to the extent appropriate to the medium by which the invitation to purchase is communicated and the product;
(b) the identity of the trader, such as his trading name, and the identity of any other trader on whose behalf the trader is acting;
(c) the geographical address of the trader and the geographical address of any other trader on whose behalf the trader is acting;
(d) either—
(i) the price, including any taxes; or
(ii) where the nature of the product is such that the price cannot reasonably be calculated in advance, the manner in which the price is calculated;
(e) where appropriate, either—
(i) all additional freight, delivery or postal charges; or
(ii) where such charges cannot reasonably be calculated in advance, the fact that such charges may be payable;
(f) the following matters where they depart from the requirements of professional diligence—

(2) 1979 c.54; Part 5A was inserted by S.I. 2002/3045. Back [5]
(3) 1982 c.29. Part 1B was inserted by S.I.2002/3045. Back [6]

(i) arrangements for payment,
(ii) arrangements for delivery,
(iii) arrangements for performance,
(iv) complaint handling policy;
(g) for products and transactions involving a right of withdrawal or cancellation, the existence of such a right.

Aggressive commercial practices

A4.04 7.—(1) A commercial practice is aggressive if, in its factual context, taking account of all of its features and circumstances—
(a) it significantly impairs or is likely significantly to impair the average consumer's freedom of choice or conduct in relation to the product concerned through the use of harassment, coercion or undue influence; and
(b) it thereby causes or is likely to cause him to take a transactional decision he would not have taken otherwise.

(2) In determining whether a commercial practice uses harassment, coercion or undue influence account shall be taken of—
(a) its timing, location, nature or persistence;
(b) the use of threatening or abusive language or behaviour;
(c) the exploitation by the trader of any specific misfortune or circumstance of such gravity as to impair the consumer's judgment, of which the trader is aware, to influence the consumer's decision with regard to the product;
(d) any onerous or disproportionate non-contractual barrier imposed by the trader where a consumer wishes to exercise rights under the contract, including rights to terminate a contract or to switch to another product or another trader; and
(e) any threat to take any action which cannot legally be taken.

(3) In this regulation—
(a) "coercion" includes the use of physical force; and
(b) "undue influence" means exploiting a position of power in relation to the consumer so as to apply pressure, even without using or threatening to use physical force, in a way which significantly limits the consumer's ability to make an informed decision.

SCHEDULE 1 COMMERCIAL PRACTICES WHICH ARE IN ALL CIRCUMSTANCES CONSIDERED UNFAIR

1. Claiming to be a signatory to a code of conduct when the trader is not.   **A4.05**

2. Displaying a trust mark, quality mark or equivalent without having obtained the necessary authorisation.

3. Claiming that a code of conduct has an endorsement from a public or other body which it does not have.

4. Claiming that a trader (including his commercial practices) or a product has been approved, endorsed or authorised by a public or private body when the trader, the commercial practices or the product have not or making such a claim without complying with the terms of the approval, endorsement or authorisation.

5. Making an invitation to purchase products at a specified price without disclosing the existence of any reasonable grounds the trader may have for believing that he will not be able to offer for supply, or to procure another trader to supply, those products or equivalent products at that price for a period that is, and in quantities that are, reasonable having regard to the product, the scale of advertising of the product and the price offered (bait advertising).

6. Making an invitation to purchase products at a specified price and then—
(a) refusing to show the advertised item to consumers,
(b) refusing to take orders for it or deliver it within a reasonable time, or
(c) demonstrating a defective sample of it,
with the intention of promoting a different product (bait and switch).

7. Falsely stating that a product will only be available for a very limited time, or that it will only be available on particular terms for a very limited time, in order to elicit an immediate decision and deprive consumers of sufficient opportunity or time to make an informed choice.

8. Undertaking to provide after-sales service to consumers with whom the trader has communicated prior to a transaction in a language which is not an official language of the EEA State where the trader is located and then making such service available only in another language without clearly disclosing this to the consumer before the consumer is committed to the transaction.

9. Stating or otherwise creating the impression that a product can legally be sold when it cannot.

10. Presenting rights given to consumers in law as a distinctive feature of the trader's offer.

11. Using editorial content in the media to promote a product where a trader has paid for the promotion without making that clear in the content or by images or sounds clearly identifiable by the consumer (advertorial).

12. Making a materially inaccurate claim concerning the nature and extent of the risk to the personal security of the consumer or his family if the consumer does not purchase the product.

13. Promoting a product similar to a product made by a particular manufacturer in such a manner as deliberately to mislead the consumer into believing that the product is made by that same manufacturer when it is not.

14. Establishing, operating or promoting a pyramid promotional scheme where a consumer gives consideration for the opportunity to receive compensation that is derived primarily from the introduction of other consumers into the scheme rather than from the sale or consumption of products.

15. Claiming that the trader is about to cease trading or move premises when he is not.

16. Claiming that products are able to facilitate winning in games of chance.

17. Falsely claiming that a product is able to cure illnesses, dysfunction or malformations.

18. Passing on materially inaccurate information on market conditions or on the possibility of finding the product with the intention of inducing the consumer to acquire the product at conditions less favourable than normal market conditions.

19. Claiming in a commercial practice to offer a competition or prize promotion without awarding the prizes described or a reasonable equivalent.

20. Describing a product as 'gratis', 'free', 'without charge' or similar if the consumer has to pay anything other than the unavoidable cost of responding to the commercial practice and collecting or paying for delivery of the item.

21. Including in marketing material an invoice or similar document seeking payment which gives the consumer the impression that he has already ordered the marketed product when he has not.

22. Falsely claiming or creating the impression that the trader is not acting for purposes relating to his trade, business, craft or profession, or falsely representing oneself as a consumer.

23. Creating the false impression that after-sales service in relation to a product is available in an EEA State other than the one in which the product is sold.

24. Creating the impression that the consumer cannot leave the premises until a contract is formed.

25. Conducting personal visits to the consumer's home ignoring the consumer's request to leave or not to return, except in circumstances and to the extent justified to enforce a contractual obligation.

26. Making persistent and unwanted solicitations by telephone, fax, e-mail or other remote media except in circumstances and to the extent justified to enforce a contractual obligation.

27. Requiring a consumer who wishes to claim on an insurance policy to produce documents which could not reasonably be considered relevant as to whether the claim was valid, or failing systematically to respond to pertinent correspondence, in order to dissuade a consumer from exercising his contractual rights.

28. Including in an advertisement a direct exhortation to children to buy advertised products or persuade their parents or other adults to buy advertised products for them.

29. Demanding immediate or deferred payment for or the return or safe-keeping of products supplied by the trader, but not solicited by the consumer, except where the product is a substitute supplied in accordance with regulation 19(7) of the Consumer Protection (Distance Selling) Regulations 2000 (inertia selling)[1].

30. Explicitly informing a consumer that if he does not buy the product or service, the trader's job or livelihood will be in jeopardy.

31. Creating the false impression that the consumer has already won, will win, or will on doing a particular act win, a prize or other equivalent benefit, when in fact either—

(a) there is no prize or other equivalent benefit, or

(b) taking any action in relation to claiming the prize or other equivalent benefit is subject to the consumer paying money or incurring a cost.

NOTE

The other Schedules are not reproduced.

---

[1] S.I.2000/2334, to which there are amendments not relevant to these Regulations. Back [11]

INDEX

LEGAL TAXONOMY
FROM SWEET & MAXWELL

This index has been prepared using Sweet and Maxwell's Legal Taxonomy. Main index entries conform to keywords provided by the Legal Taxonomy except where references to specific documents or non-standard terms (denoted by quotation marks) have been included. These keywords provide a means of identifying similar concepts in other Sweet & Maxwell publications and online services to which keywords from the Legal Taxonomy have been applied. Readers may find some minor differences between terms used in the text and those which appear in the index. Suggestions to *sweet&maxwell.taxonomy@thomson.com*